Development, Women, and War

Feminist Perspectives

Oxfam GB

Oxfam GB, founded in 1942, is a development, humanitarian, and campaigning agency dedicated to finding lasting solutions to poverty and suffering around the world. Oxfam believes that every human being is entitled to a life of dignity and opportunity, and it works with others worldwide to make this become a reality.

From its base in Oxford, UK, Oxfam GB publishes and distributes a wide range of books and other resource materials for development and relief workers, researchers, campaigners, schools and colleges, and the general public, as part of its programme of advocacy, education, and communications.

Oxfam GB is a member of Oxfam International, a confederation of 12 agencies of diverse cultures and languages, which share a commitment to working for an end to injustice and poverty – both in long-term development work and at times of crisis.

For further information about Oxfam's publishing, and online ordering, visit www.oxfam.org.uk/publications

For further information about Oxfam's development, advocacy, and humanitarian relief work around the world, visit www.oxfam.org.uk

Development, Women, and War
Feminist Perspectives

Edited and introduced by
Haleh Afshar and Deborah Eade

A Development in Practice Reader

Series Editor
Deborah Eade

Oxfam

First published by Oxfam GB in 2004

© Oxfam GB 2004

ISBN 0 85598 487 2

A catalogue record for this publication is available from the British Library.

Available from:

Bournemouth English Book Centre, PO Box 1496, Parkstone, Dorset, BH12 3YD, UK
tel: +44 (0)1202 712933; fax: +44 (0)1202 712930; email: oxfam@bebc.co.uk

USA: Stylus Publishing LLC, PO Box 605, Herndon, VA 20172-0605, USA
tel: +1 (0)703 661 1581; fax: +1 (0)703 661 1547; email: styluspub@aol.com

For details of local agents and representatives in other countries, consult our website:
http://www.oxfam.org.uk/publications
or contact Oxfam Publishing, 274 Banbury Road, Oxford OX2 7DZ, UK
tel: +44 (0)1865 311 311; fax: +44 (0)1865 312 600; email: publish@oxfam.org.uk

Our website contains a fully searchable database of all our titles, and facilities for secure
on-line ordering.

The Editor and Management Committee of *Development in Practice* acknowledge the
support given to the journal by affiliates of Oxfam International, and by its publisher,
Carfax, Taylor & Francis. The views expressed in this volume are those of the individual
contributors, and not necessarily those of the Editor or publisher.

Published by Oxfam GB, 274 Banbury Road, Oxford OX2 7DZ, UK.

Printed by Information Press, Eynsham.

Oxfam GB is a registered charity, no. 202 918, and is a member of Oxfam International.

Contents

Contributors

Lesley Abdela is a senior partner of Eyecatcher Associates/ Shevolution and is Chief Executive of Project Parity. She holds an MBE for services to women in politics and public life, an Honorary Doctorate from Nottingham Trent University for her work on human rights, and is a previous winner of the UK Woman of Europe award for her contribution to the empowerment of women in Central and Eastern Europe.

Haleh Afshar is Professor of Politics at the University of York, where she teaches Politics and Women's Studies, and also teaches Islamic Law at the Faculté Internationale de Droit Comparé at the University of Strasbourg. Recent works include *Islam and Feminisms: An Iranian Case-study* (Macmillan, 1998) and (co-edited with Stephanie Barrientos) *Women, Globalization and Fragmentation in the Developing World* (Macmillan, 1999).

Mary B. Anderson is President of The Collaborative for Development Action Inc., Director of the Local Capacities for Peace Project, and Co-director of the Reflecting on Peace in Practice Project. She has published widely on gender as well as on international emergency assistance and supporting peace-building capacities.

Glenda Caine is co-founder and Director of the Independent Projects Trust (IPT) which has, since 1990, been undertaking facilitation, training, and research work with rural communities, schools, the police service, and other institutions in transition owing to social, political, and economic changes in South Africa. She has a particular interest in peace education and training in conflict resolution.

Chris Corrin is Professor of Feminist Politics and co-ordinator of the International Centre for Gender and Women's Studies at the University of Glasgow in Scotland. She works with women's groups internationally on issues of politics, human rights, and violence against women. Her recent works include *Women in a Violent World* (Edinburgh University Press, 1996); *Feminist Perspectives on Politics* (Pearson, 1999); and *Gender and Identity in Central and Eastern Europe* (Frank Cass, 1999).

Deborah Eade has over 20 years' experience in development and humanitarian assistance, and worked for Oxfam GB and other NGOs in Mexico and Central America throughout the 1980s. She has published extensively on these issues and is Editor of the international journal *Development in Practice*.

Judy El-Bushra has 30 years' experience in development work in both governmental and non-governmental bodies, with a particular geographical focus on Sudan and Somalia. Her main areas of professional interest have been research and training in gender and development, distance education, conflict analysis, and more recently culture and performance and its relevance for development.

Sumaya Farhat-Naser is Professor of Botany at the University of Birzeit and was co-founder and former Director of the Jerusalem Center for Women, the Palestinian branch of Jerusalem Link. She is a founding member of the Women Waging Peace Global Network and has received several awards, including the 1995 Dr Bruno Kreisky Prize for Human Rights, the 1997 Mount Zion Award, and the 2000 Ausberg Peace Festival Award.

Myriam Gervais is a Research Associate at the Centre for Developing-Area Studies at McGill University, where she conducts research on human security, governance, and civil society in Africa. She has published widely on development issues in Niger and Rwanda, and consults for and lectures to government agencies and NGOs involved in aid programmes.

Rola Hamed is a Palestinian-Israeli currently working for a German Foundation in Tel Aviv. She holds an MA in Peace and Development Studies from Gothenburg University through a joint programme for Palestinians, Israelis, and Europeans conducted at the Tantur Center in Jerusalem, and is on the board of Bat Shalom.

Maria Holt worked for several years at the Council for the Advancement of Arab–British Understanding (CAABU) before joining the British Council in London as a Parliamentary Officer. Her academic work has focused on Middle East politics, Islam, women, and violence.

Ann Jordan is a freelance writer, researcher, and trainer with a 40-year background in teaching, and a particular interest in cross-cultural understanding.

Angela Mackay is Chief of the Gender Affairs Office in the UN Mission in Kosovo. Prior to this appointment, she was responsible for developing, testing, and revising the training materials described in her chapter throughout the major UN peacekeeping missions.

Donna Pankhurst is Senior Lecturer at the Department of Peace Studies at the University of Bradford. She has published on gender, democracy, and rural development in Zimbabwe; land reform and democracy in Namibia; and famine and the environment in Sudan. Her current work focuses on the causes of conflict, methods of its settlement, and peace building in Africa.

Jenny Pearce is Professor of Politics and International Development at the School of Peace Studies at the University of Bradford. She was previously Director of the Latin American Bureau, and has published extensively on Latin American issues. Her recent works include *Civil Society and Development* (co-authored with Jude Howell) (Lynne Rienner, 2001).

Elaheh Rostami Povey is a gender specialist and lectures in Development Studies at the School of Oriental and African Studies (SOAS) at the University of London. Her recent publications include *Women, Work and Islamism: Ideology and Resistance in Iran* (Zed Books, 1999), under the pen name Maryam Poya, and published in Farsi under her own name.

Hugo Slim is Reader in International Humanitarianism at Oxford Brookes University, Chief Scholar at the Centre for Humanitarian Dialogue in Geneva, and is a policy adviser to and trustee of several international NGOs, including Oxfam GB.

Gila Svirsky is a peace and human rights activist and former Director of Bat Shalom (Daughter of Peace), the Israeli branch of Jerusalem Link. She serves on the board of the Association for Civil Rights in Israel, is co-ordinator of the Coalition of Women for a Just Peace, which brings together eight Israeli and Palestinian women's peace organisations, and is an active member of the Women in Black movement.

Martha Thompson is an independent consultant on development and humanitarian issues with over 20 years' practical experience in these fields, and teaches at Brandeis University in Boston. Throughout the 1980s and 1990s she represented a range of international NGOs in Mexico, Central America, and the Caribbean, including Catholic Relief Services, Concern, Oxfam America, Oxfam Canada, and Oxfam GB.

Suzanne Williams pioneered gender and development work in Oxfam GB and has extensive experience in Brazil, Namibia, and South Africa. Author of *The Oxfam Gender Training Manual* (Oxfam, 1995), and co-author (with Deborah Eade) of *The Oxfam Handbook of Development and Relief* (Oxfam, 1995), she is currently Oxfam GB's Policy Adviser on Gender and Conflict.

Preface

Deborah Eade

After three decades of trying to get 'gender onto the development agenda', it is now widely recognised that, although the indicators of women's subordination to men are universal, persistent, and fairly comprehensive[1], this does not mean that women constitute a homogeneous group. Nor does it mean that their interests or needs[2] are identical across social, economic, cultural, political, and other divides.

In the context of humanitarian work, however, and certainly in terms of how the issues are presented in the mass media, women are commonly seen in terms of their membership of a group or community. While terms such as 'the plight of women' (be they Afghan or Albanian or Angolan) distinguish them from men, this is at the expense of insisting upon their commonality as women in ways that invariably gloss over significant differences among them. The ensuing narrative either insists upon women's victimhood and their helplessness in the face of suffering and adversity; or it stresses their resourcefulness, their 'inner strength', their stoical struggle to keep their families going, their 'natural' identification with peace. Men prosecute war to defend the homeland, and women bind the social wounds and keep the home fires burning. Men, in this dualistic portrayal, will negotiate only from a position of power that is ultimately based on violence, or the threat of violence; women will look for compromises that do not involve such zero-sum games.

This narrative finds it even more difficult to countenance the engagement of women in violence and destruction than to recognise that many men do seek peaceful dialogue rather than solutions that are based upon aggression: that suicide bombers should include women seems to turn the world upside down. But real-life problems arise when emergency interventions and post-conflict programmes are based on distorted generalisations that not only deny women and men the full range of human agency, but may also lock emerging societies into ill-fitting roles that diminish rather than enhance their development potential.

This Reader comprises two parts. The first is introduced by Haleh Afshar and is based on her guest-edited issue of the journal *Development in Practice* (Volume 13, Numbers 2 & 3) published in May 2003. A feminist scholar and activist, and a prominent commentator on contemporary Islamic affairs, Haleh Afshar is Professor of Politics at the University of York. Contributors on the overarching theme of women, war, and peace building describe the work of women (some feminist, some not) who are actively engaged in trying to (re-) build equitable and sustainable societies in the very process of living through or emerging from war.

The second part of this Reader contains a selection of papers drawn from other issues of the journal and elsewhere focusing on the ways in which aid agencies often relate to the 'victims' of conflict, who are predominantly 'womenandchildren' (to borrow Susan McKay's phrase, quoted in Karam 2001:19), and considering how external agencies might best support these 'victims' and other civilians in their own peace-building efforts.

The experience of living or working in a situation of armed conflict defies generalisation: every war or situation of political violence has its own distinct characteristics. In terms of gender-power relations, there are grounds for guarded optimism in some cases, near despair in others. Human beings do adapt to new circumstances and will devise all manner of ways to secure their survival even in the most desperate of situations. It is a piece of aid-agency lore that social disruption can, in some instances, open up new opportunities for women that enable them to break out of restrictive gender stereotypes. The legacy of women's clandestine networks in Afghanistan described by Elaheh Rostami Povey is one such case, the growing political agency and 'self-protection' capacities of peasant women during the war in El Salvador chronicled by Martha Thompson and Deborah Eade is another. These and other experiences recorded in this volume show what women can achieve when they are able to organise autonomously, as women and as citizens. And yet, the overwhelming evidence is that, although women do characteristically take on additional burdens in order to secure the survival of their families, often assuming extra economic and public (including military) responsibilities over and above their reproductive work, these changes in gender roles are generally contingent and context-specific, and as such fail to take root within a broader project of social transformation. So unless women are able to distinguish for themselves between the desirable and negative outcomes of social upheaval, and mobilise to defend what they perceive as improvements in their quality of life, the ideological undertow is all too likely to sweep away any fragile gains women may have experienced during wartime and may well usher in 'traditional' patterns of gender-power relations.

It is a sad reflection of the crisis facing political institutions throughout much of the contemporary world that this collection cannot be comprehensive in its coverage of existing armed conflicts, and that more will almost certainly have broken out than been resolved even before it goes to press. At the time of writing, the situation in post-war Iraq remains highly unstable, the peace processes in the Middle East and West Africa are at best precarious, the conflict in Colombia bleeds on almost unnoticed, and the 'war on terror' seems set to claim more lives. The need for new perspectives on conflict, new approaches to peace building and conflict resolution, could not be more urgent. If this volume helps readers to look at these issues in a more creative way, then it will have contributed in some small way to meeting that need.

Notes

1 UNDP's Gender-related Development Index (GDI) ranks countries according to the life expectancy, adult literacy, education, and earnings of women relative to men. Even in Norway, the highest-ranking country on both the Human Development Index (HDI) and the GDI, despite their higher average level of education, women still earn only two-thirds of average male earnings (UNDP 2003). The world over, from rural and urban sectors in developing countries to OECD nations, women generally work longer hours but earn less money than men. The Gender Empowerment Measure (GEM) looks at women's representation in public and professional life. High-income Japan, which ranks ninth in the world in terms of human development, drops to thirteenth position on this index: women hold only 10 per cent of parliamentary seats, compared with 30 per cent in South Africa; fewer than 10 per cent of Japanese legislators and senior officials are women, compared, for example, with 36 per cent in Honduras; and while 45 per cent of professional and technical workers in Japan are women, countries as varied as Brazil, Philippines, and Poland all do significantly better on this score. In other words, a country's HDI ranking can mask considerable female disadvantage, while a low HDI or GDI ranking does not necessarily mean that women are absent from public life.

2 A reference to the pioneering distinction between strategic and practical interests, as originally defined by Maxine Molyneux (1985), and strategic and practical needs, the approach later developed by Caroline Moser (1989).

References

Karam, Azza (2001) 'Women in war and peace-building: the roads traversed, the challenges ahead', *International Feminist Journal of Politics* 3(1): 1–25.

Molyneux, Maxine (1985) 'Mobilisation without emancipation? Women's interests, state and revolution in Nicaragua', *Feminist Studies* 11(2): 227–54.

Moser, C.O.N. (1989) 'Gender planning in the Third World: meeting practical and strategic gender needs', *World Development* 17(11): 1799–825.

UNDP (2003) *2003 Human Development Report*, Oxford and New York: Oxford University Press.

Part One: Introduction
War and peace: what do women contribute?

Haleh Afshar

Much has been written about women's suffering in times of war, but despite the lip-service, little has actually been done. Part One of this Reader is based on the guest-edited issue of *Development in Practice* (Volume 13, Numbers 2 & 3), in which contributors discuss conflicts that have raged throughout the Middle East, Africa, and Eastern Europe over the past century and highlight the commonalities of some of what women experience of women during wars and their potential to contribute both to war and particularly to peace. They consider some of the reasons why women's concerns have yet to be placed at the forefront of both analysis and practical outcomes, and present an overview of different feminist approaches to peace building and conflict resolution, and concrete policy measures to achieve these ends. The authors address major conceptual and practical problems in the hope of paving the way towards establishing effective strategies that might help us to realise hopes that have been written about for decades. They argue that is important to move beyond the myriad projects that involve women to consider the factors that contribute to the relatively poor overall impact of such projects, an outcome which often results from a failure to understand the underlying gendered power relations and the dynamics of social change.

Many of these papers were presented at two meetings held at the University of York: a February 2001 conference organised by International Alert and Dr Sultan Barakat, director of the Post War Reconstruction and Development Unit; and a subsequent meeting in May 2002 of the Women and Development Study Group of the Development Studies Association (DSA). The organisers and contributors were acutely aware of the dearth of literature and analysis concerning the situation of women in conflict, post-conflict, and reconstruction, and that what does exist remains too much at the level of rhetoric and has yet to be translated into concrete and effective measures. The papers reproduced here therefore focus on women on the ground: what happens to them during wars and what are their demands in the subsequent periods of peace and reconstruction. The authors come from both academic and practitioner backgrounds and have sought to combine their theoretical and practical knowledge in order to forge more effective measures and suggest changes that could lead to the inclusion of women at all stages of post-war and reconstruction processes. Above all, they consider the practicalities of meeting the specific gendered demands that must be taken into account, understood, and then placed at the forefront of policy making.

This section begins with papers offering an overview of the situation of women at times of war and peace which explode some prevalent myths, including the assumption that the war front is separate from the home front or that women are always victims in times of conflict. The authors argue that such analysis is simplistic and that at times the very terminology used to define conflict, war, and the war front can be misleading. Conflicts can both empower and disempower women, since women can be at the same time included in practice and yet excluded ideologically, or they may be both victims and agents of change – though they often have no effective choice in these matters. They may opt to be fighters and yet be attacked and raped; they may choose to provide back-up support and yet simultaneously find themselves and their homes in the firing line; they may be caught in transgressions – such as cross-division marriages – that could have been bridges towards peace but may instead have become causes of hatred and war. Through the hardships they experience, many women do develop visions of peace that are rooted in their shared sufferings, but that cannot be translated into negotiations which are themselves anchored in hatreds, and bounded by geographical, religious, and historical divisions that ignore the commonality of experiences that women know so well. The views and experiences of such women are too complex to be included in documents that simply divide up territories and allocate material resources.

Peace processes, whether at local, national, or international levels, seldom include the perspectives that emerge from women's shared suffering. Even the choices that many women make at times of war and conflict may still be condemned when peace is being negotiated, or be rejected once formal peace has been achieved: all too often women are expected to abandon any positions of responsibility and authority they may have achieved when the men were at war and are expected to return to the domestic realm if and when peace returns. Commonly, what the returning warriors bring home is violence, fear, and domination, while their women are expected to bear the pain and remain silent and submissive in the name of peace and unity. The crisis of masculinity and difficulties of facing 'the enemies within' make it hard if not impossible to include some of the demands that women would wish to make as part of the processes of peace making. There is as yet little hope that national boundaries will be abandoned. Nationalism and national identities are unlikely to be discarded even though women generally lack the right to bestow such identities, despite having been given the duty of protecting them.

In the first paper **Donna Pankhurst** sets out the overall framework and in the second I outline the difficulties that must still be confronted in mainstreaming women and their demands. Along with other contributors, these two authors contend that these demands are multilayered and not easily perceived, and that they will not be remedied simply by the use of politically correct language. Given that it is often impossible to use straightforward analytical categories since women cut across boundaries and cannot be defined as a single group, the task becomes all the more difficult at times of war and unrest. Pankhurst notes that women have greatly contrasting experiences of war, experiences that are also mediated by differences in age, class, and regional or ethnic backgrounds. That said, women have been less likely than men to initiate wars and have, universally, been ascribed the identity of 'victim'. But such generalisations also hide the reality that women seldom have a choice about whether they are indeed victims or active participants. There are no longer war fronts and, as it were, 'backs' or areas 'behind the lines' since homes, schools, hospitals, public highways, and even personal relationships are often part of the arena of war. Men and women who marry across the invisible boundaries of faith and ethnicity find themselves torn by subsequent conflicts, as has been the case of pre-war and subsequent marriages between Muslims and Christians in the former Yugoslavia and between Shiia and Sunni Muslims in Iraq. There is little choice about victimhood when individuals cannot break away from the constraints placed upon them by tight-gripping ethnic, religious, or regional identities.

In her article, **Judy El-Bushra** argues that to understand the problems it is important to adopt an approach based upon a gender analysis that can describe the situations both of men and of women. This analysis might well indicate that both sexes are 'excluded', albeit in different ways. She suggests that gender relations may indeed change through conflict: for instance, at moments of crisis there is often more political space for women to take on male roles in the absence of men. But positive experiences must be placed in the context of the daily pain, suffering, and deprivation that wars bring for civilians. As Pankhurst, El-Bushra, and I argue, conflicts may be simultaneously empowering and disempowering. They erode gender barriers but burden women with greater responsibilities, which are not then easily translated into power. The need to cope makes women more independent, more effective, more outward-looking, yet they also feel 'a desperate solitude'; conflicts tear asunder family units and extended kinship networks, and deprive entire communities of their beloved sons, husbands, and sometimes their daughters as well, leaving women in charge of destitute families.

However, although gender barriers may become less rigid, gender identities often do not change, and the emphasis on motherhood and domesticity remains central to the survival of the entire community. At such times women may be able to exercise more control over whom they marry and when, but they cannot shirk the maternal and family duties that become harder to meet as the conflict deprives them still further of resources and opportunities. Maternal roles are often translated into symbols of nationhood and, as in the case of mothers of martyrs, almost an emblem of conflict. But women are generally unable to use this shared suffering to form a chain to link the opposing parties through their common understanding of loss and sorrow.

Conflicts may propel women into a more active arena, but at the same time rapid changes in gender roles may create a crisis of masculinity. El-Bushra argues that conflict generates confusion for both sexes about what values should be retained, and this in turn creates a wider social crisis. The outcome of the tension between the underlying gender relations and the new relations which conflict makes necessary have a spiral effect as one consequence leads to others, making it difficult to pinpoint what is cause and what is effect. But all too often the outcome appears to be a return to ossified pre-conflict gender ideologies. Pankhurst and El-Bushra, as well as **Maria Holt**, note the importance of analysing the impact of these changing roles in relation to masculinity and of recognising the negative outcomes that a crisis of masculinity is likely to mean for post-war resolution.

But despite the many shortcomings and problems, women activists have continued to struggle to obtain a voice and improve their overall condition. The second set of papers focus on peace making and peacekeeping, and especially on developing peace in ways that comprehensively include women as participants and as beneficiaries. Here, our contributors argue that the most difficult problem is that, despite the rhetoric, development and reconstruction programmes have remained largely gender blind. Peace-building processes have frequently been focused on short-term measures initiated and administered by organisations that are themselves patriarchal and hierarchical, and whose recruitment processes continue to be anchored in the 'old boy network' and rigid hierarchies. Unless the processes and the relevant organisations change, women stand little hope of success. To achieve peace and democratisation, national and international agencies have to focus on dealing with the problems of existing power structures and seek to develop processes that might be able to reform them and thus open the way for women and their interests. As **Lesley Abdela** shows in her essay, changing the gendered nature of hierarchy is never easy and at times may appear virtually impossible; there is still a tendency for international powers to choose and appoint all-male transitional governments which, inevitably, are poorly qualified to represent women's interests in the nation-building process. Abdela suggests a complete rethinking of peace-building strategies, and supports **Chris Corrin**'s view that the democratisation process has to be properly thought through over the long term with appropriate levels and types of investment and the comprehensive inclusion of women throughout. Thus, change is needed not only within the countries experiencing conflict but also within the international agencies and their working methods.

All the above problems and challenges notwithstanding, the contributors show that it is possible to make some inroads. Working with women and seeking to reflect their views, Abdela argues that to secure women-centred democratisation, albeit fraught with difficulties, remains an important and feasible objective. However, as **Angela Mackay** demonstrates, translating aims into reality is no easy matter. Training peacekeepers, both uniformed and civilian, about gender and about the human rights of women and children is a complex and difficult process. Mackay shows that providing culturally sensitive and effective gender training for peacekeepers, a project in which she has been involved in recent years, may be hard but is nevertheless essential and can go a long way towards removing blinkered visions and enabling the trainees to understand how they can make a difference and take responsibility for their own actions. Inviting the peace makers and the peacekeepers to think through the prevailing gender blindness can in the long run open the way to more sensitive practices. Training the peacekeepers is challenging but rewarding, and gender awareness should become part and parcel of the basic skills requirements of all peacekeeping forces.

Corrin and **Elaheh Rostami Povey** highlight the necessity of including women activists who have worked at the grassroots during times of war and conflict because they have so much to contribute to peace building and to the post-war decision-making process. Perhaps the most effective means of facilitating women's access to power would be through the provision of effective training, education, and schooling. Long-term investment in such infrastructure could help to build up the basis for real democratisation, as opposed to repeated exercises in voting, which often simply reproduce existing power structures. Corrin argues that skill reconstruction, rehabilitation, and democracy building can only be effective if and when there is a gender audit in place to help identify and minimise discriminatory practices. Inclusiveness requires dialogue and understanding, and an awareness that the process is both lengthy and expensive: education systems have to be rebuilt and infrastructure has to be put in place and sustained. But these investments, and the training of women for managerial roles, all form part of the process that could 'develop peace'.

The authors believe that, despite the difficulties, the diverse and effective coping mechanisms that women have developed during situations of war and conflict could be an invaluable resource to facilitate their successful integration in the post-war context. At times of conflict, women use their family networks and friendship skills to build solidarity groups to deal with both immediate and long-term problems. Often, as in the cases of Palestinian and Afghan women among others, women assume positions which allow them to intervene not only to help with short-term needs but also to defend women's rights and seek to secure a better position for them in the long term. The articles by Corrin, Abdela, Holt, Rostami Povey, El-Bushra, and **Ann Jordan** show that, ultimately, the success and effectiveness of such groups depend largely on the prevailing political circumstances. Jordan provides clear examples of the variety of ways in which women have been effective peace workers and offers possible avenues for empowering them to continue in this role.

In all cases, the diversity of cultures and norms as well as differences in women's backgrounds, ages, and aspirations make it impossible for researchers to produce formulaic proposals for how to ensure the integration of women in peace-building processes and in any eventual democratisation. The need to include women in such processes has finally been accepted. But, as with every other feminist demand, there remains a gap between theory and practice. The articles drawn from the special issue of *Development in Practice*, together with those included in Part Two of this Reader, offer a number of proposals that advocate programmes and policies that are more culturally specific, more focused, more long term, and far more in-depth than is usually the case in dealing with women and war, and that begin with women from the grassroots upwards. These proposals come from both academics and practitioners: some of the authors have studied the problems addressed here from an academic perspective over a long period of time, while others are actively involved in building such processes and in the delivery of programmes on the ground. The hope is that funds will follow the practitioners and that practice will follow the theories, sooner rather than later.

Acknowledgements

I would like to thank Dr Sultan Barakat and the Post War Reconstruction and Development Unit and the Development Studies Association's (DSA) Women and Development group for organising the meetings at which a number of the papers published in this Reader were presented and discussed. I also thank International Alert and the DSA for their financial and infrastructural help in organising these meetings. Thanks also to my wonderful friends and colleagues who wrote and presented the papers, and then patiently accepted the comments and suggestions of the editors and referees. I am particularly appreciative of one colleague who even thought of us on her wedding day and put the finishing touches to her article before donning the blue garter! Above all I would like to thank Deborah Eade who was gracious, helpful, and forgiving. She remained positive about the project, supportive, and encouraging when the way seemed barred. She has been a friend indeed, and I am most grateful.

The 'sex war' and other wars:
towards a feminist approach to peace building

Donna Pankhurst

Introduction

For more than a decade, resolutions from the United Nations and the European Commission have highlighted women's suffering during wars, and the unfairness of their treatment upon the return to peace. Over the past few years there thus has been an increasing interest in women's experiences during war and their potential capabilities for peace, but this interest has not led to significant improvements in women's lives during and after armed struggle. They still have highly distinct experiences of conflict which tend to leave them marginalised in peace negotiations and significantly disadvantaged with the onset of peace. This paper considers the various explanations for this lack of positive change.

One of the charges which might be made against both actors and analysts of conflict is that of conceptual confusion. *Conflict* is a word often used loosely to mean many different things despite its long history in social science. Most types of social, political, and economic change involve conflict of some sort, and one could argue that many of the positive changes in world history have occurred as a result of conflict. How much more confusing, then, is the term *peace*! With much less of a social science tradition behind it, peace is a term which is not only subject to very little conceptual scrutiny, but is also declared, with little qualification, as a political objective for which compromises, and indeed sacrifices, are to be made.

In the mix of such ambiguities about these two terms, blindness about gender inequality (often among other inequalities) commonly rests unchallenged, and the inequality itself thrives. There is a sophisticated analytical literature on the history of women and gender relations during and after war which is persistently ignored by many prominent writers on conflict, conflict resolution, and peace building

First published in *Development in Practice* 13(2&3): 154–77 in 2003

in favour of newly coined terms and observations which are very seldom rooted in analyses of historical social, political, and economic change. There is now perhaps greater international political will to improve the position of women after wars end (if not actually during war) than ever before, yet there is little evidence of much positive change. Women's concerns are still rarely heard, let alone addressed, by policy makers during peace settlements.

I begin, therefore, with a preliminary review of the conceptual debates from literature on conflict and peace, and women and gender relations, and then I consider these issues during the peace-building process. The questions I seek to address in the paper are derived from concerns about sloppy conceptual thinking on conflict and peace, and on the nature of gender politics in 'post-conflict' situations. Specifically, I ask why extreme forms of gender inequality persist and what can be done to improve the situation for most women in peace-building contexts.

Concepts of conflict and peace

Accepting that no straightforward technical definition (such as more conventional approaches to the categorisations of battles and wars in terms of the numbers of casualties) is likely to encapsulate the complexities of contemporary conflicts in much of the world today, observers frequently present descriptive typologies of conflicts which feature organised and/or collective violence.[1] Violent conflicts emerging since the end of the Cold War have commonly been called *ethnic conflict, social conflict*, and *civil conflict*, along with *international social conflict* where there is some cross-border activity or other states are involved. These descriptive terms are intended to capture the much cited observation that 90 per cent of today's casualties of war are civilians (Lake 1990), as well as to convey something about their causes. Competing identities are often added to the list of root causes, whether conceived in terms of an essentialist ethnicity, or regionalism, or tensions over state formation, or marginality to the global economy (Miall *et al.* 1999:1–38).

The prevalent use of the word 'conflict', rather than 'war', is also a reflection of today's complexities, with violence characterised by stops and starts, fluid boundaries, battlegrounds in residential areas, and civilian casualties. However attractive the term 'conflict' is as a convenient device to catch all these phenomena, it also entails a lack of clarity about what exactly is being discussed. The word may thus be used interchangeably to refer to a *conflict of interest* or to the *violent expression of conflict*. The question hardly arises as to how or why this 'conflict' situation is different from what is 'normal', as typologies of conflict tend not to be connected to deeper, more sophisticated analyses of the places about which they are commenting. Moreover, there is very little discussion in much of the writing on 'conflict analysis' or 'conflict resolution' on the impact of certain types of social relations on the specific forms of violence, let alone engagement with theories of human or social behaviour.

There is an emerging common approach which divides the causes of conflict between underlying causes – which might commonly be seen as 'structural inequalities' – and 'triggers' – factors which tip such situations into violent conflict. There is as yet no comprehensive, convincing account of why difficult pre-existing conditions (including economic hardship and acute competition over resources between communities with different identities) lead to violent outbreaks of conflict in some places, but not in others. Without clarity about the significance of similarity and difference between conflicts, it will remain difficult to assess with any reliability the chances of transition to peace. For instance, while it remains unclear precisely what weight to give particular economic circumstances in assessing the causes of a particular conflict, it also remains unclear what impact they may have on the chances of success of any peace-building strategy. Improved economic circumstances always feature on wish-lists for peace, but the connections between violence and economic conditions are complex, not simple.

A rather narrower conception of conflict that is still prevalent derives from a kind of 'socio-psychological model' (Duffield 1997:90 in Annex I). Here, the cause of conflict is seen as being disagreement, or breakdown of communication, between individuals or groups. Violent manifestations of conflict are therefore viewed as irrational and, almost by definition, based upon misunderstandings. The mechanisms through which people and organisations might be able to achieve peace are therefore seen to be those which strengthen (or even establish) channels of communication between conflicting groups and individuals, such as mediation and mediation training, and conflict-resolution workshops. Such activity is focused at the micro level, and is geared towards the minimisation of violence *per se*.

Such techniques are not readily able to address the links between economic insecurity or inequality and violence. Indeed, their very logic, which often focuses on lack of understanding and empathy as the driving force behind violence, can occasionally suggest that at times there is a need to play down the significance of such economic 'root causes' and other aggravating political circumstances (such as corrupt government administration). Furthermore, where the 'psycho-social' model of conflict informs external interventions, interpreting violence as the consequence of poor understanding, it may be assumed that all people involved in the conflict are victims, no matter what role they play during the conflict. Such a view can lead to serious political and social tension if it is relied upon during the processes of peace building.

Turning to the meanings of the term 'peace', Galtung's (1985) conception of *negative peace* has come into widespread use, and is probably the most common meaning given to the word, i.e. the end or absence of widespread violent conflict associated with war. A 'peaceful' society in this sense may therefore include a society in which social violence (against women, for instance) and/or structural violence (in situations of extreme inequality, for example) are prevalent. Moreover, this limited 'peace goal', of an absence of specific forms of violence associated with war, can and often does lead to a strategy in which all other goals become secondary. The absence of analysis of the deeper (social) causes of violence also paves the way for peace agreements that leave major causes of violent conflict completely unresolved. Negative peace may therefore be achieved by accepting a worse state of affairs than that which motivated the outburst of violence in the first place, for the sake of (perhaps short-term) ending organised violence.

Galtung's alternative vision, that of *positive peace*, requires not only that all types of violence be minimal or non-existent, but also that the major potential causes of future conflict be removed. In other words, major *conflicts of interest*, as well as their violent manifestation, need to be resolved. Positive peace encompasses an ideal of how society *should* be, but the details of such a vision often remain implicit, and are rarely discussed. Some ideal characteristics of a society experiencing positive peace would include: an active and egalitarian civil society; inclusive democratic political structures and processes; and open and accountable government. Working towards these objectives opens up the field of peace building far more widely, to include the promotion and encouragement of new forms of citizenship and political participation to develop active democracies. It also opens up the fundamental question of how an economy is to be managed, with what kind of state intervention, and in whose interests. But more often than not discussion of these important issues tends to be closed off, for the sake of 'ending the violence', leaving major causes of violence and war unresolved – including not only economic inequalities, but also major social divisions and the social celebration of violent masculinities.

An egalitarian vision of 'positive peace' also embodies equality between ethnic and regional groups, and, though mentioned far less often, among the sexes. Enloe defines peace in feminist terms as 'women's achievement of control over their lives' (Enloe cited in Kelly 2000:48), which she regards as requiring 'not just the absence of armed and gender conflict ... but also the absence of poverty and the conditions which recreate it' (Kelly *op. cit.*). However, the details of these larger peace goals highlighted by Enloe are rarely discussed among those involved in conflict situations and their potential resolution, which serves to eclipse gender issues at the point of peace settlements and in post-conflict situations. Where the question of pursuing greater gender equality does arise at the point of a settlement, it is not uncommon for it to be seen as neither essential nor urgent in peace building. In some cases, changes in gender relations are even cast as jeopardising the survival of peace. For example, many women in liberation movements have commented that they were accused of thwarting their movement's aims by exposing the sexist and violent behaviour of their male comrades, or even by concentrating their political activity specifically on women's concerns.

The marginalisation of gender issues is not merely a political and tactical position of those at the forefront of negotiations, however. Scholars and analysts in the fields of conflict analysis and conflict resolution (CR) 'discovered' gender later than development studies (DS) or international relations (IR) (Pankhurst and Pearce 1997). As noted by an increasing number of scholars, the process of taking gender more seriously as an analytical category within DS seems to have responded to an 'efficiency imperative'. This 'efficiency imperative' has been illustrated most clearly and extensively by Elson (1995), and has for some time been commonplace among major organisations.[2] In essence, many development *policies* often failed because they ignored gender issues, and it became apparent (through the theoretical and empirical work of feminist academics and practitioners) that if gender were taken into account a far greater degree of success could be achieved. Clearly, this story is more complex and complicated than I can elaborate here, but, in any case, gender has as a result become more or less mainstreamed in some key areas of development work, at least to a far greater degree than in IR.

If this explanation for the gendering of DS is correct, then in order for a similar push to occur in CR (or IR, for that matter) a related 'policy-wing' would need to benefit in some way by taking gender seriously. Until recently this was not perceived to be the case; settlements to conflicts could be found not only without the involvement of women, but also at the very expense of women as a gender. It was thought that gender considerations made no difference to the ability to find a settlement, or to the chances of that settlement holding. In other words, negative peace could be achieved in conditions of gender inequality, with no 'efficiency imperative' to push for change, and sexual politics not sufficiently developed to make it a problem not to change.

More recently, with the extension of conflict resolution into post-conflict policies, gender issues have come to be seen as far more central, and as directly affecting the *efficacy* of peace-building initiatives, even if women still remain marginalised at the point of brokering a settlement, as I show below. This shift has not yet led back into reconceptions of the impact of gender relations on the conditions of conflict or peace. Nor has it led to a change in women's experiences of conflict or peace building, to which I now turn.

Women's wars

For many years, the roles of women in war and other types of violent conflict remained almost invisible throughout the world. Accounts of war, through news reporting, government propaganda, novels, cinema, etc., tended to cast men as the 'doers' and women as the passive, innocent, victims. In poor countries, wars were not portrayed in quite the same way, but stories of the courage and bravery of men as fighters have also tended to eclipse the active roles which women have played. As women's experiences have become more broadly known, it has become clear that there are many different ways in which women live through and participate in wars: as fighters, community leaders, social organisers, workers, farmers, traders, welfare workers, among other roles. Nonetheless, many conflict narratives highlight a common theme of women seeking to minimise the effects of violence through their different social roles. Stories of women actively seeking to end wars have received increasing international attention. The bravery of those women who go against the general tide of opinion, and sometimes literally place themselves in the line of fire, has come to be much celebrated.

For instance, there has been a surge of interest in women who have negotiated peace between groups of warring men (Berhane-Selassie 1994; El-Bushra 2000), or who have even courageously intervened in battles to force peace (in Ethiopia, Somalia, and Sudan, for instance). These women have sometimes called on and expressed values, behaviour, and codes which are explicitly associated with their gender. As one female peace activist commented:

> Both men and women have the potential for peacemaking and the responsibility to build and keep peace. The women, however, seem more creative and effective in waging peace ... It is the women's emotional strength to transcend pain and suffering and their predisposition to peace that provides them with greater potentials for peacemaking.
> (Quoted in Garcia 1994:45)

Similarly, discussing the importance of coalition building in the peace process of the Philippines, another woman activist commented:

> And here we see that women have played a large role. Perhaps because of their very lack of exposure to the way traditional politics has been played in this country and the way power has been used, there is in their attitude – and it is not because it's in our genes but because it is in our experience and culture – much less of a kind of 'ego-involvement' which has to be overcome in dealing with the sorts of questions that need to be answered and the consensus building that needs to be done in forging a peace for a people that have been so divided ... Moreover, women have largely been the survivors and carers of survivors, so this seems to have given them a sustained intensity of wanting to resolve the peace question ... Furthermore, through the women, there are possibilities of introducing new paradigms in conflict resolution, because, as I say, we are practised in conflict resolution and conflict transformation in the domestic sphere, that perhaps need to be played out more to become an input into the way public negotiations take place.
> (Quoted in Garcia 1994:63–4)

But some of these accounts also show that in the same wars, women – indeed sometimes the same women – have played both 'peace-making' and 'war-mongering' roles (El-Bushra 2000; Jacobson 2000; Mukta 2000). An increasing number of accounts of war highlight women's direct involvement in violence or in motivating the men in their communities to fight (El-Bushra 2000; Jacobson 2000; Mukta 2000; Vickers 1993). This is particularly so where wars are about national identities, as women in most societies take the major responsibility for passing on cultural identities to children and play active roles in supporting exclusive and aggressive ideologies about nationalism (Elshtain 1987; Ferris 1993). Accounts of some conflicts document actual violence committed by women (African Rights 1995; Bennett *et al.* 1995, *passim*; Goldblatt and Meintjes 1998 on South Africa). These accounts remain in the minority, and their authors are sometimes subject to criticism, if not censure. The extent of women's involvement in violent acts in warfare remains poorly understood, and violence is still commonly believed to be the main preserve of men (Jacobs *et al.* 2000; Kelly 2000).

It is clear from the above discussion that women have great contrasts in their war experiences, which are also mediated by differences in age, class, and regional or ethnic background. What is striking, nonetheless, is that there are also great commonalities in their experiences, regardless of the kinds of situations they find themselves in, or the kinds of roles they play in times of conflict. During war, women tend to bear a much greater burden than men for taking care of survivors, as well as children. They also carry the main burden for ensuring food provision, while keeping social and political activities going when men are fighting away from their homes. This shift of social responsibilities from men to women is common, despite the many different contexts in which conflicts occur, from remote rural villages in which most of the food has to be grown and/or gathered, to big cities where all kinds of resourceful innovations are developed by women to ensure that families have enough to eat and are otherwise well taken care of.

Even in the midst of the horrors of conflict, many women have embraced these changes as moments of liberation from the old social order (see, for example, Sharoni 2001). As the need arose for them to take on men's roles, so they had to shake off cultural restrictions and adopt new lifestyles. The relative minority of women who have joined armies (as nurses, administrators, or even fighters), have even sometimes been able to persuade their political movements to take demands for improved women's rights seriously, and to accept women's political representation. Several commentators have observed that in moments of social crisis there is often more 'political space' for radical change in social relations, including those of gender (Elson 1998 on economic crisis; Kynch 1998 on famine), and this has certainly been the case in many wars.

Nonetheless, these 'positive' experiences have to be placed in context. With the changes in the way war is normally fought, and the increasing predominance of civilians among the casualties, there is a continuing thread in the ways women experience suffering in distinct ways – not because of any intrinsic weakness, but because of their position in society (United Nations 1985). Women are not normally leaders in settings before conflict erupts, and so, in this sense at least, they are not as directly responsible as men for war violence. Nonetheless, they experience high rates of injury and death (although not usually as high as men) and the particularly brutal war injury of rape. Rapes committed in times of war have received greater attention in recent years, but they also seem to be on the increase. The proliferation of light weapons has also increased the threat of rape, as it is harder to resist male violence when faced with a gun (Abdel Halim 1998; Turshen 1998). Common effects for women, in addition to the direct trauma caused by the rapes themselves, include social stigmatisation; physical and mental injury, as many war rapes are multiple and accompanied by other forms of violence; illness (from sexually transmitted diseases, usually with negative impacts on reproductive health); and death itself (from HIV/AIDS, or assault and murder because of the stigma attached to rape survivors) (Twagiramariya and Turshen 1998).

The experiences of girls in conflicts are even less well documented than those of boys, but are often horrific and specific to their gender (Nordstrom 1997). Generational relations are also destabilised where children become soldiers (Richards 1995), a situation which is now increasingly prevalent in part as a result of the proliferation of light weapons, which can be used by almost anyone (Turshen 1998). Because these weapons have given them power over others, many children in war-torn African societies have grown up without learning to respect their elders, as was the norm before war broke out. Women, in particular, feel this loss of respect, especially when young boys commit rape and other forms of violence on older women (*ibid.*).

Women's testimonies suggest that they often feel they have had little *choice* about whether they are innocent victims or courageous participants in a war: sometimes they find that they have to actively engage in the violence, or suffer the consequences, including death. Perhaps this lack of choice is intensified because of the changes in the nature of warfare and in the types of violence that have emerged in the post-Cold War era. Jacobs *et al.* (2000) suggest that such inability to choose is not a recent phenomenon and may rightly characterise women's experiences in most wars. Certainly, where conflict is fought out in people's homes (with light weapons) and the reasons for fighting involve issues of the very survival of a particularly defined identity, women have been placed on one side or another, regardless of how they feel about the conflict. Women who are seen to 'break out' of the ethnic identity ascribed to them, for instance by having mixed marriages or joining human rights organisations, are often targeted for particular censure, if not actual violence (as in the former Yugoslavia, for example (Korac 1998)). Men also experience elements of these hardships in wartime, but women's stories still remain relatively marginal or hidden as narratives of conflicts. In addition, women's experiences do not inform the terms of peace settlements, and their concerns are not taken into account in decisions about what should happen during the peace.

A history of gendered conflict endings and gendered peace

Conflicts end in many different kinds of ways, with little analysis to understand their implications for long-term peace (Pankhurst 1999). Nonetheless, whether they are the product of a negotiated settlement or of military victory, it remains common for women's voices – either individual or organised – on all sides to be absent or marginal at the point when a settlement is reached. Many international organisations have recognised this as a problem for some time and, indeed, in some efforts to redress the balance, women have been integrated in some key peace processes in recent years. Unfortunately, such efforts are often based on questionable assumptions and resemble a drop in the ocean in terms of their capacity to effect change favourable to women, as I show below.

Women rarely receive recognition for their contributions as providers and carers, let alone for their roles as social and political organisers. They usually receive much less support than male fighters in post-conflict reconstruction and rehabilitation projects (Goldblatt and Meintjes 1998), even though women provide most of the caring for the population in post-war settings, and it would thereby seem that addressing women's basic needs would benefit society as a whole (El-Bushra 1998; United Nations 1998). Women also rarely figure in 'security concerns' in 'post-conflict' situations, even though domestic violence increases during and after war (Kelly 2000; Krog 2001).

It is common for a high proportion of women to have experienced multiple rapes and associated injuries and infections during war. Many give birth to children conceived through rape, which leads to many kinds of problems, whether the children are abandoned, killed, or kept. Health facilities which deal with the effects of rape, and specialist support for such mothers and children, are consistently given low priority, and are rarely available. Women are unlikely to make formal complaints about rape, during or after conflict, unless they are encouraged and supported to do so. Violent acts committed against girls, which are more hidden than those against adult women, also urgently require investigation in most post-war situations. What tends to happen is that girls are given even less support than adult women, and the onus for reporting rests with the children themselves (Nordstrom 1997).

Even where Truth Commissions or other kinds of justice-seeking institutions are established after a conflict, it appears that women still do not report instances of rape anywhere near the numbers which actually take place (Goldblatt and Meintjes 1998). This was true during the wars in the former Yugoslavia and the 1994 genocide in Rwanda, even though the international tribunals set up in both instances made it very clear that rape had to be taken seriously as a war crime (for Rwanda see Twagiramariya and Turshen 1998; for Yugoslavia see Cockburn 1998). One of the reasons for this reluctance to come forward and hold perpetrators of sexual violence to account is said to be that such women are commonly still under the threat of domestic and sexual violence. It is common after war for there to be no effective personal security for women, and for rape, among other forms of sexual violence (including domestic violence), actually to increase (Cockburn 1998; Kelly 2000; Krog 2001). Rather than receiving *support* at the end of wars, women usually suffer a *backlash* against any new-found freedoms, and they are forced 'back' into kitchens and fields. Where governments and/or warring parties establish new constitutions or peace processes, they often neglect the needs of women or outwardly limit or restrict the rights of women. In some cases, such restrictions may be carried out explicitly through the legal system, either by failing to repeal existing discriminatory laws or by creating new ones (Kelly 2000). This might be called a 'gendered peace' (Pankhurst and Pearce 1997).

Furthermore, women often experience a backlash in their relations with men. It is not uncommon for there to be public outbursts of protest – and even violent assaults – against women who are economically independent, or are employed in traditional 'male' roles, or persist in living in urban areas and pursuing an education in predominantly rural communities. Many of the women who were active in liberation struggles in places like Algeria, Vietnam, Zimbabwe, Namibia, Eritrea, and Mozambique bitterly experienced widespread instances of discrimination and backlash, although in each case the extent to which the state and/or government has played a role is still subject to debate (De Abreu 1998; Jacobs and Howard 1987). Many such women have to adjust to a new situation in peacetime in which they have less political space to challenge gender relations than they did during wartime or even beforehand. In a similar vein, women commonly find their historical contributions minimised in both official and popular accounts of war, as happened in Europe after the Second World War (Kelly 2000).

At times, official policies are themselves part of the backlash, even if the state is not evidently orchestrating it. The state can bring to bear many of the policies observed in 'normal times' in many parts of the world to intervene in gender politics in favour of men. The state, for instance, is instrumental in enforcing controls over women's sexuality; in failing to provide adequate security to women (especially in terms of protection from violence, sexual and otherwise); in imposing and/or supporting restrictions on women's movement, access to housing, jobs and property (especially land); and in neglecting women's health needs. In many cases, such official policy outcomes are also reinforced by the practices of international organisations.

Such states are intervening in contexts of social crisis where violence against women is very high, and at both social and individual levels there are great battles to define surviving women's roles and rights as secondary to those of men. Attempting to answer the question 'why?' is certainly challenging. It seems as though the challenge posed to traditional gender relations during times of war becomes too great for patriarchal societies to accept it in times of peace. The ideological rhetoric is often about 'restoring' or 'returning to' something associated with the status quo before the war, even if the change actually undermines women's rights and places women in a situation that is even more disadvantageous than it ever was in the past. This is often accompanied by imagery of the culturally specific equivalent of the woman as a 'beautiful soul', strongly associating women with cultural notions of 'tradition', motherhood, and peace (Pierson 1989).

In this post-war situation, the *differences between women* often reassert themselves again, especially in many countries where women are divided along ethnic and/or regional lines (Korac 1998).

New divisions may also emerge as a result of the different roles that women play during the war, e.g. whether they are perceived to have been on the side of 'victors', or 'perpetrators' or 'collaborators', and whether they have given birth to children of 'the enemy' as a result of rape.

All of these issues can determine who qualifies for aid and other forms of support (Turshen 1998), as can women's marital status. Marital status is highly significant in situations where women do not have strong legal rights (including access to land and credit). Where the majority of the surviving population is female (as in Rwanda, where it is 70 per cent), this can lead to heightened tensions among women, who compete over men and resources. Tensions also arise over whether children survived the war or not. For these reasons, it is not unusual for there to be very little trust among women as a group, thereby weakening their capacity to act collectively to meet their needs and protect their rights. Peace-building strategies do not usually directly address these tensions and divisions between women, but rather tend to focus either on 'women' as a category, or assume their existence as genderless members of other groups.

The new celebration of 'peaceful women'

In many contrasting social and cultural contexts, it is commonplace for the conceptualisation of *femininity* to include some of the 'opposite' qualities ascribed to masculinity. Such qualities – which include things like seeking non-confrontational methods of conflict resolution, willingly working for the good of the collective, and even remaining passive – are assumed to be embodied by all women (United Nations 1985, 1995). These assumptions have a long tradition of identifying female qualities with a rejection of war and conflict (Byrne *et al.* 1996; Ferris 1993). Accounts of war which highlight the violence directed at women tend to reinforce the assumption that all women are always pro-peace and anti-violence. There are also echoes here of the essentialist 'mother' figure who stands for peace, and the central place of the mother figure in many societies' cultural ideal about 'tradition' (Cockburn 2001).

Recently there has been a surge of international interest in 'peaceful women', also featured in much of the writing on war-torn societies – both in analysis and in policy debates. This seems to have occurred partly as a revulsion against the violence of war, and in the hope that a focus of attention on women might reveal the way towards a more peaceful, less violent world. Multilateral aid organisations have therefore increasingly assumed that policies that integrate women in their work are fundamental to peace building (United Nations 1985, 1995), and that women 'hold the key' to peace building. For instance, International Alert's Code of Conduct (1998) states:

> We explicitly recognise the particular and distinctive peacemaking roles played by women in conflict afflicted communities. Women and women's organisations are often reservoirs of important local capacities which can be used in peace-building activities ...
>
> (International Alert 1998:6)

Thus, some of women's distinctive qualities (whether these are thought to be biologically or socially determined) become identified with the way forward in peace building. Strategies therefore focus on ways to enhance, support, and extend the work that women are thought to be well equipped to undertake, alongside all their other responsibilities, as 'women's work'. And, in effect, many women are themselves taking up this mantle.

Some women's organisations have developed the capacity to work openly to protect and extend human rights (especially in Latin America). Others have extended the work they undertook during conflict to ensure that the social fabric did not collapse, including, for example, various forms of community organisation and welfare provision in refugee camps in Northern Ireland, El Salvador, Guatemala, Rwanda, and Burundi. Others focus more directly on the need to talk about, and participate in, strengthening peace in the name of women (such as the Federation of African Women's Peace Networks, the Femmes-Africa-Solidarité, and other groups in Israel and the Occupied Territories, as well as in the former Yugoslavia – see Cockburn 1998 for more examples). Finally, there are those women's organisations which explicitly attempt to challenge women's oppression and gender inequality in post-conflict situations (such as those which facilitate women's participation in war-crimes' tribunals and truth processes). Many of these organisations also attempt to build bridges between groups of women with very different experiences of conflict, who might otherwise be separated by their ethnic, regional, or political identities.

All these types of organisations can therefore be of fundamental importance in addressing common weaknesses in existing peace-building strategies: the lack of attention to women's needs; the marginalisation of gender analyses; and the absence of efforts to challenge particularly discriminatory practices in institutions and in society more widely. Furthermore, women's organisations have within themselves the potential to achieve many of the goals that peace-building efforts should strive to fulfil: to increase women's (and thereby household) income; to increase women's abilities to participate in political processes and civil society more generally; to increase the number of women who become leaders and representatives; and to reinforce efforts to challenge masculine cultures in institutions and society more widely.

These challenges and changes do not happen on a large scale at present because many women's organisations face great difficulties in ensuring their continued survival, let alone in achieving all of their objectives. Such problems include chronic under-funding and lack of training in the areas of management, leadership, and lobbying. In practice, new women's organisations often have to deal not only with marginalisation and stigmatisation by powerful government and non-government organisations, but also with direct physical harassment from local men and security forces, especially common in post-conflict situations where gender tensions are already running high.

The provision of external funding for grassroots organisations is of great potential help, but it often creates tensions as well. In allocating scarce funds to such groups, there is sometimes an expectation that they should 'deliver the peace' single-handedly, which is unrealistic. Moreover, participation in such groups can sometimes lead to unsustainable increases in a woman's workload. Lessons from the development field suggest that those women's groups that stand the greatest chance of success and make the best use of external funding tend to be those that were initially formed and established their objectives in the absence of (or with minimal) external funding; those that acknowledge the differences between women; and those that set themselves clearly achievable objectives. These lessons also suggest that when states support women's organisations as part of a policy to enhance women's participation in development, they avoid taking women seriously in other ways. This implies that a successful strategy of supporting women's organisations needs to be complemented by other gender-aware policies.

Supporting women as groups of individuals (rather than in organisations) is also a common strategy in trying to promote peace building (United Nations 1985, 1995, 1998). A common request from peace activists and commentators is that there should be more of a female presence at the sites of peace making, as well as at discussions that may take place as part of peace building (European Commission 1996b; United Nations 1995). There is a general tendency for the leaders of institutions and political organisations to be the only participants at peace settlements, with very little grassroots participation. Women in general are thus marginalised, as they are always poorly represented at the leadership level. Outside parties have had some limited success in enabling women to participate in peace talks. For instance, the Life and Peace Institute ensured that women's peace groups gained access to some of the Somalia peace and reconciliation talks (even though they gained observer status only). Similar initiatives have also occurred in Burundi, Sudan, and Northern Ireland.

Merely being invited to attend talks or peace conferences is insufficient, however. Very few women have the education, training, or confidence to participate fully, even if they are in attendance. This has been stressed not only by women activists and observers in the South, but also in the North (especially Northern Ireland – see Mulholland 2001). As one peace activist expressed it:

> ... there is very much technically that women have to learn. In terms of the technical capability to discuss the issues, women are much less prepared because we have not had the luxury of all the education and study that men have had when they go out and take long years to discuss these issues ... we are going to bring the women in and we are going to have to provide support to bring them in. It is not going to happen automatically.
> (Quoted in Garcia 1993:65)

There are lessons here from development policies which have attempted to expand the participation of women in the political process by offering them special training and educational opportunities. Providing training and support for women activists who might then be able to participate at peace talks and in decision-making bodies, and to train other women in turn, could, in time, generate enormous benefits (United Nations 1995, 1998). Where levels of women's basic education are low, other approaches are required to increase women's participation in the short term, such as special meetings which solicit women's views. These remain rare. There is clearly some positive potential for such women in increased education, potential income, and even political power. What they argue for, or achieve politically, is bound to include the same variety of experiences and pressures for and against speaking on behalf of different constituencies (all women, poor people, people from 'their' region, etc.) as has been elucidated by the literature on 'women in politics'. Discussion about the potential for peace-making women all too often takes place not in this intellectual and political context, however, but in a conceptual vacuum. What difference might it make to take on a feminist analysis in developing such policy?

And yet 'tradition' remains untouchable?

Many international organisations seeking to assist particularly African countries in peace building have become very enthusiastic about promoting so-called 'traditional' methods of conflict resolution (in the sense of searching for an end to organised violence). 'Traditional' methods in this context are distinct from the identification of historic roles played by 'peaceful women' in the previous section, and are associated with responses of community representatives and people in positions of authority. International organisations often have multiple, and not always clear, objectives in these contexts and are confused about what exactly might be promoted. Examples of international support for such initiatives exist in Kenya, Mozambique, Uganda, and Somalia, for instance.

The description of *'traditional' conflict-resolution mechanisms* includes many different activities, like long, stylised discussions, public hearings, ritual blessings, symbolic acts of forgiveness, corporal punishment, and material compensation (symbolic, property and/or labour) awarded to an injured party to be paid by the 'guilty' party (whether individual or collective). All can be intended to achieve a range of outcomes between different parties, including a shared understanding of different points of view; retribution; compensation; forgiveness; and trust building. These mechanisms do indeed work sometimes to build understanding and consensus, but they may also work to the benefit of the office holder and his family or community. All these types of activities are to be found somewhere in the remembered, if not recent, past of many African countries, and are increasingly described in the literature in terms that verge on adulation and reification (see Duba *et al.* 1997, for example).

These 'traditional' mechanisms are increasingly being packaged within an international terminology of peace building, not least to access funding from international donors. Legitimately, some of them have been in constant use for several generations. More commonly, however, many of them have been recently resurrected from the memory of elderly people, while others are actually being self-consciously invented for the first time. In itself, this is not surprising: history is studded with examples of political leaders who have used the invention and/or re-invention of tradition as a tool of mobilisation and legitimisation (Jacobs and Howard 1987; Vail 1989). The term 'traditional' is therefore often misleading, but tends to have the effect of placing a particular 'tradition' off-limits to outsiders. Instead, very local politics determines what actually happens.

One thing which these 'traditional' activities often have in common, however, is that office holders are almost universally men, which is also normally claimed as part of the tradition, and they are not easily held accountable for their decisions or actions. Where these practices are seen to 'work' they tend to be about peace building among men, with little to offer women *per se*. Since these practices commonly regulate relationships between communities of people, rather than simply among individuals, women often find that they are affected, and even bound, by outcomes over which they had little or no influence. A key challenge for the future will be to 'modernise' so-called 'traditional' mechanisms and approaches. In a context where international organisations are supporting attempts to 're-discover' (and reify) remembered versions of past practice, this struggle will be arduous indeed.

Feminist analyses of conflict and peace: debates continue

A significant number of feminist writers on issues of conflict and peace have come from the development field. This is not a coincidence, as so many of the struggles we have witnessed recently have taken place in the South. There has been an outpouring of writing in this area which stands as a direct, and largely unmet, challenge to contemporary policy interventions in conflict and peace building. At the same time, key theoretical and analytical issues remain problematic and unresolved. Below, I consider the implications of the widespread use of the term 'gender'; analyses of masculinity and of femininity; and the prevailing confusion about how to think about rape and sexual violence.

Abuse of the term 'gender'

Where the term *gender* is self-consciously used in relation to conflict and peace, the working definition that is usually offered is that gender denotes all the qualities of what it means to be a man or a woman which are socially and culturally, rather than biologically, determined. Gender includes the way in which society differentiates appropriate behaviour and access to power for women and men. In practice, this has entailed the privileging of men over women. This working view of gender is summarised in Box 1.

The most nuanced studies of gender address this problematic of gender disadvantage directly, with attempts to measure, explain, and review ways of challenging it, and they tend to focus almost exclusively on the behaviour and experiences of women. Studies that explore the differences between women are particularly useful in that they help break down the tendency to see women as a uniform, homogeneous category (United Nations 1998). However, this remains the exception rather than the rule in studies of conflict, in contrast to DS, where a far more sophisticated literature exists. With the increasingly widespread use of the term gender, two key political challenges persist. First, there is a need to ensure that the complexities and differences in women's experiences are kept in view alongside the commonalities that are articulated through an analysis based on gender. Second, it is equally important to make sure that feminist challenges to power relations,

---

Box 1: Gender or sex?

Gender is a term used in contrast to sex, to draw attention to the social roles and interactions between women and men, rather than to their biological differences. Gender relations are social relations, which include the ways in which men and women relate to each other beyond that of personal interaction. They include the ways in which the social categories of male and female interact in every sphere of social activity, such as those which determine access to resources, power, and participation in political, cultural, and religious activities. Gender also denotes the social meanings of male and female, and what different societies regard as normal and appropriate behaviour, attitudes, and attributes for women and men. Although the details vary from society to society, and change over time, gender relations always include a strong element of inequality between women and men and are influenced strongly by ideology.

There are some 'grey' areas about what is and is not biologically determined which are still subject to debate, not least among feminists. Some people have argued that women tend to be less predisposed to aggressive and violent behaviour because of certain biological characteristics. These include lower testosterone levels, and the differences in women's brain structure and development. Such characteristics are believed by some to make most women less likely to behave in challenging and competitive ways than most men. However, no scientific study argues that all forms of different behaviour patterns and roles in society can be explained by biological factors alone.

and a feminist project to transform society, do not get completely marginalised. Both of these challenges remain as central in the area of development as they are in peace and conflict studies, as highlighted in a recent major review (Jackson and Pearson 1998). The review suggests that part of the problem is that practitioners coming into the development field are freely using the term gender while they lack basic familiarity with the key literature, concepts, and methods of feminist research (Baden and Goetz 1998:22).

Feminist scholars have argued that as gender was taken into development-policy processes, particularly as part of an effort to 'mainstream' gender issues, the focus was originally on women as the target group to be brought into development (Jackson and Pearson 1998). This process was based on the common and mistaken assumptions that: (a) women were not already involved in some way; (b) their labour was a 'free' good readily available for new activities; and (c) women would automatically control the fruits of their labour in any such activities.[3] As the crudest mistakes were addressed, policy makers persisted with the need for a more careful inclusion of women, as it was recognised that successful use of women's labour could make development occur more efficiently (see Note 2).

This misunderstanding of gender relations in the policy process is analysed in the field of environmental policy in the South, in a way which has even closer parallels with peace building, by Green et al. (1998), who have extensive experience in environment and development policy and analysis. These authors argue that because policy makers in the environmental field have only borrowed selectively from gender research and analysis, they have consistently failed to improve women's command over natural resources or to contribute to the effectiveness of projects (ibid.). Such policy makers tend to identify women as a homogeneous group with some natural affinity as guardians of natural resources and therefore potentially the most effective group to carry out environmental projects.

Policy makers in the environmental field thus often target women and exclude men in their projects (e.g. tree planting and seed conservation), recognising women as victims, but then also as effective environmental managers (Davidson et al. 1992, cited in Green et al. 1998). Environmental policy makers' assumptions therefore echo some of the perspectives put forward in 'ecofeminist' writing which emphasises the innate feminine qualities of women that make them the most appropriate guardians of natural resources (e.g. Mies and

Shiva 1993; Shiva 1998). In effect, such policies identify environmental projects as part of 'women's work' within established gender divisions of labour (Green *et al.* 1998). In practice, such policies tend to make the same kinds of errors described above – assuming that women's labour is free, when actually there are commonly already many claims on it and many opportunity costs to consider if they don't use their labour on other crops or other activities. It is also commonly assumed that women automatically benefit from 'community activities', when there is considerable evidence to refute this (*ibid.*).

The parallels with policy makers' expectations of women in peace building are very strong here. Drawing on images of women's supposedly innate qualities described in the sections above (in this case, the predisposition to work against violence and for peace), interveners conceive of projects which rely on women's (free) labour and exclude men. This occurs in a context where analyses show that women are far more diverse as a group and that the issues need to be tackled by men as well. Moreover, they assume that this work is self-evidently a priority for women and that it will inevitably help tackle gender inequality. On the contrary, evidence shows that women whose subsistence needs are barely secured tend to have other more pressing calls on their time. Further, gender inequality, which can actually increase during phases of peace building, severely limits what women are able to do from very marginal positions in society.

Even in contexts where gender does have prominence in the peace-building discourse, the problems of categorising women as a homogeneous group tend to be replicated – as I have tried to show above with the 'peaceful women' approaches. Moreover, none of the common approaches to peace building take on the challenges of the feminist project of transforming gender relations, as they do not tend to consider how to work towards positive peace in the wider sense.

Is it all down to masculinity?

Feminist research has shown the ways in which many large institutions across the world are not gender neutral, but rather tend to be masculine in culture and practice. State bureaucracies and security services, as well as international bodies, tend to be structured and to function according to norms of masculinity, and they do not have a gender-neutral culture of their own (El-Bushra 2000). For instance, they tend to be hierarchical in structure, to militate against cooperative and consultative working patterns, and to encourage individualistic, competitive behaviour. They also typically have top-down leadership and management styles. Such institutions also seem to have a stake in preserving differences between women's and men's economic and political roles, which are continuously reinforced by the active use of symbols of masculinity and femininity. Appropriately, images of success and achievement tend to be associated with masculine images of force and strength (Elshtain 1985, 1987; Peterson 1993; Steans 1998).

The effects of such types of masculinity are not only seen directly in the commission of violent acts, but also in the structure and functioning of key institutions which are responsible for organising war, and indeed many of those which are meant to manage the peace. The logical policy implication is that transformation of the masculine nature of such institutions is of central importance in any peace-building strategy. It is certainly difficult to see how positive peace could be achieved without significant changes in the way certain institutions and policy-making bodies operate. In reflecting social norms, such institutions (private, state, and international) are typically dominated by men, with few women being in decision-making positions. Such a pattern was until recently almost globally universal and it has now come to be seriously questioned and challenged in countries of the North. This is not only because of the desire for greater equity between women and men for employment and power, but also in the hope that this can lead to changes in the way that such institutions operate.

Security institutions are usually those most in need of reform in different post-conflict contexts (United Nations 1995). Without adequate personal security (for women and men), it is very difficult to reduce violence, or even sometimes to prevent a return to war. All too often such organisations are part of the problem, rather than the solution. They typically embody the aggressive values of masculinity outlined above, both in the way internal decisions are taken and management issues are resolved, and in the way that services are delivered to the public. Several countries have begun to tackle these problems by focusing on reducing violence and corruption within the police force, and they have incorporated the retraining of officers to deal with rape, which has been identified by international institutions as a priority in peace building (United Nations 1997). Policies which have been taken up on a small scale include: using women as key trainers; increasing the number of women employed, especially in more senior positions; and training and promoting women as investigators of gender crimes (El-Bushra and Piza López 1993).

What is not known with any certainty is what difference it would make if there were to be a far stronger presence of women in positions of authority in some other institutions, such as government ministries and other parts of the civil service, although it is commonly assumed that this would change institutional cultures (e.g. United Nations 1995). There are, of course, no guarantees that a greater presence of women *per se* would even lead to a sustained challenge in the masculine culture of such institutions in the short term, let alone prevent the re-emergence of conflict. Unless one has a clear analysis of exactly *which* institutions are responsible for the fragility of peace, it is also not clear how change should be prioritised. A lot of work remains to be done in this area.

What feminist writers seem to agree on, however, is that existing patterns of entrenched masculinity are highly *unlikely* to change without considerably increasing the representation and participation of women as an essential precondition. There is still a strong debate about the significance of increasing women's participation, membership, and/or representation in the corporate and public sectors of countries in the North, but one position suggests that some changes may be achieved in key locations of major institutions (see Pringle and Watson 1992). Even where this is agreed, however, increasing the number of women in key institutions is generally not believed to be enough to bring about changes in institutional culture in societies which still highly value norms of masculinity based on aggression and violence.

Writers within the development field have long argued that in trying to challenge the ways in which gender relations develop, it is necessary to look at the ways in which men are socialised to become part of a male gender. Research focusing on the construction of *masculinity* has also revealed cross-cultural tendencies, and some of these are highly pertinent to studies of conflict (Lentin 1997; Steans 1998). Egotistical, aggressive, and dominant behaviours are common features of cultural definitions of masculinity, as is men's dominance over women (Byrne 1996). War of all types creates militarised societies, and in many different cultural contexts militarisation is linked to masculinity – not as a socio-biological attribution but rather as 'cultural constructions of manliness' (Turshen 1998).

Several writers have argued that at times of socio-political tension prior to conflict, as well as during conflict itself, some types of masculinity come to be celebrated and promoted more than others (Cockburn 1998, 2001; El-Bushra 2000;). Maitse (2000) argues that nationalism *per se* tends to emphasise aspects of masculinity which are more likely than others to lead to violence. In some conflict situations, the more violent aspects of masculinity are played out in all aspects of men's lives to an extreme degree, in what Hague (1997) calls a 'hetero-national masculinity' with reference to the Serb and Bosnian Serb military. In other words, a culture of masculinity means that for a man to be a 'real man' he also has to be aggressive, egotistical, dominating, and, when necessary, violent.

While the analytical debate about masculinity is therefore quite developed, it has not yet significantly influenced peace-building policy – nor indeed development policy – beyond attempts to reform security organisations. Theoretically, it might be possible for people to reclaim positive cultural traditions of masculinity which have been lost or undermined during conflict (Large 1997), but this would probably require true leadership, or at least tolerance, and there are very few examples where this seems at all likely.

Women as the peace makers: constructions of femininity

One of the most challenging implications of the proposition that certain types of masculinity are more prone to be evoked at conflict moments is that, in many societies, one of the main institutions for promoting one or another type of masculinity is the family – a site where *women* play a leading role in educating young people and indeed in encouraging adults to live by a certain set of values. As was described above, in some cases this leads women to exert great pressure on male relatives, including sons, to embrace violence. It is important to recognise that some writers are keen to avoid blaming women entirely for this phenomenon, stressing that this role has to be weighed against the role of other institutions. El-Bushra (2000), for instance, stresses that political parties, nationalist movements, and age groups also play key socialising roles in different contexts. She cites Richards' work (1995) on Sierra Leonean 'warboys', which highlights child abuse through several generations as a major cause of their extremely violent behaviour.

I have already highlighted some of the problematic assumptions made about femininity in the policy context of the 'peaceful women' approach. A growing number of writers seek to explore the variety of women's experiences of violence, as perpetrators and collaborators in addition to victims and survivors. Jacobs *et al.* (2000) highlight this tendency as an outcome of casting women as innately peaceful, non-violent individuals who are sometimes coerced against their will to play certain roles in conflict situations. These authors are keen to force consideration of the fact that sometimes women can and do engage in violence, ranging from complicity to agency (see Butalia 2001; Jacobs 2000). Denying women's agency is also a potential outcome of the crude deployment of a 'gender' concept in policy, where all women are presumed to act in the same way and are powerless to do otherwise. Highlighting the common difficulties that women face as a group can easily degenerate into seeing them as innocent victims and prevents an appreciation of the great variety of roles women actually embrace. Clearly there is a need for more refined analysis of concepts of *femininities* – of what it means to be a woman in different contexts – and for further consideration of how these might lead to different types of peace-building policies.

Analysing rape and sexual violence

As I have tried to show above, violence against women (including rape) during war remains severely under-reported (Drakulić 1994). Rape is recognised as a war crime – and, indeed, war itself is assumed to be a 'cause' of rape. However, there is little agreement on exactly what the difference is between war rape and other forms of rape. Rape as a war crime can be linked to attempted genocide, but may not always be so. From some of the writings about it, one might deduce that war rape is less personal, is part of a military plan, and has a different motive from rape in other circumstances. The explanations for rape at other times are hardly straightforward, however, and they are rarely taken into account by non-feminist writers on conflict. Male rape has received more attention recently, and seems to have been present in many wars in the past, as part of the 'normal' behaviour of heterosexual male soldiers. But since research on male rape in 'normal' times is scanty, it is difficult to make a judgement about how different it is in war.

There is an emerging debate about whether war rape is intended to undermine sexuality or activate it. The perpetrators' sexuality is said to be activated as part of the development or even transformation of war-like masculinity. Enloe (1988) has been influential in highlighting that military commanders have commonly regarded rape against women, particularly in public, as a significant bonding experience (the same argument is not made about male rape, however). War rape is also commonly assumed to be an attempt to undermine the sexuality of the victim/survivor, whether male or female. Both of these types of analysis are commonly used in studying rape in other contexts, however, and so do not assist in clarifying what is unique about war rape.

Turshen (2001) takes the debates somewhat further by considering the case of Rwanda and Mozambique in more detail. She suggests that there has been a neglect of men's motivation to gain access to property through women, and see women as property. Through rape and other forms of assault on women, men were able to gain rights to women's land and access to their labour through forced 'marriage'. They were also able to deny other men access to these goods by disabling and murdering women. She suggests that this motivation might be restricted to societies where gender relations are so unequal that women are not legally autonomous individuals – that is, where colonial and customary legal codes have combined to create the current situation (ibid.). Perhaps an additional context is one of poverty, where access to very small amounts of property has great significance. Turshen provides a careful analysis of the outcome of such violence in these two African countries, but the extent to which it constituted a conscious, premeditated motivation on the part of the perpetrators remains an open question, as does the issue of whether this constituted simply the opportunism of individual perpetrators, or whether there was some self-conscious collective understanding that this action was acceptable or inevitable during wartime. It is worth noting that explanations offered for rape in other places, e.g. the former Yugoslavia (Cockburn 1998), while not conclusive, do not mention gaining access to property or labour as motivations. Finding 'explanations' for war rape remains as complex and challenging as explaining rape during peacetime, a situation that hardly helps to minimise or prevent it.

Giving women a better deal: policies and proposals

I have tried to illustrate some of the ways in which sloppy thinking about concepts of peace and conflict has served to limit the effectiveness of peace-building policy processes in addressing the needs of women. Clearly there are additional, contextual explanations for the persistence of gender inequality and the injustices women suffer in peace building. For instance, in contexts with higher levels of urbanisation and education, issues concerning labour laws are of far greater importance than in predominantly rural, non-literate societies. Nonetheless, in an international context where there is a widespread perception that gender imbalances are a problem, and there is considerable official concern to change things for the better, it is worth taking the analysis a stage further to think through how and where change could best take place.

A great deal more care needs to be taken in determining the conditions of a peace settlement. I have argued elsewhere (Pankhurst 1999) that this is necessary in order to increase the chances of movement towards positive peace and even of lasting negative peace. Any attempts which facilitate more consultation from women have to be an improvement on the current situation, with the provisos about increasing participation given above. Any international support which might be offered to limit the effects of a 'backlash' against women would also make a great deal of difference. Any 'blueprint peace agreements' which are used internationally ought to follow the guidelines about women's needs that have been agreed at UN level and other international forums. The capacity of women to articulate their views could be promoted through initiatives that are neither about personal security nor about economic policy. El-Bushra (2000) argues that rather than seeking ways to achieve a feminist agenda of increased economic autonomy, many women in African countries prioritise ways to restore 'respect' through mended social relations between women and men, even where these are evidently unequal and exploitative. The key improvement in all of these approaches would be to have women's voices heard.

I list below a few examples of what might be feasibly attempted in the near future in some key policy areas, provided a suitable political context is developed. By this I mean that there needs to be increased pressure internationally to ask why and how different forms of violence become more intense and organised under different circumstances; and what the fundamental conditions of peace are. Comparative lessons about peace and conflict – positive or negative – are rarely learned between countries, but they should be. Conflict analysts and peace activists similarly could learn about gender from those practitioners and analysts who have been working in this area for many years. Fostering the space for 'making sense' of gender relations is essential. In this context outsiders might wish to support men as well as women in their efforts to challenge gender stereotypes. Working with men who are also peace activists, community workers, parents, and carers is a useful peace-building tool (United Nations 1995), if rarely taken advantage of.

Macro-policy shifts need to be made by developing 'gender mainstreaming' in post-conflict, peace-building policy processes, alongside 'special' policies specifically geared towards women. This is a goal that has been accepted as appropriate by key international organisations for some time (European Commission 1996a; United Nations 1995). At its simplest, a gender-aware approach requires asking, 'Does this policy affect women and men differently?', and if the answer is affirmative, then it is necessary to explore what can be done to prevent or correct women's disadvantage (Elson 1995). Asking this question would lead to a complete overhaul of the way a policy is developed and implemented in some cases, and in others it would require only minor adjustments. A few governments and international organisations have recently begun to 'engender' budgets to ensure that at least there are no unforeseen consequences of tax and expenditure plans that would penalise women more than men (Elson 1998), but there is considerable potential for further development in this area.

Some general economic policies have more acute implications for gender politics than others. For instance, it is very common to consider *land reform* necessary for peace building. Nowhere in the world has land reform been implemented where gender was not an issue, yet gender has yet to be mainstreamed into its implementation. It is not uncommon for women's previous land rights to be lost or undermined, while new land titles are granted exclusively to men. Women may have some access in their own right but it is usually less secure than men's and often dependent on the women's marital status. International donors have often been very influential in deciding the type of land reform which should be adopted and so there is a great deal of potential for gender to be taken up as an issue in cases where land reform is considered an important part of peace building.

Welfare policies needed to address post-war problems in the short and long term are often developed in a gender-blind way. For instance, in the immediate post-war context, special measures to provide support to ex-combatants are made, but it is very common for women (and child) ex-combatants to be relatively marginalised, if not completely neglected. Similarly, the needs of women to be protected from the violent behaviour of demobilised (yet possibly still armed) male fighters are rarely considered. Furthermore, women ex-combatants' welfare needs rarely receive the same attention as do men's. As women are the main carers of survivors, neglect of their basic needs has knock-on effects throughout society. An alternative approach that *prioritises* women's welfare requirements would have positive knock-on effects in times of peace building.

Such neglect is sometimes a function of the broad macro-economic context where international assistance to governments is conditional on economic reform measures which tightly restrict welfare spending. There is a growing lobby which argues that such conditionalities ought to be looser in post-war economies (Stewart and Fitzgerald 2000) to allow governments to address the specific needs of peace building. As yet, this argument has not been accepted by donors. The same budgetary constraints also often restrict government spending on *education* and it is still the case that girls benefit less than boys in countries where rehabilitation of educational provision is taking place. There are many ways in which this perpetuates an already existing gender inequality and is therefore a useful point of intervention. Moreover, where peace education is taken seriously as part of the new curriculum, this frees women from what might be seen as a private responsibility (that of educating their children for peace) and makes it a public activity, in which men can also play a part. Where peace education also contains explorations of gender issues, there is a direct, long-term input to helping to transform gender relations, and thereby helping to build positive peace.

Nurturing a human-rights culture through the establishment of and support for human-rights organisations is a common mechanism used in peace building. There is room for a very positive input from donors here, especially in terms of incorporating women's rights into human-rights work (European Council 1995). It is more common for women than men to be unaware that they have human rights which are recognised internationally. Children's rights have received much publicity in recent years, but they still tend to be marginalised within the work of many human-rights organisations. Where they are taken up, they are much more concerned with boys' experiences than with girls'. There is therefore considerable room for improvement in this area.

If making politics 'more democratic' is considered important in peace building, then increasing the representation of women should be an objective. However, it is often only when the mainstreaming gender question is asked about apparently gender-neutral changes that any problems with achieving this objective become apparent. For instance, requirements for the registration of voters may affect men and women differently if high degrees of literacy, or long distances of travel, are required. Similarly, attempts to encourage civil society organisations to participate in public debate, or consultations with government, may marginalise the views of women if most organisations are dominated by men. In both cases, special activities involving women may be required (*ibid.*).

As discussed above, so-called 'traditional' reconciliation and conflict-resolution mechanisms need to be handled with care, even as they are being embraced with increasing amounts of enthusiasm internationally. There are perhaps two gender-based reasons why donors should exercise caution in providing support. First, these mechanisms tend to be much more a reflection of highly gendered local politics and power relations than they are part of some value-free traditional cultural context. Second, women's needs are normally completely marginalised in their practice and may even be undermined by them. There are notable exceptions, where the re/invention of traditions has incorporated important roles for women, and even given women and young men space to influence outcomes, but it requires sensitivity to distinguish between the two approaches.

Truth Commissions are coming to be seen as a central plank of peace building, but they usually omit specific consideration of violence against women or else handle it very badly. Women's experiences tend to be marginalised or ignored (United Nations 1998), either because they include specific things which do not happen to men in the same way (sexual violence), or because women find it difficult to bring complaints forward, or because commissioners, the government, or the general public do not want to acknowledge the truth about women's war experiences. The South African Truth and Reconciliation Commission recognised some elements of all of these problems once it was well into its investigation, and it did try to address them by holding some hearings where only women were present, an act which many women regarded as successful in addressing the problem (Goldblatt and Meintjes 1998). The point is not merely to avoid omitting the particular sufferings of women, but also for their experiences to be integrated into the whole story.

In other countries, different kinds of truth processes work outside national commissions. At local levels, sometimes with the help of national or external organisations, communities of people record and mark their conflict histories in different ways (see, for example, REMHI 1999 on Guatemala). Some accounts tend to emerge more spontaneously than others, and it is common for women's experiences to remain undeclared in the absence of proper encouragement (Goldblatt and Meintjes 1996). Although it is difficult for supporting outsiders to shape processes of reconciliation and justice with sensitivity, it is an important task that may, among other things, open up the possibility for women to articulate their histories too.

Conclusion

In general, the plight of women in war attracts international attention, sometimes to a greater degree than men's, and it is often used as a symbol of the horrific barbarism mankind is capable of. Women's roles in working towards peace have become increasingly celebrated (while their other roles are downplayed). As a consequence of this attention, women in 'post-conflict' peace building have been thrust into unprecedented prominence in the policy processes of many international organisations. Yet women remain marginal, as a group as well as as individuals, in peace negotiations and in consultations about 'post-conflict' strategies. Whether in specific peace-building activities, or in more general macro policies, women's needs are consistently marginalised in 'post-conflict' societies, while they also suffer a 'backlash', often with physical and legal ramifications, not only from male citizens but from the state itself.

This unjust and unequal situation persists as an outcome of intense gender politics in 'post-conflict' contexts, where the 'sex war' often becomes more acute than it was 'pre-conflict'. Nonetheless, it is important to register that the persistent reluctance of many analysts and advisers to take on lessons about gendering analysis and policy processes – from feminist histories of other conflicts and from feminist studies of development – has itself allowed, if not facilitated, the playing out of such intense gender politics.

Notes

1 And explicitly exclude situations where there are merely high levels of individual violence, such as that against women (Kelly 2000).

2 For instance, the World Bank has stated that 'women ... often perform better than men because they are less likely to migrate, more accustomed to voluntary work and better trusted to administer funds honestly' (World Development 1992, cited in Green et al. 1998:264).

3 Subsequently, as gender has come to be seen as a generic term referring to either male or female in the development field, some writers have argued that it has even tended to neglect women's issues once again, and that the analysis of power relations between genders has become completely lost (see Baden and Goetz 1998).

References

Abdel Halim, A. (1998) 'Attack with a friendly weapon', in Turshen and Twagiramariya (eds.) (1998).

African Rights (1995) *Rwanda Not so Innocent: When Women Become Killers*, London: African Rights.

Baden, S. and A.M. Goetz (1998) 'Who needs [sex] when you can have [gender]? Conflicting discourses on gender at Beijing', in Jackson and Pearson (eds.) (1998).

Bennett, O., J. Bexley, and K. Warnock (eds.) (1995) *Arms to Fight, Arms to Protect: Women Speak Out About Conflict*, London: Panos Institute.

Berhane-Selassie, T. (1994) 'African women in conflict resolution', *Center Focus* 120 (March): 1–3.

Butalia, U. (2001) 'Women and communal conflict: new challenges for the women's movement in India', in Moser and Clark (eds.) (2001).

Byrne, B. (1996) 'Towards a gendered understanding of conflict', *IDS Bulletin* 27(3): 31–40.

Byrne, B., R. Marcus, and T. Powers-Stevens (1996) *Gender, Conflict and Development. Case Studies*, BRIDGE Report No. 35, Brighton: IDS, University of Sussex.

Cockburn, C. (1998) *The Space Between Us: Negotiating Gender and National Identities in Conflict*, London: Zed Books.

Cockburn, C. (2001) 'The gendered dynamics of armed conflict and political violence', in Moser and Clark (eds.) (2001).

Davidson J., D. Myers, and M. Chakraborty (1992) *No Time to Waste: Poverty and the Global Environment*, Oxford: Oxfam GB.

De Abreu, A.A. (1998) 'Mozambican women experiencing violence', in Turshen and Twagiramariya (eds.) (1998).

Drakulić, S. (1994) 'The rape of women in Bosnia', in Miranda Davies (ed.) *Women and Violence: Realities and Responses Worldwide*, London: Zed Books.

Duba, K.R., Y.G. Kalacha, J. Riganao *et al.* (1997) *Honey and Heifer: Grasses, Milk and Water. A Heritage of Diversity in Reconciliation*, Nairobi: Mennonite Central Committee Kenya and the National Museum of Kenya.

Duffield, M. (1997) 'Evaluating conflict resolution: Context, models and methodology', in Gunnar Sorbo, Joanna Macrae *et al.* (eds.) *NGOs in Conflict – An Evaluation of International Alert*, Annex 1, Bergen: Chr. Michelsen Institute.

El-Bushra, J. (1998) 'Gendered Interpretations of Conflict: Research Issues for COPE', Working Paper, London: ACORD.

El-Bushra, J. (2000) 'Transforming conflict: some thoughts on a gendered understanding of conflict processes', in Jacobs *et al.* (eds.) (2000).

El-Bushra, J. and E. Piza López (1993) *Development in Conflict: The Gender Dimension*, Oxford: Oxfam GB and ACORD.

Elshtain, J.B. (1985) 'Reflections on war and political discourse', *Political Theory* 13(1): 39–57.

Elshtain, J.B. (1987) *Women and War*, New York, NY: Basic Books.

Elson, D. (ed.) (1995) *Male Bias in the Development Process*, Manchester: Manchester University Press.

Elson, D. (1998) 'Talking to the boys: gender and economic growth models', in Jackson and Pearson (eds.) (1998).

Enloe, C. (1988) *Does Khaki Become You? The Militarisation of Women's Lives*, London: Pandora Press.

European Commission (1996a) *The European Union and the Issue of Conflicts in Africa: Peacebuilding, Conflict Prevention and Beyond*, Brussels: European Commission.

European Commission (1996b) *Linking Relief, Rehabilitation and Development*, Brussels: European Commission.

European Council (1995) *Integrating Gender Issues in Development Cooperation*, Brussels: European Council.

Ferris, E. (1993) *Women, War and Peace*, Research Report 14, Uppsala: Life and Peace Institute.

Galtung, J. (1985) 'Twenty-five years of peace research: ten challenges and responses', *Journal of Peace Research* 22(2): 141–58.

Garcia, E. (1993) *Participative Approaches to Peacemaking in the Philippines*, Tokyo: United Nations University.

Garcia, E. (ed.) (1994) *Pilgrim Voices: Citizens as Peacemakers*, London: International Alert.

Goldblatt, B. and S. Meintjes (1996) 'Gender and the Truth and Reconciliation Commission. A Submission to the Truth and Reconciliation Commission', Pretoria: Truth and Reconciliation Commission.

Goldblatt, B. and S. Meintjes (1998) 'South African women demand the truth', in Turshen and Twagiramariya (eds.) (1998).

Green, C., S. Joekes, and M. Leach (1998) 'Questionable links: approaches to gender in environmental research and policy', in Jackson and Pearson (eds.) (1998).

Hague, E. (1997) 'Rape, power and masculinity: the construction of gender and national identities in the war in Bosnia-Herzegovina', in Lentin (ed.) (1997).

International Alert Gender Campaign (1999), *Women Building Peace: From the Village Council to the Negotiating Table*, London: International Alert (available at www.internationalalert.org).

Jackson, C. and R. Pearson (eds.) (1998) *Feminist Visions of Development*, London: Routledge.

Jacobs, S. (2000) 'Globalisation, states and women's agency: possibilities and pitfalls', in Jacobs *et al.* (eds.) (2000).

Jacobs, S. and T. Howard (1987) 'Women in Zimbabwe: state policy and state action', in H. Afshar (ed.) *Women, State and Ideology: Studies from Africa and Asia*, London: Macmillan.

Jacobs, S., R. Jacobson, and J. Marchbank (eds.) (2000) *States of Conflict: Gender, Violence and Resistance*, London: Zed Books.

Jacobson, R. (2000) 'Women and peace in Northern Ireland: a complicated relationship', in Jacobs *et al.* (eds.) (2000).

Kelly, L. (2000) 'Wars against women: sexual violence, sexual politics and the militarised state', in Jacobs *et al.* (eds.) (2000).

Korac, M. (1998) *Linking Arms: Women and War in Post-Yugoslav States*, Uppsala: Life and Peace Institute.

Krog, A. (2001) 'Locked into loss and silence: testimonies of gender and violence at the South Africa Truth Commission', in Moser and Clark (eds.) (2001).

Kynch, J. (1998) 'Famine and transformations in gender relations', in Jackson and Pearson (eds.) (1998).

Lake, A. (ed.) (1990) *After the Wars*, Somerset, NJ: Transaction Publishers.

Large, J. (1997) 'Disintegration conflicts and the restructuring of masculinity', *Gender and Development* 5(2): 23–30.

Lentin, R. (ed.) (1997) *Gender and Catastrophe*, London: Zed Books.

Maitse, Teboho (2000) 'Revealing silence', in Jacobs *et al.* (eds.) (2000).

Miall, H., O. Ramsbotham, and T. Woodhouse (1999) *Contemporary Conflict Resolution*, Cambridge: Polity Press.

Mies, M. and V. Shiva (1993) *Ecofeminism*, London: Zed Books.

Moser, C. and F. Clark (eds.) (2001) *Victims, Perpetrators or Actors? Gender, Armed Conflict and Political Violence*, London: Zed Books.

Mukta, P. (2000) 'Gender, community, nation: the myth of innocence', in Jacobs *et al.* (eds.) (2000).

Mulholland, M. (2001) 'The challenge to inequality: women, discrimination and decision-making in Northern Ireland', in Moser and Clark (eds.) (2001).

Nordstrom, C. (1997) *Girls and Warzones: Troubling Questions*, Uppsala: Life and Peace Institute.

Pankhurst, D. (1999) 'Issues of justice and reconciliation in Complex Political Emergencies', *Third World Quarterly* 20(1): 239–56.

Pankhurst, D. and J. Pearce (1997) 'Engendering the analysis of conflict: perspectives from the South', in H. Afshar (ed.) *Women and Empowerment*, London: Routledge.

Peterson, V.S. (1993) *Global Gender Issues*, Boulder, CO: Westview Press.

Pierson, R.R. (1989) 'Beautiful soul or just warrior: gender and war', *Gender and History* 1(1).

Pringle, R. and S. Watson (1992) '"Women's interests" and the post-structuralist state', in M. Barrett and A. Phillips (eds.) *Destabilizing Theory: Contemporary Feminist Debates*, Palo Alto, CA: Stanford University Press.

REMHI (Recovery of Historical Memory Project) (1999) *Guatemala: Never Again!*, London: Latin American Bureau.

Richards, P. (1995) 'Rebellion in Liberia and Sierra Leone: a crisis of youth', in O. Furley (ed.) *Conflict in Africa*, London: I.B. Tauris.

Sharoni, S. (2001) 'Rethinking women's struggles in Israel–Palestine and in the North of Ireland', in Moser and Clark (eds.) (2001).

Shiva, V. (1998) *Staying Alive: Women, Ecology and Development*, London: Zed Books.

Steans, J. (1998) *Gender and International Relations*, Cambridge: Polity Press.

Stewart, F. and V. Fitzgerald (eds.) (2000) *War and Underdevelopment*, Oxford: Oxford University Press.

Turshen, M. (1998) 'Women's war stories', in Turshen and Twagiramariya (eds.) (1998).

Turshen, M. (2001) 'The political economy of rape: an analysis of systematic rape and sexual abuse of women during armed conflict in Africa', in Moser and Clark (eds.) (2001).

Turshen, M. and C. Twagiramariya (eds.) (1998) *What Women Do in Wartime: Gender and Conflict in Africa*, London: Zed Books.

Twagiramariya, C. and M. Turshen (1998) '"Favours" to give and "consenting" victims: the sexual politics of survival in Rwanda', in Turshen and Twagiramariya (eds.) (1998).

United Nations (1985) *Report on the World Conference to Review and Appraise the Achievements of the United Nations Decade for Women: Equality, Development and Peace*, Nairobi, 15–26 July.

United Nations (1995) *Beijing Declaration and Platform for Action*, Fourth World Conference on Women, 15 September.

United Nations (1997) *Report of the Expert Group Meeting on Adolescent Girls and their Rights*, Addis Ababa: United Nations, Division for the Advancement of Women.

United Nations (1998) *Resolution on Women and Armed Conflict*, United Nations, Commission for the Status of Women.

Vail, L. (1989) 'Introduction: ethnicity in Southern African history', in L. Vail (ed.) *The Creation of Tribalism in Southern Africa*, Oxford: James Currey.

Vickers, J. (1993) *Women and War*, London: Zed Books.

Women and wars:
some trajectories towards a feminist peace

Haleh Afshar

Women as revolutionaries and combatants: the Islamic experience

When analysing the role of gender in conflict, the first myth that needs to be exploded is that of the absence of women from the battleground. It is too simplistic to assume that it is in the nature of men and women to be situated in the public and private arenas, respectively, and that it is in the essence of their beings that men become associated with wars, revolutions, and rebellions, while women become associated with peace. In addition to the flourishing feminist literature that argues against such assumptions, in the context of Islam and the Middle East, history empirically counters such views. Throughout the ages, women have been active participants in wars, not only as camp followers, carers, and providers, but also as combatants.

The recorded participation of women in wars preceded Islam and became central to Islamic politics at the time of the Prophet some 14 centuries ago; and both the majority Sunni Muslims and the minority Shiias have historical memories of female warriors. The Prophet was accompanied by women in the wars that he waged, and after his death his youngest and cherished wife Ayisha took to the battlefields heading an army against the Shiia *imam* Ali. Though she was defeated, Ayisha's experience both as warrior and as king maker has been central to the history of Islam. After the death of the Prophet, it was Ayisha who decided that caliphs should be selected by consensus (*ijma*), rather than by descent. She facilitated the choice of first her father and subsequently Omar and Othman as caliphs. When eventually the Prophet's cousin and son-in-law was selected as the fourth caliph, Ayisha raised an army and went into battle against him.

Muslim women have continued to participate in wars and struggles across the centuries. To take Iran as an example, there has been both a long history of women's participation in protests, revolutions, and rebellion, and often a close association between their actions and those of the religious establishment. It may be argued that revolutions can demonstrate that they have real and extensive popular support when the women take to the streets. In the case of Iran, back in the late nineteenth century, veiled women led riots demanding cheaper bread. Their presence convinced the Qajar king that he needed to respond positively to that demand. Similarly, women played an important role in the tobacco revolution of 1881. The Qajar king Nasseredin shah granted a tobacco monopoly to a British company to control the industry from the point of production to consumption. The handing over of such a lucrative industry to a foreign company met with intense opposition among the merchant classes and their close allies in the religious establishment. As a result, the eminent Shiia leader Haj Mirza Hassan Shirazi issued a *fatwa*, or religious order, banning the use of tobacco. The entire nation obeyed. Women of all classes, including the royal entourage, felt so outraged that they broke their water pipes and gave up smoking. When the Shah smoked a water pipe (*qualyan*), in the presence of his favourite wives and ordered them to follow his example, they refused pointing out that they would not touch alcoholic drinks because it was forbidden by Islam: 'Right now tobacco has been forbidden by the senior religious leader. It cannot be made licit for us by the monarch's command' (Ravandi 1336:719). The king revoked the tobacco concession.

In 1906, veiled women mobbed the royal carriage, demanding that the king pay attention to the demands of the religious leaders who were leading the constitutional movement. There were even some redoubtable tribal women who took up arms against the king's forces and beat them in battle. Later in the century, Iranian women continued to play their part in the military occupation that ravaged the country during the Second World War and were active in the subsequent revolutions of 1953 and 1979. In 1979, the presence of veiled women by the millions in anti-shah demonstrations spelt the downfall of the Pahlavi rule in Iran.

Even in the post-revolutionary period and under the Islamification laws, during the war against Iraq women served as nurses, cooks, and washerwomen behind the front lines. But the feminine nature of their tasks contributed to the enduring wartime picture of 'man does, woman is'.

Women warriors

Universally, women have participated in the wars and revolutions embroiling their homelands. Their contributions have ranged from providing practical support for the combatants to being used as important symbols of nationhood and motherhood, to becoming embattled courageously and fighting alongside men. They have done so in Latin America, Southeast Asia, Africa, and elsewhere. Women were freedom-fighters in Nicaragua, Vietnam, and in South Africa, where they were trained and fought along with men in the ANC forces. The ANC offered the same military training for men and women. Women and men slept in separate barracks but the women wore the same uniforms, attended the same physical fitness, engineering, and map-reading courses, and did the same chores and daily routines as the men. In Vietnam and among the rebel factions of Southern Sudan, women were also active combatants. They furnished much of the infrastructure of resistance, acted as couriers, and provided intelligence and refuge.

In times of war, gender barriers were diluted. Where they were active combatants, women's participation often helped during the time of war to create a sense of equality and erase gender differences. Sometimes individual women have even been propelled into positions of authority. But those were the exceptions. All too often in the post-war era women have found it harder to maintain their positions. This may in part be because their participation was always seen as marginal; they were 'helpers' and not policy makers or frontline combatants. Women who enlisted to serve with the conventional armed forces, as in the South African SADF or in the Israeli army, for example, remained subservient to men and were employed in feminised tasks and medical and civilian ranks. In some cases, as that of Iran during the eight-year war with Iraq, the presence of armed women at the front line and in army processions was merely a propaganda ploy. Though much photographed on parades, women covered in the full-length *chador* veil never took part in active combat. Thus it can be argued that, on the whole, whether real or symbolic, the presence of women in the formal and informal armed forces has not fundamentally changed their social position (Abdel Halim 1998; Cock 1992).

However, even when women are not present in direct combat, they continue to play important roles in supporting the cause. Usually they have been operating within their traditional frameworks providing the men with vital support and back-up. In Palestine, women belonging to Amal and the Islamist Hizbollah seem to have been liberated by the war. They have shed their invisible domestic role to participate actively in the public sphere, albeit veiled and segregated. They smuggled food, kept watch and, when necessary, created diversions so that the men could get away. They did not join the military, but they were and remain an integral part of the resistance movement. Similarly, Vietnamese women were viewed as an asset to their men. They cultivated the fields while the men went to war, provided food and support, carried medicine, served as air-raid wardens in the north, and fought along the men in the south (Taylor 1999:125).

War and femininity

In their long struggle against apartheid, some ANC and South African guerrilla women chose to be both lovers and fighters. But they did so against the prevailing opinions and had to defend their position by arguing that such relationships did not 'weaken' them, even though it 'softened' them (Cock 1992:152). This exercise in the niceties of terminology is indicative of the problems that women experience when they try to combine their roles as carers and warriors.

The sense of masculinity which is anchored in the very conception of wars and revolutions remains almost uncontested. A change in the role of men from breadwinners to combatants entitles them to more rights. But femininity sits uncomfortably with wars and conflicts. The change of the role of the woman from a housewife to a combatant is without clear precedence and has taken differing trajectories in different contexts. The move may provide a path towards equality but it can also cause a further decline in a woman's status. Those few women who achieve a position of leadership often feel very vulnerable. They find it necessary to prove their commitment and valour all the time (Cock 1992:162). This may explain why, while the Iranian resistance leader Rajavi could leave to work in exile, his wife, Khiabani, was the partner who stayed behind to continue the fight to the death. But for those women who survive, once they have been identified as 'strong women', it becomes difficult for them also to acknowledge having a heart (Atwan 1993); the masculine stereotype of battles works to deprive women of all vestige of femininity.

Yet many women do not wish to abandon femininity. Even warrior women sometimes tire of the uniformly male attires that denote their military rank by denying their femininity. Sometimes women who have lived with and dressed like their male counterparts find it liberating to regain their femininity. But even among revolutionaries, when such women wear short skirts and feminine clothes, they find that their brethren in arms may revert to type and begin whistling and cat-calling (Cock 1992:152). There are times when women find their traditional clothes useful as a protection. Muslim women have used their all-enveloping veils to secure their anonymity and also to hide the arms and ammunition that they carry for the fighters. They did so in Iran in the course of the 1906 and 1979 revolutions and in the post-revolutionary struggles in the 1980s, and they did it as well during the civil war in Algeria and in other Muslim countries. The redoubtable South African woman Thandi Modise has been called 'the knitting needles guerrilla' because, while she was operating underground as an Umkhonto we Sizwe guerrilla, she tried to look as ordinary as possible and carried a handbag from which protruded a pair of knitting needles (Cock 1992:149).

Front and back

A further myth that needs exploding is that of valiant men at the battlefront defending the honour of their wives and protecting the family back home. Increasingly, wars are fought on the home fronts. In Iraq, it was marketplaces and bridges that were bombed, as well as underground refuges in which women and children would hide to protect themselves from the bombardment of the cities. In Afghanistan, it is the towns once again that are bombed and the women and children that trail across mountains and borders to reach refugee camps, where invariably they live in abominable conditions.

The invisibility of women's participation in wars and revolutions, their unacknowledged, low-profile contributions to the protection of the combatants, and their hidden complicity in the construction of the fighting forces have all helped to uphold the myth of the silent cowardly woman in need of protection from male warriors. Were the details of women's activities more broadly known, it would become more difficult to maintain these kinds of stereotypes (Turshen 1998:1).

Militarism is disenfranchising; it is politically as well as economically and physically debilitating. In militarised zones and during civil wars, violence becomes a crisis of everyday life, especially when 'dirty war' strategies are used by different factions contending for power

(Nordstrom 1992:261). It becomes difficult, if not impossible, to separate combat from non-combat, and the frontguard and rearguard are not clear-cut, either. Most women in such situations experience violence as a matter of daily life and devise strategies to cope with it. To live under military occupation is to live in a permanent state of war with no place to hide and no ceasefires.

When nations live under military occupation, be it by foreign or by coercive internal forces, the traditional divides between feminine and masculine roles and spaces are blurred. During the *intifada* uprising in Palestine, for example, women confronted Israeli soldiers in their homes and neighbourhoods more often than men did during the day: 'Usually soldiers come each day in the morning ... this is the usual routine: the soldiers come, enter some houses without knocking and take the men and boys away' ('Adi 1993:124).

The attacks and destruction of camps and villages in the 2002 Israeli invasion have further obliterated any notion of divide between home and war fronts or any gender divide in terms of death and destruction. Rita Giacaman, Professor of Public Health at Birzeit University, reported 'rampant' stealing of people's belongings and valuables and the stealing of food from stores by the army as a matter of everyday experience (reported in her e-mails of 11 and 15 April 2002, among many more). Homes became mass graves (*Guardian* 16 April 2002). At such times and in such battles, men, women, and children can be labelled as 'terrorists' and murdered indiscriminately. Children as young as four years of age were accused of terrorism and murdered with impunity (interview with an Israeli squadron leader on the BBC Radio Four 'Today' programme 16 April 2002).

Once the distinction between the home and the battlefield has been eliminated, it is not surprising that the armed forces should lose sight of boundaries: not only do the homes become the targets of invaders but also sexuality becomes the domain of power struggles. Rape is used to rip apart the fabric of society not only by undermining women but also their men. Male soldiers invade homes, attack women physically and sexually, and force themselves on women who had until then lived a private life. Women who are taken prisoner are humiliated physically and emotionally. Male interrogators use concepts of shame and honour when questioning women prisoners and do not stop at words. Honour and shame become central to the lives of women prisoners. The divide between masculinity and femininity remains crucial, particularly in terms of these concepts. Women who are arrested and refuse to be broken down by their prison interrogators may be raped or assumed to have been raped.

There are, for instance, extensive reports of Iranian prison warders raping virgin girls in order to make sure that they would not be allowed in heaven after their execution (Goldbatt and Meintjes 1998). Palestinian women resistance fighters were often not welcomed back to their communities, even if they had not been sexually violated by their interrogators. Women trapped in these and other situations of conflict have often found that, once freed from prison, it is difficult, if not impossible, for them to regain their honoured positions within the family. Many are, or are accused of being, pregnant with illegitimate children (Mayer 1994:78).

Marriage

One of the practical problems imposed on women by the prevalence of value systems grounded on honour and shame is the impossibility of women activists and combatants to return to normality. Since often they are seen as having been tarnished either physically or emotionally, they become 'un-marriageable' in societies where marriage is the norm.

Moreover, the sexual vulnerability of women is not confined to the activities of invading forces. Among combatants, too, the relationships between men and women can be difficult. Sudanese women fighters found themselves subjected to forced marriage and rape (Abdel Halim 1998:96). Iranian women working with the resistance movements were more or less compelled to marry their comrades in order to make them respectable and enable them to work alongside men. In fact, the only possible path to women's rising up the ranks of the Iranian resistance fighters was through marriage. When Ashraf Khiabani, the wife of Massoud Rajavi and leader of the Islamic *Mujahidin* forces in Iran, was killed in a street battle, he married Maryam, the wife of his second in command. Maryam divorced her husband, married the leader, and subsequently displaced him as the leader of the *Mujahidin* in exile. But she could not have done so without the formality and protection of marriage. Nicaraguan women fighters got married informally while under arms, but at the end of the Sandinista revolution found it difficult to re-integrate into their society. Some South African women guerrillas chose to marry and have children at the same time as they engaged in the resistance movement, arguing that marriage and children were necessities, not luxuries, and that they deepened the commitment of the combatants.

At times of war and crisis, the role of women is to give solace to soldiers by marrying them, or in some cases by comforting them in the euphemistically named 'rest and recreation zones'. Those who marry must give solace to the nation by giving birth to sons and demonstrating the need for further combat by shadowing the coffins of those killed in combat.

But marriage has also been designated a place where women are expected to perform their duties as carers and providers. In war, they become carers of the sick, wounded, and disabled men who can no longer fight, and the providers of future warriors. During the eight-year war against Iraq, the Iranian state was offering widowed and single women a small dowry and a great deal of encouragement to marry disabled and wounded soldiers, thus freeing the state of its obligation to care for its heroes.

Motherhood

Perhaps the most difficult demands placed upon women at times of war regard motherhood. Warring states and revolutionary leaders adopt a language that reifies motherhood and defines a woman's worth in terms of her ability to have children. For example, the Iranian religious leader Khomeini, like Hitler and Mussolini before him, considered motherhood to be a full-time occupation rooted in the core of the family. Khomeini instructed women to return to their homes and concentrate on being good teachers 'in the family'. He advised them most strongly to avoid cluttering their minds with 'unnecessary' subjects taught in the formal educational institutions. The Germans limited female enrolment in the universities to 10 per cent, Mussolini and Khomeini barred women from studying technical subjects, and Khomeini expelled all female law students. Like Hitler in 1936, Khomeini in 1979 sacked all women judges and made the law the exclusive domain of men. Thus, though a powerful and evocative symbol, motherhood was defined in these contexts as the unavoidable destiny as well as the national duty of women.

Women in post-revolutionary Iran were to be 'elevated' to the honourable task of motherhood. They were to become the pillars of society by being 'strong forts of virtue and chastity' and by 'raising brave and enlightened men and meek and united women'. Such praise of motherhood echoed Hitler's statement that entrusted women with the life of the nation by making them responsible for caring for the body and mind of their men. So strong was the call for women to espouse motherhood that some national papers in Iran began referring to young women as 'future mothers of the children of the revolution'. Hitler in *Mein Kampf* makes a similar assertion, contending that young women achieve full citizenship only when they marry and particularly when they bear children to maintain and perpetuate the Arian race. Similarly, Khomeini felt that mothers should be the cornerstone of the nation's future by raising 'brave men in the laps'.

But it is not only fascists, Christians, or Muslims who place motherhood as the central contribution of women to war efforts. In Israel, Geula Cohen, founder of the extreme-right Tehiya Party, reminded women that it was in their 'nature' and their 'reserve duty' to be 'a wife of a soldier, a sister of a soldier, a grandmother of a solider' (Hazleton 1977:63).

Thus motherhood, which in peacetime is often a natural progression and a happy event, becomes a burdensome duty during a crisis, and even the forerunner of death and devastation. Women fighting at the front feel the need to justify having children. Women who are left behind are expected to give birth to sons and to future warriors and to sacrifice those very sons to the cause. They become the guardians of cradles and coffins. Motherhood, the unpaid job of women at home, is rewarded by the death of their children. Thus, mothers universally become the symbol of sorrow and suffering, and children the cause for sacrifice. Some warrior women adopt the same language as men in singling out motherhood as such an emblem. The South African guerrilla fighter Ruth Mompati, who had given her whole life to the struggle, said that she has 'done it for our children' to create a better life for them (Cock 1992:178).

Some women fighters, however, have seen motherhood as a celebration of their femininity and as the humanising aspect of their lives. Jacqueline Molefe, a leading member of the Umkhonto we Sizwe guerrilla movement in Southern Africa, was proud to say that, in addition to being a soldier, she was the mother of two little girls who had 'introduced something new' in her life (Cock 1992:162). The well-known fighter Thandi Modise felt that giving birth enabled her to keep hold of reality, of pure and absolute love, and of the reasons why she was fighting. In her view, it was important for fighters also to understand the emotions and experience the love of parenting (Cock 1992:152). But in the battle between femininity and war many women had to abandon their children and fight.

Martyrdom

Celebration of death and martyrdom becomes the hallmark of suffering and achievement for women across cultural and national divides. In Israel and Palestine, as in Iran during the war with Iraq, funerals are major political occasions where it is women and their suffering that are paraded as justification for further wars and further grief.

In Iran, public funerals were central from the inception of the 1979 revolution, which orchestrated a recurring theme of public mourning ceremonies held at 40-day intervals to remember those gunned down by the shah's soldiers. These mourning marches began in the holy city of Qum and spread throughout the main urban centres and finally led to public demonstrations of over two million people in Tehran. Thus, it can be argued that the Iranian revolution was anchored in the ceremony of death and mourning. The massive presence of women, veiled in the traditional black *chador* (veil), played an important symbolic role in affirming not only their support for the cause, but also the willingness of the nation's homes and hearths to move out of their allotted domestic sphere and give public backing to the Islamic revolution.

However, it was during the war with Iraq that this powerful symbolism was played to its fullest. As more and more men were called to the front and killed, ever greater importance was given to motherhood both as a symbol of resistance and of heroism. Public funerals were held every week with mothers of martyrs heading the mourners while promising more sons for the cause. Thus, motherhood became a sign of survival and defiance: mothers of martyrs announced that it was their aim in life to produce more martyrs. They paraded their young sons as evidence of the unending supply of heroes. At the time, death was a very likely future for these boys since the Iranian untrained militia forces, *basiji,* were recruited from children of school age and despatched to the front; some were barely 14 years old and had about a fortnight's training before they were sent to fight. Death was probable and the belief that martyrdom would secure a passage to heaven was absolute. Iranian resistance fighters, and subsequently the Iranian government at war with Iraq, publicly 'congratulated' the mothers of these 'martyrs'. Mothers of martyrs were celebrated, filmed, and interviewed. The rhetoric was backed by official government encouragement and pro-natalist propaganda as well as by financial rewards. Even though the rewards were negligible, the hype and publicity verged on the hysterical. Women who had many martyred sons were offered pensions for their achievements, given prizes, hauled up at Friday prayers, and praised for offering their sons to the war and helping them achieve martyrdom. Through motherhood, then, these women became heroines. Women were not warriors, their battles were emotional; they were the ones who sacrificed their loved ones for the nation and for the cause.

This same symbolism remains extremely powerful in Palestine, where the mood of sacrifice and martyrdom has become embedded in the *intifada*. Religious leaders continuously announce to the world that their highest aspiration is to achieve martyrdom, and the mothers of martyrs proclaim proudly that they are prepared to offer their remaining sons to the cause.

Although the celebration of martyrdom is not exclusively an Islamic custom, the concept of martyrdom is deeply rooted in the theology of the Shiia sect. There is a long-standing belief that giving one's life for a just cause is a noble act that is rewarded in heaven. But martyrdom and heroism in the early days of Islam were not the exclusive domain of men. Almost all the descendants of the Prophet – men as well as women, and children – took to the front in the Battle of Karbala to fight against the Caliph Muaviyeh, whom they accused of usurping power. Almost all the men were killed. Though soundly defeated, their massacre in Karbala created the powerful symbolism of martyrdom, which has remained a central motive among the minority Shiias in general, and Iranians in particular. Female descendants of the Prophet not only took part in battles but also made history by denouncing Muaviyeh and publicly declaring the right of the descendants of the Prophet to lead the *umma*, community of Muslims. There was nothing quiet, veiled, absent, or enclosed in the private domain about these women in the golden days of Islam. They went into an unequal battle against the usurpers of power and, when taken prisoner, they made brave speeches denouncing Muaviyeh for his savage and disrespectful treatment of the descendants of the Prophet.

This deeply rooted symbolism came very much to the fore during the revolution and the war against Iraq. But it is sad and ironic that 14 centuries later the Islamic revolution should use images of veiled secluded women as the symbols of success and in many cases seek to enclose and exclude them from the public domain as an indication of progress and Islamism – when these women participated in the revolution, they did so for ideals that did not include their exclusion from the public domain.

Post-war reconstruction

Wars don't simply end
And wars don't end simply
Wars have their endings inside families.

(Enloe 1996:299, 306)

For too long, wars, revolutions, and militarist governments have been seen as male affairs with men fighting for masculine causes, ranging from defending specific classes or ideologies to protecting the interests of groups or nations. In these contexts, women – defined in terms of their function as wives, mothers, and keepers of the nation – are used as incentives to make male soldiers obedient, willing to kill for the sake of maintaining the socially constructed notions the woman embodies (Enloe 1988:20). The presence of women as icons is celebrated, but often their active contribution to the cause is shaded out by history and by subsequent political developments. In post-conflict periods, ideas of national security are redefined in terms of safeguarding the political and social status quo, rooted in the practical and symbolic mobilisation of gender identities, roles, and bodies, in the service of the new polity.

In the post-war and post-violence phases, women are expected to make the necessary practical and emotional adjustments to go back to their traditional role of 'homemakers'. Ideologies do not change during wars; they are simply suspended. Emerging post-war nations very frequently reconstruct an idea of nationalism which is heavily dependent on control over their women 'in the effort to protect, revive and create nations' (Basch 1997:5). Even where women have been active participants in liberation struggles, more often than not the aftermath of violence appears to result in their confinement to the domestic sphere where it is assumed they will be 'protected'. Embedded in this notion of protection is the idea of securing the safety of women and children. The protection of the home and family becomes central to peace-building efforts even when, as is often the case, homes have been attacked and ravaged.

Wars break asunder once-integrated communities, which may fracture along lines of racial, ethnic, or religious identity or party affiliation, whether real, imagined, or reconstructed. The wars in Bosnia, Ethiopia, and Lebanon are but a few examples. Such wars manipulate identity and make it much harder for women to maintain their place in society and continue in their time-honoured function as cultural transmitters and socialisers within their families. The Iraqi invasion of Iran immediately made 51 per cent of the Iraqis, who like Iranians are of the Shiia Muslim sect, into the enemies of their own nation. Marriages amongst Sunnis and Shiias in Iraq, which had hitherto been commonplace, suddenly became sites of contestation. As elsewhere, the war in Iran fractured homes, families, and women's sense of identity.

A feminist perspective on post-war definition of citizenship

Exploding the myths about women's absence from wars and conflict also entails recognising that they may well bring a different perspective on how to end the violence and work towards peace. Although women all over the world have different views about war and militarism, it can be argued that many of them share a strong commitment to peace and nurturing. This enables them to survive wars, which are not of their making, and devastation and revolutions, which do not benefit them. Feminists, who perceive the commonality of women's experience as superseding man-made national boundaries, thus offer an alternative approach. They often see beyond the 'abstractions and deceptions' of borders and boundaries which enflame the intertwining, swirling circles of violence and are able to identify overarching symbols of unity and shared values that transcend those artificial divides.

Lebanese women authors have blazed a trail by writing about ways of analysing and surviving wars without rancour, and seeing them instead as life experiences of a historical continuum. Authors such as Jean Said Makdisi, Etel Adnan, and Emily Nasrallah have created a 'narrative of peace politics'; they write out of war and about war, but most of all they write *against* war (Cooke 1999:84). Writing from the margins, they reveal the artificiality of the Lebanese War Story that imposed an order 'on the chaos of emotions, motivation and outcomes of the war' (Makdisi 1990:76). They highlight the reality that in Lebanon there were no clear boundaries between war and peace, but rather periods of calm which embodied 'different degrees of being at war' (Makdisi 1990:76). For them, stark categorisations like war and peace are not useful in describing their lives, which instead moved along a continuum between 'war and not-war' (Cooke 1999:84).

Using the traditional craft of storytelling and their traditional roles as keepers of memories, these women use the power of words to create a different understanding. They conventionalise a new centre, which does not break down along neat distinctions between 'friend and foe, victory and defeat, front and home front' (Makdisi 1990:76). These writers see the 'static' definition of nationalism as irrelevant. They argue that there should be different criteria of belonging to a nation. They want to explode the myth that men go to war to protect their women and that women prefer that their men die in combat rather than return in defeat (Cooke 1999:76).

The poet and painter Etel Adnan has used women's traditional role as witnesses and keepers of memories to write a different story about motherhood and suffering (Adnan 1993:159). She attributes a 'magical power' to motherhood, to suffering for the deaths of martyrs and survival: the power to heal societal wounds with words. She writes about the insight that such suffering brings to understanding war and peace as holistic processes. In this alternative vision, motherhood is seen not as an emblem of war, but as a symbol of peace building. Here, motherhood at times of war ceases to be merely about cradles and coffins and becomes also about healing.

The absence of a clear boundary between the war and the home fronts means that ordinary women live as mothers of militiamen and also 'chid[e] them as naughty sons for wreaking such havoc'. As scolding mothers they undermine the glories of gun-toting and put themselves in a position of authority over the generators of the violence. In other words, they become involved in and assume responsibility for trying to stop the war (Makdisi 1990:76).

Lebanese women authors have created a perspective whereby the heavy burden of grief and suffering is seen as a means of enabling them, and potentially enabling nations, to gain a new understanding of the wasteland that wars create. The survivors should have the strength to move towards a 'humanistic nationalism'. This is very different from the male perception, which defines nationalism as an absolute sense of belonging that is constructed within a binary framework of differentiation and recognition. Whereas in this male perception the nation is the undisputed birthright only of those who 'naturally' belong to it, the feminist humanists define the nation as dialectic, as both produced and productive. Citizenship ceases to be a birthright or a reward for military service; it becomes an identity that can be acquired by shared suffering and grief. The survivors do not have allegiance to a single polity, but rather to the diverse and fragmented realities that form and re-form in different alliances and networks to ensure survival. It is the sorrow of those who stayed and survived that forms the nucleus of allegiance and support. Their shared suffering unites them and creates a sense of shared identity. Suffering and survival create new roots in new places and bring with them old experiences and understandings. No one feels entitled to any particular piece of the earth. Their suffering and shared identities as mothers and wives give women access to the whole world as a homeland, while they keep 'a very tiny place' into which they can 'sink their roots'; roots which are both ancient and modern, firm and flexible (Nasrallah 1985:16). The women Nasrallah writes about have uprooted and re-rooted themselves, and continue to keep a sense of belonging.

When women themselves take charge of their own identity, they often celebrate motherhood as a harbinger of peace, an experience that could bridge the gap between women across wide religious and national divides. In Argentina, the Madres de la Plaza de Mayo (mothers of the disappeared) used the powerful symbol of mother-hood to demand justice and peace. Like the Madres, the Black Sash organisation in South Africa gathered about 2000 women who took to the streets demanding peace in the name of motherhood. These largely English-speaking and middle-class women used motherhood as a banner for peace and reconciliation. For such women, motherhood entails responsibility for life and not death.

Movements like the Black Sash, the Madres, and the Detainees' Parent Support Committee (DPSC), among many more, have created a new form of resistance to the state, to tyranny, and to death-mongers: a resistance based on the notion of motherhood, parenthood, and the family. Wars, revolutions, and injustice politicised mothers and family relations, and proved important in mobilising women. Mothers as protectors of their children and of the nation can and have used the maternal image to oppose war, forced conscription, and militarism. These are the women who identify themselves as the voice of nurturers and preservers.

In Iran, where there was a counter-movement of nurturers, individual mothers on occasion laid siege to the barracks where their conscripted sons were being trained to be sent to war. The story of Khatoun, a young mother from a village in the central province, has become legendary. Khatoun followed the conscription lorry by begging a lift from a distant relative who owned a van. She then stayed on the pavement outside the barracks crying the traditional scream, *shivan*, which women do in ceremonies of mourning. She stopped passers-by to ask them to share in her grief and think about a war and a revolution that deprived peasant women of their invaluable young sons only to squander their lives at the front. She cried and screamed for almost a week. Although few newspapers reported her vigil, every day crowds gathered around her in support. Eventually the authorities invented a bureaucratic excuse for releasing her son and both mother and son returned to their village.

Women across the Palestinian–Israeli divide have linked hands physically both by keeping vigils as mothers on public squares and by sewing shared patchwork quilts across the length and the breadth of the two nations. Women across the divide in former Yugoslavia are seeking to forge common bonds. Muslim women across the world, even across the Iranian and Iraqi borders, have united in their abhorrence of what the Taleban did to women in the name of Islam.

These and other symbolic gestures may as yet be too few and far between, but feminism has a vital contribution to make to peace building and post-war reconstruction around the world. The first halting steps have been taken, the bigger strides are yet to come.

References

Abdel Halim, A. (1998) 'Attack with friendly weapon', in Turshen and Twagiramariya (eds.) (1998).

'Adi, S. (1993) 'Fifty-three days' curfew in Kufr Malek', in Agustin (ed.) (1993).

Adnan, E. (1993) 'Letters from Beirut', *Mediterraneans* 5:107–10.

Agustin, Ebba (ed.) (1993) *Palestinian Women: Identity and Experience*, London: Zed Books.

Atwan, T. (1993) 'Life is struggle inside and outside the Green Line', in Agustin (ed.) (1993).

Basch, L. (1997) 'Introduction: rethinking nationalism and militarism from a feminist perspective', in Constance Sutton (ed.) *Feminism, Nationalisms and Militarism*, Arlington, VA: American Anthropology Association.

Cock, J. (1992) *Women and War in South Africa*, London: Open Letters.

Cooke, M. (1999) 'Mapping peace', in Lamia Rustum Shehadeh (ed.) *Women and War in Lebanon*, Gainesville, FL: University Press of Florida.

Enloe, C. (1988) *Does Khaki Become You? The Militarization of Women's Lives*, London: Pluto Press.

Enloe, C. (1996) 'Women after wars: puzzles and warnings', in Kathleen Barry (ed.), *Vitna's Women in Transition*, Basingstoke: Macmillan.

Goldblatt, B. and S. Meintjes (1998) 'South African women demand the truth', in Turshen and Twagiramariya (eds.) (1998).

Hazleton, L. (1977) *Israeli Women: The Reality Behind the Myths*, New York, NY: Simon & Schuster.

Makdisi, J.S. (1990) *Beirut Fragments: A War Memoire*, New York, NY: Persia Books.

Mayer, T. (1994) 'Heightened Palestinian nationalism', in M. Tamar (ed.) *Women and the Israeli Occupation*, London: Routledge.

Nasrallah, E. (1985) quoted in Cooke (1999).

Nordstrom, C. (1992) 'The backyard front', in C. Nordstrom and J. Martin (eds.) *The Path to Domination, Resistance, and Terror*, Berkeley, CA: University of California Press.

Ravandi, M. (1336, 1957) *Tarikheh Ejtmayieh Iran*, Volume 3 (2nd edn.) Tehran: Amir Kabir Publications.

Taylor, S.C. (1999) *Vietnamese Women at War*, Lawrence, KS: University Press of Kansas.

Turshen, M. (1998) 'Women's war stories', in Turshen and Twagiramariya (eds.) (1998).

Turshen, M. and Twagiramariya, C. (eds.) (1998) *What Women Do in Wartime: Gender and Conflict in Africa*, London: Zed Books.

Developing policy on integration and re/construction in Kosova[1]

Chris Corrin

Introduction

While I have addressed post-conflict reconstruction and gender analysis in Kosova using the Gender Audit (GA)[2] elsewhere (Corrin 2000, 2001), my focus in this chapter is on the impact that changes in dialogue have had on the policy toward and support for local women's work in reducing gender imbalances and gender-based violence in Kosova. A central area of concern in undertaking the GA was to assess the extent to which women's social, economic, educational, and political participation has been encouraged – both in 'informal' civic forums and organisations, and at the formal levels of power. For continuity and in the interests of follow-up projects, the GA assesses 'gaps' in policy making, service provision, data collection, and the co-ordination and monitoring of projects designed to increase the participation of women and girls. The GA suggests additional monitoring, investigation, and collaborative efforts to bring about the full integration of women and girls in the re/construction of societies in southeast Europe. In view of the fact that the critiques and some recommendations from the GA have been taken up in two recent UN reports (one by the Secretary General and the other by UNIFEM), as well as in the Kosovo [sic] Women's Initiative (KWI) Review, the GA has already made some input to the analytical decision-making framework.[3]

The situation in which the UN Mission in Kosova (UNMIK) came to be the governmental power was one of tension and turmoil following the NATO bombing of Kosova and Serbia. Much has been written about this intervention and the gendered aspects of conflict and post-conflict developments (see Hasani 2000; Judah 2000; Maliqi 1998; Mertus 1999; Waller *et al.* 2001). Peacekeeping has evolved to include areas of humanitarian relief, refugee return, demining, civilian policing,

 First published in *Development in Practice* 13(2&3): 189–207 in 2003

demobilisation, human-rights monitoring, elections, and nation building.[4] Contrasting, and sometimes competing, agendas and perspectives highlight ongoing tensions between international and local needs and interests, and between short-term crisis aid and long-term development planning. The various official international groups, including those involved in UNIFEM, KWI, and UNMIK (Gender Affairs), were working with these tensions to varying effect. Cross-collaboration seemed to be something that was difficult to implement or maintain but clearly had a highly significant impact. Through the work of feminist international NGOs, it has been possible to develop a somewhat more sustainable collaboration with local women's organisations (see Corrin 2000 for more detail on this and on how the work of UNIFEM succeeded in bridging some of the gaps between the bilateral collaboration with local and international NGOs and international organisations within UNMIK).

Coping with violence and conflict

For many millions of women throughout the world, the vital struggle they engage in every day is for freedom from external aggression. Kosovar Albanian women[5] were centrally involved in resisting state oppression – both in the parallel social and economic systems that began in 1989 and in non-violent resistance. During the armed resistance, women fought in the Kosova Liberation Army (KLA) and actively supported the struggle.[6] The legacies of such involvement remain in women's realities today.[7] Because democratic politics cannot develop under oppression by external powers, gaining freedom from Serb rule was a basic necessity in order to develop a political, social, and economic system that was democratic and participatory. Ideas regarding peaceful resistance were the subject of much discussion throughout Kosova in the ten years preceding 1999, as most people desperately wanted the non-violent resistance led by Ibrahim Rugova to succeed (for more details on this movement, see Waller *et al.* 2001). War was viewed as the failure of this resistance.

The ways in which the struggle was carried out determined something of the outcome regarding gender relations, but the lack of a national government presents an unusual environment for developing a democratic system. Women are involved in the new and expanding police forces, in de-mining projects, in running farms, and in businesses. There is growing recognition of the need to deconstruct certain attitudes towards violence, and to include women's cultural experiences alongside those of men. And because the Kosovar population is predominantly young, with around half being under 25 years of age, there is great potential to revolutionise gender relations, especially with experience from the diaspora.

Peace is not just the absence of war, and the violence experienced in war remains part of a continuum of gender-based violence that threatens many women in their daily lives (Corrin 1996; Davies 1994; Jacobs *et al.* 2000; Meintjes *et al.* 2001). Distinctions between war and post-war often remain unclear. In Kosova, the difference was brought about by a very fragile 'peace' negotiated at Rambouillet. This negotiated cessation of violence privileged the 'men at war' while it excluded women and other civil society representatives. But it is vital for civic groups, especially feminist organisations, to be involved in discussions and policy making regarding the peaceful reconstruction of their societies, especially given their expertise and their political will to talk across differences towards agreement. That Milosevic would not accept peacekeepers did not make the bombing necessary. Having threatened such military action, however, it was believed that NATO authorities would have lost credibility if they had failed to carry through. While (formal) armed conflict could be said to have ceased after the end of the bombing campaign, Kosova was by then awash with weapons and military personnel, and revenge attacks continued. Inter-ethnic and political violence was UNMIK's main focus, yet police crime statistics reported violence against women as equally common (see **www.civpol.org/unmik**). Heightened levels of public violent crime are not uncommon in post-war situations.

In such circumstances, survivors are traumatised and, most importantly for the purposes of this paper, the trauma is gendered. Cynthia Cockburn (2001:25) points out that many men who were wounded in conflict are doomed to unemployment, and that women and children in rural areas are highly exposed to landmine accidents. In the case of Kosova, women were additionally traumatised by war rapes and by the loss of their menfolk.[8] Many Kosovar Albanian women and men were also betrayed by lifelong Serb neighbours (for instance, several families remained concealed in cellars without food and light for days before their neighbours directed Serb military and paramilitary soldiers to their hiding places). It is because of such specificities of war that the 'hard talking' of peace needs to include women's voices. Hannan Ashrawi, a former participant in Israeli–Palestinian peace talks, has stated that women bring to the table the need to talk directly about the most difficult issues rather than postponing them or getting entangled in bureaucratic logic (cited in Karam 2001:11). Needless to say, the hard talking of re/construction also needs to include women, but UNMIK authorities took some time to recognise their absence in the case of Kosova.

Much suffering from physical violence is experienced on a large scale at the international level and is caused by governments and those who oppose them, as well as by vigilantes, traffickers in people, and traffickers in body parts. Other types of violence – such as increased levels of domestic violence and civil conflict – have been viewed by some analysts as 'side-effects'. A common response to violence and to the suffering it produces is to downgrade and deny it. This has been particularly apparent in the context of male violence against women in all of its forms – the most common aspects being violence in the home and rape in times of war and domestic peace. Rape and abuse of 'enemy' women in war seem to have a history as long as war itself. In the particular case of Kosova, thousands of women and girls were assaulted because systematic rape was seen as a central part of the war strategy.[9] The urgent need for the comprehensive support of local women's groups willing to work on trauma counselling has been apparent since July 1999. However, such groups were initially frustrated in their efforts to carry out their work in their own ways to develop their society.

When the bombing ended and re/construction began in Kosova, there were 100,000 'internationals' in place, including 60,000 aid workers and 40,000 military personnel. Some attention was paid to the (ab)use of women's bodies by internationals and to the collusion between local and international 'entrepreneurs' for profit. That the UN Police managed to rescue even 50 women in the year following the war was possible basically because local women working on these issues had campaigned and raised their concerns at many different forums. Rather than a route for traffickers, Kosova became a destination. Cynthia Enloe (1993) assessed the symbiotic relationship between military bases and prostitution, with soldiers developing expectations of local conditions, including the availability of particular women for their 'use'. With the basis of the legislative and judicial processes undermined and without restrictions on entry or exit, Kosova quickly became recognised as a new market for trade in women's bodies.

When war crimes have taken place, co-existence among sufferers from all sides requires thinking through ideas about 'peace with justice'.

The scope of criminal responsibility needs to be widened to include leaders and commanders who lend their influence to encourage crimes against women. Such case law becomes all the more important in light of the fact that current paramilitary and militia command structures are not easily defined and are often organised covertly. During post-conflict reconstruction, general discussions about enforcing 'co-existence', with pressure often coming from international military officials, often serve to exacerbate existing tensions. The lack of a fully functioning legal system has gender implications, as judges have extensive powers of decision making, often much to the disadvantage of women. In Kosova, for example, with poorly functioning courts, women seldom receive a favourable decision in custody cases. Similarly, women's right to property is not generally recognised and, in cases of violence against women or children (including incest), despite the presentation of photos and witness statements, the courts tend to free the husband and/or father on the grounds of 'lack of evidence'. Local women's groups have worked very hard to change these circumstances and to educate women and girls about their rights.

Although women frequently constitute the majority of targeted civilian war casualties, they are not solely war victims, as their active contributions and commitment to peace and re/construction processes testify. Given that many military conflicts are continuations of previous wars, the roots of these conflicts require analysis, and civic organisations, especially feminist groups, need to be involved in such inquiries. International-community perspectives tend to view wars as inevitable, with military alliances, such as NATO, building their strategies on deterrence. Yet the shifting political administration of UNMIK means that, given the necessary opportunities and information, women's groups *do* have the possibility of exerting some influence on the processes of social, political, and economic reconstruction. Many women's organisations are working towards changing the way people think by their own example in constructing local, national, and international coalitions. Several groups in Kosova exemplify the transformation of the grassroots nature of women's experience of war into coalition work on reconciliation and co-existence in many different ways (Corrin 2001). More than 50 indigenous Kosovar NGOs have been at work in civic initiatives since 1999, and at least 15 are currently working to support women's needs. Several of these organisations were active before 1998, and below I give examples of good practice from several groups belonging to the Kosova Women's Network (KWN).

The KWN was founded in 1998 by *Motrat Qiriazi* (Sisters Qiriazi or MQ) in alliance with *Lejenda*, *Aureola*, and *Elena* in order to co-ordinate their work (see Corrin 2000 for further details on these groups). MQ has been working since 1989 to support rural women and girls, enabling them to take control of their lives and make positive changes for themselves and their communities. This group is a founding member of a network that has formed the core of much co-ordinated local work with Kosovar women, and its activists work alongside international feminist colleagues and sustain a dialogue with UNMIK politicians. Education for girls and women has been a key focus of MQ and within the KWN. This work is now increasingly recognised within international organisations such as the KWI as vital for taking forward women's inclusion at all levels of Kosovar society. Since November 2001, the KWN *Voices* newsletter and website have testified to the enormous energies women show in their community activism. With profiles of women's groups, popular chart songs against violence and harassment, and articles about the national players' travelling performances, the Network addresses all sorts of issues ranging from war rape to street harassment. Supported by the Open Society Institute and others, this initiative has a multi-dimensional character and has achieved an enormous impact throughout society (for more information, see **www.womensnetwork.org**).

As can been seen from the UN Secretary General's report, all of these areas of work are of prime importance for a society emerging from war into a post-conflict situation. With rapid and ongoing change taking place throughout a formerly tight-knit society such as that of Kosovar Albanians, women will be able to overcome some of the traumas their society has experienced only if they have access to services and educational opportunities provided locally and within a supportive framework. Working across different ethnicities is something that the KWN has been encouraging for some years in the communities it works in; having gained local trust and support before the war, its work since then has proved invaluable. In the violence of the immediate post-war phase, MQ was working in Mitrovica and continuing its activities with Serb and Roma women. Enabling the continuation of such work is something to which all 'peacekeepers' could usefully aspire. As victims of war rape and violence, many women remain in need of support, and the lack of a rule of law can easily encourage the rule of the physically powerful. Sustained, direct support for long-standing local women's groups that can network widely would alleviate some of the problems concerning disclosure of the previously undisclosed 'hidden violence'. Local groups are also aware that they need structures in place to sustain their work after the international presence is withdrawn. Several international feminist organisations have generated bilateral links in support of local women's groups – among others *Kvinna till Kvinna*, *Medica Mondiale*, and the 'STAR' Network (although according to an October 2002 report in KWN News, donors have discontinued support for the latter's local groups' network).

One of the reasons why women's work in the KWN has added importance is that the Network has a feminist ethos in its focus on education and consciousness-raising activities at the local, national, and international level (in its attendance of international human-rights conferences and seminars, for instance). Despite some very poor experience with several aspects of the international administration, reported in the GA, Kosovar activists are still able and willing to recognise when useful links need support (such as the KWI work with the emerging Women's Councils). Local women activists continue to build bridges between the UNMIK administration and local organisations. The 25 November 2002 news on the UNMIK website, for example, talked about KWN activism on the International Day Against Violence Against Women (see **www.unmikonline.org** for more details). There has also been much support among feminist organisations across the former Yugoslav republics. Work such as that of the Centre for Women War Victims in Zagreb (which has extended its work with refugees into Albania) and the Autonomous Women's Centre in Belgrade (Mladjenovic 2001:172–88) show that creative, caring collaboration continues across the region. Throughout the region, feminist solidarity work and friendship networks are strong and persist across the many differences, either real or imposed.

The work of the KWN in providing a powerful momentum to community consolidation has become increasingly recognised internationally. Certainly the UN Secretary General's remarks at the Beijing+5 Conference in 2000 indicate that:

> *Five years ago, you went to Beijing with a simple statement: 'We are not guests on this planet. We belong here'. Five years on, I would venture that we all know this is an understatement ... not only do women belong on this planet ... the future of this planet depends on women.*
> (Rehn and Sirleaf 2002:86)

The report by UNIFEM (Rehn and Sirleaf 2002) tackles many of the issues facing women in war and negotiated peace, highlighting the gaps in policy and in liaison procedures on overcoming the underlying reasons for women's oppression. While increasingly meetings of the Organisation for Security and Co-operation in Europe (OSCE) consider issues of human trafficking, they do not explicitly tackle trafficking as a gendered phenomenon.[10] Trafficking in human beings explicitly targets women in specific ways, and international organisations need to acknowledge this in both their information services and their policy negotiations. There are slightly greater grounds for optimism in work from the Informal Group on Gender Equality and Anti-trafficking in Human Beings in terms of its focus on gender analysis.[11] That these issues are on public political agendas that include input from experienced women gives reason for some hope. However, there is room to work toward the inclusion of a specifically feminist focus to inform gender analysis. Without a feminist focus, gender analysis can be misunderstood as 'just add women and stir' (Moser 1993). Indeed, many senior administrators with whom I spoke in March 1999 believed that 'gender' was a particular type of work that specialists can/should do without 'impinging' upon others. Ideas and comprehension about mainstreaming policies for gender equity were not widely apparent. Initiating the Gender Taskforce as a multi-agency group or forum to bring gender issues to the forefront of public dialogue and debate, UNIFEM took a much more inclusive approach to local consolidation work. This Taskforce also worked to convene key agencies on issues of importance to women. UNIFEM carried out its initial mainstreaming mandate through various forums (which successfully brought together UNMIK pillars and heads of agencies) as well as through its programmes (see Surtees 2000; Wareham 2000).

Evaluation of the KWI

Developed during the emergency phase to focus on the reintegration of women into the reconstruction process, the KWI was funded through the US Department of State's Bureau for Population, Refugees and Migration. A budget of US$10m was provided for humanitarian and emergency assistance, to be managed by UNHCR, with the intention that it be spent very quickly.[12] From the outset, this much-publicised initiative created tensions within local communities. Although the fund was 'for women', it was actually aimed at poor families. Undoubtedly, since women form a large part of such families, especially as war widows and heads of household, this kind of assistance does support women. However, other civic groups tended to view 'women's groups' as having privileged access to funding. This was quite clearly not the case. Funds were channelled through international 'buffer' organisations, which itself often created difficulties of access for local women, who felt that many of the projects could have been more suitably managed locally. Four international umbrella agencies (Oxfam, Maltheser Hilfdienst, the Danish Refugee Council, and the International Rescue Committee) co-ordinated local women's organisations to develop budget proposals. Some of these local groups came into existence simply in order to gain access to funds and some deemed it unlikely that their organisation would survive the termination of grants. That the work of the KWI was given to an already busy UNHCR officer as just a part of her remit, and was inadequately staffed or resourced, says much about the importance attached to managing this initiative. It is known that 'women' cannot be conceived as a homogeneous group, and that their identities are neither given nor unchanging. Kosovar women may be rural workers, urban professionals, older wives, young widows, translators, politicians, and so on. As Karam (2001:14) points out: 'women's interests need to be *prioritized*, not because they are gender-specific, but because they are the basis of the articulation of the needs of any society' (emphasis in the original). Some recognition of this need to prioritise, coupled with a fully supportive framework, would have made it possible to use the US$10m to create and develop a truly enabling set of programmes and policy initiatives for Kosovar women.

The independent evaluation of the KWI was finalised in October 2002 (Baker and Haug 2002). Through focus groups, interviews, and document reviews during September/October 2001, the evaluation considered the appropriateness, cost effectiveness, impact, and sustainability of KWI-funded activities. Comparison with similar processes in Bosnia, conducted through the Bosnia Women's Initiative (BWI), was a key focus used to assess management, co-ordination, and the impact of donor requirements. This focus was intended to address the broader aspects of what worked and what did not in terms of gender mainstreaming. However, whether or not conditions in Kosova at the end of conflict were similar to those in Bosnia is not considered overtly. It is true that many organisations present in Kosova were drawing on experiences from Bosnia, but it was mainly the OSCE that did the learning in Bosnia, whereas the United Nations had to start from scratch in post-war Kosova. The entire Kosova administration was initially run by internationals (something that occurred haphazardly in Bosnia as the United Nations stepped in only when all else was blocked). The fact that UNHCR had found it difficult to work with small women's groups in Bosnia did not necessarily indicate that working with women's networks in Kosova would pose similar difficulties. Having worked together for some years before the war, as part of the alternative civil society in Kosova, several of these women's groups had wide outreach and community trust and would have been capable of implementing projects. The representation made directly to UN senators by Kosovar women activists also challenges any idea that women could not manage funds.

Noting the range of project documents relating to the KWI, and the range of goals and objectives, over the 1999–2000 period, the evaluation took two goals from a 2001 UNHCR document in order to assess the KWI:

> to help mobilise women throughout Kosovo, with a specific focus on returnee, displaced and war affected women; to assist them and their families in rebuilding their lives and livelihood; and to empower women to become agents of change and solidarity through raising awareness, fostering the development of women's networks and enhancing the principles of gender equity at all levels of government and civil society.
> (Baker and Haug 2002:iv)

Had these principles been the main, clear thrust of the KWI's work from mid-1999 – and had they been supported by strategic thinking, using gender analysis for mainstreaming throughout UNHCR institutions – it would have been possible to develop a broader, sustained framework of support for generating assistance with a gender balance. It is an insight into the crisis nature of KWI funding that such a profusion of project documents exists. When I visited the KWI staff in March 2000 they were working on six strategic areas for needs assessment: immediate survival needs; psychosocial and community support; special healthcare services; empowerment; livelihood; and legal rights and legal protection. Attention in all of these areas could have benefited local women greatly if a focused gender analysis had been employed to generate a gender-sensitive framework for decisions concerning proposals and support for continuing work. That the KWI would provide support to a war-torn country in the midst of the crisis it faced in the return to peace is not in doubt, yet the self-starting nature of Kosovar society (through their alternative arrangements since 1989) meant that there was already much to build on in terms of community collaboration.

The failure to include local, experienced, and motivated women community leaders in the implementation of the KWI's work was a missed opportunity. This is so not just for management and local ownership of the aims and goals, but for the viability and sustainability of the ethos of developing peace and re/construction. A management and supervision committee that included local women could have helped the early implementation stages of KWI funds during 1999–2000. Local women had proved themselves capable in many arenas in the years following 1989, then later during the war with their work in Kosovar communities in refugee camps, and then again from 1999 with returnees. Lessons that had been applied from the BWI about its institutional capacity and procedures not being suited to productive interaction with large numbers of small women's groups meant that KWI funds went into sub-projects with NGOs for various sectors (such as reproductive health and microfinance) and into small project grants that were channelled through international NGOs operating as umbrella agencies. These decisions determined much in the critical 1999–2000 phase. Without an analytical frame for gender mainstreaming, the KWI was viewed as 'just a project for women', though the broader focus was on poor families and later minority-ethnic communities. Sadly, these misunderstandings concerning how the project was envisioned and implemented meant that, as stated above, considerable resentment was generated among many civic groups that 'women' were 'given' US$10m. Organisations and networks that had been active for some years resented having to go through international umbrella groups, the staff of which were sometimes very new and inexperienced – not only in Kosovar affairs but also in international work.

Assuming the lead role as head of the Humanitarian Pillar of UNMIK, UNHCR devoted much of its capacity at the beginning to rebuild housing and infrastructure against the oncoming winter of 1999. The KWI was not prioritised at this early phase:

> Implementation in this already highly complex politicised setting was under-mined by a combination of conflicting priorities, low capacity, high staff turnover, lack of a detailed needs assessment, diverse goals and objectives, [and] donor pressure to disburse funds rapidly and provide special reports.

(Baker and Haug 2002:iv)

There is much to be considered in the above statement, not least that the staff attempting to implement KWI initiatives were not given priority in terms of support or 'space' to present ideas and infuse some policy priorities into UNHCR and UNMIK institutions about good practice with regard to gender mainstreaming. Gender mainstreaming need not take up great resources but begins with using a gender lens and being open-minded enough to consider assessments of strategic and long-term value. UNHCR staff were not able to take on these gender-mainstreaming priorities in highly charged contexts. When a senior OSCE official attempted to do so by networking with local women, she was replaced. This was not a positive image for those who remained. However, the work of UNIFEM staff did generate some successful contributions through the Gender Taskforce. The lack of apparent KWI input into such processes was a loss for all in terms of consolidating work in this area with a view to future development. It is difficult to find the root cause of the lack of cohesion between units working on gender, but there seemed to be a reluctance to collaborate, as if such work would involve competing projects in a way that would not happen under the UNMIK umbrella.

In the evaluation, the umbrella-agency funding staff placed a low priority on 'specialised key technical support, sustainability, strengthening of networks and monitoring of reintegration and empowerment indicators' (Baker and Haug 2002:v), despite their status as overarching goals. This was an area of much frustration for local women's groups, which spent considerable time briefing international staff only to feel marginalised when decisions were made about how to give ongoing support; or whether, why, and under what conditions new women's groups should be started. It was in this climate that local women made interventions to US politicians, and this in turn raised questions both ways – for local groups and for international staff in Kosova. Gender funding became something of a 'hot potato' so that there were mixed reactions to the findings of the GA when it was published in May 2000. At the first all-Kosova women's conference in Priština in July 2000, local women were very appreciative, particularly of the GA's broad overview of reconstruction programmes and specific information on UNMIK procedures. It was also vital for the GA to be translated into Albanian and Serbian in order for the document to be as widely available and useful as possible to women's groups and other civic organisations.

International reception of the GA was cautious, and even defensive in some quarters, as it was viewed as too critical of UNMIK efforts and

KWI activities. At the June 2002 Fourth World Conference on Women (Beijing+5) held in New York, presentations of the GA met with a good reception among the NGO Forum groups, though with slightly less appreciation at the international formal proceedings. For women's groups in Kosova to have so much high-level information about how UNMIK was being administered and how women's issues were being incorporated (or not) into larger agendas was crucial in giving them the power of knowledge. Information such as who the local and international co-heads of the Education Department are and how to contact them is vital for groups that are trying to push forward agendas on the education of girls. Working so hard at the grassroots rural level without such information is disempowering, so the GA worked on many levels to disseminate important, detailed information to local groups and to analyse the various reasons why members of the international mission seemed unable to prevent gender-mainstreaming issues from falling through loopholes.

Much seemed to hinge on the importance given to gender-equity issues when there were crises concerning demilitarisation and refugee resettlement. Women were affected by such crises in differentiated ways and gender equity was, of course, important. Here my interview with a senior UN official was indicative not just of defensiveness in Kosova regarding gender politics at that time, but also of a lack of understanding about the positive aspects that mainstreaming can bring to enhance programmes and processes.[13] What transpired was a fundamental lack of comprehension about the intellectual requirements of 'thinking through gender' at budget levels, in terms of both personal security and violence issues. This is clearly not a major resource issue but is something that closed, hierarchical, institutional cultures find great difficulty incorporating into their agendas. There is certainly much room for opening up discussion on these issues given the wider remit of 'peacekeeping'. The UN Secretary General's report also sets policy agendas that are inclusive and expansive in their thinking on mainstreaming issues, and that do not focus just on numbers but also incorporate other ways of thinking and being. This is where the real change lies.

During 2000, there was some strengthening of staffing and technical support for the KWI within UNHCR headquarters, to help improve implementation. However, UNHCR's overall focus by then was on minority-ethnic communities, and the KWI followed its lead. Local women's groups had been active in this area for quite some time (see, for instance, the chronology of women's groups on **www.womensnetwork.org**). It has also been possible to see positive change since February 2001 when the KWI established six multi-ethnic regional Women's Councils to assume responsibility for review and appraisal of KWI grant-funded projects. The KWN newsletter gives full details of this initiative, regarding it as very positive in terms of Kosovar women's inclusion. This boost in female empowerment, achieved through their active inclusion and respect for their knowledge, could have been undertaken earlier, yet still augurs well in terms of future collaboration on similar agendas.

KWI sectoral and project funds

Figure 1 shows that by 2000 more than US$8m had been allocated by the KWI to sectoral support and small projects via the four main international umbrella NGOs. As Figure 1 shows, the bulk of this money (US$7.2m) was allocated to the sectors of reproductive health, psychosocial well-being, and microcredit, with project grants through the umbrella agencies amounting to approximately one-third of the total. These umbrella agencies had a mixed record, with unsatisfactory performance

> ... linked mainly to both lack of technical capacity and inconsistent management ... The choice of some partners as Umbrella Agencies who, like UNHCR, specialise in provision of relief and rehabilitation assistance may be disadvantageous in the medium to long term ... many of these agencies subsequently have difficulty in accessing development funds as UNHCR begins to phase out.
> (Baker and Haug 2002:45)

Of these project grants, almost half were for vocational training, with sewing, knitting, and handcrafts making up 50 per cent of the total. Performance on KWI grant-funded income-generation projects was disappointing: 'less than 30% showing indications of being viable ... 80% of sewing and handicraft projects funded during 1999–2000 were still operating in 2001 by virtue of a second grant from KWI' (Baker and Haug 2002:vii). This is a familiar story in small income-generation projects of this kind, though other possibilities for grants for alternative activities such as Internet projects seem not to have been fully explored. Certainly, income generation was often highlighted to me in March 2000 in discussions on the inclusion of women in the new institutional arrangements. This was particularly significant for

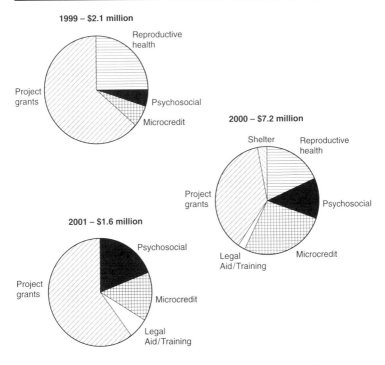

Figure 1: KWI fund allocations

1999 – $2.1 million

2000 – $7.2 million

2001 – $1.6 million

1999 and 2000 are reported expenditures. 2001 is budgeted amount. 'Project grants' refer to projects by individual women's groups.

Source: Baker and Haug (2002:19).

women heads of household, but was also viewed as a necessity for those young women who wished to continue their education as a gateway to business life. Some of the UNIFEM Gender Taskforce work in Peja in 2000 highlighted this (detailed in the GA; see Corrin 2000). However, the KWN organised a successful conference for local women in 2001 on gaining funding for activities aimed at enabling women to achieve economic independence (see KWN News at **www.womensnetwork.org**).

A key focus for sectoral funds involved health workers on issues of reproductive health. Long-term impact in this field depends on other factors such as girls' and women's education. The GA and others argued for development funds to be used from the KWI to support girls' schooling to ensure that young women could take up gains made through advocacy and awareness training. Strong funding in this area from KWI activities now seems less likely to be forthcoming due to the timeframe of UNHCR's exit strategy, despite the fact that education was noted as a key concern from 2002. There is perhaps a danger that giving priority to reproductive health can in turn place the emphasis on maternity/motherhood as a 'key focus' for women, whereas children's needs are a family and community concern, not solely a woman's responsibility nor a concern to be financially supported via funding to promote gender equity. In addition, the wealth of experience gained during the ten years of providing alternative 'Mother Theresa' community care and cottage hospitals may be overlooked if primary healthcare and sex education for women and girls are not given high priority (see Corrin 2000 for more information on health service re/construction). Obviously these points link closely with gender awareness in a predominantly young population, one-third of which is under 15 years of age, and where the ratio of men to women aged between 20 and 50 years is 86:100 (Baker and Haug 2002:iv). Under such circumstances, the possibilities for change are potentially enormous, not limited to attempts to reconstruct old ideas about patriarchal, hierarchical ways of working but enabling the generation of nuanced and inclusive values that aim toward equity across all areas.

In certain respects, the ways in which KWI staff work was viewed as counter-productive to progressing gender agendas. On sexual and gender-based violence (SGBV) work, for example, KWI staff monitor outputs rather than impact. In this area, outputs are much less tangible than are gauging and monitoring impact, though the latter is central. Here, the KWN shows excellent results in assessing the impact of its community-based educational programmes in rural areas, in urban awareness-raising campaigns, and of course in its popular-music success and theatre performances. This work is particularly successful in making links with community awareness, education, and the reduction and prevention of violence. Recommendations from the GA, regarding a holistic appraisal (using UNIFEM's Gender Taskforce idea), were to give broader support to local and other international activities in this field. Ideas arose from local staff to have health specialists visit the centres where women were based, rather than expect the women to go to the specialist centres – a daunting prospect for women in any community. Again, education is important here with a key strategy in 2002 for the KWI to invest in girls' education. Rural groups such as MQ have been implementing educational projects for many years and the KWI could have built on their knowledge and set funds aside in 2000 for educational trusts.

Political dialogue

The gendering of democratic processes in Kosova provides a good example of women's varying political involvement in re/construction and democracy building. Analysing the greater inclusion of women in peace and democracy building involves consideration of 'developing peace' (Corrin 2002). Analysts have long been aware that ideas of 'development' cannot be reduced to economic growth, or even to structural economic change. Instead, 'development' typically represents a vision of societal progress, a 'better' life, which includes various components such as comfort, peace, environmental balance, and more. In this context, 'developing peace' is made up of various threads that can make such things come into being, with the absence of war being just one component. For women's lives, issues of violence are often central, yet the suffering from violence is often neglected, particularly in matters of personal security. Our societies remain largely ruled according to economic figures about gross national product in which women's unpaid work (including cleaning homes, caring for children, cooking, and farming) is not counted. Monetary activity is an unreliable measure of welfare, while the suffering from violence cannot be analysed in a cost–benefit analysis, because the costs are experienced by specific people (war widows, for example) who are very different from those who benefit. The human-development concept is a better indicator of the fate of women, since it includes several dimensions targeted at capturing the status of women in a given society – empowerment through expansion of capabilities and participation; equity in distribution of basic capabilities; opportunities for everybody to have at least a certain minimum; sustainability of people's opportunities to freely exercise their basic capabilities; community membership, belonging; and security, notably in their daily lives (for further discussion on this topic, see *Journal of Human Development* (2000:1(1)). All of these aspects are significant in analysing women's participation in developing peace in Kosova.

Kosovar society is often described as never having experienced democracy, yet in the parallel system from 1989 there were democratic developments at the community level that mirrored 'national' governance. Much was learnt in this decade and expectations for a democratic future were high. After getting off to a very poor start in many ways, not least by not including any women in the top decision-making bodies, lessons were at last being acted upon. The 30 per cent quota for women in elections run by the OSCE is one response to the realisation that all citizens suffer through the lack of women's input. After violent conflict, many people want to move on, not just stay in the same situation. However, feminist studies again show that, in electoral terms, 'giving up' power to women is not a linear or straightforward process (Corrin 2002).

With no elected government, state building and electoral grounds remain strongly contested areas among groups in Kosova that compete from positions of varying strength in a shifting legal environment. At such times, relations of inequality between men and women can impede women's abilities to gain a political voice. Upset by violent change, during periods of flight, exile, displacement, and return, traditional aspects of gender balance lead many women heads of household to differing expectations. In analysing these changes, key areas that need to be addressed include political culture, movement 'from below' in terms of women's participation, and the significance of gender balance in politics. The incorporation of motivated women, across the spectrum of political affiliations and styles of participation, creates progressive political changes in areas in which women are under-represented. The involvement of Kosovar women in governmental and community-level politics identifies their deepening involvement across these arenas. Their work in coalitions that combine local, national, and international elements is also making a positive contribution.[14]

One of the most concerted attempts to bring together local women involved in work across wide sections of Kosovar society, and particularly among united Albanian and Serb women in Kosova, took place in meetings convened under the auspices of Women Waging Peace held in Priština in September 2000.[15] These meetings were extremely well organised by Swannee Hunt (former US Ambassador to Austria) and Vjosa Dobruna (Kosovar co-head of the Department for Democratic Governance and Civil Society Support). Local women worked together in mixed groups to outline a strategic plan to work for the peaceful improvement of everyday life in Kosova. The following day, their plan was presented to the international gathering with senior UNMIK and OSCE officials, women politicians, and community activists from Bosnia and Herzegovina, Croatia, Slovenia, Northern Ireland, and elsewhere. Five crucial areas identified in the strategic plan were: economic development and job security; rule of law and judicial-system reform; safety and security; social welfare, including health, education pensions, and orphans; and women in the political system. Concrete steps to meet targets were outlined, along with discussion of ways to take plans forward.

Beyond the group discussion were plenary sessions attended by 'top brass', including the head of the OSCE, the Security Council, and other senior UNMIK officials. These senior personnel recognised in the course of the fiery debates and forthright statements that this was not a 'PR' exercise nor a 'women's issues' meeting, but rather a gathering concerned with major socio-political problems facing Kosovar society, and with outlining ways to tackle even the most intractable issues of sustainable security (personal and societal). The head of UNMIK security offered to meet with the group working on safety and security at the end of the month, and these meetings continued throughout 2001. The wealth of diverse experience and personal courage shown by members of these meetings was awe-inspiring. Challenging from a position of knowledge is something in which some local women in Kosova are well versed. Slowly, their voices are being heard and their suggestions acted upon.

The October 2000 municipal elections were a first step in realising UNMIK's agreement on power sharing in Kosova, leading to 'the progressive dissolution of the parallel structures'. These elections marked a watershed in Kosova's political transition, conferring international legitimacy on the local administrations. However, as can be seen in detail elsewhere (Corrin 2002), while women did gain representation, only 8 per cent of them (76 in total) were elected. The significance of this peaceful transfer of power in municipalities was significant not only for the process but as a precedent for future electoral developments. In the 'all Kosova' (not 'national') parliamentary elections in November 2001, the proportion of women elected was much higher. Overall, 34 women won seats in the three parties that gained the largest shares of the votes. Of the 47 Democratic League of Kosova (LDK) seats, 15 went to women; in the Party of Democratic Kosova (PDK), eight of the 26 seats went to women, including Flora Brovina, dubbed Kosova's First Lady;[16] and among the 26 Coalition Return (KP) seats were seven women. In the November 2002 municipal elections, women candidates saw an upturn, making up 28.5 per cent of the new municipal assemblies, 262 having been elected. Nearly all of Kosova's smaller communities received representation in the municipal assemblies for the areas where they live. Voter turnout, however, was down, from a high 79 per cent in 2000 to a more modest 54 per cent in 2002. There is some media speculation now that even the anomalous position of Kosova with regard to Serbia may be changing, with international discussions being proposed that offer the Serbian administration the possibility of EU membership in exchange for letting Kosova 'go' (for a full report on simulated negotiation, see **www.usip.org**). For Kosova and Serbia to reach an agreement on the independent status of Kosova would be a significant step forward in consolidating the political framework.

Conclusions

A more open, inclusive process in the implementation of international humanitarian programmes could have avoided frustrations experienced by local NGOs, some of which have worked with Kosovar women in their communities for many years. The tendency to establish new groups to offer rural communities short-term 'choices' was often made without taking into account what already existed or examining other options. Piecemeal, short-term projects cannot substitute for longer-term planning. Local women are aware of the importance of creating sustainable forms of support before the internationals depart – a reflection of their anxiety that no long-term social and attitudinal changes will be made otherwise. Legislative change is only part of a process in dealing with, for example, issues of violence against women. Changes in attitudes, and recognition of the gendered nature of violence in war and domestic peace, are essential for the implementation of gender-sensitive laws and policies. Some of the partial failures of the international effort are related to the lack of a gender perspective while others are more common to the humanitarian arena. It is essential that international organisations learn from previous post-conflict situations, especially from others from nearby regions such as, in this case, Bosnia. This means examining what is comparable, however, and not assuming that Bosnian and Kosovar peacekeeping interventions and societies are identical and that 'blueprints' can be followed.

Too often women's needs and potential contributions are marginalised or minimised, not regarded as a vital ingredient in *all* reconstruction processes. This can perpetuate a belief that women in Kosova are not 'culturally attuned' to becoming partners in community or regional politics, but remain victims and, therefore, recipients of aid and assistance rather than active partners in reconstruction efforts.

There are always specific aspects to take into account within a global human-rights framework. Some of the OSCE work in schools in relation to human-rights campaigns is contributing to widening knowledge.[17] With regard to girls' education, post-war trauma, poverty, and insecurity will prevent some girls from completing eighth-grade schooling. Given the high percentage of under-15s among Kosovar citizens, this is an area in urgent need of international support. With EU funding, groups such as the Amsterdam-based Academic Training Association are undertaking higher education reforms at both undergraduate and postgraduate levels. The Canadian International Development Association (CIDA) has put many millions into teacher-training programmes and support. Education within the international media is also important, to portray positive images of Kosovar women – as capable, courageous, and confident – in order to *strengthen* rather than undermine their activities and aims. Here, KWN performances support stronger perceptions of women that are in turn reported through the various media. Little attention had been paid to the tendency of the international media, from 1991, to portray 'Balkan women' and/or Muslim women in negative terms (see Corrin 1996). Attitudes concerning 'traditional' societies could usefully be discussed, certainly within the context of how war rips apart closely knit communities with loss of life, trauma, and material devastation. New ways of bonding and supporting 'in community' develop slowly in such awful circumstances, yet they do develop, and within this women's strengths can become recognised afresh.

An assessment of how women's groups in Kosova can enter the political dialogue from a more empowered position links with activities in other post-conflict situations. Women active in this area are keen to share findings and discuss comparisons and differences in ways of working towards similar goals across different regions. Enabling the inclusion of local women requires international support at various levels, rather than official decisions being made about what women need (or do not need) without any reference to *women themselves*. An example of this was apparent in the case of tractors for families in Kosova.[18] Many women were not considered suitable for training in how to drive tractors and operate heavy machinery within an agenda where gender and ethnic bias coalesced to prevent women from making their own choices. Ideas concerning 'Muslim women' and 'traditional cultures' have often been put forward as concrete *reasons* not to empower rural women in Kosova and elsewhere (see, for example, Walsh 2000). Rather than considering women generally as targets for short-term low-level funding, or primarily humanitarian crisis funds, it is also necessary to train them in many other areas, including management. Translating theory into practice proved both complex and problematic in certain sections of the international mission in Kosova. Clearly, processes of gender mainstreaming must be both two-way (i.e. happening within international and local structures) and transparent. Key aspects include the need for sex- and age-disaggregated statistics so that ratios of women/girls and men/boys can be studied in a range of settings, engendering policy-making implications for different groups, and gender mainstreaming throughout administrative and political decision making. The lack of gender balance and gender analytical skills within the international administration had clear 'knock-on' effects in decision making in post-conflict Kosova.

The pace of change is important, but the need to include, and show respect for, local knowledge and the involvement of Kosovar personnel cannot be overemphasised. Many local women spent much time and energy giving information and advice to the small team of gender specialists in UNMIK, only to be frustrated by the lack of co-ordination and feedback, and the continued failure to draw upon their expertise in the implementation phase. The current KWI evaluation is a good start in learning from this process in the case of Kosova, yet the excellent report on successes in gender inclusion from the UNTAG mission in Namibia took ten years to gain serious consideration (Olsson 2001:97–110). Forming a base for mainstreaming the training of gender analysis would help ensure equitable progression for women and men in any reconstruction and reintegration processes. Working with gender issues considers the needs, involvement, and decision making of women as well as men in a community, in order to understand how unequal power relations are shaped by and built into social institutions of family, legal structures, religious systems, and beliefs. The reaction from some senior UN officials exemplifies a mind-set that persistently regards issues concerning women and girls as secondary, and views gender-equality policies as being in competition with other 'important' (often 'national') issues. Yet gender analysis is an integral part of the solutions, a lens through which to view the development of just and equitable policies, the implementation of which does not depend on vast resources. Basically, all the arguments over funding and projects come down to an issue of respect. Local women who resisted external oppression are not prepared to be patronised by US officials in Kosova nor treated as aid recipients or victims. Engendering an inclusive dialogue on this will certainly help to develop strategies for supporting women in emergencies as being central to reconstruction, with gender a key factor in mainstreaming equity issues, instead of putting 'aid' into scattered women's projects. The failure to engage in partnership with local women's groups emerging from war has proved a major loss for achieving such goals in Kosova. In 2002 the KWI is now working more closely with the KWN in various reconciliation projects.

At an international level, there are grounds for optimism with regard to the movements towards the full inclusion of women's interests and voices in future peace negotiations and reconstruction processes. It is clear that during situations of crisis and reconstruction, donors and international organisations in the field are beginning to give greater appreciation to and consideration of women's initiatives within their remits. In recommending the report on Women, Peace and Security to the UN Security Council, Kofi Annan proposed that: 'Just as your work can promote gender equality, so can gender equality make your work more likely to succeed' (UN press release, 4 November 2002). With their online newsletter the KWN show the enormous creative energies going into their various projects. Their popular song *Fundi im I shkurte* (My Short Skirt) was in the charts. This came out of stories based on the Vagina Monologues (international work to eliminate violence against women around V-Day[19] by playwright and activist Eve Ensler). Requests for their performances of women telling their stories have been made from Switzerland and other countries with sizeable Albanian populations. In these and other ways, they are proving the adage that women's empowerment is community empowerment!

Acknowledgements

I wish to thank those who patiently took time in Kosova to discuss their situation and to answer many queries. My gratitude also goes to Mary Diaz (WCRWC) and Ariane Brunet (UAF) for facilitating the initial visit to Kosova for collaboration on the Gender Audit; as well as to various readers and all the feminist friends throughout central and south-east Europe without whom this work could not have been done.

Notes

1. I use the term 'Kosova' because this is the term that the majority Kosovar Albanian community uses. Using 'Kosova' (rather than 'Kosovo') during the hostilities with the former Republic of Yugoslavia, particularly since 1998, signalled a move towards independence for many groups and individuals.

2. The GA was commissioned by the Women's Commission for Refugee Women and Children (which, since 1989, has sought to improve the lives of refugee women and children through vigorous programmes of public education and advocacy, and by acting as a technical resource) and the Urgent Action Fund (created in October 1997 to promote the human rights of women within the context of strategies outlined in the Beijing Platform for Action).

3. See websites in the references for the full text of both UN reports and the KWI review.

4. Judith Hicks Stiehm emphasises how these new activities directly affect women and women's opportunities for participation in international operations, with opportunities for women to direct these new aspects of peacekeeping being more in accordance with gender-main-streaming policies. The author argues that the implementation and institutionalisation of these new policies requires commitment, resources, and sound strategies to overcome institutional inertia and, sometimes, resistance. (See Olsson and Tryggestad 2001:39–48.)

5. The term 'Kosovar Albanian' distinguishes Albanians in Kosova from those from Albania. As explained in Note 1, Albanians

generally spell this 'Kosova', although 'Kosovo' is often used within the international community and is acceptable to the Serbian regime. The issue of which of the two spellings to adopt was a highly political one in the context of resistance to Serb domination.

6. More research is needed to consider the links between the terms on which women participated in the resistance struggle and the transformation of gender politics during peacetime under the UNMIK administration.

7. As is fully discussed in feminist discourses, 'women' are not a homogeneous entity. In Kosova the struggle against Serb aggression involved Kosovar Albanian, Serb, and Roma women in differing ways. This is true of the impact of the NATO bombing and most certainly apparent in the post-war situation. While many Serb and Roma women fled Kosova in the immediate post-war period, many also stayed behind. It is those who remained who are working across major divisions (both physical and psychological) to achieve a constructive engagement for peaceful reconstruction.

8. In one village in eastern Kosova only eight men returned.

9. See Fitamant (2000); Human Rights Watch (2000); Wareham (2000); and 'War and rape: a digest of referenced articles' at www.flora.org/flora.mainot/17300.

10. Neither the Tirana meeting of the newly formed OSCE Victims Assistance on 27 November 2002 (giving assistance to trafficked women sent back from Italy), nor the workshop in Skopje on 25 November 2002 (on human trafficking

investigation) highlights gender as a key variable in the analysis of human trafficking.

11 See summary of the 8 October 2002 meeting by H.E. Ambassador Del Marmol and Dr Gracheva, Chairpersons of the Informal Group on Gender Equality and Anti-trafficking in Human Beings, PC.Del/904/02, 5 November 2002.

12 Similar initiatives had been implemented in Bosnia (BWI US$5m) and in Rwanda (RWI US$7m). In each of these projects, it remains unclear how economic projects such as income-generating initiatives aimed at the most vulnerable groups of women redress wider inequalities in gender relations.

13 In a rather bizarre conversation, the official told me that he could not discuss gender issues as there were not enough police*men* in Kosova (!). Ironically, I soon discovered (March 2000) statistics showing that 24 per cent of the Kosovar police force was women, while the UN police force had only 6 per cent women.

14 Various case studies in Moser and Clark (2001), particularly those of Simona Sharoni and Urvashi Butalia, detail the work of such coalitions towards sustainable peace. Cynthia Cockburn (1998) also analyses women's often difficult and dangerous work across differences towards ending conflict and violence. In the context of south-east Europe, the work of the Gender Taskforce of the Stability Pact under the direction of Sonja Lokar has been significant in post-war electoral political campaigns. Here regional coalitions have been formed to support women standing in various elections under the networking banner of 'Women Can Do It'.

15 This is a global initiative hosted by the Women and Public Policy Program of the Kennedy School of Government at Harvard University.

16 Flora Brovina, a doctor and women's activist, was sentenced in 1999 to 12 years' imprisonment under the Milosevic regime, and was released in 2001. She was put in the ballot by the PDK as a presidential candidate and her campaign caused much discussion, not least about having a 'woman President'. Her humanitarian work has won international recognition and she won the UN Millennium Peace Prize for Women. For more details, see 'Kosovo's First Lady' in the *Guardian*, 15 November 2001.

17 A year-long human-rights campaign in Kosovar schools concluded in June 2002. Every month of the year, 150 classes representing around 1800 pupils in grades seven and eight, from all regions and communities of Kosova, prepared calendars in a human-rights awareness campaign. Using interactive media to promote discussion and activities, the children reported on the texts and drawings they produced (see OSCE press release, 7 June 2002).

18 All families who had owned a tractor before the war were entitled to receive one afterwards, but some UNMIK officials decided that for those women heads of household who were not themselves able to drive tractors, men could be hired to do ploughing for them. There are several misunderstandings here about what women are entitled to and about what they can do. Firstly, women heads of household were entitled to tractors regardless of what they used them for; and, secondly, many women wished to be trained to drive tractors

and to operate other heavy farm machinery.

19 V-Day is a global movement to stop violence against women and girls. For more details, see www.vday.org.

References

Baker, J.M. and H. Haug (2002) *Final Report: Independent Evaluation of the Kosovo Women's Initiative*, Geneva: UNHCR (text available at www.unifem.undp.org).

Butalia, U. (2001) 'Women and communal conflict: new challenges for the women's movement in India', in Moser and Clark (eds.) (2001).

Cockburn, C. (1998) *The Space Between Us: Negotiating Gender and National Identities in Conflict*, London: Zed Books.

Cockburn, C. (2001) 'The gendered dynamics of armed conflict and political violence', in Moser and Clark (eds.) (2001).

Corrin, C. (1996) *Women in a Violent World: Feminist Analyses and Resistance Across 'Europe'*, Edinburgh: Edinburgh University Press.

Corrin, C. (2000) *Gender Audit of Reconstruction Programmes in South Eastern Europe*, New York, NY: Women's Commission for Refugee Women and Children and Urgent Action Fund (text available at www.gla.ac.uk/centres/icgws).

Corrin, C. (2001) 'Post-conflict reconstruction and gender analysis in Kosova', *International Journal of Feminist Politics* 3(1): 78–98.

Corrin, C. (2002) 'Developing democracy in Kosova: from grassroots to government', *Parliamentary Affairs*, Special Issue: Women and Politics Revisited 55(1): 99–108.

Davies, M. (ed.) (1994) *Women and Violence: Realities and Responses Worldwide*, London: Zed Books.

Enloe, C. (1993) *The Morning After: Sexual Politics at the End of the Cold War*, Los Angeles, CA: University of California Press.

Fitamant, S. (2000) *Assessment Report on Sexual Violence in Kosovo*, New York, NY: UNFPA.

Hasani, E. (2000) *Dissolution of Yugoslavia and the Case of Kosova: Political and Legal Aspects*, Priština: Albanian Institute for International Studies.

Human Rights Watch (2000) *Kosovo: Rape as a Weapon of 'Ethnic Cleansing'*, New York, NY: Human Rights Watch.

Jacobs, S., R. Jacobson, and J. Marchbank (eds.) (2000) *States of Conflict: Gender, Violence and Resistance*, London: Zed Books.

Judah, T. (2000) *Kosovo: War and Revenge*, New Haven, CT: Yale University Press.

Karam, A. (2001) 'Women in war and peace-building: the roads traversed, the challenges ahead', *International Feminist Journal of Politics* 3(1): 2–25.

Maliqi, S. (1998) *Kosova Separate Worlds: Reflections and Analyses 1989–1998*, Priština: Dukagjini PH.

Meintjes, S., A. Pillay, and M. Turshen (eds.) (2001) *The Aftermath: Women in Post-conflict Reconstruction*, London: Zed Books.

Mertus, J. (1999) *Kosovo: How Myths and Truths Started a War*, Los Angeles, CA: University of California Press.

Mladjenovic, L. (2001) 'Caring at the same time: on feminist politics during the NATO bombing of the Federal Republic of Yugoslavia and the ethnic cleansing of Albanians in Kosovo 1999', in Meintjes, Pillay, and Turshen (eds.) (2001).

Moser, C. (1993) *Gender Planning and Development: Theory, Practice and Training*, London and New York, NY: Routledge.

Moser, C. and F. Clark (eds.) (2001) *Victims, Perpetrators or Actors? Gender, Armed Conflict and Political Violence,* London: Zed Books.

Olsson, L. (2001) 'Gender mainstreaming in practice: the United Nations Transitional Assistance Group in Namibia', in Olsson and Tryggestad (eds.) (2001).

Olsson, L. and T.L. Tryggestad (eds.) (2001) *Women and International Peacekeeping,* London: Frank Cass.

Rehn, E. and E.J. Sirleaf (2002) *Women, War and Peace: The Independent Experts Assessment on the Impact of Armed Conflict on Women and Women's Role in Peace-building,* New York, NY: UNIFEM.

Sharoni, S. (2001) 'Rethinking women's struggles in Israel–Palestine and the North of Ireland', in Moser and Clark (eds.) (2001).

Surtees, R. (2000) *Women at Work: The Economic Situation and Opportunities for Women in Kosovo,* Priština: UNIFEM and DFID.

United Nations (2002) *UN Security Council: Report of Secretary-General on Women, Peace and Security:* S/2002/1154, 16 October 2002 (for full text see www.un.org).

Waller, M., K. Drezov, and B. Gokay (eds.) (2001) *Kosovo: The Politics of Delusion,* London: Frank Cass.

Walsh, M. (2000) 'Aftermath: The Impact of Conflict on Women in Bosnia and Herzegovina', Working Paper No. 302, Center for Development of Information and Evaluation, Washington, DC: USAID (text available at www.dec.org/pdf%5Fdocs/PNACJ322.pdf).

Wareham, R. (2000) *No Safe Place: An Assessment on Violence Against Women in Kosovo,* Priština: UNIFEM and DFID.

Kosovo: missed opportunities, lessons for the future

Lesley Abdela

The dogs of small war

The speed with which international affairs switched from the relative tranquillity that characterised the Cold War to incipient anarchy and untrammelled aggression has taken most of us by surprise, leaving us much to reflect upon in terms of dashed hopes for sustainable and lasting peace. Pandora has reopened her box and let loose the dogs of small war.

One important consequence of all these changes has been an explosion of bush wars (with more to come) and a loss of belief in the art of diplomacy. Some of these wars can be loosely identified as tectonic plate wars, breaking out after decades of rigid rule, as in the Balkans; others are more straightforward power-plays, whether in the form of outright attacks on divided units as in Chechnya and East Timor, or of rivalry over Kashmir.

A mushrooming of small wars ahead implies a mushrooming of post-conflict reconstruction efforts. The experience in the Balkans with post-war reconstruction can provide a significant contribution to further learning, as much learning still needs to be done from the messy, poorly conceived, and chaotic manner in which the outside world stepped in and tried to help in the 1990s. Among the most important lessons that transpired is the need to include women fully in peace building. But as shown in ALNAP's latest annual report, there are serious difficulties in achieving this.[1]

Becoming an actor in Kosovo's drama

Getting there

I first 'parachuted' into Kosovo with the Organisation for Security and Co-operation in Europe (OSCE) in the immediate aftermath of the

NATO campaign. Being an actor in the drama is an eye-opening experience, and one that is impossible to gain at a distance. One of the lessons that became most obvious to me as a result of my involvement is that women must stop being added on as an optional extra, bolted on as an afterthought or half-day excursion to a West End play, and must instead be an integral part of the peace-building process. Organisations such as International Alert have launched campaigns like 'Women Building Peace: From the Village Council to the Negotiating Table' which explicitly set out to place women 'at the heart of reconstruction and reconciliation'.

My first-hand experience in conflict and post-conflict situations started in 1993 when I was a journalist in a Bosnian war zone, in the Bihac enclave. I conducted over 300 interviews with Bosnians, Serbs, and Croats. Then, from August to December 1999, I was seconded by the British Foreign and Commonwealth Office to be Deputy Director for Democratisation for the OSCE in Kosovo. This was in the dramatic immediate aftermath of the NATO campaign against Milosevic's forces. At the invitation of the British Council in Freetown, I followed this with a ten-day visit to Sierra Leone in November 2000 to carry out an initial needs assessment on gender and governance in the uncertain and still-troubled aftermath of the diamond-and-drug-fuelled conflict.

For three years I had discussed with NATO/SHAPE (the Supreme Headquarters Allied Powers Europe – NATO's training school for military and civilian personnel), the British Ministry of Defence, and representatives of NGOs how to improve coordination and cooperation between formal and informal sectors in conflict and post-conflict situations – and how to include women as well as men in decision making and planning.

I arrived in Priština as part of the United Nations Mission in Kosovo (known by its acronym UNMIK) at the end of August 1999, 14 weeks after the NATO bombing had ended. From my office on the seventh floor of the OSCE Mission headquarters, a former bank, I could see the ruins of the main police station, shattered by a NATO precision bomb, though Priština was not as badly damaged as other places. People sat out at cafe tables in the warm sunshine. Among the indigenous Kosovar Albanian population there was a strong sense of optimism. People had reopened shops and cafes and were rebuilding their homes with remarkable speed (when they could get the materials to do so). To my surprise, there did not even appear to be problems of law and order. I felt safer walking around Priština in the evening than walking around London. There were plenty of local women walking around shops and cafes in the evenings.

A squandered honeymoon

By the time I left Kosovo in December 1999, however, UNMIK had squandered its honeymoon period, producing few results and acting in a cumbersome, clumsy, and bureaucratic manner. The United Nations was responsible for running the municipal governments, while the OSCE was supposed to be training Kosovar administrative staff.

By mid-October, it had become clear that the international community was fast losing credibility. Tales of intimidation and shoot-outs between rival criminal gangs had become part of everyday life. The crime rate increased dramatically and women were regularly getting kidnapped (an estimated five a week from Priština). I no longer saw women out after dark because by then they were too afraid. I heard reports from reliable sources that lack of sufficient and properly trained international police meant that, near the Albanian border, girls as young as 16 were being snatched from their beds for forced prostitution.

'Women came last – after everything else came women'

Despite an absolute immensity of warnings signalling that the overwhelmingly men-dominated international missions were getting things wrong, the women of Bosnia and Kosovo remained excluded from any concrete involvement in negotiations, post-conflict reconstruction planning, and policy making, and even from the democratisation process itself.

At the OSCE conference on gender held in Vienna in June 1999, Martina Vandenberg of Human Rights Watch warned the OSCE in no uncertain terms of the urgent need to reform:

> The OSCE region is one of conflict. These conflicts and the complex reconstruction issues they leave behind have a profound impact on women's lives. Many women in these conflicts have lost male members and find themselves heads of households for the first time. Other women have faced rape and torture at the hands of state or non-state parties to the conflict.

> Discrimination against women during the reconstruction period is legion. Our experience with the OSCE indicates that field personnel urgently need

*a tremendous amount of training on human rights – with special emphasis
on women's human rights ... Women's absence from leadership positions
within the OSCE as well as the failure to include women's human rights
in the OSCE is reflected in the lack of reporting on women's human rights
flowing in from field missions in Bosnia, Croatia, Tajikistan, FYROM/
Macedonia, and elsewhere.*

(Vandenberg 1999)

As one Bosnian woman leader interviewed by Human Rights Watch
said bitterly, 'Women came last – after everything else came women'.

Mistakes repeated in Kosovo: the male-as-leader culture

Where were the women?

One year after this report was written, the same mistakes were to be
repeated in Kosovo. With one exception, all senior posts in the OSCE
and the UN missions in Kosovo were held by men, most of whom had
got there through traditional male hierarchies. The most senior
individuals had been government ministers, while many had a
background in military or diplomatic service. None had any
substantial gender-awareness training or experience.

During my time in the field with the OSCE in Kosovo, I realised
that this exclusion of women from the senior decision-making
structures of the OSCE and United Nations, combined with the very
damaging gender ignorance/blindness of the senior men posted to
these missions, were key contributing factors to the chaotic and costly
mess that ensued in the civilian reconstruction process. The men in
the United Nations and the OSCE missions were deeply imbued in an
old-fashioned, male-as-leader culture that was clearly ignorant of the
female majority and therefore particularly ill-suited to face the
imposing challenges ahead. At roundtable discussions I attended,
top UNMIK and OSCE officials regularly and earnestly discussed
what percentage of Serbs and other ethnic groups and 'minorities'
should be represented on judicial, political, and public bodies, without
ever mentioning the inclusion of women.

I pointed out this discrepancy repeatedly, stressing that hundreds
of documents had been drafted emphasising the importance of
incorporating women fully in peace-building and reconstruction
processes. For example, an early paragraph in the unanimous Security
Council adoption of Resolution 1325 (2000) states:

Reaffirming the important role of women in the prevention and resolution of conflicts and in peace-building, and stressing the importance of their equal participation and full involvement in all efforts for the maintenance and promotion of peace and security, and the need to increase their role in decision-making with regard to conflict prevention and resolution ... urges Member States to ensure increased representation of women at all decision-making levels in national, regional, and international institutions and mechanisms for the prevention, management, and resolution of conflict.

In addition, I also pointed out that the UN Global Platform for Action recommended that at least one-third of decision-making positions at all levels of politics and public life be women. And in September 1999, Elisabeth Rasmusson, one of the few women in the upper ranks as Deputy Head of OSCE Mission in Bosnia and Herzegovina, and Madeleine Rees, a lawyer with the OSCE in Sarajevo, organised a meeting in Sarajevo for the explicit purpose of discussing lessons learned about the exclusion of women in the OSCE Bosnia Mission.

Too complicated to include women?

I returned to Priština to remind the men at the OSCE Mission that the post-mortem of Bosnia Herzegovina had shown that it had been a serious error not to include women properly in the first elections and that at the second elections there had been a specific stipulation that at least one-third of candidates should be women. And yet, in a spectral echo of what must have been received wisdom in Bosnia, the men in the OSCE in Kosovo justified excluding women by saying that the situation was 'complicated enough without having to think about representation of women as well', and that women in leadership posts would be 'alien to local culture and tradition'. It was precisely the savage, musket-driven consequence of this 'local culture and tradition' we were all there to help put right.

In a further display of their biased awareness of reality, these 'liberal' male Europeans added that in any case 'no women in Kosovo are interested in participation in politics or public life'. In believing this, these men showed an unacceptable ignorance of the fact that – as in other former communist countries – many Kosovan women of all ethnic backgrounds were well educated and were qualified professionals in all fields, including medicine, engineering, and teaching. For instance, Luleta Pula, the Albanian Kosovan leader of a social democratic party, told me that in 1990 she headed the 60,000 women-strong wing of the LDK (Democratic League of Kosovo) Party.

She pointed out that ethnic Albanian Kosovan women had been very active for ten years or more in running the alternative society under the Serbs. Kosovan women also told me that they had been involved in running 'underground' municipalities and judiciaries. Kosovan women had risked – and even lost – their lives working as language assistants and advisers to the OSCE Verification Mission prior to the NATO bombing.

The complete exclusion of women from the democratisation process was highlighted by the fact that Dr Bernard Kouchner, the then special representative of the UN Secretary General in Kosovo, appointed the 17-person Kosovan Transitional Governing Council with not a single woman on it.

'Never as pushed aside as we feel now'

Frustrated and puzzled by the fact that the men at the top of the international community continued to ignore the voices of Kosovan women, I sent out a note asking if any women's NGO representatives would be interested in attending an exploratory meeting to discuss women's political empowerment. Around 30 women from 16 local women's NGOs and international organisations came along. This included representatives from rural women's networks, and from Serb, Roma, and ethnic Albanian communities.

We held a series of meetings with the purpose of working together to develop a programme of activities to increase women's participation in politics and public life. Each meeting was attended by an increasing number of women from NGOs across the province and from the Albanian, Serb, and Roma communities, as well as from the wings of political parties – the LDK and the UCK (Kosovo Liberation Army) and from international organisations.

Some 60–80 women from 22 Kosovan NGOs across the province attended the meetings, and they told me that these meetings were the first time that Kosovan women's NGOs had been able to come together to work on anything. Igbal Rugova, leader of Motrat Qiriazi, an umbrella of four rural women's networks said: 'The international community has marginalised us women in a way we never had been before. We have never felt as pushed aside as we feel now.'

Prompted by the frustrations of the Kosovan women, a UN colleague and I sent a fax to UN Secretary General Kofi Annan to ask him to intervene. As a direct consequence, three Kosovan women NGO leaders were invited to meet with Annan and Kouchner, who agreed as a result that UNMIK would in future hold regular consultations with women NGO leaders. Three women were subsequently invited to join the new joint interim governing group, and six women were appointed to the new interim transitional council.

The diamond ceiling

An unexpected consequence from the actions outlined above affected me directly: I was fired from the Mission for breaking protocol by sending a fax requesting Kofi Annan to intervene. I had been 'uncollegiate'. The fax was considered a 'major breach of protocol' by the men in senior posts. It had embarrassed the male hierarchs of the OSCE in Kosovo. As a result, the Dutch Head of Mission told me a few weeks later to leave Kosovo. Ironically, when I heard the news, I was away for ten days in Russia, working on a prior contract training future women leaders. I was told through e-mail not to return.

I have published two books on women in the workplace, *Breaking Through the Glass Ceilings* and *Do It! – Walk the Talk*. Yet I had not realised how precarious a place a sole woman higher up in the hierarchy is in if the men around and/or slightly below her find her presence disturbing. Ruefully, I'm thinking of calling this less examined phenomenon 'the Diamond Ceiling': at that height in the 'company' you can buy diamonds if you wish, but you had better buy them fast.

Trading places

One root cause of the exclusion of women from senior posts is the way in which international organisations function and the way they recruit and promote their personnel. Before each mission, horse-trading takes place between nations for prestige posts. Foreign Offices play games harking back to Richelieu or Rome. One Italian diplomat told me that he had, over a period of years, happily backed Denmark, The Netherlands, France, and other countries in their bids to put their men in place, with an eye on calling in the favour down the line.

Thus, senior posts in peace missions are subject not to finding the best and most appropriate person with the character and outlook for the job, but rather by Buggins' turn and trading places. And, once in place, hierarchy is all. No matter how ill-suited for the job the person mandated by his country may be, he (and, as I have pointed out, it is overwhelmingly 'he') can and does veto any ideas from lower down without any fear of mutiny in the ranks. Mission 'junkies' want to junket off to Aceh, if it blows further, or Madagascar if the civil war continues, or ... The wretched and immoral concept of collegiality – a conspiracy of *omertá* (the code of silence practised by the Mafia) regarding your colleagues and especially your bosses – clicks seamlessly into place.

Of course the mere inclusion of more women in the post-conflict reconstruction processes is not enough to ensure a smoother ride towards a rebuilt polity and economy. The very structures that somehow arrive like a flat-pack from Mission control to the field have yet to manage to fit the place and circumstance.

Problems resulting from poor or inadequate pre-planning and inappropriate senior personnel are further compounded by the fact that a most vital ingredient, communication, is hard to come by when it is needed the most. Let me provide an example. One day, in September or October 1999, I saw a distraught Kosovan woman outside the UN police headquarters in Priština. Three UN police officers were telling her to go away, mocking her. I went up and asked what was happening. One of the police officers said:

> *'This is a crazy woman – ma'am. She has come to us three days running. She says her family is being nasty to her. We keep telling her that's nothing to do with us and she should go away. She's just a crazy woman.'*

I asked them if it had occurred to them that she may well have returned despite them telling her to go away because she was desperate for someone to help her. At the very least they could advise her which agency in Priština could offer assistance and possibly counselling. They said they had no idea where to send her or how to find out.

I asked an experienced UN police peacekeeper in Kosovo to tell me why UN missions often go so wrong. His response mirrored the frustrations of other competent professionals angered by the organisational mish-mash:

> *'No clear sense of purpose; muddled and contradictory goals and objectives crafted by amateurs, implemented by incompetents, and defended by bureaucrats whose sole purpose in life is to move up the food chain. Make no waves, admit no mistakes, accept no responsibility, and demand no accountability. Appearance is everything; never mind the substance. Pay no attention to the man behind the curtain.'*

In late 2000 I received an e-mail from a relatively new Mission member in Kosovo. She wrote:

There have been a lot of mistakes and problems in the Kosovo deployment
(mostly from the civilian side) – coordination and communications
between agencies and organisations being one of the most outstanding.

This lack of communication, combined with gender ignorance/
blindness within the Mission in Kosovo, had a wide variety of negative
consequences for women.

Sex trafficking

Along with drugs, sex trafficking has become a huge, criminal trade
whereby women are forced into prostitution whenever clients with
cash can be found. This involves the transport of women and girls
across state lines, and, like with the drugs trade or the illegal cash
flows from Russia to banks in the Mediterranean region, it helps to
maintain fuzzy borders in south-east Europe to facilitate this movement of human beings.

The following is taken from a report in *The Times* dated 5 February
2000:

*The women, some as young as 16, are held captive by gangsters, often
Albanian, and forced to sell sexual favours to troops and businessmen
in the nightclubs opening around Kosovo. In the past Kosovo was not a
destination for the east European sex trade, which began with the collapse
of communism in 1991, but the presence of a 45,000 strong army has
proved an irresistible draw.*

*In one bar just outside Priština, near the HQ of Russian forces, 12 young
women were rescued in early February. Their duties included dispensing
sexual favours to Russian and American K-For troops and other foreign
clients. The girls, who were rescued by the International Organisation of
Migration (IOM), were said to be terrified.*

Barely four months after the international forces arrived, the Kosovan
population began to feel impeded rather than liberated. A woman
NGO leader summed up the mood:

*'You "internationals" are polluting our air and clogging up our roads with
all your white vehicles,' she said. 'You refuse to employ us as professionals
in your organisations. There are thousands of you. You all make promises
but we neither see action from you nor do you provide us with funds to get
on with things ourselves.'*

How could matters be improved? Some suggestions

What would be the best structures and vehicles in future post-conflict situations to fulfil tasks of strengthening democracy, human rights, free media, good governance, and society based upon law and order and the mainstreaming of gender in all activities?

Even though missions write excellent evaluation reports about lessons learned, this knowledge is either not passed on to the next mission, or simply not incorporated. The exclusion of women by senior males in the Kosovo Mission happened despite repeated strong warnings and reports about attitudes to women on previous OSCE missions.

There are three ways in which matters can be improved:

- Post-conflict elections should be crafted to ensure the inclusion of women. There should be, for instance, a format mandating that at least 40 per cent of all candidates be women. In elections with list systems there could be alternate men and women's names on the lists of candidates. These mechanisms are both democratic and inclusionary.

- It is crucial to ensure that women have fair access to resources. It is pointless to 'empower' women and pass protocols, directives, resolutions, or statute laws without providing the ancillary funding required to make the changes operational and effective.

- Co-ordination, co-operation, and understanding between formal and informal sectors need to be dramatically improved. The military, NGOs, international institutions, politicians, and local populations are all key stakeholders in producing a satisfactory outcome. The lack of interface and co-ordination among them must be addressed urgently.[2]

Other recurrent problems that are not directly addressed in this paper but that nonetheless require attention include the following:

- The military and the large international organisations such as the United Nations tend to be contemptuous of the hundreds of little ants – 600 or more NGOs were active in Kosovo even in the early post-conflict days.

- The small NGOs are disdainful and increasingly critical of the large, over-funded, and endlessly ineffectual bureaucracies.

- NGOs are often suspicious of the military.

- In Kosovo, the NATO military with their well-practised, well-thought-out command and control structures were confused and annoyed by the *ad hoc* ('chaotic') work culture of the hundreds of NGOs and by the cumbersome structures of the United Nations and the OSCE.

The military, which have extensive training resources, may be able to assist NGOs and civilian consultancies with pre-Mission training in team building, planning skills, logistics know-how, and simulation exercises. At the same time, NGOs may be able to help train the military in developing a greater understanding of communication between military and civilian personnel in order to better interact with and assist the civilian population, including women and men, different ethnic groups, and so on.

Addendum and concluding remarks

The following article appeared in *Business Week* online on 23 May 2002:

> *First Lady Laura Bush made headlines when she took to the airwaves of Radio Free Europe on May 21 to urge the women of Afghanistan to play a major role in the reconstruction of their battered nation. Mrs. Bush isn't alone. She was echoing a growing school of thought among foreign policymakers that the key to fostering democratisation and economic development, especially in impoverished Muslim and African nations, may lie in the empowerment of women.*
>
> *In state after state plagued by civil war or ethnic cleansing, thousands of men have been killed. That has left women as the majority of the population. And it sometimes means there's no one else to shoulder the leadership role in both politics and economic development in what are often conservative, patriarchal societies ... The statistics can be stunning. In Bosnia, 67 per cent of the population is female, and the figure is 70 per cent in parts of Kosovo. Women and children account for 80 per cent of refugees. And the men who don't get killed often live abroad and send money home.*
>
> *The good news is that several ... NGOs – some run by women – have been focusing for years on helping women with such issues as political involvement and microeconomic projects. And the experience has paid off. 'NGOs run by women are more successful than NGOs run by men', says Joseph Presel, a former American ambassador to Uzbekistan. 'There has been fairly rapid and measurable success. It's not readily apparent but is very much the case.'*

But despite this potential for leadership, women in Kosovo were for the most part left out of the post-conflict reconstruction process. Among other things, women lacked equal access to:

- administrative power;
- participation in all levels of the democratisation processes;
- planning, implementation, and monitoring of policies;
- funding and resources.

As a result, women did not enjoy the same respect as male survivors of conflict did – men wounded in conflict are perceived as heroes, while women raped in conflict are seen as shameful and are expelled by their communities. In addition, the needs of (thousands of young) widows have been overlooked, and women continue to lack equal access to retraining and employment opportunities.

Neither men nor women should be allowed to be deployed on an international mission as civilians, police officers, or military personnel unless they can prove as an entry qualification that they have attended a minimum of three days' training in gender sensitivity and gender mainstreaming – and this must include Heads of Missions and Heads of Departments. Clear evidence that an individual lacks gender awareness should be grounds for refusing promotion or redeployment until this has been remedied or the person removed.

Acknowledgement

The full report on which this paper is based, *Kosovo – Opportunities Missed, Lessons Learned*, may be requested from tim.symonds@shevolution.com free of charge.

Notes

1   The Active Learning Network for Accountability and Performance in Humanitarian Assistance (ALNAP) is an inter-agency forum working to improve learning and accountability in the international humanitarian system. ALNAP (2002) Section 4.3.4 on Gender Equality noted the following:

- While most agencies now have gender-equality policies, they are clearly not being translated into practice. Gender-analysis tools and training appear to have been largely ineffective in the face of highly resistant bureaucracies. The exception is UNHCR (June 2001), where structural barriers to gender equality such as cultural norms and practices are analysed in depth.

- For the most part agency reports, while themselves critical of a lack of gender analysis, do not adequately analyse how interventions might be improved. Again, the focus is on what happened, and not on why it happened.
- The ActionAid summary report (2000) comments that gender issues tend to be de-prioritised in emergencies and tend to be confused with initiatives targeted toward women. Targeting women may result in immediate impact but does not necessarily address structural and rights issues, which is one important objective of a gender-equality approach.
- In the reports that do consider gender equality, poor practice and failure to mainstream gender adequately appear to be the norm, even in interventions that were successful overall.

2 Better forward planning needs to go into any civilian responses in the future, and I recommend Schoenhaus (2002) on this extraordinarily important matter.

References

ALNAP (2002) *Humanitarian Action: Improving Performance Through Improved Learning*, ALNAP Annual Report, London: ALNAP.

Schoenhaus, R.H. (2002) *Training for Peace and Humanitarian Relief Operations: Advancing Best Practice*, Peaceworks Reports 43, Washington, DC: United States Institute for Peace (available free of charge from usip_request@usip.org).

Vandenberg, M. (1999) Keynote address at the OSCE Supplementary Human Dimension Meeting on Gender Issues, Vienna, 14–15 June, www.osce.org.

Training the uniforms:
gender and peacekeeping operations

Angela Mackay

A complex setting, a difficult task

At face value it is a simple idea – training peacekeepers on 'gender'. At the same time, the suggestion that peacekeepers should be required to receive training on 'the protection, special needs, and human rights of women and children in conflict situations'[1] is close to revolutionary. That the idea was initiated by leading national politicians and advanced vigorously within the United Nations only adds to the surprise that this project should be deemed so radical.

Approximately three years ago, former Canadian Minister of Foreign Affairs Lloyd Axworthy and former US Secretary of State Madeleine Albright agreed to support the development of a training programme on 'gender' for civilian and military personnel working on peacekeeping missions. The preamble to the Charter of the United Nations – 'We the peoples of the United Nations determined to reaffirm faith in fundamental human rights in the dignity and worth of the human person, in the equal rights of men and women' – had proved difficult to live up to. Peacekeeping missions in the previous decade, including Cambodia, Somalia, Rwanda, and Bosnia, embodied graphic demonstrations of the failure of member states to honour their commitments. At the same time, peacekeeping forces had been found wanting in their own behaviour, both in terms of flaunting such undertakings and of failing to protect the populations they were sent to serve.

The complex environment of modern, multifaceted, and multi-organisational missions makes the expectations enunciated in the Charter particularly ambitious and challenging. All the rules have changed from earlier traditional peacekeeping missions. The days in which UN peacekeepers merely patrolled a dividing line between two opposing forces in an attempt to create a space in which peace might

First published in *Development in Practice* 13(2&3): 217–22 in 2003

be explored and developed are long gone. These days, peacekeepers face mass movements of displaced people, of whom the vast majority are women and children. They also have to deal with war crimes such as torture, rape, and ethnic cleansing on an unprecedented scale, as well as turn their hands to disarmament and demobilisation campaigns, provide security to besieged settlements, and confront vicious, armed, and traumatised child soldiers. And they have to do all this often with little or no specific preparation or training.

Nevertheless, the changes in social structures as a result of conflict are beginning to be understood. The fact that war changes roles and responsibilities within society, while exposing men and women of all ages and classes to new threats and opportunities, has become increasingly recognised. Civil wars disrupt and destroy civilian life. Men leave, die in combat, are brutalised, lose employment, or resort to despair, violence, or apathy. Women assume enormous burdens of work and all manner of different tasks and responsibilities, they lose their security and their protectors, and they are also victimised and marginalised.

Into this confusing and dynamic mix come the peacekeepers, scarcely trained for the nature of their interface with civilians and certainly unversed in the gender implications of an unknown society. Axworthy and Albright's idea came at an opportune moment. That moment was almost jettisoned when Senator Jessie Helms found out about it, and then blocked any financial contribution by the USA to a project with Canada, declaring that Canada was not a 'developing' country. Luckily, the UK Department for International Development (DFID) joined the project with Canada. In February 2000, the sponsors shared the first draft of the training package with a number of UN agencies, military bodies, governments, and NGOs. Following comment and revision, the final product was delivered in late 2000.

This initial training package, titled *Gender and Peace Support Operations*, was developed to cover a three-day training session and was aimed at a broad cross-section of the peacekeeping community – not specifically military or civilian institutions – and to serve as a body of reference material to be delved into, developed, and customised by interested organisations. The project undertaken by the Training and Evaluation Service (TES) of the Department of Peacekeeping Operations (DPKO) at the United Nations has done just that, embarking on a customised training package specifically for the 'uniforms' – military and civilian police.

This initiative has been reinforced by surprising moves within the United Nations. Since its inception, the United Nations has developed conventions, issued guidelines, defined strategies, and issued resolutions to strengthen the hand of all the actors seeking to uphold fundamental human rights principles. Since 1948 and the Universal Declaration of Human Rights, great distances have been travelled in the continuous efforts to keep the issues relating to equal rights for men and women not only in the spotlight, but moving forward. The series of conferences on human rights and specifically on the advancement of women – which have been held in Mexico, Copenhagen, Nairobi, and Beijing – have focused on efforts to achieve gender equality, to eliminate obstacles and discrimination against women, to end violence against women, and to respect women's human rights.

Moreover, in June 2000, the UN General Assembly held a special session titled 'Women 2000: Gender, Equity, Development, and Peace for the Twenty-first Century', and in October of that year, in a more unusual move, the Security Council, in open debate, focused on gender, equality, and peace. This resulted in Security Council Resolution 1325 (2000), a strong affirmation of the role of women in the prevention and resolution of conflict. It stresses the importance of the full involvement of women in all aspects of promoting and maintaining peace and security and the need to increase their role in decision making. It specifically recommends specialised training for peacekeepers on the protection, special needs, and human rights of women and children.

Training packages for 'the uniforms'

Simultaneously, in October 2000, the TES began developing a customised training package for 'the uniforms'. This initially involved seeking out any existing suitable materials and discussing the needs and key features of such a training package with various personnel from the DPKO and other UN agencies.

It rapidly became apparent that there existed little or nothing on the subject that could be used or transformed for military purposes. At the same time, there was unanimous consensus that the material should be practical and concrete and that the training should last for no more than one day. This material is to be provided to trainers in the nations that contribute troops, since the training of peacekeepers is always a national responsibility. The task of the United Nations is to provide training materials and advice and to train trainers. The 'gender' project involved developing a package for use by trainers for pre-deployment and ultimately a handbook to be given to all troops to keep in their pockets or in their kit.

The aim was to provide adequate background reading material for the trainer to become familiar with the subject; to provide a variety of options for presenting the material, with questions pitched at participants of different ranks and levels of responsibility, and additional materials to stretch the minds of those with a particular interest or to use at further training sessions. Very little, if any, reading was expected of the participants, who would be provided only with a basic record of the key points covered in the course.

The material was developed using a 'rights-based approach'. This approach was used for a number of reasons. It allows the presenters to distance themselves from the material so that discussing human rights does not become a case of the trainer's version of morality, or anyone's view of what is 'right' or 'wrong'. It allows for an emphasis on the fact that, as UN staff, peacekeepers are supported and protected by human rights conventions as well as expected to uphold and promote human rights. Those rights provide a standard by which they are expected to operate and the standard by which they will be assessed. The aim was also to foster the notion of personal responsibility as well as the response of the military within the mission.

In the best of training traditions, the course, somewhat ambitiously, intended to do three things – provide knowledge and information on how the relationships between men and women and their gender roles and responsibilities are transformed by violent conflict; develop basic skills of gender analysis and a recognition of the differing needs, capacities, and expectations of men and women; and make peace-keepers aware of the implications of their actions.

The content focused on three principal topics. The first was *What is Gender?*; the second *Gender and Human Rights*; and the third *What Can I Do?* The general feeling was that a considerable amount of time needs to be spent on the definition of gender, on clarifying the distinction between gender and sex, and on clearly establishing in the participants' minds that gender is socially constructed, that it changes, and that war creates a dynamic environment in which all social roles, responsibilities, and expectations can be dramatically altered. Once this is well understood, the participants get to test their analytical skills by examining simple case studies to identify the 'gender' issues and their implications.

Gender and Human Rights is the next piece of the puzzle, providing participants with a list of objective criteria upon which to base their actions and a universal set of standards to help them through the contradictory maze of options they need to consider in a peacekeeping operation. Once more, after a discussion and exploration of what human rights are all about, specific gender-based issues are presented as problems for participants to discuss. Resolution of these problems is often difficult, if not impossible. This is intended to underline once again the ambiguity of the environment in which the participants will operate.

In the concluding module, the participants are encouraged to assume personal responsibility by thinking of the actions they themselves may take in a peacekeeping mission in order to ensure their own gender sensitivity – as well as of tasks they might assign others in their command or suggest to senior officers.

An emotional, political, and cultural challenge

The issue with gender training material is the emotional rather than the intellectual challenge it presents. From the outset, it is at some level a politicised discussion. It strikes at the centre of everyone's being, male or female, because it is about beliefs, values, practices, expectations, and attitudes that identify every one of us. Long-held assumptions are likely to be challenged, issues of power and control confronted, and a demand made to look at the world from a different perspective. Another area of potential trouble is that, given the military propensity for checklists, there is always a danger that material on gender sensitisation is simply ticked off from a list alongside landmines, HIV/AIDS, or driving skills.

At the same time there is a lack of tough, clearly defined and enforceable standards for the behaviour of military and police peacekeepers. A code of conduct exists but its effectiveness is ultimately guaranteed only by the commanders who enforce it. In addition, no matter what training material is produced, the issue of sovereignty prevents the United Nations from making it enforceable. UN personnel can suggest, request, persuade – but not enforce or insist on the delivery of training. This may change in the future with 'lead' nations suggesting that they draw up a list of training requirements for all incoming contingents, who will be rejected if they do not comply. This proposal has been mentioned by senior Australian officers as a result of the experience in East Timor.[2]

Field testing the training package

This training package was piloted during field tests conducted in the United Nations Transitional Administration in East Timor (UNTAET) mission in February 2001. Three sessions were conducted for international military peacekeepers, one for UN civilian police, and one for the Timor Lorosa'e Police School cadets (in translation). Each class had approximately 25 participants.

The principal lesson learned from this pilot is that material needs to be presented in the utmost simplicity. Language, concepts, and examples need to be discussed in the most basic of formats and a variety of different training techniques need to be used to convey the material. Most participants in the pilot were first-time peacekeepers with no previous experience on which to draw, little knowledge of other peacekeeping efforts, and remarkably little imagination. There was also a wide range of participants in the classroom, from corporal to colonel, a fact that inhibited discussion among the more hierarchical cultures, in which senior officers are always shown deference.

Poor English-language skills prevented many participants from joining the discussion, asking questions, or registering their understanding. This would not be a problem, of course, in a monolingual group in which a single language could be used.

Working as self-starting groups exploring problems together was not a developed skill in most cases. Participants would generally defer to the senior person present and were reluctant to voice an opinion.

For pre-deployment training, the material should be broad and generic, incorporating a wealth of different examples. For in-mission training, it will be important to contextualise and offer local examples whose relevance the peacekeepers will immediately be able to test.

Overall, the training was well received but was too ambitious, seeking to fill an enormous void in the thinking and worldview of the majority of the peacekeepers. The tension between gender and culture was expected and inevitable, and discussions on the topic needed to be managed skilfully in order to avoid lapsing into using culture as an excuse for inaction. The contradictory views of those who professed they cannot interfere to stop violence against women because 'wife beating is a part of the local culture' but at the same time declared they 'wanted to help' and 'make a difference' seemed to be missed without being properly problematised.

An enormous distance remains to be covered for this material to be understood in any meaningful depth. There is need for repetition and reinforcement at the national and the international level, among all ranks of peacekeepers, and in particular among the senior ranks who, it is too often assumed, know and understand. Without their commitment, the 'simple soldier' lacks support and reinforcement for any positive steps taken in the gender arena.

However, merely having a first draft in addition to all the lessons learned from the field test is a great step forward for the DPKO. Backed by Secretary General Kofi Annan's response to the recent Brahimi Report,[3] which analysed the way peacekeeping is currently done and how it can be improved, this training project is in good company and strikes a timely chord. Annan's response made three specific references to the gender question: there should be more training on International Humanitarian Law (IHL) and gender issues; there should be a mixed-sex team to go from HQ to missions to conduct training for senior managers; and there is to be a strengthened mandate for integrating a gender perspective in peace operations – including a better gender balance in senior appointments and greater attention to sensitivity among personnel in their interactions with the population.

Now the work continues to incorporate the necessary changes identified from the field test and to be tested again and again in different settings before making the package available to all member states and to the new mission training cells.

Sustainable peace and gender relations

It is essential that peacekeepers of all nations, be they military, civilian police, or civilian, understand the significance of gender relations in the work they undertake. Without an understanding of how the relations between women and men are structured, how they are affected by violent conflict, and how the mere presence of peacekeepers further affects those relations, there can be little meaningful progress in the effectiveness of peacekeeping operations. Sadly, recent experience has demonstrated the negative effects on a population that is experiencing conflict with the presence of peacekeepers who lack sensitivity, or who in some way betray the principles and standards established by the United Nations. Their failure to conform to these standards and to respect the interests, needs, and desires of the population, particularly the women, has weakened their legitimacy and their effectiveness.

Women, who constitute the bulk of the civilian population affected by warfare, have typically been either overlooked by the warring parties and peacekeepers alike, who in both cases regard them as 'victims', as helpless bystanders, as targets for abuse, or as dispensable commodities. This overwhelming disregard for over 50 per cent of the population in situations of armed conflict has resulted in the iniquitous treatment of women by those expected to act in their interests.

An additional tragedy is that the resources committed to peace-keeping – both human and material – fail to realise their potential. A 'peace' that neglects the interests of a large part of the community, or that supports, reconstructs, and in some cases strengthens the inequities in the power structure, relegating women to roles of subordination and inferiority, cannot truly be called a peace worth having – and is unlikely to be sustainable.

It is important that peacekeepers reflect and practise the principles for which the United Nations stands, that they ensure that a society in conflict is in better shape after they leave than it was before they came, and that all members of society have equal access to the blessings of peace. That much of the reconstruction effort is about the relationships between men and women is easy to say, harder to understand, and even harder to practise. To grasp the fact that almost every activity, policy, programme, or project is in some way 'gendered' is extremely challenging. To appreciate the enormity of this fact takes time, interest, and intellectual energy.

This training manual is designed to enable instructors to read, prepare, and deliver basic training on the meaning and implications of gender and peace support operations. It is intended to be practical, concrete, and useful. It provides numerous examples, based on real-life experiences or situations, so the participants can constantly test their understanding of the concepts and their ability to discover responses and ideas for solving problems.

There are often no right answers, only better ones. In the disruption and confusion that accompany violent conflict and its aftermath, it is supremely difficult to determine and retain clear priorities. Some will argue that, at such times, gender considerations are not high on this list of priorities. This would be a profound mistake, for gender relations, their implications, and their outcomes are at the root of any society, and to neglect them will not only be to our collective detriment, but will also be wasteful, counter-productive, and will not contribute to a lasting peace.

Notes

1   United Nations Security Council Resolution 1325 (2000), New York.

2   Conversations with Mike Smith, Deputy Force Commander, UNTAET, and Andrew Mackinnon, Department of Defence, Canberra, Australia.

3   The Report of the Panel on United Nations Peace Operations commissioned by the United Nations Secretary General and first published in October 2000 (A/55/305 – S/2000/80) is commonly known after its chairperson as the Brahimi Report.

Palestinian women, violence, and the peace process

Maria Holt

Introduction

In September 1993, an astonished world watched as Palestine Liberation Organisation (PLO) leader Yasir Arafat and Israeli Prime Minister Yitzhak Rabin shook hands on the lawn of the White House, sealing what seemed at the time to be the beginnings of a peace agreement that both sides could live with. But the ensuing process of peace building between Israel and the Palestinians has failed to live up to early expectations, and, particularly since the outbreak of violence at the end of September 2000, hopes for a permanent peace settlement seem to have been extinguished altogether. The seven-year 'peace process', however, provided a space in which the Palestinian population of the West Bank and Gaza Strip could move away from resistance to start planning for self-government.

For their part, Palestinian women sought to consolidate the gains they had made as participants in the national struggle; they also looked ahead to their own position in the anticipated independent Palestinian state. In this chapter, I propose, first, to analyse the roles played by Palestinian women in the conflict and in the peace process; and, second, to examine how their participation has been influenced by the many forms of violence to which they have been exposed. I shall argue that a routine and systematic use of violence over a prolonged period of time has had the effect of placing women at a disadvantage when it comes to imagining and constructing the future state. They have been excluded, in other words, from effective participation in their own society.

By *violence*, I mean both the violence of the Israeli occupation, and the physical and psychological violence which women experience within their community. Violence affects Palestinian women in several ways: first, they are discouraged, on the whole, from engaging in direct violence, but they may sometimes – and in gender-appropriate ways – assist the men of the community who are at the forefront of the fighting; second, women are also disadvantaged by violence aimed at them directly. This comes from the occupying forces, in the form of beatings, verbal harassment, torture, and imprisonment, but also from their own men, in the form of domestic abuse; and, third, while Palestinian women are victims of violence, they are also agents, in the sense that they make choices and frequently act on their own behalf.

The story of Palestinian women's participation in their long-running national struggle is a well-documented one. At first sight, it appears to be an inspiring model of female inclusion in and positive contribution to an anti-colonial movement. If one delves below the surface, however, a number of inconsistencies begin to emerge and these have had an adverse effect on women's role in the peace process. To begin with, although men and women might be expected to employ different modes of struggle, these have tended to perpetuate an imbalance in power relations. Like all members of the community, 'Palestinian women have directly suffered the pains of Israeli arbitrary measures, compounding the suffering they already endure as women living in a patriarchal and conservative society' (WCLAC and WSC 2001).

Male and female roles derive from traditional ways of behaving, which in turn are rooted in Islamic culture.[1] Moreover, the masculine character of Palestinian nationalism has meant that female qualities tend to be undervalued and very particular conceptions of masculinity and femininity established. One result of this is a belief that women should, as far as possible, be protected, which has caused a conflict between the desire to shield women from the ugly reality of violence and the need for every member of society to add their effort to the struggle. A third problem lies in the lack of consensus within women's organisations themselves. Disagreements have arisen between those who believe that the national liberation struggle must take precedence and those who feel that national liberation should go hand in hand with women's liberation; between those who support the Oslo peace process and those who do not; and between some women who support the Islamic movement in the West Bank and Gaza Strip and others who believe it has had largely negative implications for women.

In order to address these questions, I will begin by discussing, in general, women's experiences of violence in conflict situations. I will then review the historical and current involvement of women in the Palestinian struggle, with reference, first, to the issue of violence in Palestinian society and the impact it has had on women; second, to the role of Islam in Palestinian culture, and in particular the phenomenon of Islamic resurgence as a political movement; and, third, to the scope of women's political activism, in the *intifada* period and beyond.

It is clear that, generally speaking, women have not fared well. While they have worked hard in many areas, their efforts have been impeded both by the violence of the Israeli occupation, which still continues, and by the masculine character of the liberation struggle, which includes strong elements of both structural and actual violence. At the same time, although women are victimised by the male-defined character of both the society and the conflict, one should not lose sight of the fact that they are also contributors in the sense that their support is active and deliberate. While I am not suggesting that women in the West Bank and Gaza Strip have by any means succumbed to a masculinist agenda, and although I am well aware that Palestinian men are also victims of the policies of the Israeli government, I believe women's efforts have been distorted and undermined by the prevailing male-dominated culture, which 'often means women internalise a sense of shame and self-blame. This is accentuated in "honour" cultures, since sexual assault and failed marriages are seen to dishonour not just the woman or girl, but her family as well' (British Council 1999:18).

Women, war, and violence

In war, women are likely to experience two types of violations: first, the violence that is done to them that is also done to men, in other words, 'dignified' violence, which is named as an abuse of human rights and widely condemned; and, second, violence that is enacted upon women because they are women, which is not usually counted as a human-rights violation since 'what was done to them smells of sex' (MacKinnon 1998:44). Sexual violence has been described as 'one of the most extreme and effective forms of patriarchal control, which simultaneously damages and constrains women's lives' (Kelly 2000:45).

In late 1992, stories began to emerge from Bosnia about the mass rape and forced impregnation of Muslim women and young girls by Serbian soldiers, as a form of 'ethnic cleansing' (Vickers 1993:23). After the Iraqi invasion of Kuwait in August 1990, there were reports of rape by Iraqi soldiers of Kuwaiti and non-Kuwaiti women, some of which led to pregnancies, an event so shocking in a conservative Muslim environment that some women killed themselves rather than give birth to enemy babies. In the occupied Palestinian territories, too, according to various sources, 'dozens of Palestinian women and girls have reported that Israeli interrogators have threatened them with rape and subjected them to sexually humiliating practices' (Vickers 1993:32).[2] It prompts the question as to why this particular method of violence is so routinely employed as a weapon of war. One possible answer, according to Seifert, is that sexual violence against women 'is likely to destroy a nation's culture' (Seifert 1999:150). But it is also the case that male violence against women

> ... is so pervasive, across so many historical eras and cultural differences, that it seems only explicable by reference to something intrinsic in men as men, some fear, some insecurity or aggressiveness which also inclines men to sustain formal institutions – military forces – which embody and legitimise these violent attitudes and behaviours.
> (Enloe 1988:209)

Violence against women in war is two-pronged: by humiliating individual women, it aims to reassert male power in a general sense; and it is intended to demoralise the enemy by striking at its weakest point. Thus, war-related violence against women is inextricably linked to domestic violence and to sexually violent crimes against women. Indeed, it has been argued that the 'questions of women and peace and the meaning of peace for women cannot be separated from the broader question of relationships between women and men in all spheres of life and in the family' (United Nations 1985:8). In light of events in Bosnia and other parts of the former Yugoslavia, the role of sexual violence in war has been re-evaluated. Rape and sexual violence against women, as Seifert says, are nothing new (Seifert 1999:145). What is different is that the causes of sexual violence in war are now being examined, and that the rape and sexual torture of women in conflict situations has been redefined as a war crime.

But women are not only victims of sexual abuse by enemy men; they also participate in conflicts in a variety of more proactive roles, from giving support to fighters and acting as substitutes for absent male workers to engaging in combat. When discussing women and violence in war, it is necessary to acknowledge women's agency. It can be argued, as Pettman says, that 'women's moral and political support and war work are essential parts of war-making' (Pettman 1996:127).

However, even when women are willing participants in their nation's struggle, they cannot altogether escape the shadow of victimisation and are still liable to become the targets of more private violence (in the shape of domestic abuse or ostracism) by their community as a result of their treatment by the enemy. Women tend to be at a disadvantage in national struggles regardless of what they do, and part of the explanation for this is 'the contradictions men demonstrate between their revolutionary political consciousness and their reactionary social-gender consciousness' (Abdo 1991:20).

In situations where women have played an active role in the liberation struggle, for example in Eritrea and Nicaragua, they may still find themselves encouraged to go back and adopt more 'traditional' roles once the fighting has ended, for 'whatever women's participation in wars and armed struggles, even as combatants, they are routinely pushed "back home" and their contribution erased when the fighting stops' (Pettman 1996:126).

Palestinian women, although they have gone some way towards challenging gender stereotypes, have fallen into similar patterns when it comes to moving from struggle to state building. One reason for this has been the problematic role of violence in Palestinian society, both as a means of patriarchal control and as an ubiquitous fact of daily life. Women are said to face 'double oppression', in the sense that violence comes from both the Israeli occupation and their own society.

Women, Islam, and honour

Throughout the long period of struggle, Palestinian society – violated and threatened with extinction – has clung to certain familiar structures. One of the most important of these has been the Islamic framework within which Palestinians have traditionally lived their lives. However, in times of extremity, even such primordial attachments tend to become distorted and used to justify inappropriate behaviour. Moreover, a number of scholars have argued that allegiance to a system of honour and shame, as manifested in the behaviour of women, has had a detrimental effect on the Palestinians' ability to wage an effective liberation struggle. Peteet, for example, has referred to the concept of honour as 'a defining frame for masculinity' (Peteet 2000:107). Arab masculinity, she notes, 'is attained by constant vigilance and willingness to defend honour (*sharaf*), face (*wajh*), kin and community from external aggression and to uphold and protect cultural definitions of gender-specific propriety' (Peteet 2000:107).

According to Afshar, the concept of honour killing (the killing by men of female family members who are believed to have committed 'crimes' against the honour of the family, for instance engaging in adulterous relationships or even speaking to unrelated males) is seen in many Middle Eastern countries as 'the national duty of men' (Afshar 1998:173). Among Muslims, she suggests, 'women have traditionally been the appointed site of familial honour and shame and the representatives of the public face of the society's commitment to its faith' (Afshar 1994:129).

However, in the Palestinian context, by expending disproportionate energy on the protection of their women, it could be argued that men have failed to make use of women's potential contribution to the defence of the nation and, in addition, are themselves handicapped from playing a full part.

In the 1930s, for example, the uprising following the death of Shaykh Izz al-Din al-Qassam, through its use of Islamic symbols and language, encouraged the participation of the masses in social action; Qassam's ideology has been described as 'Islamic populism' and was aimed at all levels of society (Johnson 1982:54), including women. It was fuelled by a sense of desperation at the rapidly deteriorating situation and the threat to Palestinian national identity. Yet even though women took part in the 1936 revolt, they tended to be protected from the general violence and insecurity that was besetting society. Already a masculine-based nationalism had taken root, or rather a process by which masculinity is nationalised (see Massad 1995), and this was achieved, at least in part, as a result of the honour system.

The Zionists were well aware of the Palestinian Achilles' heel of honour and used it to their advantage during the hostilities of 1947 and 1948. For example, in December 1947, Palmach forces, during an attack on the village of al-Khisas, near the Lebanese border, deliberately targeted women and children (Benvenisti 2000:103). In October 1948, in an attempt to force the occupants of the village of al-Dawayima, on the western slopes of the Hebron highlands, to flee, the Israeli army murdered women and committed rape during a brutal assault on the village (Benvenisti 2000:153).

According to Warnock, the demands of the honour system prevented Palestinian society from preserving itself when threatened with the overwhelming Zionist force in 1948. She argues that 'many of the Palestinian families who fled their homes did so primarily out of fear that their women would be raped by Zionist soldiers ... For many Palestinian men, saving their women from rape was more important than defending their homes or showing personal bravery and defiance' (Warnock 1990:23). In Warnock's view, defence of the land and defence of women are closely connected. Peteet, too, suggests that, as the 'conflict spread and intensified, women were becoming victims of war precisely because they were women, the crucial repositories of family honor' (Peteet 1991:59).

In Palestinian society, as elsewhere in the Islamic world, honour is a concept 'that is laden with culturally specific semantic connotations' (Afsaruddin 1999:9). Closely bound up with constructions of masculinity and femininity, the demands of the honour system continue to govern relations between the sexes and within families. Zahira Kamal speaks of 'an ideological structure ... based on ancestral traditions ... [which] derives its strength from Arab religious practices and is filled with superstitions ... One result of this structure is that Arab women are ... considered weak, incapable creatures, mere shadows of their men' (Kamal 1998:79). Thus, to a large extent, honour 'is rooted in the sexual behavior of women' (Afsaruddin 1999:9). For Palestinian women, like the majority of women in Arab societies, family honour 'is the concept in whose name most of the restrictions upon ... women's freedom of movement are imposed' (Ein-Gil and Finkelstein 1984:171).

It is important to distinguish, however, between an honour system that victimises and restricts women and one that enables them to play a fulfilling part in their society. For Palestinians forced into exile after 1948, the concept of honour became more than a framework through which to live their lives; it defined the loss of the land and the idealisation of women as guardians of national dignity. The shock of being abruptly removed from their land and dumped into the alien and crowded environment of refugee camps gave rise to feelings of despair and powerlessness among Palestinians, particularly among men. Having lost everything, many men found themselves with only one outlet through which to express their authority – the family – and, in some cases, this led to abuses of male power within the home. It is conceivable that such conditions, supported by a belief that Islam permits, under certain circumstances, the physical punishment by men of their wives, have been at least partially responsible for providing a basis for violent treatment. When traditional structures are combined with oppressive and humiliating conditions in daily life, the outcome is likely to be a deterioration of women's rights and status.

National struggle, dispossession, and exile

Despite the restrictions placed upon them, Palestinian women have embraced roles other than that of victim. From the beginning of the twentieth century, what may be termed 'resistance' activities by women have evolved through various stages. These began as charitable and social-welfare work by a small group of upper- and middle-class ladies. After 1918, when Britain obtained the mandate for Palestine, women started to take part in demonstrations against British policies. Fleischmann argues that, although Palestinian women's activity during the British mandate period has been described as 'politically unaware', these women 'established an organized and often militant movement that was actively involved in social, political, and national affairs' (Fleischmann 2000:16). She reports that women's 'frequent participation in demonstrations signified their willingness to engage in "unladylike" and even violent behavior, thereby defying cultural norms that prescribed limited public visibility of women' (Fleischmann 2000:24).

After the 'catastrophe' of 1948, the majority of Palestinians had to leave their homeland. Women 'describe the first decade of exile in terms that evoke death and a state of mourning. The loss of country and home and a refugee status were akin to the loss of a loved one' (Peteet 1991:26). Losing Palestine, in the words of one exile, 'was like losing a husband or a son' (Madame Haddad, a middle-aged woman from Jaffa, quoted in Peteet 1991:26). On the other hand, in terms of empowerment, the refugee camps provided women with a new set of roles. As the pivot of family life and the symbol of what it means to be Palestinian, they struggled to keep their families together, to maintain their fragile sense of identity, and to respond to the many hardships of everyday life.

Palestinians in exile realised the vital importance of education – for girls as well as boys – if they were to regain their homeland.

As they became better educated, women started to look beyond home and marriage. Many were keen to participate in the embryonic resistance movement. The PLO was founded in 1964, and under its umbrella, the General Union of Palestinian Women (GUPW) was created in 1965. However, although barriers between the sexes began to break down, traditional values continued to play a central role. This was partly because they were too deeply embedded to change easily and partly because they were an essential component of the attachment to the land of Palestine and, therefore, closely entwined with national identity.

During the 1960s, although the character of the resistance remained militantly masculine, Sayigh and Peteet suggest that some of its leaders, particularly in Lebanon, were committed to the inclusion of women. These men 'campaigned against traditional notions of honour and fostered new symbols of a culture of resistance. The slogan *al-ard qabl al-ird* (land before honour) became part of everyday speech and had a strong effect by putting the two sacred values in opposition, thus forcing people to choose between them' (Sayigh and Peteet 1986:118). But this development is less clear-cut than it appears. Hatem, for example, argues that, like its Algerian counterpart in the 1950s and 1960s, the Palestinian liberation movement 'resisted significant changes in personal values women were expected to uphold. The preoccupation with women's honor as part of the definition of a respectable wife was not challenged' (Hatem 1993:42–3). Certainly there was some shift in attitudes towards 'honour' and, as a result, some women were able to participate in the resistance, but enlightened attitudes on the part of a few male leaders failed to transform the status of women substantially. A contradiction remained between the demands of living in a society threatened with obliteration, a 'war zone' in which actual or anticipated violence circumscribed every aspect of Palestinian life, and the existence of an idealised realm in which traditional values continued to occupy a central position.

The occupation: coming to terms with intrusion in the private sphere

The 1967 Israeli occupation brought the Palestinians of the West Bank and Gaza Strip into a more intimate proximity with those who had taken their land. Suddenly the Israelis were no longer simply 'the enemy outside'; they were in Palestinian villages, on Palestinian streets, and even in Palestinian homes, which inevitably had a profound effect on women. They suffered violation – both physical and psychological – and trauma. From the early days of the occupation, women had no choice but to confront the Israeli military authorities. They protested against the seizure of Palestinian land, the demolition of houses, and the ill treatment of their children, and, in response, they were arrested, imprisoned, and sometimes physically abused by the occupying forces.

Although one side effect of the occupation was a growth in feminist consciousness among certain sections of society, women were still expected to occupy a traditional position in society. Even though a few women became fighters, some turned to political activism, and many others contributed to the resistance, they continued to be lauded, above all, as the 'mothers of martyrs and Patriotic Mothers' (Cooke 1996:174), rather than being accepted – alongside men – as defenders of their nation. This was because, while 'the mobilization of women in the struggle was needed, it had to be reconciled with the equally important task of cultural preservation. The results were contradictory expectations of women, who were to take on new public tasks in the struggle, but without challenging the old value systems or the roles they played in the personal arena' (Hatem 1993:42–3).

In many ways, this period marked an important transition for women. While conservative attitudes certainly did not disappear and life undoubtedly became more difficult in many respects, opportunities for women increased. The female illiteracy rate in the West Bank declined from 65 per cent in 1970 to 37 per cent in 1983 and in Gaza from 65 per cent to 39 per cent for the same period. A growth in the number of Palestinian universities gave more women access to higher education (Kamal 1998:80). Increasing numbers of women chose – or were forced – to take paid work outside the home. During this period, too, women established new types of organisation. The year 1978 'witnessed the birth of a more progressive and "feminist" women's movement – namely, the women's committees' (Ameri 1999:36).

A crisis of masculinity

The Palestinian uprising – or *intifada* – which began at the end of 1987 witnessed the Palestinian residents of the West Bank and Gaza Strip making a concerted effort to resist Israeli occupation, politically, economically, and culturally. In this section, I will discuss the effects of the *intifada* on Palestinian women, in terms of victimisation and agency. The *intifada* started as a display of spontaneous anger and a reassertion of national dignity, and has been described as an attempt by the 'young, armed only with stones and facing death and pain, ... to sweep away the older generation in terms of political relevance and actual leadership' (Peteet 2000:113). The effects it had on Palestinian women were mixed, and their responses and activities can be divided into several phases. Although they added their efforts to the general communal rejection of the occupation, women also experienced victimisation both from the enemy and their own society. One should bear in mind, however, that Palestinian males, too, were the victims of brutality and humiliation.

Since the Palestinians lack a state and an army, they have been unable to wage war in the conventional sense. Theirs has been an unequal struggle, using non-violent means, such as civil disobedience and peaceful resistance, and, on occasions, violent methods, such as armed struggle and terrorism. Although there have been some successes in the fight against Israeli occupation, on the whole the Palestinian struggle can be said to have failed, and, in the process, Palestinians in the West Bank and Gaza have experienced bitterness and disillusionment, as well as extreme forms of violence, in terms of forced removal from the land, the humiliation of occupation, negation of identity, and denial of basic human rights. As men have traditionally been responsible for defending the community, their inability to do so and their apparent powerlessness in the face of a militarily superior enemy has caused a crisis of masculinity.

The Israeli occupation, as Peteet suggests, 'seriously diminished those realms of practice that allow men to engage in, display and affirm masculinity by means of autonomous actions. Frequent witness to their fathers' beatings by soldiers or settlers, children [became] acutely aware of their fathers' inability to protect themselves and their children' (Peteet 2000:107). In response to feelings of powerlessness and shame, young Palestinian boys and men took it upon themselves to confront the occupation. They did it by asserting their own strength, in the form of stone throwing and verbal taunts, and by turning the beatings, torture, and imprisonment inflicted on them by the occupying Israeli authorities into something positive, 'a critical rite of passage into adulthood' (Peteet 2000:114).

Indeed, the *intifada* has been described as introducing

> ... a new masculine image, which immediately caught the attention of
> the international media ... The image was that of young boys confronting
> Israeli soldiers, kaffia masking their faces, throwing stones with one hand
> and carrying a Palestinian flag in the other ... This conception of youthful,
> assertive and defiant masculinity, captured in such metaphors as the
> 'generation of occupation' or the 'children of the stones', inspired both
> media coverage and popular narrative of the intifada.

(Sharoni 1998:1077)

Although it was undoubtedly the case that the uprising by young boys and men provided a liberating and hopeful interlude for the Palestinian population demoralised by the Israeli occupation, it did little to challenge the status quo. More a gesture of desperation than a seed of revolution, it failed to develop an alternative leadership or a radically different strategy for combating the occupation.

The so-called 'new Palestinian masculinity' also had a number of negative implications for Palestinian women. To begin with, it reinforced the existing presumption of a masculine-based nationalism. Massad argues that 'the mobilizing metaphors of nationalist movements ... reflect the fundamental assumptions of nationalist thought, which establishes the future gender constitution and gender roles of nationalist agency. History shows that other revolutions have foundered on a "nation first, women after" strategy' (Massad 1995:469). Despite the fact that women's active participation in the *intifada* undoubtedly 'pressured the secular leadership into changing part of its conceptual framework, the masculine still reigns supreme in Palestinian nationalist thought' (Massad 1995:482–3). Indeed, as Massad says, although the anti-colonial struggle has transformed the lives of Palestinian women, they 'are still considered subordinate members of the nation' (Massad 1995:483).

Another outcome has been a rise in domestic violence, as some Palestinian men have turned their anger and frustration on female members of their own family, a situation that finds parallels in conflict situations elsewhere in the world. The men,

> under tight discipline that [forbade] the use of weapons other than stones,
> [were] frustrated. The shortened workday, limited to prestrike hours,
> [meant] that they [were] home more often rather than working and then
> meeting male friends in coffee houses. The closure of West Bank schools ...
> resulted in children also being home all day. In addition, military curfews

*[forced] the entire family to stay inside for days at a time, often in very
cramped quarters. The battering that [followed] in some homes [was]
unsurprising.*
(Strum 1992:160)

One reason for this is that Palestinian society, 'like all patriarchal
societies, discriminates between the sexes in, for example, the
upbringing of girls and boys' (Yahya 1992:5). While boys are raised to
be assertive and powerful, girls are taught to be 'blindly obedient to
male family members' (Yahya 1992:5). As Palestinian psychiatrist
Eyad Sarraj puts it, although women suffer from the impact of the
occupation,

> *they also suffer as a result of tradition … In [Palestinian] patriarchal
> culture, women and children have always been in a weaker position than
> the patriarch, the male head of the family. When a husband can no longer
> contain his anger, his humiliation, his frustration due to the conditions
> of occupation, he is likely to find an outlet for his anger within the home.
> Women are often the victims of this anger.*
> (Quoted in Sabbagh 1998:175)

Second, humiliations inflicted on Palestinian men by the Israeli
authorities have also contributed to a heightened aggression against
female family members. It is claimed that '[s]ome men who were
subjected to beatings and torture return home to inflict violence upon
women' (Peteet 2000:120). A third explanation for the violent treatment of women has been 'the growth of fundamentalist movements
whose ideologies advocated traditionalism in family relations [and] re-
establishing a more authoritarian attitude towards women …
[F]undamentalism reinforced the traditional paternalistic setting
where the father is fully authorized to control the conduct of his family
members even by violent means' (Jad 1998:59–60). It is likely that
violence against women in the home can be attributed to a combination of these factors. Although a 'hot line' for victims of domestic
violence has existed in the West Bank since 1994, general awareness
of the problem remains relatively low and physical violence against
women is tolerated as 'a fact of life' in some sections of the community.

Women, activism, and the peace process

Nonetheless, despite the element of victimisation, one of the most
significant effects of the *intifada* 'was the transformation that took

place in women's consciousness of their roles. As they struggled with the soldiers to free their children, women overcame the internal barrier of fear that often prevented them from joining organized activities such as women's work committees' (Sabbagh 1998:3). Such developments, it has been suggested, encouraged women to challenge their position in the patriarchal structure, a process that had already begun. But women were forced to confront not just the traditional and patriarchal character of their society; they also found themselves up against the triumphantly masculine image of the *intifada*, which meant that, whatever successes they may have achieved in the early stages, these were unlikely to be sustained.

Abdo notes that 'the discourse on women and the *intifada* has focused largely on one particular image of social relations, that [of] "the heroic mother" ... The actions of such women have given rise to the national heroine known in the literature as "*Um al-Shaheed*" or the "Mother of the martyr"' (Abdo 1991:25). But the concept 'motherhood-nationhood', she says, 'became a prominent feature in Palestinian popular culture when it was taken up by the national male leadership. Motherhood and the glorifying of the "mother of the martyr" were incorporated in the national ideology of the movement, and particularly in the ideological construction of its armed struggle' (Abdo 1991:26–7). Another – later – female image was '*Um al-Asirah*' or the 'Mother of the female political prisoner', which, Abdo suggests, was 'a liberating image. Taking pride in a daughter in prison presumes a willingness on the part of women to confront some age-old repressive traditions embodied in the concept of "women's honour"' (Abdo 1991:30). Although these images of motherhood may be regarded as positive, they do little to challenge the underlying patriarchal structure of society.

Enloe's analysis of the role of women in nationalist struggles is useful in helping to understand the dilemmas experienced by Palestinian women. She suggests that 'a woman who begins to go out of her home in the evening to attend nationalist meetings in the name of securing a better future for her children may meet strong resistance from her husband ... He may even beat her to stop her from attending such meetings' (Enloe 1988:55). Experiences such as this may lead to a heightened feminist consciousness. When women became involved in nationalist activities, Enloe argues, many of them may not have imagined that 'critiques of foreign rule ... would lead to critiques of relations between husbands and wives. In fact, many women became involved *as* good wives and good mothers. It was only later that they concluded that they would have to overcome male resistance in their homes and neighborhoods if they were to be able to participate fully in the movement' (Enloe 1988:55). But for women in the West Bank and Gaza Strip, there was a wide gulf to be negotiated between understanding the confining structures of their patriarchal society and acquiring the necessary power to challenge them.

Women and the Islamist movement

Since the late 1980s, a political Islamist movement has flourished in the West Bank and Gaza Strip. As Roy suggests, its strength, especially in Gaza

> is rooted in the territory's extreme poverty, isolation, and traditional social structures, and its growth has been nourished by a profound sense of popular despair over the steady disintegration of daily life and the consistent failure of the nationalist movement to achieve any political resolution to the Palestinian–Israeli conflict and to end the occupation.
> (Roy 1995:22)

But one could argue that Islamism, far from being a foreign implant or merely a response to 'bad times', is woven into the fabric of Palestinian society.

As with Islamic movements elsewhere, the tendency has been for Islamists to take women and the family as the starting point of an ideal Islamic community. To some women, the Islamist trend is empowering. They see it as the only realistic hope of liberation for the Palestinian people. The confrontational brand of Islam espoused by groups such as Hamas[3] presents both a challenge and a compelling alternative to the apparent failure of the secular nationalist movement to achieve any significant progress. But while many women welcome the growing popularity of militant Islam, others regard it as an imposition. In the Palestinian territories, Islamist groups have sought to impose upon women a set of rules that some people – both male and female – argue are not Islamic.

The so-called '*hijab* campaign' in the Gaza Strip in the early part of the *intifada* is an illuminating example of what many women see as the removal of choice. Hammami describes it as 'fundamentally an instrument of oppression, a direct disciplining of women's bodies for political ends' (Hammami 1990:25). She argues that the Islamists have used the *hijab* as an instrument of social pressure. It is clear, she says, that the *intifada hijab* is 'not about modesty, respect, nationalism or the imperatives of activism[,] but about the power of religious groups to impose themselves by attacking secularism and nationalism at their most vulnerable points: over issues of women's liberation' (Hammami 1990:28). On the other hand, as Abdo suggests, 'the issue of *hijab* and Muslim fundamentalism [may have been] overplayed by the Israeli and Western media to divert attention from the major struggle against Israeli aggression' (Abdo 1991:33). It is important to separate the political programmes of groups such as Hamas from day-to-day religiosity. As Ameri notes, 'the question of Muslim fundamentalism goes beyond a dress code. It touches people's daily lives through its impact on institutions such as schools and the law' (Ameri 1999:43).

Nonetheless, the question of control remains a central one. By enforcing a particular mode of dress on women, Hamas supporters have been able to assert their power. When one looks more closely at the movement, it is clear that many of the young men drawn to it perceive themselves as powerless and lacking in the means to improve their situation. By using coercion and even violence against the female members of the community in the name of religion, they are able to gain some sense of self-respect. It has little to do with Islam and more to do with the struggle for power or dignity.

Women's political struggles

Many analysts of the Palestinian women's movement concur that women experienced a degree of empowerment through their involvement in the *intifada*. But although women from all segments of society were mobilised to take part, both spontaneously and by way of political organisation, it proved difficult to sustain their gains. Following the 1993 Oslo Accords between Israel and the PLO, Palestinians acquired partial autonomy in the West Bank and Gaza Strip and started to plan for government and eventual statehood.[4] But Palestinian women leaders found 'themselves outside the male-dominated political circles where official policy regarding the future of autonomy in Gaza and the West Bank [was] being determined' (Shalala 1995).

Anxious not to be excluded from the process, women's organisations worked hard to draw attention to their own demands. The potential for achieving women's equality in the new era of Palestinian self-rule, according to Ameri, is shaped by two factors:

'first, the past and present efforts of women's organizations to stimulate feminist consciousness and, second, their successes and failures in building participatory structures and traditions capable of realizing women's sociopolitical rights' (Ameri 1999:29). While she is correct to identify women's organisations as a key element in enabling the mass of women to participate in the political process, the lack of consensus among organisations has led to a dilution or fragmentation of women's aspirations.

Under the terms of the Cairo Agreement of May 1994, the newly created Palestinian National Authority (PNA) promised to operate within the framework of a draft Basic Law for the National Authority in the Transitional Period. The Basic Law has come under fire from some Palestinian women's organisations that criticise it for making no mention of equality between men and women. Afraid of being marginalised in any future Palestinian entity, in January 1994 some of the women's committees, the GUPW, human-rights NGOs, and others formed an umbrella group to produce a 'Women's Charter' to be presented to the PNA for inclusion in the constitution. The document aimed at 'cancelling out the laws that discriminate against women, guaranteeing the rights of women in the political, economic, social and educational spheres, and their equality in front of the law ... [It] also demand[ed] that the state of Palestine comply with international women's rights laws' (Rimawi 1994). Finally published in August 1994, the Charter is 'tellingly circumspect on the crucial issues of family law and personal status' (Usher 1994:17). One reason for this omission was the continuing struggle between the secular and Islamist versions of a future state.

The greatest problem, in the words of one critic, is that 'given the male-dominated Palestinian cultural tradition, there is a sharp lack of women with the kind of political and leadership skills needed to advance the women's agenda' (Ghada Zughayyar, director of the Jerusalem Center for Women, quoted in Nolen 1996:20). In order to address this omission, women's groups were again galvanised into activity. Co-ordinating their efforts was the Women's Affairs Technical Committee (WATC), formed in 1992 after protests that women were not adequately represented in the various PLO technical committees. In 1995, the WATC implemented a project entitled 'Palestinian Women and the Electoral Process', with the objective of 'improving women's abilities to participate in public life' (*Palestinian Women's Network* 1995:10). In January 1996, the first Palestinian election, for an 88-seat Legislative Council, took place in the autonomous areas. Twenty women ran for office and five won seats in the new parliament. Although the project had aimed at achieving 30 per cent female representation on the PLC and only five women (5.7 per cent) were elected, the project was judged to have been a success. It will be remembered, the organisers commented, 'for having offered a combination of comprehensive, well-balanced and much needed skills, techniques and information that satisfied the participating women's needs and encouraged a number of them to participate in the elections as candidates' (Candidate Training Project, West Bank and Gaza, 14 April – 15 May 1995).

Some Palestinian organisations suggest that domestic violence continues to present an obstacle to women's development. A recent public-opinion survey carried out in the West Bank, Gaza Strip, and East Jerusalem on violence-related issues revealed that 49.3 per cent of respondents believe that Palestinian customs and traditions are a stumbling block to women's progress; and 56.8 per cent do not accept that the Palestinian man's treatment of his wife is characterised by violence. At the same time, 50.7 per cent support a man's right to punish his wife physically if she does not obey him; 41.3 per cent believe a man may beat his wife if she lies to him; 49.2 per cent approve of the physical mistreatment of a woman by her husband if she 'underestimates his manhood'; and 61.7 per cent claim that intervention by the police in marital disputes is undesirable (PWWS and PCPO 2001).

Precise figures on the extent of domestic violence in Palestinian society are not available since, as al-Haj notes, 'when a woman is physically abused by her husband and asks for support and protection from her relatives, [they] often force her to return to her husband under the pretext of the children's welfare' (quoted in Yahya 1992:5). However, a number of measures have been taken by women's organisations to highlight the problem; to combat its effects; and to educate women about their rights. For example, a Women's Centre for Legal Aid and Counselling has been set up in the West Bank to advise women on their rights under Islamic law in matters such as marriage, divorce, and the custody of children. The extreme conditions of the *intifada* left little room for the observance of such rights and some male community leaders took advantage of the situation to impose their own notion of social order. In 1995, the Women's Empowerment Project, which runs vocational and counselling courses for women victims of violence, was created in the Gaza Strip. But in the opinion of its director Shadia Sarraj, real protection for women needs the support of the Palestinian Authority, 'especially in education and law' (Usher 1997).

Future hopes

Palestinian society has experienced a broad range and different forms of violence, both from outside and from within. For men, the traditional defenders of national and family honour, there has been little they have been able to do either to save their society from harm or themselves from humiliation. Palestinian women, as a result, are doubly victimised. They are victims of Israeli state violence and also of violence within their own society. Their experiences are bound to confuse them. They have seen their male kin brutalised and humiliated, their children terrorised, and their homes destroyed. They have become accustomed to living in an environment of relentless violence.

But Palestinian women face another form of violence. Within their own society, they are subjected to a seemingly insoluble conflict between 'tradition' and 'modernity'. They have been exposed to theories of women's rights and feminism, and, at the same time, to the 'fundamentalist' agenda of the Islamists. Tugged in several directions, they must maintain family stability, act as an example of appropriate female activism in a conservative Arab-Muslim society, and avoid threatening the precarious authority of their men. A final variety of violence to which Palestinian women are exposed is the international violence of gender oppression which dictates, first, that violence is an acceptable method of dealing with disputes; and, second, that women are destined always to be the victims of such violence. Sharoni suggests that an 'ongoing systematic gender-sensitive analysis of the contents and multiple effects of peace agreements, the processes designed for their implementation and the obstacles they face is necessary if peace is to become more than the mere end of physical violence and military confrontation' (Sharoni 1998:1089).

As the Palestinians continue to struggle for a state of their own in the West Bank and Gaza Strip, thwarted at every turn by Israeli intransigence and the creation of facts on the ground, women are concerned about their own rights and how these might best be protected by law. There is no doubt that their strong involvement in anti-occupation activities, particularly during the *intifada*, bestowed upon them both experience and a degree of empowerment. Unfortunately, however, this has failed to translate into tangible political gains. Although some women's groups united to produce the 'Women's Charter', a number of women 'expressed their frustration over the way [it] was written without consultation with the grassroots membership ... While women in general feel betrayed by the [Palestinian Authority], political women feel betrayed by the male leadership of their political parties, and women at the grassroots level feel betrayed by their women leaders' (Ameri 1999:47). As Sharoni notes, the signing of a peace agreement 'in and of itself does not create the conditions for gender equality' (Sharoni 1998:1089).

By considering the trends and developments discussed above, it is possible to gain some idea of where the Palestinian struggle is going in terms of future female involvement patterns, whether in the struggle for a state or the process of state formation. At the heart of this speculation lies a debate on whether 'the *intifada* propelled women into public life ... [or] succeeded only in provoking a conservative backlash which has driven women back into their homes' (Usher 1992:37). Giacaman believes that, although repression inflicted massive damage on women's organisations during the *intifada*, 'in the course of the resistance women mounted against both Israeli repression and Islamicist reaction, something emerged which is in fact genuinely irreversible. And this was the qualitative change in consciousness these struggles wrought' (quoted in Usher 1992:39). It has been, in other words, 'an experience of empowerment' (Usher 1992:39).

At the same time, the latest outbreak of violence between Palestinians and Israelis, ignited by Ariel Sharon's visit to al-Haram al-Sharif at the end of September 2000, is a cause for great concern. According to Sharoni, the militarisation of Palestinian society has been overlooked, as have been 'the new conceptions of masculinity that have emerged as a result, and the relationship between militarised masculinities and violence against women' (Sharoni 1998:1083).

In view of these factors, the outlook for women's political activism would appear to be grave. A combination of external aggression and repression from within has, in my view, marginalised women's organising, and there is a danger that this state of affairs will persist even when – or if – peace negotiations are restarted. In the present precarious situation, as Ameri notes, 'women's issues are of extremely low priority and one fears ... that the derailed women's movement may not get back on track for some time yet' (Ameri 1999:52–3).

As the formal peace process appears to have collapsed, and with it any semblance of law and order, Palestinian women are exposed to new threats of violence. Between the end of September 2000 and the end of January 2002, 42 Palestinian women and girls (including two 3 year-olds, one 2 year-old and one 4 month-old infant) were killed by Israeli security forces and settlers (Miftah 2002). Most of these were 'accidental victims' – women or girls who happened to be in the wrong place at the wrong time or who died as a result of being prevented from reaching a hospital – although it was reported on 27 January 2002 that a suicide bombing in West Jerusalem had been the work of the first-ever female bomber. It is difficult to predict how relations between Israelis and Palestinians will now progress. If some form of peace process is able to proceed and the Palestinians are allowed to resume the business of state building, women may have the opportunity to consolidate some of the gains they have made.

Although the present situation gives little cause for optimism, women's achievements over the last 50 years are heartening. Palestinian women have struggled for greater access to education, for the right to work, for broader participation in the political process, and for the realisation of their rights as human beings. They have been both courageous and outspoken. The most positive message to take from Palestinian women's involvement in the national struggle is that, unlike Algerian women in the 1950s and 1960s, Palestinian women are unlikely to be forced back into the home. Although there is a long way to go in terms of equal rights and participation, women in the West Bank and Gaza Strip have made impressive progress in that direction.

Notes

1   See also reports by the Women's Organisation for Women Political Prisoners (WOFPP) in Tel Aviv, Amnesty International, and *Palestinian Woman's Experience of Violence*, published by the Women's International League for Peace and Freedom (WILPP), Palestine Section, June 1991.

2   Although the majority of Palestinians in the West Bank and Gaza Strip are Sunni Muslims, there is a significant Christian minority (estimated at between 3 and 10 per cent).

3   Hamas, which is the Arabic acronym of the Islamic Resistance Movement (*Harakat al-Muqawama al-Islamiyya*), first appeared in February 1988 as 'the *intifada* wing of the Muslim Brotherhood (*Ikhwan*) in Palestine'.

4   The Israel–PLO Agreement on the Gaza Strip and Jericho Area, 4 May 1994.

References

Abdo, N. (1991) 'Women of the intifada: gender, class and national liberation', *Race & Class* 32(4): 19–35.

Afsaruddin, A. (ed.) (1999) *Hermeneutics and Honor: Negotiating Female 'Public' Space in Islamic/ate Societies*, Cambridge, MA: Harvard University Press.

Afshar, H. (1994) 'Muslim women in West Yorkshire: growing up with real and imaginary values amidst conflicting views of self and society', in H. Afshar and M. Maynard (eds.) *The Dynamics of 'Race' and Gender: Some Feminist Interventions*, London: Taylor & Francis.

Afshar, H. (1998) *Islam and Feminisms: An Iranian Case-study*, Basingstoke: Macmillan.

Ameri, A. (1999) 'Conflict in peace: challenges confronting the Palestinian women's movement', in Afsaruddin (ed.) (1999).

Benvenisti, M. (trans. M. Kaufman-Lacusta) (2000) *Sacred Landscape: The Buried History of the Holy Land since 1948*, Berkeley, CA: University of California Press.

British Council (1999) *Violence Against Women: A Briefing Document on International Issues and Responses*, London: British Council.

Cooke, M. (1996) *Women and the War Story*, Berkeley, CA: University of California Press.

Ein-Gil, E. and A. Finkelstein (1984) 'Changes in Palestinian society', *Forbidden Agendas: Intolerance and Defiance in the Middle East*, a collection of articles from the journal *Khamsin*, selected and introduced by Jon Rothschild, London: Al Saqi Books.

Enloe, C. (1988) *Does Khaki Become You? The Militarisation of Women's Lives*, London: Pandora Press.

Fleischmann, E.J. (2000) 'The emergence of the Palestinian women's movement, 1929–39', *Journal of Palestine Studies XXIX*(3): 16–32.

Hammami, R. (1990) 'Women, the Hijab and the intifada', *Middle East Report* 20(3&4): 24–8.

Hatem, M. (1993) 'Toward the development of post-Islamist and post-nationalist feminist discourses in the Middle East', in J. Tucker (ed.) *Arab Women: Old Boundaries, New Frontiers*, Bloomington, IN: Indiana University Press, in association with the Center for Contemporary Arab Studies, Georgetown University.

Jad, Islah (1998) 'Patterns of relations within the Palestinian family during the intifada', in Sabbagh (ed.) (1998).

Johnson, N. (1982) *Islam and the Politics of Meaning in Palestinian Nationalism*, London: KPI.

Kamal, Z. (trans. R. Khalidi) (1998) 'The development of the Palestinian women's movement in the Occupied Territories: twenty years after the Israeli occupation', in Sabbagh (ed.) (1998).

Kelly, L. (2000) 'Wars against women: sexual violence, sexual politics and the militarised state', in S. Jacobs, R. Jacobson, and J. Marchbank (eds.) *States of Conflict: Gender, Violence and Resistance*, London: Zed Books.

MacKinnon, C.A. (1998) 'Rape, genocide, and women's human rights', in S.G. French, W. Teays, and L.N. Purdy (eds.) *Violence Against Women: Philosophical Perspectives*, Ithaca, NY: Cornell University Press.

Massad, J. (1995) 'Conceiving the masculine: gender and Palestinian nationalism', *The Middle East Journal* 49(3): 467–83.

Miftah (2002) 'Palestinian human and material losses inflicted by Israel during the intifada (uprising): September 28, 2000 until January 27, 2002', *Special Report: Intifada Update No. 36*.

Nolen, S. (1996) 'Women leaders call for unity', *Palestine Report*, 8 March.

Palestine National Council (1989) 'Palestinian Declaration of Independence', Algiers, 15 November 1988, reproduced in *Journal of Palestine Studies* XVIII(2): 213–16.

Palestinian Women's Network (1995) 'Palestinian women and the electoral process', *Palestinian Women's Network* 1(1) November.

PWWS (Palestinian Working Women Society) and PCPO (Palestinian Center for Public Opinion) (2001) *Public Opinion Survey on the Issue of Violence Against Women*, Ramallah and Beit Sahour, 19–22 April.

Peteet, J.M. (1991) *Gender in Crisis: Women and the Palestinian Resistance Movement*, New York, NY: Columbia University Press.

Peteet, J.M. (2000) 'Male gender and rituals of resistance in the Palestinian intifada: a cultural politics of violence', in M. Ghoussoub and E. Sinclair-Webb (eds.) *Imagined Masculinities: Male Identity and Culture in the Modern Middle East*, London: Saqi Books.

Pettman, J.J. (1996) *Worlding Women: A Feminist International Politics*, London: Routledge.

Rimawi, M. (1994) 'Palestinian women activists draft an equal rights document', *Jerusalem Times*, 1 July.

Roy, S. (1995) 'Beyond Hamas: Islamic activism in the Gaza Strip', *Harvard Middle Eastern and Islamic Review* 2(1): 1–36.

Sabbagh, S. (ed.) (1998) *Palestinian Women of Gaza and the West Bank*, Bloomington, IN: Indiana University Press.

Sabbagh, S. (1998) 'Palestinian women and institution building', in Sabbagh (ed.) (1998).

Sayigh, R. and J. Peteet (1986) 'Between two fires: Palestinian women in Lebanon', in R. Ridd and H. Callaway (eds.) *Caught Up in Conflict: Women's Responses to Political Strife*, Basingstoke: Macmillan Education, in association with the Oxford University Women's Studies Committee.

Seifert, R. (1999) 'The second front: the logic of sexual violence in wars', in M.B. Steger and N.S. Lind (eds.) *Violence and its Alternatives: An Interdisciplinary Reader*, Basingstoke: Macmillan.

Shalala, N. (1995) 'Women leaders sceptical about elections and civic policies', *Jerusalem Times*, 10 November.

Sharoni, S. (1998) 'Gendering conflict and peace in Israel/Palestine and the North of Ireland', *Millennium Journal of International Studies* 27(4): 1061–89.

Strum, P. (1992) *The Women are Marching: The Second Sex and the Palestinian Revolution*, New York, NY: Lawrence Hill.

United Nations (1985) 'Nairobi forward-looking strategies for the advancement of women', in *Report of the World Conference to Review and Appraise the Achievements of the United Nations Decade for Women*, Nairobi: United Nations.

Usher, G. (1992) 'Palestinian women, the intifada and the state of independence: an interview with Rita Giacaman', *Race & Class* 34(3): 31–44.

Usher, G. (1994) 'Women, Islam and the law in Palestinian society', *Middle East International*, 23 September.

Usher, G. (1997) 'Palestinian women tackle domestic violence', *Guardian*, 1 March.

Vickers, J. (1993) *Women and War*, London: Zed Books.

Warnock, K. (1990) *Land Before Honour: Palestinian Women in the Occupied Territories*, Basingstoke: Macmillan.

WCLAC (Women's Centre for Legal Aid and Counselling) and WSC (Women's Studies Center) (2001) 'Stories from Women Living Through the Al-Aqsa Intifada', www.grassrootsonline.org (accessed May 2001).

Yahya, M. al-Ha (1992) 'Violence against women leads to oppression', *Sparks*, April.

Women and conflict transformation: influences, roles, and experiences

Ann Jordan

Introduction

This chapter is based on my current research project, 'Hidden Voices: Working Towards a Culture of Peace'. Using an oral-testimony approach and a multicultural perspective, I am interviewing grassroots peace workers, giving priority to women's testimonies, and exploring a range of transformational processes. These processes include mediation, advocacy, education, self-help, music and the arts, reconciliation, spirituality, storytelling, and bridge building. By publishing this collection of inspiring and informative personal stories, my aim is to raise awareness, stimulate further debate, and enhance understanding of the complexity of peace processes, for both the worker in the field and the layperson.

Here, I focus on the women I have interviewed. My particular interest is to explore what influences and drives women to become actively involved in peace-building processes, including their roles, sustaining factors, and transformational experiences. I analyse all of these within the framework of their working contexts. I begin by providing an overview of these women, followed by a presentation of the findings of key aspects including areas of experience that are reflected within a number of broad themes. Drawing upon other relevant research and peace projects, I also focus particularly on the roles that such women play in transformational peace-making processes. Finally, I highlight what can be learnt from these women's peace experiences and the contribution they are making towards the concept of a culture of peace.

Defining the research project

The participants

So far, I have interviewed 22 people – including 14 women – who have narrated 20 different peace stories in total. The women all work in peace building in various capacities. Many are directly involved in post-war or conflict areas or are working with others who are. Fifty per cent of the interviewees are based in the UK but work internationally. The others were interviewed in Israel, Australia, South Africa, the USA, and Ireland. Their ethnic backgrounds include white British, Irish, Jewish-British, Jewish-American, Cherokee of mixed ancestry (Anglo/Celtic), black South African, Italo-American, and a person from New Zealand. Their institutional affiliation and/or work include:

- a grassroots women's aid peace group working on post-war reconstruction in the Balkan states, specifically Bosnia and Croatia. The work now focuses on support for human rights, regeneration, self-help schemes, and peace and reconciliation;

- a housing co-operative in the British Midlands which constitutes a community peace and environmental centre. The centre offers support to asylum seekers and refugees, and provides resources and information. Members run peace workshops in schools, and campaign on peace and environmental issues;

- research undertaken for a PhD, entitled 'Mending the web' (Walker 2001), which addresses peace building between indigenous and non-indigenous Australians. The research uses a process of listening intently to the stories of indigenous people involved in processes of conflict transformation as well as those of non-indigenous people working in solidarity with them through a reconciliation programme;

- a training team based in the UK that promotes the exploration and use of active non-violence for positive social change and sustainable peace;

- a training programme with local organisations in Bosnia promoting peace through sustainable community development and supporting training and networking opportunities;

- a collaboration of Jewish, Moslem, Christian, and Hindu musicians living in Israel and working with music as a cultural bridge and powerful force for peace. The 'Voices of Eden' ensemble is described as a living example of peace in the Middle East;

- training workshops in Art and Conflict in the UK, Africa, Israel, and Central America. Using art therapy, mediation, and restorative justice, the workshops explore the ways in which art can contribute to conflict resolution and peace making (see Liebmann 1996);

- working for peace by providing training, especially for young people, in conflict-handling skills, mediation and negotiation, and relaxation and meditation in Britain, Eastern Europe and the Balkans, Russia, Africa, Ukraine, and the USA;

- education for and about peace, in which the aim is to support, encourage, and promote peace education and the promotion of a culture of peace in schools and the wider community in the UK;

- volunteering with Peace Brigades International (PBI) in Colombia, whereby internationals accompany and provide protection to human-rights defenders who are under threat as they go about their work;

- positive action and bridge building to break down cultural barriers and advance understanding on peace issues, especially disarmament. A group of UK mothers, using the collective identity of motherhood, has reached out and networked with groups of mothers from a number of countries including those in the former Soviet Union, the USA, Japan, and Cuba;

- a community development organisation in south Belfast which is involved in many different kinds of work, runs a variety of projects to match the relevant needs of the mixed urban community, and does things that probably could not be done anywhere else in Belfast. This is because the organisation is not 'owned' by any religious body or political party, but rather embodies a form of local democracy;

- an alliance of African peace builders that works to ensure that African women have the tools to participate in promoting peace, development, and human security in Africa as strongly and as frequently as men. Staff in the organisation provide human rights and legal education to women within government and civil society, conduct research, and support networking efforts on the continent; and

- the Friendship Association, a volunteer, non-profit organisation formed for the specific purpose of creating bridges that will enable citizens of St. Augustine in Florida to make connections with the citizens of Baracoa in Cuba. By constructive example, members are proving that citizen diplomacy based on true friendship and mutual respect can transcend political differences. They hope to sensitise those who currently oppose entering into true diplomatic relations with Cuba in the USA.

Parallel projects

In presenting my findings, I draw upon four peace projects that parallel my own in a number of respects. These include:

1 Cynthia Cockburn's action-research work with women of polarised ethno-national groups who were able to transcend their differences to find commonalities in their peace work (Cockburn 1998).

2 The Panos Institute's international collection of oral testimonies of women's many roles during and after conflict, in which women 'speak of their experiences of armed conflict as fighters, participants, refugees, and organisers for peace and reconciliation in addition to their various roles as family carers'. These show that women 'are on the move, proactive, making decisions. They are not victims. They became activists for peace where they could see an alternative way of resolving issues' (Bennett *et al.* 1995).

3 The International Fellowship for Reconciliation's 'Women and Peacemaking Programme' (IFOR 1998), which is developing a gender perspective within peace work, based upon the recognition that women fulfil multiple roles in conflict but could be seen mainly as leaders with innovative ideas about peace building.

4 International Alert's Gender Campaign, *Women Building Peace: From the Village Council to the Negotiating Table* (IAGC 1999), which highlights the roles and capacities of women contributing to sustainable peace.

Both IFOR's programme and International Alert's Gender Campaign were established specifically to promote women's contribution to peace.

These projects, like my own, all aim to find out and highlight the ways in which ordinary civilians work towards making peace in their everyday life. There is a strong focus on hearing their 'voices' and on collecting and disseminating good practice so that people, both locally and internationally, can gain from these positive stories, campaigns, and achievements.

Roles and ways of working

Cockburn (1998) points out that women may not necessarily be directly involved in formal peace-building processes but very much underpin them. The fact that they are not visible does not mean that they are absent. This is my main departure point. Although there is still a long way to go for women to have equal power and participate on equal footing to men in the highest levels of decision making, they are nevertheless deeply involved. A major point raised in International Alert's Gender Campaign is the scepticism and ignorance concerning women's contributions and potential role in preserving peace. This needs to be addressed in order to attain gender equality and achieve sustainable peace.

The women in my project do not necessarily work only with women, but through their work they bring women peace makers to the fore. While allowing for some degree of interchange, their roles can be grouped into four broad categories:

- *Supportive*: enabling, assisting, facilitating, supporting, accompanying, and building up.
- *Directive*: organising, training, managing, advising, and providing resources and information.
- *Networking*: promoting, liaising, disseminating, publishing, and influencing.
- *Representing*: acquiring the roles of ambassadors and advocates.

The woman affiliated with the UK-based training team on non-violence is team co-ordinator and trains resource people. She allocates work among them, provides advice, back-up, materials, etc. to enable them to provide training among social-change activists.

The co-ordinator of the training programme in Bosnia responds to a wide and diverse range of needs. Using trainers from Bosnia or Croatia, her key role is to help them organise seminars and workshops in the local communities.

The woman who belongs to the grassroots women's aid peace group has seen her role develop over the years from that of supplying aid and working in partnership with local women in social reconstruction work to that of supporting human rights, regeneration, self-help schemes, and peace and reconciliation initiatives. The local women with whom the peace group has worked have taken on organisational, managerial, and decision-making roles. They have relished the opportunity to empower themselves, which has let them use skills they didn't know they had.

Many of the women involved in peace-building work directly on influencing policy themselves or on empowering other women to use their initiative and adopt proactive approaches. Overall, the women consider that they have enhanced or acquired many skills through their work, including, for example, active listening and speaking, negotiation, mediation, and lobbying. The major point here is that the peace women are actively involved. They are in charge, both as leaders and as co-ordinators. They are dynamic – proactive rather than reactive – and often act as catalysts. In comparison with the men I interviewed the position/power/influence of women in these peace processes was equal, if not stronger.

Motivation and influences

Factors that drew these women towards their chosen peace-building area fall into four broad categories: prior experience, pragmatism, emotional/spiritual motivation, and compelling need. For many of the women there is some overlap between and within these categories. However, early or formative experiences, spirituality, and subsequent long-term involvement in and commitment to peace building are key factors.

The women's aid worker had been involved in peace work for years, including the women's peace movement. She, like her co-workers, responded emotionally to the crisis in the Balkans but also rationally by thinking about the issues and deciding that there was something practical that she could do.

The manager of the peace house has always been involved in the peace movement, even while raising a family and working full-time, and has always been deeply involved with marginalised people. She claims that her own sense of marginalisation is very much part of her identity. She has always seen the importance of connecting and communicating with everybody.

The researcher, a Cherokee woman of mixed ancestry, was raised in a very Western environment but was always involved in learning about and participating in Cherokee ways of knowing and in evolving Cherokee culture. These experiences have brought on a process of conflict transformation within her family and herself. Her personal experiences continue to deepen her commitment to understanding ways of over-coming conflict between indigenous and non-indigenous peoples.

The co-ordinator of the women's positive action programme was already involved in the peace movement before she was appointed to that post. For example, alongside other women from the Campaign for Nuclear Disarmament (CND) and the Quakers, she was involved in raising awareness about and money for the women at Greenham Common (in the UK) who were protesting against the deployment of cruise missiles in the 1980s.

Doing something practical and looking for something meaningful were also quite prominent factors influencing women to become involved in peace building among the group I interviewed. The volunteer with PBI had been looking for work that had a purpose. One of the main things that attracted her was the idea that by being an international observer she could do something that Colombians could not do for themselves.

These motivating factors indicate a desire to act upon initial influences/experiences and to participate in a positive way as part of what they do. They also convey a belief that peace is worth working for – and also essential – as a way of effecting social change. Responding to a perceived need clearly responds to a commitment that goes much deeper than simply seeking something to do. These initial influences, especially 'compelling need' and 'strong emotional/spiritual' drive, sustain many of the women throughout the work that they take upon themselves.

Main themes of the research

A number of strands have emerged in my research which fit within broader themes: relationships and communication; approaches and methods to achieve sustainable peace; race and gender; and trans-formation. The themes emerge in the four main parallel projects. They also match the criteria set out in a number of notable peace-research works on effective peace building. This particular set of women's stories exemplifies what they consider makes for effective peace-building practice.

Relationships and communication

The main theme that emerged from my research concerns relation-ships and communication, with a particular focus on partnership, collaboration, interconnection, alliances, and networks. All the women I interviewed mentioned the importance of working collaboratively and in solidarity with others – in other words, developing good solid relationships and understanding. The main values underpinning all of these include trust, acceptance, good will, respect, forgiveness, compassion, and humour, with trust as the underlying key factor.

Much was made of reaching out to others and finding common ground by recognising our mutual humanity. One woman stated that whatever you do individually is part of the larger picture. The need for active listening was also widely expressed. The researcher in Australia believes that true peace building involves hearing, supporting, and acknowledging the views and opinions of others, especially among the most disadvantaged members of our societies.

Self-awareness features as a necessary prerequisite to positive relationship building and appropriate action. The women talked about being prepared, having prior information, having realistic expectations, and seeing their work as a long-term commitment. This means taking responsibility for and care of oneself. In their view, it is essential to address conflict both inside one's self and within teams. It is also equally important to realise that working in a post-war context is extremely demanding emotionally because one absorbs many strong feelings.

In her paper 'Insiders/Outsiders in Conflict Areas', Mary B. Anderson (2000) speaks about 'local capacities for peace', which she believes every society has, and she calls for a new collaborative effort and a need to learn from experience. Mari Fitzduff (2000) also discusses the 'what, who, and why' of conflict resolution. She emphasises that positive emotional strategies are required to resolve conflicts, and that partnerships can work well.

The women in my study who are involved in post-war community social reconstruction especially highlighted the need for effective partnership and participation. They talked about flexible, dynamic teams using initiative, sharing tasks, balancing work overload, and having non-hierarchical structures. They recommended employing local people, providing safe environments, being vigilant about power inequities (including gender and race), and addressing imbalances.

Cockburn (1998) found that themes of alliance, democracy, and identity wind through the accounts of the women involved in her study. Although each of the three projects she carried out is distinct, they share a number of commonalties, especially the fact that the projects are themselves alliances. She maintains that the most important resource for an alliance is a participatory democratic process characterised by the careful and caring management of interaction and decision making. This in turn involves fostering good communication, inclusive activity, and supportive relationships.

The Panos research (Bennett *et al.* 1995) highlights the importance of alliances among women in fostering empowerment through solidarity and the pooling of resources. International Alert collaborated with over 100 NGOs to launch its international Gender Campaign (IAGC 1999). IFOR's women's programme is part of a large international alliance that includes All Africa Women for Peace (AAWP) (IFOR 1998), where one of the participants in my research plays a key role. She, along with other professional women from different African countries, is working to consolidate a base which will act as a contact, networking, and resource centre for women peace builders in Africa.

Alliances and networks are central features in virtually all the peace projects in my research.

The Friendship Association is a strong alliance between US citizens and Cubans. The co-ordinator believes that through bonds of friendship and joint programme activities a more humane and mutually beneficial bilateral relationship will result for both Cuba and the USA. The two women who are working in education and training in peace are members of wider peace networks which provide forums for the exchange of ideas and the promotion of good practice. The co-ordinator of the group of peace women/mothers states that, via positive action and bridge building, the group was able to reach across a wide cultural divide. Among other things, the group successfully linked women from the USA with women from the (former) Soviet Union either in the USA or in Britain.

Louise Diamond (1999) describes 'multi-track diplomacy' as a systems approach to peace building that embraces a large network of organisations, disciplines, and methodologies working flexibly towards non-violent approaches to sustainable peace. The women in my research have formed multiple networks/links with allied projects. For instance, the co-ordinator of the community development association in Belfast has taken part in IFOR's programme. She maintains political links with the Women's Coalition in Northern Ireland. The peace house manager has stated that, while maintaining links is time consuming, sustaining such networks is an essential element in being able to have a wider impact. She now has a website whose whole purpose is to disseminate information. The women's aid project has always forged links and built networks with other groups and projects, and also issues a regular newsletter.

The women in these examples believe that it is essential to integrate fieldwork and ideas using a multidisciplinary/agency approach;

to have a forum for the exchange of good practice that includes comprehensive access to and dissemination of information (including the Internet); and to maintain continuous support, especially financial.

Towards sustainable peace: approaches and methods

Discussing the path to sustainable peace via a peace-building framework, John-Paul Lederac (1999) stresses the need for interdependence and relationship building at all levels. His 'process-structure' approach to peace is dynamic and changing while at the same time it carves a structure with direction and purpose so that it is truly sustainable. He believes that, in order to achieve sustainable peace, it is vital for peace to be seen as a creative process and for structural change to take place.

The peace women in this study clearly show an understanding of peace as a creative process. There is an emphasis on flexibility, adaptability, and open-mindedness, for example responding to actual rather than perceived needs, having choices, and always being willing to learn. Improvisation emerges as a major element. Most women recognise that aspects of conflict transformation are holistic and overlapping.

The following examples illustrate Lederac's 'process-structure' approach at work.

Creativity approaches

The musician who is part of 'Voices of Eden' believes that her ensemble's performances make a very real and practical contribution to the solution of conflict in Israel by, among other things, refusing to be stopped by the violence and by providing musical harmony, which relieves stress and reduces anxiety. She asserts that clarity allows us to come up with more creative solutions to our very dramatic problems.

The researcher involved in storytelling as the key process in a reconciliation programme in Queensland maintains that stories shed light on the interconnectedness of all things. They are holistic and enable conflict transformation. Through her work, the researcher has come to know effective processes of transforming conflict between indigenous and non-indigenous people more deeply. Her completed research looks at what we can learn from the stories that live within cultures. She says that we must acknowledge the complexities of colonisation and be aware of the ways in which indigenous concepts and ways of knowing are silenced by Western methods of processing conflict.

From my experience working with art and conflict, I firmly believe that people gain insights through artistic approaches that they can then use to contribute to conflict resolution and peace building. Cultural appropriateness regarding certain approaches and the use of materials is always a consideration.

Community reconstruction and development

The co-ordinator of the training programme for local organisations in Bosnia has stressed that the workers involved in the project are recruited from the local communities, and that the programme is ongoing and responsive to the needs of the group. The training ranges from organisational management, development, and reporting to human-rights education, advocacy, and community building. Aware that supporting women's groups in Croatia and Bosnia is a long-term project, the programme's policy is to develop enduring links with each group individually and really get to know what each group needs and aspires to. The programme now supports a number of self-sufficiency projects, including a peace and reconciliation project in Pakrac that focuses on health education, as well as a non-violent conflict-resolution project in a local secondary school. The Croatian government has continued to fund this project.

The manager of the peace house and community centre has talked about the 'practical peace work' that her organisation carries out with young people and with refugees, stressing that its activities should be seen not only in terms of campaigning but also in terms of offering practical helpful work at the community level.

At the community association in Belfast, the co-ordinator has described the work of her organisation in helping local people to 'open their minds', look for creative options, and use their talents within their 'culture of peace' community. She uses social-conflict energy as a way of producing some positive social interaction at the local level and also within the wider community.

Education and training

The non-violence training programme is not about denying conflict. Rather, it is about working through conflict on non-violent and neutral terms, and about channelling conflict properly so as not to be thwarted by it. The co-ordinator believes that conflict needs to be resolved through a creative process that can take advantage of its positive energy.

The co-founder and partner of the peace project that is focused on education and training has emphasised practical approaches to the project's work. One of these is not to lecture groups but to give them practical experience, e.g. listening skills. Another is to use practical skills to build relationships, e.g. contacting, getting to know people, and helping people in post-war areas.

Working on education for and about peace, the co-ordinator uses interactive discussion in her workshops, with all pupils having an input. In terms of sustainability, she insists that the peace programme must permeate the whole school and the wider community. It is an ongoing process that requires much reinforcement.

AAWP works to ensure that African women acquire the tools and capacity they need to work toward peace, development, and human security in Africa on an equal footing to men. The research co-ordinator works with other AAWP staff in providing human-rights and legal education to women within government and civil society, conducting research, and supporting networking efforts throughout the continent.

Information exchange and solidarity
In protecting human-rights work in Colombia, the PBI volunteer has stressed that the non-interference approach is about being as visible as possible. The whole purpose is just to be physically there, to enable the human-rights workers to go about their work safely. She has also claimed that, in many cases, the leading workers are women, a reflection of the fact that women in general are doing really important and effective grassroots human-rights work at the community level all over the country.

The Friendship Association divides its outreach efforts into three groups: local educational events, awareness-building delegations to Cuba, and support of programmes in both St. Augustine and Baracoa. Specific projects and programmes have been created or revitalised, covering a number of areas of mutual interest including communications, environment, and humanitarian aid.

One of the achievements of the Mothers for Peace has been helping women who were trying to set up voluntary organisations in the former Soviet Union after the fall of the Iron Curtain. Among other things, they helped to set up a scheme for women to engage in conflict-resolution training. Over the past two years, a number of the Russian women have come to the UK to do Alternative to Violence training, and Mothers for Peace, who are themselves trainers, have gone to Russia to train women there.

The diversity and variety of the peace-building activities described above demonstrate the commitment of all these women to social, economic, and political justice, as well as to non-violent processes of structural change. Their experiences have yielded various recommendations on how to work towards peace most effectively, including the use of various methods to influence policy outcomes, such as the involvement of high-profile people such as MPs and policy makers. For example, the women's aid worker invited her local MP to visit the partnership in Croatia. A second recommendation is to ensure that the reconciliation process is fully in the hands of those directly involved in the conflict. A third is to adopt a peace model that will enable all involved to achieve greater depth and focus. And a final insight is to ensure that effective monitoring, review, and assessment procedures are in place.

Evaluation was difficult to implement rigorously. Most of the women interviewed use more informal procedures, but they see evaluation as an ongoing, multi-dimensional, and intrinsic component of any change process. They have used various techniques to evaluate the effectiveness of their projects, including, for example, qualitative personal feedback using an evaluation form and/or brief meetings with a sample range of users to get a sense of how the work had influenced ideas and improved the effectiveness of peace practice. Other methods or indicators include the number of successful follow-up schemes, increased co-operation and networking, increased leadership, and positive change in people's lives. According to the Panos research (Warrington 1999), the key to measuring qualitative objectives is consultation with those involved, without which it is virtually impossible to measure them.

Race and cultural issues

The main factors in this theme are awareness, sensitivity, and appropriateness in working across cultural boundaries; all these being integral to peace building.

Virtually all participants in my research highlighted the need for self-awareness or self-knowledge. This includes having a profound understanding of issues related to ethno-centricity and racism, of cultural frames of reference or worldviews, of the ubiquitous and often inappropriate use of Western models of peace building, and of the need to ensure that different racial and cultural perspectives are fully incorporated in both documentation and practice.

It is interesting to note that most people interviewed talked as much about cultural similarities as they did about differences, mentioning things such as 'having similar needs but doing things differently' and 'connecting through our common humanity'. It was felt that cultural diversity should be embraced and celebrated. One woman talked about her strong realisation, through ordinary conversation, that what people fundamentally care about is actually the same, irrespective of cultural, religious, or political differences. In the end, we are all human beings.

General comments about dealing with differences and culture-bound misunderstandings included getting to know the people and the culture, recognising that culture-bound behavioural differences are with us all the time, and trying to stay with and in some way 'process' the culturally different behaviour. The human-rights worker in Colombia said that the key element for her was adaptability, being able to adjust to any situation, and she added that tiny things can cause huge friction when living and working in stressful situations. Those working in community social reconstruction as well as some working in education and training referred to the range of difficulties embedded in the 'insider–outsider' issue. Trust emerged as a key factor to overcome such differentiations, especially for those working in culturally diverse environments.

Specific ways of overcoming cultural barriers, particularly in settings where the women in my research were working in close proximity with ethically mixed local communities in Bosnia, Croatia, Uganda, Ukraine, Colombia, and South Africa, were illustrated in three main aspects:

- *language*, i.e. learning local languages, or using official translators or local volunteers who speak English or other international languages;

- *behaviour*, i.e. conducting oneself in a way that displays sensitivity, respect, and appropriateness (including attention to dress, habits, and gestures);

- *cultural bridges*, i.e. doing practical things such as placing welcoming signs on doors, contacting local families, and showing respect by speaking to local people in their own language where possible. The co-ordinator of the training programme in Bosnia stated that there can be a dilemma regarding the need to respect people's identities without promoting nationalistic agendas. Collaborative participation in a common cause was seen in itself as a cultural bridge.

Gender issues

In her discussion of the UNESCO Women and a Culture of Peace Programme, Ingeborg Breines (1998) strongly emphasises gender equality as a precondition for a culture of peace, and speaks of the need to fully use women's experiences, talents, and potential at all levels of society.

Through its Gender Campaign, International Alert was one of the five organisations pressing the UN Security Council to adopt the resolution regarding gender sensitivity in all UN missions (including peacekeeping) and for women's full participation in peace processes.

Cynthia Cockburn's women's bridge-building project (Cockburn 1998) is underpinned by gender perspectives including identity and difference, nationalism and ethnicity, and international relations.

In my research, a number of women highlighted the intersection between race and gender. Discrimination in their peace-building work was experienced not so much by them personally but by women in certain communities, especially in the Balkan states, Northern Ireland, Eastern Europe, and Colombia.

At the UN World Conference against Racism held in South Africa in 2001, the session chaired by Mary Robinson, 'Intersection of Gender and Race', explored discrimination against women, and its complexity and multi-dimensionality – especially when race was involved (Robinson 2001). A compilation of best practices for dealing with discrimination was called for. While emphasising the intersection of race and gender, Gay McDougall of UN/CERD asserted that racial discrimination does not necessarily affect men and women equally.

As stated above, the women interviewed in this study showed more evidence of their position, power, and influence in their peace-building work than of their low-profile status or subservience to men. Many work directly on influencing policy making and policy outcomes, or on empowering other women to be proactive and get involved in peace-building initiatives. For example, the community association in Belfast has recently run a productive development programme focused specifically on women. It was a major success because its individual training programmes were personally developed, and the women supported each other. Other examples abound as well: there are increasing successful self-help schemes supported by the women's project in Bosnia, women's empowerment is a cornerstone of the AAWP's programme, and Mothers for Peace has empowered numerous women over the years.

Negative factors, sustaining factors, and personal transformation

Negative factors

All of the women interviewed have experienced opposition, obstacles, and setbacks in their peace work. On the whole, they consider that significant progress has been made, but that there is still much more to be done. Some women, for example, have experienced great antagonism towards them, while two have received threats. All of those working in teams or organisations have experienced conflict within the teams. Owing to the stressful nature of much of their work, several women have also experienced 'burn-out' at some point. Under-funding and serious lack of resources remain the all-pervasive problems. But despite all the obstacles, these women carry on undeterred, even if in one or two cases their involvement has lessened. They find strategies to combat their difficulties, and draw strength from sustaining factors.

Sustaining factors

Good relationships at all levels appear to be the *sine qua non* in sustaining these women throughout their peace-building work. These include support from family and friends as well as solidarity and camaraderie within teams. The need for support was strongly emphasised, including counselling and debriefing, especially for those directly involved in post-war contexts.

The second major factor is the belief in the effectiveness of the work these women are doing in conjunction with long-term commitment. This is particularly sustaining during times of high stress, doubt, frustration, etc.

Enjoyment and empowerment are illustrated through a whole set of 'Ss' – satisfaction, stimulation, solidarity, spirituality, seeing results, and a sense of achievement. Spirituality, in particular, is a strong feature in many of these peace stories. Some simply refer to their faith in God, while others talk about drawing upon 'an inner sense or inner peace', or about having a deep spiritual aspect in their psyche.

Most of the women share the conviction that feelings and healing are of central importance to peace building, and that proper structures and mechanisms need to be in place within the working environment for expressing such feelings. Samuels (1993) states that qualitative work requires addressing both internal and external factors but that we need to concentrate on what he calls the 'inner world' of feelings and sensitivities. Mindell (1995), writing about conflict transformation through 'processing' or 'inner work', maintains that to achieve sustainable peace we need to break through to a new level of communication. He adds that structural work is only a bandage unless feelings are properly healed. Indeed, feelings were explored extensively throughout the interviewing process of my research work, and a whole range of experiences of both positive and negative emotions was discussed.

Personal transformation

Unequivocally, the foremost response to the question of how the work these women carry out has personally transformed them relates to the whole experience of peace building, referring to 'the journey itself', 'the process itself' – 'all the experiences were a natural development'. Some women talked about early experiences, the onset of and transition to using skills in peace making, learning about oneself, working with women on a different basis with a degree of success, having a new concept of war, and seeing other people gaining new insights from their work on conflict. This is a clear indication that working holistically towards conflict transformation and sustainable peace has been in itself transformational for these women.

Conclusion

Albeit a small-scale study, 'Hidden Voices' provides a good diversity of ideas and practices. The women who participated in my research are clearly neither victims nor marginal spectators. On the contrary, they have a range of often overlapping, but essentially leading and strongly proactive, roles. Working at the grassroots level, they endeavour to influence policy and decision-making processes.

My research participants do not reflect a wide pool of women involved in sustainable peace building on a global scale, but alongside all those referred to in this paper and beyond, I believe such women are plentiful and growing in strength and number. While all participants are keenly aware that their personal experience is but a tiny contribution to peace in general, and that it is not always possible to generalise from the specific, they also know that collectively they may help to make a difference.

As the peace researcher involved in storytelling put it, 'Individual stories are synthesised with other stories to create themes. These themes tell the larger story of peace building ways. Therefore story is a process of weaving individual experience into a larger web of meaning.' I would suggest that the themes discussed in this paper also form a larger picture about women and sustainable peace: what motivates and influences them, what drives and sustains them, their roles, their diverse and effective practices, and their experiences in conflict transformation.

Diamond (1999) believes that exercising our power to empower means generating more stories and building a base of success from which we can all learn. The second component of International Alert's Gender Campaign is about public awareness strategy, the 'know-how' of peace. This focuses on women's achievements and experiences in conflict situations, as well as on their contributions to peace building.

The peace education co-ordinator in my research made a most pertinent comment, 'Peace can be gained if we know how to do it.' I very much hope that the publication of this inspiring collection of peace stories will make a valuable contribution to the 'know-how'.

References

Anderson, M.B. (2000) 'Insiders/ Outsiders in Conflict Areas', paper presented at the Conflict, Development and Peace (CODEP) conference on Critical Partners for Peace: Dynamic Collaborations in Conflict Situations, London, 14–16 February 2000.

Bennett, O., J. Bexley, and K. Warnock (eds.) (1995) *Arms to Fight, Arms to Protect: Women Speak Out About Conflict,* London: Panos Institute.

Breines, I. (1998) 'A gender perspective on a culture of peace', *International Peace Update* 63(3): 1–2.

Cockburn, C. (1998) *The Space Between Us: Negotiating Gender and National Identities in Conflict,* London: Zed Books.

Diamond, L. (1999) 'Multi-track diplomacy in the 21st century', in EPCP (ed.) (1999).

EPCP (ed.) (1999) *People Building Peace: 35 Inspiring Stories from Around the World,* The Netherlands: European Platform for Conflict Prevention 1999.

Fitzduff, M. (2000) 'A Multi-faceted Approach to Critical Partnerships for Peace', paper presented at the Conflict, Development and Peace (CODEP) conference on Critical Partners for Peace: Dynamic Collaborations in Conflict Situations, London, 14–16 February 2000.

IAGC (1999) *Women Building Peace: From the Village Council to the Negotiating Table,* London: International Alert (available at www.international-alert.org, accessed January 2002).

IFOR (1998) 'Women and Peacemaking Programme: Developing a Gender Perspective into Peace Work', www.ifor.org (accessed January 2002).

Lederac, J.-P. (1999) 'Just peace – the challenge of the 21st century', in EPCP (ed.) (1999).

Liebmann, M. (1996) *Arts Approaches to Conflict,* London: Jessica Kingsley.

Mindell, A. (1995) *Sitting in the Fire,* Portland, OR: Lao Tse Press.

Robinson, M. (2001) 'Gender Dimensions of Racial Discrimination', discussion document at the World Conference Against Racism, Racial Discrimination, Xenophobia and Related Intolerance, Durban, 31 August – 7 September 2001.

Samuels, A. (1993) *The Political Psyche,* London: Routledge.

Walker, P.O. (2001) 'Mending the Web: Sustainable Conflict Transformation Between Indigenous and Non-indigenous Australians', PhD thesis, University of Queensland.

Warrington, S. (ed.) (1999) *Giving Voice: Oral Testimony Training Manual,* London: Panos Institute.

Fused in combat: gender relations and armed conflict

Judy El-Bushra

Introduction

Do gender relations change through conflict? How might conflict itself be fuelled by aspects of gender identity? A research project carried out by the Agency for Co-operation and Research in Development (ACORD) that combined oral testimony with more conventional research methods concluded that conflict has undoubtedly given women greater responsibilities, and with them the possibility of exerting greater leverage in decision-making processes and increasing their political participation. The research also sheds light on the role of 'ordinary' citizens (in contrast to military and political leaders, who are usually the focus of conflict analysis) as 'actors' responding to crisis, and describes how gender identities are woven into a complex web of cause and effect in which war can be seen as a 'conflict of patriarchies'.

The research holds lessons for both gender analysis and conflict analysis, and highlights the need for interventions addressing the cycle of violence in proactive ways. This paper focuses on conclusions relating to gender analysis and the implications of using an open-ended and discourse-based research methodology. The implications of the findings for conflict analysis and for policy and programme design are discussed in the original reports.[1]

Methodology

The project 'Gender-sensitive Programme Design and Planning in Conflict-affected Situations', carried out by ACORD during 2000 and 2001, aimed to enhance gender awareness in development projects in contexts affected by conflict. Field research was carried out in Sudan, Somalia, Uganda, Mali, and Angola, and desk studies were used for Eritrea and Rwanda. Using oral testimony and PRA as its main research methods, the research describes the experiences of 'ordinary'

First published in *Development in Practice* 13(2&3): 252–65 in 2003

women and men in armed conflict and aims to identify the link between gender relations and conflict through their eyes.

Methodologically, the research addresses four questions. First, what methods are appropriate for understanding the experiences of men and women in conflict, given the sensitive nature of these experiences and the possible consequences of disclosure to informants? Second, what methods enable non-academic researchers, namely staff of development and humanitarian agencies, to acquire insights into the complexity of social change in conflict, given their pressures of time and other responsibilities? Third, how can such agencies combine 'extracting' research findings for planning purposes while at the same time affording dignity and 'ownership' to the informants, given that the nature of the subject under study is potentially deeply personal or politically risky? Finally, ACORD's previous research on gender and conflict had pointed to the weakness of conventional social science analysis in developing an understanding of people's behaviour in conflict, for example the lack of attention paid to the affective domain and its relationship with the economic and political domains (El-Bushra 2000). The methods adopted therefore needed to be susceptible to analysis that uses a broad framework.

Drawing on the experience of the Gulu programme in Uganda, a long-standing collaborator of the Panos Institute's Oral Testimony programme,[2] the ACORD project's researchers[3] decided to adopt oral testimony (OT) as their main research method, complemented as appropriate by PRA and standard survey methods, and by data from secondary and official sources. The project collected around 125 testimonies from the five locations. In addition, a desk analysis was carried out of testimonies already taken for other purposes in Rwanda. PRA exercises included focus group discussions, some structured around social exclusion analysis,[4] and transect walks. Research teams in each of the localities analysed the testimonies and other material, with the whole being synthesised at a joint analysis workshop involving all five of the main case studies. The principal elements of this joint analysis are presented below.

Panos Institute (2001:1) defines OT as ' ... the result of free-ranging, open-ended interviews around a series of issues, drawing on direct personal memory and experience'. No formal questionnaires are used; the 'narrators' are encouraged to give their own views and inter-pretations as a reflection on the events they perceive to have affected their lives. Interviewers do not direct the narrators, though they can start by asking open-ended questions and allow people to follow their own train of thought thereafter.

OT brings out the narrators' personal experiences, memories, and perceptions of reality, enabling them to identify what is important and true for them in their specific context. These have a validity of their own, whether or not researchers agree with them or believe them to be 'true'. The opportunity to give testimony may give narrators the courage to address sensitive political and social topics that are difficult to address through other methods: it therefore gives a voice to the powerless and to those who are too often ignored or spoken for, and hence can become a tool for empowerment.

OT proved its worth as a method capable of eliciting deep insights into the perceptions of people whose lives have been battered by conflict, and researchers (all ACORD staff) viewed it as a method that provided an important resource for programme development, highlighted previously unaddressed issues, and pointed out new programme directions. Almost all respondents were keen to take part in the project, wanting their stories to be told.[5] There were problems, however, with the method. First, not all the interviewers felt able to approach the task in an open-ended way. The aim of OT is not so much to gather data but to build a relationship between the interviewer and the narrator within which issues can be explored and understanding enhanced. Such open-ended research is relatively new in the experience of operational NGOs, who generally carry out research to finesse an existing programme plan. It therefore requires a change in researchers' expectations of what the research can yield, and in turn puts a premium on experienced staff (often the ones in charge of most other responsibilities) as interviewers.

Second, analysing OT material presents unusual difficulties, since the material is unpredictable, broad ranging, and susceptible to many different interpretations. In addition, it is the whole interview (including the context and the style of discourse) which needs to be analysed, not just the factual information contained in the text. The emotive content of OT is at once its strength and a problem area for analysis. Analysis is therefore a lengthy process, involving alternations between intense discussion and letting the material 'lie fallow' in the researchers' minds. Indeed, the use of OT is inconsistent with linear notions of the research process: it works best in a context in which the design of research questions, data collection, data analysis, dissemination, and, finally, application are seen as elements in a circular and iterative whole.

It is too early at this stage to comment on the 'empowerment' potential of OT. The issue of appropriation is a major question in development research and requires a separate debate. What would the project have looked like if it had been designed in collaboration with respondents from the beginning? Although some instances of participatory research are found in development work, they tend to be small in scale and designed in response to local dynamics. More extensive sharing of experience on the methods of participatory research, between agencies and between the practitioner and academic communities, would be beneficial.

A thumbnail sketch of the case studies

Uganda

The war in Acholiland, northern Uganda, began in 1986 and since then has been waged between the Ugandan armed forces and a succession of rebel groups who have in general terms worked for the moral regeneration of the Acholi community as well as against the Ugandan government. Human rights abuses of the population have been recorded on both sides. About half the population of Acholiland now lives in 'protected villages' or camps for displaced people, where self-sufficient agriculture is no longer possible because of lack of space. The war has resulted in gross impoverishment through the loss of livestock and land. The traumatic experiences to which the population has been exposed (including intimidation, torture, harassment, killings, captivity, inhumane displaced living conditions, sexual abuse of different kinds, and duress in captivity or in hiding) have brought intense suffering to individuals and have in turn rendered Acholi society vulnerable to breakdown. Out-migration from Acholiland (both within and outside Ugandan borders) is extensive and reflects popular disaffection with both warring parties. A particular feature of this conflict is the alienation of youth (both male and female), many of whom decide to join the military of either side in response to abuses they have experienced or in the absence of other prospects.

The main research objective of the ACORD project was to gain a deeper understanding of the impact of armed conflict in Acholiland (1986–2001) on gender socialisation processes, and of the ways in which the latter have contributed to the dynamics of the war, with a view to initiating a debate on the sort of society Acholi men, women, and young people would want to have. In the perception of the majority of informants, Acholi cultural identity (including values, beliefs, and practices), which was once strongly maintained by social systems ensuring adherence to accepted norms, has become eroded. Though this erosion may have begun early on during the colonial era, the armed conflict has exacerbated and hastened the process of social breakdown.

The war has led not only to the material impoverishment of Acholiland but also to the breakdown of previously well-regulated relationships both between men and women and between generations. Elements of Acholi cultural practice that have proved beneficial in promoting improved relations and resolving conflicts have been eroded through state-formation processes. There is widespread resentment amongst adults of 'modern' influences, including the current favourable economic position of women and moves towards guaranteeing the rights of women and children. Testimonies show how frustrations and tensions caused by people's inability to fulfil their expected roles generate further sources of conflict, gripping Acholiland in a vicious circle of violence.

Angola

Angola has been divided by conflict since independence in 1975, in a war in which struggles for political control were particularly exacerbated and prolonged during the Cold War by proxy warfare between the two superpowers over Angola's rich mineral resources. Fighting has been bitter and has resulted in massive displacement as well as loss of life and resources. Agricultural production has suffered significantly and the informal sector in towns is the economic mainstay for a largely uprooted and proletarianised population, of which an estimated 80 per cent is not formally employed.

The Angola study took place in Viana, a settlement housing a high proportion of the war-displaced population on the outskirts of Luanda. It examined the social, economic, political, cultural, ideological, and psycho-emotional dimensions of the conflict as experienced by individuals and also at the household and community levels. The findings reveal that, while everyone without exception is affected by conflict, individual experience appears in addition to be influenced by gender and other factors. The timing of displacement is one such factor, with the more recently displaced more affected than those displaced prior to the recent, more violent phase of the conflict in Angola.

Although there was evidence of increased polarisation between groups on the basis of political affiliation and ethnic origin, as well as of the loss of traditional kinship networks and the rise of individualism, the findings also revealed a tendency towards homogenisation through, for example, the adoption of a common language, Portuguese. Similarly, traditional forms of saving (known as the *kixiki*) have been collectively revived by women from different ethnic backgrounds as a means of survival under harsh economic conditions.

Women are bearing the main financial burden of providing for the family while men are being forced into taking on responsibility for children and domestic chores. However, this gender role reversal has not been accompanied by an ideological shift, and for the most part women's status outside (and even, in many cases, within) the household remains subordinate to that of men. Men appear to be experiencing more difficulty than women adjusting to the new situation. Patriarchal norms underpinning gender identity are at the heart of the problem, as they not only aggravate men's sense of failure and frustration, but also allow both men and women to be used as pawns in the pursuit of thinly disguised political objectives.

Sudan

Civil war has ravaged Sudan for most of the country's 46 years since independence in 1956, resulting in enormous loss of life and resources (especially in the south) and in severe political, social, and economic crisis throughout. The south of Sudan is effectively divided into separate administrations controlled by the government and by different rebel groups, respectively. In addition to an estimated two million dead from fighting and famine in the south, large numbers have been displaced to the north or to other countries.

The Sudan case study was based on material collected in displaced communities in Juba and in Khartoum, exploring their livelihoods and survival strategies and the impacts of these on gender roles and relations. Among the social and psycho-social impacts of the war are the fragmentation of households, displacement, demoralisation and trauma, intergenerational mistrust, and discrimination against the displaced and the younger generations, with very limited opportunities for schooling or employment. The shift from subsistence farming to an urban cash economy has brought about increased dependence on women's work in petty trade, along with reduced living standards. Domestic violence has increased, as have destructive coping strategies like violent crime and sex-work, which in turn exacerbates the spread of HIV.

The findings of the study emphasise changes in gender roles caused by conflict, displacement, and poverty, as well as in certain aspects of people's values and attitudes. Testimonies describe how gender identities are contributing to the aggravation of conflict among political players at both the national and local levels.

Mali

The conflict in northern Mali broke out in 1991 between the state and rebels representing the Azawad movement for Tamasheq independence. Although it quietened after the signing of the National Pact in 1992, fighting broke out again that year, this time between factions within the north, with the army attempting to keep the peace. This second round, which lasted until 1994, deepened splits both between ethnic groups and within them, and hastened a long-term process whereby hierarchical divisions within northern Mali's highly stratified societies progressively broke down.

Communities in the area found themselves impoverished after losing their livelihoods, assets, and resources (land, animals, equipment, etc.) in the war, although some people managed to learn and engage in new activities. The conflict affected the quality of relationships between sedentary communities and nomadic groups, and has resulted in the massive displacement of populations, the creation of slums on the outskirts of urban centres, and flows of refugees to neighbouring countries. These displacements in turn have led to family breakdown, changing or disappearing sites of residence, and changes in nomadic settlement patterns. Refugees, women, and young people, in particular, have had their way of life influenced by other cultures.

Conflict aggravated the erosion of traditional ways of life, already affected by economic and environmental crises. Some of the changes that have taken place within the country involve changes in gender roles and relations, as well as in relationships between former masters and former slaves, with many of the latter becoming completely independent. Nomadic women have become less subdued and more involved in the management of economic activities and in decision making at household and community levels. However, ideologies of superiority and masculinity remain unaltered.

Somalia

The Somalia study was carried out in the Lower Shabelle region, the location of bitter fighting between clan factions during the last ten years of civil war. Though some attempts at resolution have taken place at the national level, tensions remain high among local groups in the Lower Shabelle, in large part because issues of access to and control over resources between local clans have not been solved. One of the findings that emerged from the research is that the international community needs to invest in peace at both local and national levels.

The conflict had a devastating impact on both individuals and groups in the Lower Shabelle. Individuals suffered death, injury, rape, trauma, and the loss of family members and possessions. The different clans present in the area gained or lost power and influence according to the fortunes of the war: generally those who had previously been powerful became even more so, except for the Hawiye, who saw their power rise considerably in the local political structure as a result of the clan's national ascendancy. Groups such as the Bantu and the Brawaanis, already the victims of discrimination, became even further disadvantaged as the few resources they once held began to whittle away.

Gender roles have changed significantly, with women taking on more economic responsibilities (often becoming the sole bread-winners for the household) and entering occupations such as money trading which were previously the preserve of men. Men, on the other hand, have lost access to their resources and with it their customary role of providers for the household. However, there appears to have been little change either in the traditional exclusion of women from community decision-making structures or in the ideological basis for this discrimination. If the state succeeds in re-establishing its structures, it is unclear whether women's enhanced economic autonomy will increase their scope for influence, or whether gender ideologies will become further entrenched when men have the opportunity to return to their former positions.

How do respondents describe the impact of conflict on their lives?

The case studies, describing the experiences of the respondents in armed conflict and their assessment of how their lives have changed as a result, reveal appalling human suffering, loss of livelihoods, erosion of social relations, and loss of faith in the future. Testimonies call overwhelmingly for peace. As a displaced male community leader from Khartoum, Sudan, put it: '[i]f all the people in the camp were out in this big yard, and you asked them what they need, they would all say "PEACE". But who listens?'

Ordinary people are knowledgeable about the factors – local, national, and international – that foment conflict, and they make considered and proactive adaptations to bewilderingly rapid change. Testimonies also demonstrate how violence leads to, and is fuelled by, poverty and the denial of rights:

> 'They claim that we are the ones who sent our children to the bush, is that true? We did not send those children to the bush. The children got disgruntled with the present way of doing things, that is why they went to the bush. It was harassment inflicted upon the people that caused the going to the bush.'
> (Interview with a man from Bungatira, Uganda)

Men view women's increasing power within the household, and their own parallel disempowerment, in various ways, depending on their context. Male respondents in Somalia and Angola, for example, accept their dependence on women passively, acknowledging that women's resourcefulness and industry have pulled them through crises. In Rwanda, conflict blurred previously sharp role distinctions: 'Women can do whatever men can do, while men can no longer do whatever they want ... All people have become the same.' In Mali, sedentary communities declare no change in household decision making, while the previously pastoralist Tamasheq men view women's increased responsibility for family affairs positively. In some cases, notably in Sudan and Uganda, this shift in roles has contributed to increased alcoholism among men and to domestic violence.

Women also view their situation in different ways. For instance, Tamasheq women in Mali are excited about new possibilities opening up for them:

> 'Frankly, since these events we women are no longer ashamed, we are no longer cold in the presence of men. I'm aware that the men are not all that happy about this, it makes them nervous, furious, and none of that was done in the past. We came back [from exile] because we were promised consideration and respect. The most notable impact for me was that I learned to read, cook well, that wasn't possible [before].'
> (Interview with an elderly woman in Agouni, Mali)

However, women in Rwanda speak of the desperate 'solitude' accompanying their new-found autonomy. In other cases, women deplore the burden of work, the breakdown of services, the deterioration in social relations, and the risks to women's health and security implicit in new livelihoods and new expectations of behaviour:

'Women are almost competing with men. This war is an advantage to women in some ways because they have learnt a lot about business, while on the other hand it is a disadvantage because you get a number of schoolgirls dropping out.'

(Interview with a divorced woman in Juba, Sudan)

Do gender relations change as a result of conflict?

Both the violence of warfare and its consequences – displacement, impoverishment, demographic imbalance – have given rise to changes in gender roles at the household level in all cases studied. This has led in turn to limited increases in women's decision-making power and political participation: however, the ideological bases underpinning gender relations appear to have remained unchanged or have even been reinforced.[6]

Consistently across the case studies, women take on increased economic responsibilities within the household. Reasons for this change include:

- inaccessibility of economic resources that men previously controlled (e.g. agricultural land in Uganda);
- displacement into urban cash economies where women's income-generating opportunities are greater than in rural areas (Sudan, Angola);
- exposure during displacement to different ways of life and new skills (Mali); and
- growth in the proportion of female-headed households (to around 30 per cent in Sudan and Mali).

The degree of change has varied. For sedentary communities in Mali, for example, reduced access to resources for both men and women means that neither can fulfil their gender roles adequately, while in Somalia, women have often taken over the role of principal breadwinners:

'I maintain my husband plus his father in Mogadishu. He is unemployed. What else can he do if the government service is not available? He has retreated to the house and the mosque, he doesn't come out. He and his father sat and waited for me just like my children for the 10 years of the civil war.'

(Interview with a woman in Kurtunwarey, Somalia)

Women have gained increased respect and decision-making power within the household as a result of men's growing economic dependence on women, although this trend is less consistent and more contested throughout:

> 'I think people's thinking has changed. We came to Khartoum with
> different perceptions and traditions. Our old customs and traditions
> prohibited men from entering certain places such as the kitchen.
> Men also thought that women could not think, were useless, and had no
> right to have their voice heard. All these are things of the past; they have
> changed. This is one benefit of the war, if wars have benefits. All family
> members have to work, both women and men. We cannot maintain
> the division of labour because there is no room for that.'
> (Interview with a separated displaced woman in Khartoum, Sudan)

> 'Now we obey our women. Women sell tomatoes, maize etc., and men are
> supported by their wives. They are taking us through this difficult time.
> There is no other support we are getting. Nobody is bringing us food.
> That is how we are living.'
> (Interview with a male elder from Brava, Somalia)

> 'The difference now is that women have caused a lot of problems.
> Suppose you do not give her what she wants, she will just sit there and
> watch. So the problems are on men. If there is money she will go to the
> market but if not she will stay hungry. In the past women used to struggle
> in every way to look after the home. They had the responsibility to care
> for the family. That is different nowadays, so the men are in trouble.'
> (Interview with a man from Pabbo, Uganda)

Changes in marriage practices are particularly evident in the Uganda and Rwanda studies, with the general trend being greater freedom of decision making for women about marriage partners and stronger legal rights to property. In this context, there may be a connection between marital status and openness to notions of women's autonomy. For example, the Rwanda study noted that married women and their husbands are generally more 'traditional' in their outlook than women who have lost their partners.

The case studies provide evidence that, for both men and women, sexuality can become an economic strategy or can secure protection in times of stress. Women marry soldiers, resort to prostitution, or re-marry frequently. Men often seek to marry women who are richer than them. Young people may be prey to the advances of 'sugar-daddies' and 'sugar-mummies'. Militarisation and access to guns enhances young men's capacity to take sexual partners forcibly. Long-term consequences may include family breakdown and the spread of sexually transmitted diseases.

Gendered power structures have changed as a result of conflict, though to a limited degree. Women's increased economic power, highlighted above, has sometimes enabled them to exert greater influence and become more involved, mainly within the household but in some cases also outside. Examples exist of women taking political roles at community and national levels (Sudan, Uganda), or becoming involved in trade (Angola, Somalia):

> 'I ... made good money from the farm. I then ventured into business. I collected US dollars from Mogadishu and brought them to Kismayo. I bought US$100 at 630,000 shillings in Mogadishu and sold at 880,000–900,000 shillings in Kismayo. My capital was then between US$600–900. After some time in this trade my capital rose to 21 million shillings. It was then that I thought of buying a shipload of dates together with seven men. I gave the money to the men who had a new ... station wagon. I told them that I would proceed to Mogadishu and make arrangements for the stores. But some people got information and waylaid the men, killing two and seriously injuring the third, who later died in Nairobi. The money was taken. I remained with only 50,000 shillings out of my capital of 21 million.'
>
> (Interview with a businesswoman from Kurtunwarey, Somalia)

Changes of consciousness among women have resulted in the formation of women's associations (e.g. in Rwanda). However, in general, changes in gender roles at the micro level have not been accompanied by corresponding changes in political or organisational influence. *De facto* gains have not been translated into *de jure* changes in women's status: women have taken on responsibility but have not been granted power. (The studies were carried out at the community level and did not set out explicitly to trace linkages with national trends, where women's increased involvement in politics and formal reconciliation mechanisms is observed more frequently. In general, however, the studies would support the view that there is in practice little linkage between local and national processes of policy reform and reconstruction.)

Women's direct involvement in armed struggle was limited largely to Eritrea, where both women and men joined armed forces as fighters as well as support personnel. Women were also involved in the genocide in Rwanda. These examples of challenges to essentialist stereotypes do not appear to have had a significant impact on attitudes towards women in general, nor to have gained them additional respect or led to long-term changes. Indeed, the Eritrea study describes the difficulties of supporting female ex-combatants in the post-war period, many of whom had become destitute and socially isolated as a result of their participation in the armed forces.

In addition to seeking to understand changes in men's and women's everyday behaviour and relationships, the research also sought to investigate possible changes in the ideals and values which underlie this behaviour. Has conflict changed accepted concepts of masculinity (what it means to be a man in a particular social context) or of femininity (what it means to be a woman in such a context)? Do the values with which parents educate their girls and boys change as a result of war, and do social institutions such as the market or the state reinforce these changed expectations in men's and women's behaviour? The conclusion reached by the research teams is that conflict does not appear to have led to shifts in gender identities, but rather to growing tensions between people's ideals (of masculinity and femininity) and the practical reality available to them when their lives are restricted by violence, displacement, impoverishment, and personal loss. Trying to live up to people's expectations imposes increasing stress on both men and women. The Uganda team's analysis, for example, indicates that:

> [i]n the internally displaced camps, men have lost the power to provide for and protect the family, or to exercise authority, leadership, or control over resources (including wives and children). The resultant frustration may be channelled into aggressivity in various highly destructive forms.
> (Uganda case study: 27)

In fact gender ideologies do not appear to have changed, and may rather have become further entrenched. Stereotypes persist, backed by values that can be seen in proverbs, songs, and other socialisation methods. It could be argued that although gender roles have changed, they have done so in line with existing gender ideologies. Women's increased economic responsibilities thus result from, rather than challenge, the notion of women as pillars of the family:

> 'If you see him arrive and you beat the kids, quarrel, and ask "How much up-keep money do you give to feed the family?", you are provoking the

situation. That is why women are the walls of the house and men are the roofs. If women understand all this, families will stay well.'

(Interview with a female politician from Juba, Sudan)

Furthermore, the gap between what role the men play and what role they ideally should play serves only to underline the ideal, rather than transform it. However, we cannot conclude that there is no scope for lasting change: changes in consciousness among women and men are in evidence and can potentially be built upon: many respondents declared that things will never be the same again.

To what extent do changes in gender relations brought about by conflict represent positive opportunities for change? Which changes are to be deemed 'positive', and by whom? Respondents were divided about whether they preferred their present life to that of the past. In Malian Tamasheq and Maure communities, for example, few people doubted the value of women acquiring new skills and ideas as a result of displacement: indeed, men and women of all ages considered their old life to have been characterised by isolation and ignorance. On the other hand, in Uganda there was a 'rights backlash' in which respondents blamed 'the West' or 'television' or 'education' for trends they perceive to have rendered children and women uncontrollable as a result of rights and equality policies:

> *'What makes most women not submissive to their husbands is the issue of gender equality or women's rights ... Women who are educated and employed are the worst group of people because ... after they get pregnant, they throw out the man. They have enough money to look after themselves.'*
> (Interview with a chief from Paibona, Uganda)

This they saw both as a product of conflict (an aspect of the resistance of Acholi culture to its incorporation into the Ugandan state) and as a factor contributing to future conflict. The widespread desire to return to old values poses problems for development policy makers and strategists. The desire to reclaim one's cultural identity may constitute a 'people's definition of durable peace', and the thwarting of that desire may be a key factor behind violent resistance. Satisfying that claim may contribute to a reduction of tension; on the other hand, those same cultural values may include elements which reinforce the subordination of women, children, and relatively powerless men, and may also conflict with international human rights standards.

These findings raise questions about the assumption, often made by development practitioners, that women's increased economic responsibilities during and after conflict can lead to their empowerment. While there is no doubt that this may happen in individual cases, these gains tend to be scattered and temporary – the process of women being sent 'back to the kitchen' is as frequent as the empowerment scenario. The *ideological* basis sustaining traditional gender relations seems resistant to change even when its outward manifestations are reordered. Interventions aimed at taking advantage of rapid change in conflict and post-conflict situations to encourage transformations in gender relations may therefore be unrealistic. Conflict may create some space to make a redefinition of social relations possible, but in so doing it seems to rearrange, adapt, or reinforce patriarchal ideologies rather than fundamentally alter them.

How have gender identities contributed to conflict?

The research undertaken for this project generated some insights to begin addressing this question, but further analysis is required. Figure 1 is an impact flow diagram indicating some of the possible causes and effects the research team members teased out from their analysis. One important caveat is, of course, that this interpretation of the contribution of gender identity to cycles of violence remains tentative. The case studies describe violent struggles over the control of resources (land, trade, women, children, labour, natural resources, cultural identity, and access to state power). The view from the field is that war is a conflict between patriarchies or established power structures. Violence both generates and is generated by poverty, humiliation, frustration, loss of livelihood, failures of governance, political manip-ulation, and breakdown of intercommunal relations (trade links, shared labour/production arrangements, intermarriage, etc.). Gender differences within and between groups are threaded through all these. Distorted and threatened gender ideologies encourage aggressiveness and revenge.

The Uganda study lists the following among internal causes of the conflict: erosion of the negotiating power of Acholi culture in general and traditional leadership in particular, which weakens the mechanisms for conflict resolution; the value placed on aggressiveness in the socialisation of children; and impoverishment and the consequent frustration felt by both men and women at being unable to provide for and protect their families, i.e. to fulfil their gender roles – in other words, ' ... aggressivity and militarisation represent both a vision and a strategy to restore the possibilities of ethnic and gender identity'

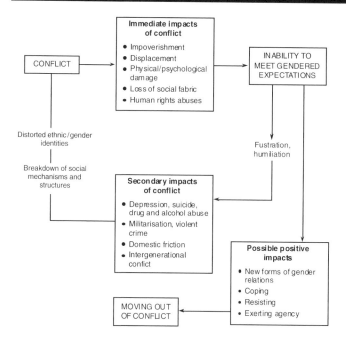

Figure 1: Gender identities and conflict – a tentative model of possible links

CONFLICT

Immediate impacts of conflict
- Impoverishment
- Displacement
- Physical/psychological damage
- Loss of social fabric
- Human rights abuses

INABILITY TO MEET GENDERED EXPECTATIONS

Distorted ethnic/gender identities

Breakdown of social mechanisms and structures

Frustration, humiliation

Secondary impacts of conflict
- Depression, suicide, drug and alcohol abuse
- Militarisation, violent crime
- Domestic friction
- Intergenerational conflict

Possible positive impacts
- New forms of gender relations
- Coping
- Resisting
- Exerting agency

MOVING OUT OF CONFLICT

(Uganda case study: 27). This same sense of frustration leading to violence and militarisation appears in the case of Sudan, where researchers concluded that gender and other identities link at the ideological level to fuel ongoing violence. Some respondents made such a link explicitly, emphasising gender-based conflict, or, as one of the respondents put it, a struggle of

> 'man against man fighting for position. This dismantled societies and sent them into wrangling, wrangling, wrangling ... Nowadays you find that there is a lot of quarrelling in families, quarrelling about the care of children. This is how I noticed gender-based conflict between men and men, between women and women, and even between children and children.'

(Interview with a male politician in Juba, Sudan)

Conflict appears to exacerbate tensions and inequalities between generations. Cycles of violence perpetuate themselves over generations: the impact of war on future generations, with the vision of a permanently militarised society as children grow up in violence, poses a massive challenge. Respondents believed that the influence of elders is declining. Conflict may also generate or exacerbate intergenerational splits by forcing (perceived) distortions in gender identities among the young, paving the way for socially unacceptable and destructive behaviour on their part. Institutionalised socialisation processes (such as the Acholi firesides, for example) fall into disuse, partly as a result of the inability of parents to fulfil their gender roles, and this contributes further to intergenerational tension:

> 'In the old days the Acholi people would teach their children around the fireplace in the evenings. These days that doesn't happen anymore. As a result, many children are now thieves, and women no longer have respect for their husbands. Parents can no longer effectively teach their children because of the life they are experiencing at the camps ... So the children behave the way they like and as a result parents feel helpless ... Girls put on slit skirts and short skirts, exposing their private parts ... This is very shameful.'
> (Interview with a woman from Pabbo, Uganda)

Similarly, war erodes local-level inter-communal relations, even if it originates elsewhere. Northern Mali is a case in point, where inter-communal differences have erupted into outright mistrust, and relations have not improved even after the cessation of hostilities:

> 'The biggest lesson I've learned? The crumbling of the age-old very solid links which used to unite the red skins and the black skins: the fragility of the confidence between them, because even today when there is calm, we still don't have confidence in each other.'
> (Interview with a Songhoi male ex-fighter from Kano, Mali)

> 'I don't believe in my country like I did. I understand now that I was wrong about it. I also understand that people can change face as and when they want; that's why I always keep to myself because I don't trust anyone.'
> (Interview with a married Tamasheq woman from Ebang-Sorho, Mali)

In the case of Somalia, previous power hierarchies between the leading clans have been rearranged according to the fortunes of the war at the national level, while discrimination against the 'minority' clans has been accentuated further. Conflict exacerbates the powerlessness of the poor and of the targets of discrimination, whether they be male or female.

Conclusions

The negative impacts of conflict are felt by all – men, women, children, and the elderly. People's ability to recover from the shocks of war is determined, at least in part, by their position in evolving power structures: in this sense, women are more likely than men to have to struggle to survive. However, this applies equally to members of minority or subordinate groups. The research carried out for this project thus confirms the importance of embedding gender analysis in a cultural and social context, and of seeing gender as an analytical lens through which wider social relations can be understood. It further indicates that if gender analysis is to 'dismantle patriarchy', as one workshop participant put it, it needs to set aside the narrow focus on women's autonomy with which it is often associated and instead adopt broader, more inclusive parameters. This would permit context-specific analysis of the various gender identities to which both men and women are expected to conform, and of the relationship of both to violence and militarisation.

The research has confirmed the hypothesis that one of the impacts of conflict is a clear change in gender relations, with women taking on greater and more extensive responsibilities at the household level while men substantially relinquish theirs. However, the institutional changes which would provide women with decision-making power consistent with these new and more responsible roles have been slow in coming. A particularly important finding, and one which has implications both for policy and for the design of assistance programmes, is that the ideological underpinnings of gender relations have barely been touched at all and may even have become further reinforced through conflict. The expectations of development practitioners that conflict provides opportunities for the radical improvement of the position of women need some rethinking. This does not mean that change is not possible, or that attempts to influence change should not be made: the implications are, rather, that radical change will be difficult to bring about in the short term, and that it will require dialogue and debate around fundamental values.

The efficacy of oral testimony for conducting research in contexts that require sensitivity to personal feelings and security has been validated. However, it also raises a number of methodological questions. First, the use of testimonies in this project has not produced neat answers; rather, it has illustrated the breadth and variety of people's perceptions of change. In relation to gender dynamics, there is no doubt that change is happening, but how should this be interpreted? Are we seeing fundamental or superficial change? Do people see their lives as being better or worse than before, and how far is their interpretation of this question coloured by their gendered experiences? How far are the interventions of development agencies coloured by *their own* perceptions and values?

There is a potential conflict between the open-ended process involved in OT and the needs of development research to explore relatively precise questions. In focusing analysis on our research questions, discarding extraneous material, and quoting selectively, have we distorted the voices of the respondents? The methodology of OT as a developmental tool needs further elaboration.

The research has begun a process of hypothesising the relationships between gender and conflict, a complex subject that requires further in-depth study. Issues for future enquiry include constructions of masculinity and its relation to militarisation and the state. The complex linkages between gender and other factors of difference, notably ethnicity and age, in a context of rapid social upheaval, is another. Further research might also explore the scope for lasting transformation in gender ideologies resulting from changes in gender roles and identities, as a basis for developing NGO interventions and strategies. Are new or alternative masculinities and femininities emerging, and, if so, should they be encouraged? Finally, the voices of young adults and children have not been adequately heard in this research and should be incorporated in the future.

Notes

1   The research report and annexes can be found on the ACORD website (www.acord.org.uk).

2   Staff of ACORD's Gulu programme contributed the Uganda section of Olivia Bennett *et al.* (1995). Panos' approach to oral testimony projects is described in Panos Institute (2001).

3   Judy El-Bushra, Asha El-Karib, Angela Hadjipateras, Ibrahim Sahl, with Idah Lumoro (Uganda), Ibrahim Nur (Somalia), Norma Fodul (Sudan), Fadimata Aya Toure (Mali), and Mariana de Souza and Tyiteta Avelina (Angola).

4   ACORD has adopted a framework for social-exclusion analysis developed originally by Organisational and Social Development Consultants (OSDC), and it has applied this framework in strategic planning and research processes.

5   The security of respondents and their testimonies was recognised as an important concern throughout the project. Some respondents in Somalia asked to be interviewed in the ACORD offices rather than in their homes. In Uganda, transcripts indicate that some resisted what they saw as

pressure to come up with controversial opinions. Otherwise, most respondents were willing to be interviewed.

6 The project defined 'gender relations' as combining:

- *gender roles:* the activities that men and women are expected to carry out within a given household or community, differing according to socio-cultural context;
- *gender identities:* expected or idealised characteristics and behaviours of different sexes, further distinguished by other categories such as age, ethnicity, economic class, and social status;
- *gendered power structures:* social institutions which control resources (e.g. the household, the community, the school, the state) when examined from the point of view of how men and women respectively gain access or membership to them, contribute to them, are influenced by them, and receive or are denied support, status, resources, or protection from them; and
- *gender ideologies:* the system of values which underpins gender roles and identities and which validates gendered power structures in a system of social relations, framed within a particular culture.

References

Bennett, O., J. Bexley, and K. Warnock (eds.) (1995) *Arms to Fight, Arms to Protect: Women Speak Out About Conflict,* London: Panos Institute.

El-Bushra, J. (2000) 'Transforming conflict: some thoughts on a gendered understanding of conflict dynamics', in S. Jacobs, R. Jacobson, and J. Marchbank (eds.) *States of Conflict: Gender, Violence and Resistance,* London: Zed Books.

Panos Institute (2001) *Giving Voice: A Practical Guide to Implementing Oral Testimony Projects,* London: Panos Oral Testimony Programme, Panos Institute.

Women in Afghanistan:
passive victims of the *borga* or active social participants?

Elaheh Rostami Povey

Introduction

Since the early 1990s there has been a flourishing literature on gender, war, violent conflict, and reconstruction (see, for example, Benjamin and Fancy 1998; Bennett *et al.* 1995; Bunch and Carrillo 1992; Jacobs *et al.* 2000; Lentin 1997; Nikolic-Ristanovic 1996; Turshen and Twagiramariya 1998; Wallace 1993). Moser and Clark (2001), in particular, provide a comprehensive global understanding of the complex gender issues in armed conflict and political violence.

This paper has particularly benefited from Moser and McIlwaine's analysis of gender and social capital, which the authors define as 'the rules, norms, obligations, reciprocity, and trust embedded in social relations, social structures, and ... institutional arrangements that enable its members to achieve their individual and community objectives' (Moser and McIlwaine 2001:179; Narayan 1997:50). They argue that, in the wake of war and violent conflict, it is essential to reconstruct social capital within communities as well as to intervene to improve economic and physical capital (e.g. infrastructure, employment opportunities, etc.), political infrastructure (formation of state and other institutions), and human capital (education, health, etc.) (Moser and McIlwaine 2001; Simpson 1998).

In the context of Afghanistan, this analysis is important because, with notable exceptions (for instance, Collett 1996; Langen 2001; Mertus 2000; Moghadam 1994a, 1994b; Shah 2001; Wolfe 1992), the dominant portrayal of women has shown them as passive victims of war, violence, and political repression, to be liberated only by Western military intervention. Twenty-two years of war and violent conflict eroded social capital in Afghanistan. However, women organised around gender-related survival strategies and, in the process, became aware of more gender-specific concerns. They worked together in groups and organisations, generating networks, norms, and trust in their communities. I hope, therefore, that by articulating the voices of women in Afghanistan, their views and demands will be incorporated in the shaping of the agenda for the process of reconstruction, rather than allowing the agenda to be set solely by facilitators, academics, and aid workers.

This paper is based on qualitative participatory research, principally involving six days of detailed observational study and 126 interviews – 11 with individual women leaders of organisations, and eight group interviews in different institutions with 123 women and three men.[1] This approach enabled me to ask questions that encouraged women to express their feelings and share their experiences. However, my work was confined to six days in Kabul, and further research is needed. For example, Participatory Urban and Rural Appraisal (PRA) (Chambers 1994; Moser and McIlwaine 1999, 2000) could provide useful tools for an appropriate quantitative and qualitative analysis of the needs of women and men in Afghanistan in the process of reconstruction. The PRA approach has been criticised for failing to reach the poorest of the poor and to redefine the hierarchical relationship between local communities and development organisations (Cooke and Kothari 2001). However, it could be useful, to some extent, to give prominence to the voices of men and women in Afghanistan.

Women and men experience war and violent conflicts differently

Many of my interviewees argued that in some ways women's situation was worse during the civil war than during Taliban rule. This is because so many women were murdered and raped by the Mujahidin. The Taliban disarmed the warlords and brutally enforced its own model of law and order. It imposed the *borga* on women and executed those women who did not obey its law. Those who did obey had some freedom of movement. But, during this period, economic activities came to a halt, poverty and hunger led many women to become sex workers, and some were forced to marry members of the Taliban, as its way of 'ending prostitution'.

Reliable statistics are scarce. According to my interviewees there are approximately 35,000 women-headed households in Afghanistan, mainly because so many men were killed during the war years and under Taliban rule (1996–2001). These women are called *zanane bee sarparast* (unprotected women), itself a derogatory term. In the post-Taliban era, they have been cast out by both family and community. They constitute the poorest of the poor and intra-familial violence against them has increased. Many women believe that there is a real danger of a large number of women being socially excluded because they are beggars, sex workers, or household heads.

A section of the Refugee Centre in Kabul is set aside for *zanane bee sarparast*. When I was there for a visit, the women refugees claimed that between 2500 and 3000 women-headed households lived there. They were separated from the other households and lived as a separate community. They said: 'Because we are *bee sarparast* we receive less food from the aid agencies. This is because many of us are not registered and do not possess an official card to receive help.' Also 'there is no soap or cleansing materials and we suffer more than men because of our monthly menstrual period'. When I asked them how they survived, they replied, 'We produce handcrafts and sell them to raise some money for ourselves and our children and we go begging in the streets.' Indeed, Kabul's streets were full of beggars, especially women and children.

After 22 years of war and violent conflict in Afghanistan, women, men, and children are suffering from malnutrition and various diseases. There are also specific health problems deriving from the war, both physical and psychological. Years of repression, deprivation, and dire socio-economic conditions have severely affected the mental well-being of most citizens. As Soraya Parlika, head of the National Union of Women of Afghanistan, explained: 'We all suffer from the psychological pains of the war and destruction. It is going to take a long time to reduce and cure the pains of Afghan women, especially the women-headed households and the orphanages.'

It is important to analyse the health issues facing women and girls in relation to the cultural specificities of Afghanistan. Many women have been subjected to rape, forced marriage, torture, killing, fear, domestic violence, social exclusion, and separation from their home and family members. Any interview that I conducted, be it with individuals or groups, often resulted in the women bursting into tears and wanting to talk about their losses. This is, for example, what Zakereh Asgarzadeh had to say:

'I was a school teacher. I lost my leg and my arm when a bomb went off eight years ago, during the civil war. Despite this I got married and had two children. My older son was born with a heart problem linked to the incident, which gives me recurrent nightmares. Some members of my

family, friends, and neighbours believe that it was a good thing that I got married and had children; others think that I should not have.
I don't know what is wrong and what is right. Sometimes I feel like committing suicide.'

Sohayla, a journalist, said: 'My three brothers were killed during the civil war and under Taliban rule; this is a terrible loss.' A woman in the Kabul Refugee Centre also expressed her sense of loss: 'I was not a poor woman, I had a nice home, [but] we lost everything. Years of unemployment, war, and destruction led me to go begging in order to feed myself and my children.' I did not meet any sex workers to interview, but many of the women I did speak to told me that they knew of many women 'who had no choice but to sell their bodies to feed themselves and their children'.

Issues frequently mentioned by my interviewees concerned inter-familial violence against women; the isolation and marginalisation of women-headed households; and men's derogatory perceptions of women in society at large. As a number of women in the Ministry of Women explained, 'most men were and are against Taliban and fought against Taliban (some of them died for their cause). But they have the same [backward] attitude as Taliban about women's place in the society'.

The low social status of women, and the consequent power imbalances between women and men that it generates, are the underlying reasons for harmful and discriminatory practices and physical and sexual abuse against girls and women in Afghanistan. The responsibility for this injustice and violence lies not only with the immediate family but also with individual communities, religious organisations, health and education institutions, professionals, and law enforcers.

The provision of resources and opportunities for women to tell and share their experiences as part of a healing process is a vital element in the post-war reconstruction effort. Many women may not want to voice the truth about what they have had to go through for fear of wider personal and political reprisals,[2] especially for sex workers in the context of Islamic law. But with the assistance of women's organisations, women's media, and NGOs, women could feel more empowered to break the taboos and thereby work towards changing gender relations at a deeper level. For example, the case of Iran, analysed by Rostami Povey among others (Rostami Povey (Poya. M.) 1999:122–57, 2001:44–73), demonstrates that the negative image of *zanane bee sarparast* can be eradicated. As a result of efforts by women's media and the encouragement of debates over the issue, this term is no longer used in Iran and has been replaced by *zan sarparast*, which means simply women-headed households.

Women's coping strategies and empowerment

Survival strategies are deeply embedded in the material conditions of life. It is usually the poorer sections of society which remain in the war-stricken areas during times of violent conflict, while those with economic opportunities usually migrate elsewhere. However, significant minorities of professional women remained in Afghanistan or have returned to their country. For these women, survival strategies were based on forming networks and groups in solidarity with poorer women. For over 20 years, and especially under Taliban rule, these networks and forms of solidarity became mechanisms for women's empowerment.[3] Based on women's life and work histories, this section will discuss the circumstances under which this happened.

Professional women's survival strategies

Many prominent women chose to stay in Afghanistan and work, either openly or clandestinely, towards empowering other women (as well as children). For example, Soraya Parlika, head of the National Union of Women of Afghanistan, became an integral part of the women's movement there:

> 'We witnessed 22 years of war, terror and bombing. We have an ancient saying, Shenidan Kay Bovad Manande Didan (it is one thing to hear about something, but quite another to see it with your own eyes). Under the Mujahidin, the weapon of one community against another was to attack, to jail, to rape, to hit in public the female members of the other community. Under the Taliban, women were denied their basic rights to education. Throughout, we continued our activities, openly and secretly, and this allowed us to hold hands with each other and survive.'

Other examples abound. The non-governmental Women's Vocational Training Centre has been active for 20 years and has offered women in Kabul courses in English and German as well as computer-skills courses. Its activists have also provided courses in handcrafts, animal husbandry, bee-keeping, and honey making in rural areas outside Kabul. They created income-generating activities for women. Shafiqa Moaber, the director, told me, 'we had 6000 students from seven to 35 years of age. When Taliban came to power, they closed down our institution. But we continued our underground activities in our homes. Many times we were threatened with imprisonment and torture, but we continued.'

Ghamar, another active member of this organisation, also explained how the group is attempting to include children who face social exclusion because of their different forms of disability: 'There are a large number of children who are blind, deaf, and/or maimed because of the civil war and the bombings of 2002. We have started to identify them in different parts [of the country], teach them different skills, and include them in our projects according to their abilities.'

During Taliban rule, the Women's Association of Afghanistan funded and managed secret sewing, knitting, and handicraft courses for women. Shafiqa Habibi, a leading member of this organisation, explained:

> 'These courses took place in the homes of the teachers. Sometimes we had to change our venue for fear of persecution by the Taliban, but we continued. Our activities enabled many women to make clothes and other necessities for themselves and their families, and sometimes they sold or exchanged their products with other women.'

After the fall of the Taliban, the Association was planning to extend its activities to include literacy classes.

The doctors in the Rabee Balkhi Women's Hospital were all educated in Kabul. Setting up the hospital had the advantage of allowing these women to perform surgery. Dr Rahimeh Zafar Setankazi, the hospital manager, explained:

> 'surgery was the domain of male doctors. During Taliban rule, only female doctors were allowed to attend to female patients. Throughout this period we remained in Afghanistan and worked in the hospital with barely minimum facilities and without being paid. We did it to serve our people and the poorest of the poor in our country.'

Mahbobeh Hoghoghmal is a lawyer and the assistant commissioner in charge of organising Loya Jirga, the Grand Council of 21 people chosen by the United Nations out of 1000 names put forward. This body will decide how the Council should convene and how the transitional government should be formed. It is hoped that the transitional government will be more representative of the diverse class, ethnic, and religious groups that exist in Afghanistan. Before Taliban rule, Hoghoghmal taught law at the University of Kabul. Under the Taliban, she taught in Peshawar and worked with women's NGOs in Peshawar on gender legal issues. She explained:

> 'In my profession I learnt how women in Afghanistan are denied many rights. Under the Taliban, even the basic rights to education were taken away from them. My aim is to raise these issues in Afghanistan and at the international level to make women aware of their rights and to change the legal position of women in Afghanistan.'

Seddighe Balkhi is the head of the Islamic Centre for Political and Cultural Activities of Afghan Women. She was a teacher. She left Afghanistan in 1981 and went to Khorasan in northeast Iran. She stated:

> 'A large number of Afghan people migrated to Iran. I therefore decided to go and work with refugee women. We set up schools for Afghan women and provided opportunities for different groups of women to be in touch with each other. In cooperation with UNHCR in Iran, we identified 2500 female-headed households in Mashhad, the capital city of Khorasan, [although] I am sure there are many more that we did not reach. We set up courses for these women and provided opportunities for them to be involved in income generating activities.'

Balkhi returned to Afghanistan in 1991 and continued her work with women in Mazare Sharif, Herat, Ghandehar, and Kabul.

Poor women's survival strategies

The majority of poor women in urban and rural areas never left Afghanistan. Those with the necessary skills turned their homes into underground schools. They were paid for these services by their neighbours, friends, and families. In this way, they were able to survive financially.

In a group interview with 39 women in the Ministry of Communication, women explained how they turned their homes into clandestine schools. They also knew the stories of other women:

> 'Ghamar Jaan's husband was killed in the civil war. She had a daughter. She secretly taught more than 800 students in her home. Many of us paid her as much as we could, sometimes 20,000 Afghan [approximately US$1.85 in 2002] a month to teach our children. This was very little money – she could hardly manage the household expenses – but it was better than nothing. Without her our daughters would have been illiterate.'

Poverty in Afghanistan is predominantly the result of war and the collapse of economic activity. In an interview with six women journalists, they argued:

> 'we are from middle-class backgrounds. We have university degrees. During the Taliban we worked in our homes, teaching, knitting, sewing, producing, and exchanging goods and services. Had we not done this, we would have been in the streets begging. Many poorer women with fewer skills were begging and some became sex-workers.'

Networking and group solidarity enabled these women to remain in touch with each other. After the fall of the Taliban they began to work for different newspapers. In February 2002 they set up the *Cultural Journal of Afghanistan Women* and published the daily *Seerat* (Nature) to promote women's issues.

As stated above, women living under extreme forms of poverty who possessed few skills or who lost their male head of household had often no choice but to become beggars or sex workers. On 13 February 2002, I visited the Shrine of *Shahe Do Shamshireh* (the king with the two swords). Every Wednesday, a large number of very poor women visit the Shrine to pray for their dead, make wishes, and ask the saint (*Shahe Do Shamshireh*) to make them come true. I interviewed ten women at this Shrine. All of them were heads of household who had lost the men of their families in the civil war and during Taliban rule. They explained: 'We are *zanane be sarparast*, no male kin to look after us, we are outcast because of this, we are even ignored by the aid agencies; we only receive food and clothes from our female neighbours.' As the basis of their daily coping strategies, these poor women rely only on women's support networks to meet their bare necessities.

Despite the horrors of war and violent conflict, many women in Afghanistan have emerged empowered from such circumstances. They became aware of their own capacities to organise and found ways to survive. Organising in this way was an empowering process. As will be discussed in the next section, women's secret organisations and networks in Afghanistan were the only functioning organisations that were trusted by the community.

Women in Afghanistan as social participants

As we have seen, a great many women school and university teachers were engaged in teaching girls, young women, and some boys in their neighbourhoods. Every single woman that I interviewed said that she taught between ten and 60 students over a period of time, offering them different courses according to their skills. Some taught as many as 100–800 students at different times. The homes of these women and others with specific skills became community homes, mainly for girls and women, but also for boys, and were financed and managed entirely by women. It was by word of mouth that women and girls spread the news about the secret schools to their peers. They hid their books, notebooks, pens, and pencils under their *borgas*, and risked their lives by going to the secret schools every day. Here, many young women and girls, as well as some boys, not only received basic literacy and numeracy training, but also studied different subjects at various levels (biology, chemistry, engineering, English, German, Arabic, Quranic Studies, cooking, sewing, knitting, hairdressing, and other skills).

The levels of trust and support generated by these secret organisations can be measured by the widespread incidence of teaching in women's homes and the support they gave each other to ensure the survival of these secret meetings. In my discussion with 17 women in the Literacy Corps, I was told that they are organising tests so that girls and young women can obtain certificates for the skills they acquired during the Taliban years. Mohtarameh Najieh Zohal Zareh, the head of the Literacy Corps, said that 'to date, we have identified 2000 students in Kabul who can be awarded certificates'.

Of course, many women involved in education were caught by the Taliban. But even though they were persecuted, jailed, and tortured, they continued their bitter struggle. Marzia Adil, a journalist, related the following story:

> '*Hadeya Malekzad taught 150 students in her home. Despite many threats from the Taliban, she continued her work. Now she is the leader of a group of women in her area and discusses with them the significance of education and employment. In a meeting with Soraya Parlika, the head of the National Union of Women of Afghanistan, 3000 women gathered together on top of the one of the hills around Kabul to raise their demands with [her].*'

Shukkria Barekzai Dawi, chief editor of the weekly newspaper *Ayeene Zan* (Women's Mirror) in association with the Asia Institute, also described the impact of her secret organisation: 'We were 23 women working as teachers. We taught 650 students [who] ... did not know about our NGO ... [But] I am proud today that they have realised that their secret lessons were organised by our NGO.'

These women became an inspiration for other women who risked their lives under Taliban rule to give cohesion and solidarity to their communities. Their secret organisations have gained the trust and support of their communities. Many men also supported the secret schools. Shukkria Barekzai Dawi, for instance, has said that her husband 'devoted his wealth to our institution'.

Women's determination and optimism enabled them to reclaim their rights following the fall of the Taliban regime. Some began publishing newspapers. In February 2002 there were two women's newspapers in Kabul, *Women's Mirror* and *Nature*. When I visited the Ariana Women's Vocational Training Centre, the centre's members were planning to launch a newspaper on 8 March 2002 to celebrate International Women's Day. They said, '[w]e are hoping to continue to publish our paper either as a weekly or daily after 8 March, depending on our limited budget'. Many women are also actively participating in rebuilding their organisations, regrouping their members, and creating new opportunities for women to learn skills in order to engage in income-generating activities. The high level of trust placed in such networks and associations demonstrates that women and women's organisations can play a critical role in the reconstruction of Afghanistan.

Under Taliban rule, women's activities were concentrated on running these secret schools, which could be described as meeting the practical gender needs of women (see Molyneux 1985; Moser 1989). In the post-Taliban period, they have begun to move towards addressing women's strategic interests by challenging patriarchal gender relations in Afghanistan. They have also challenged the Western perception of Muslim women, especially in relation to the *borga*.

When I was interviewing a group of 15 women in the Ministry of Women, a woman who came in from the street shouted, 'all I hear since the fall of Taliban is *chadory, chadory, chadory* (*borga, borga, borga*). My problem is not *chadory*, my problem is that I don't have any food to feed myself and my children.'

I asked several women at the Ministry of Women and at the Rabee Balkhi Women's Hospital about the issue of the *chadory*. They explained that, historically, the *chadory* is the traditional cover in most parts of Afghanistan, especially in rural areas. One of the doctors explained how diverse women's attitudes towards the *borga* and other traditions were in the pre-Taliban era: 'My sister went to school with *chadory*, [and] I went to school without [one]; ... some young women cycled to schools and universities.'

In urban areas, especially in Kabul, most women did not wear the *chadory*. The Taliban imposed it on them. However, women felt that:

> *'after five years, ... [it has] become part of our culture, we feel comfortable with it. Our community and society do not accept women without chadory. We will not take it off just because the West wants us to ... Some of us may take it off once we are ready and our society is ready. To be pressured by the West to take off our chadory is as bad as Taliban imposing [it] on us [in the first place]. We have the right to choose what to wear.'*

The role of women leaders such as Sima Samar, the Minister of Women in the interim government, Mahbobeh Hoghoghmal, Soraya Parlika, Seddighe Balkhi, Shafiqa Habibi, Shukkriq Barekzai Dawi, and Shafiqa Moaber is crucial in the process of reconstruction. However, as was strongly expressed by the doctors at the Rabee Balkhi Women's Hospital and the women staff at the Ministry of Communication:

> *'this is not enough. Half of the population of Afghanistan deserves more Sima Samars and more women leaders, especially taking into consideration the needs of diverse classes and ethnic and religious groups in Afghanistan. We need more women in the process of negotiations and decision making.'*

Women's demands on the reconstruction process

Many women I interviewed welcomed the end of Taliban rule. But they wanted the world to know that 'we have not forgotten that the Mujahidin were supported by America and Pakistan, who defeated the Soviet-backed ruling regime and came to power. It was the civil war which led Afghanistan to complete destruction and paved the way for Taliban rule.'

Indeed, the Soviet-backed regime was a repressive one, and in addition a degree of uneven socio-economic development occurred under the Stalinist model of modernisation. As this regime disintegrated, gender traditionalism, refurbished by the US-backed Mujahidin, with its concomitant violation of women's rights, resurfaced (see also Moghadam 1994a, 1994b).

Many women believe that a number of factors can threaten the sustainable reconstruction of Afghanistan. Among the difficulties and challenges they identified in a group interview at the Communication Centre were:

'The continuing existence of different warring factions within the interim government; ... foreign military presence; the arming of different factions of ... warlords by the Americans and the Russians; the existence of Mujahidin and pro-Taliban individuals and groups within society; ethnic inequalities and conflict.'

Many women feel that economic development is essential to a successful reconstruction project, since 'with economic reconstruction the conflicts may be less violent, as different groups will not feel so marginalised economically, politically, socially, and culturally'.

Many of the women I interviewed were also critical of the aid agencies. They perceived the international agencies as overcrowding Kabul, using the scarce resources for themselves without as yet producing anything. In the words of a staff member of the Ministry of Communication:

'they come here, take over our houses, pay high rents, [and] create such high rates ... that we cannot afford to rent a room for ourselves [anymore]. They consume our water and electricity with their generators and we have no electricity and very little water. They eat our food, and we can't afford basic food for ourselves and for our children.'

The question of evaluating development agencies in terms of their legitimacy and their capacity has been debated widely (see, for example, Korten 1990). Many Afghan women are demanding that the aid agencies take into account their local conditions. Seddighe Balkhi, for instance, believes that these agencies 'could help develop a sustainable [form of] agriculture. We have oil, gas, copper, coal, gold, precious stones; we could be a rich country. We have been attacked by all sides for too long; today we need help reconstructing our economy.'

Mohtarameh Najieh Zohal Zareh from the Literacy Corps argued that:

'With the fall of Taliban our children are ready to go to school. But there is no school. In Kabul, which is less ruined than other parts of Afghanistan, you will not find one school that is not completely or half ruined. We need our schools to be re-built.'

Zakereh Asgarzadeh, who lost her arm and leg in the bombing, expressed the demands of the large number of disabled people and argued that access to certain resources – such as the provision of wheelchairs, buses with wheelchair access, and ramps – could enable them to become economically active. 'If I am provided with these facilities, I can teach again', she said.

Sharifeh Halim and Ziba Popol, who are active in the National Union of Women of Afghanistan, work closely with Zakereh and other disabled women. They argued that there is a great need for co-operation among women's organisations, women leaders, and the grassroots to properly articulate women's voices and demands.

Some women believe that the process of reconstruction must take into consideration the gender dimension of the needs of women and men. As Soraya Parlika has argued, there is great potential to engage women in income-generating activities: 'Traditionally, women have been involved in animal husbandry, dairy products, and handicrafts – these are areas where we could help women.'

The importance of building a channel of communication between women political leaders and ordinary women and/or of creating links among women and women's groups, including those who are facing repression (for example, *zanane bee sarparast*), are topics that are constantly discussed among women. At the Ministry of Communication, for example, I was told the following:

> 'Many women have no security in the home or outside of the home.
> We also need equality of opportunity in education and employment ...
> Now that we have the Ministry of Women, we must organise a branch of
> this Ministry in every workplace to look into women's needs and demands.'

Throughout the violent conflict, women's NGOs also remained in touch with each other and with female members of the community through networking and solidarity groups. In the post-Taliban era, these organisations have become important agents for reconstruction. In a post-conflict period in which the state does not yet exist in any real sense, women's NGOs are playing a crucial role, particularly in relation to education, training, and skills to create opportunities for women to have access to income-generating activities, thus contributing to household well-being. As Shukkria Barekzai Dawi explained:

> 'there are 136 women working in our NGO. We work with the refugees;
> we work as health workers in the hospitals. We have literacy classes
> in poorer areas and we teach women handicrafts in order to generate
> incomes for themselves and their families.'

These organisations do not receive funds from any national or international institution, but rely instead on the support of individual Afghan citizens. Reflecting on this situation, Shukkria told me: 'We have asked for financial help, but nobody has helped us financially.

If we [were to] receive financial help, we [would] have great potential and opportunities to expand our work and help our people.'

Some women expressed their willingness to be role models for other women in order to break the taboo about women-headed households and to explain why certain women were forced to become sex workers. They were willing to tell their stories on radio and television programmes, either sharing them themselves or having their stories written by other women in newspapers and magazines. When I asked them why they feel it is so important for women to tell their stories, their answer was that, through sharing common experiences, 'we understand each other's pain better'. They also want their voices to be heard by the whole world.

Despite years of war and violent conflict, I felt incredible optimism and hope listening to all the women I spoke to. Women's willingness to participate in the process of reconstruction is indeed very exciting, and promises to be quite rewarding. Their optimism and willingness is the result of their years of struggle as social actors, and policy makers would do well to take note of their remarkable achievements. As Mayra, a Ministry of Communication worker, put it:

> 'I was in my last year of completing my PhD when the Taliban took power. I did not have the opportunity to leave the country and I suffered many years of war and terror [along with] millions of others. I feel that I know more about the needs of our community than those who left the country. I feel that people like me should be involved in the process of reconstruction.'

Conclusion

As I have attempted to show in this paper, women in Afghanistan have bravely shown their capacity to devise ways of coping with life, even under the most extreme forms of coercion. As social actors, women have experienced 22 years of war, civil war, and violent conflict, and have sought alternative ways of surviving and formulating their objectives within a context of restricted resources and restrictive cultural practices.

The most immediate need of women, men, and children in Afghanistan today is for economic reconstruction. However, as the findings of this research demonstrate, the gender dimension is also crucial in this process. Women experienced war and violent conflict differently from men. Their secret organisations empowered many women; creating networks of trust and reciprocity in their neighbourhoods, among their friends and relatives, and also within their communities. To ignore women and their organisations in the process of reconstruction would deny women in Afghanistan the right to rebuild and solidify their new reality. It is vital for policy makers and aid workers not to ignore economic and social issues, particularly at the present time, when the interim government in Afghanistan and countries in the West seem to be so preoccupied with political and military issues.

Acknowledgements

This project was funded by the BBC World Service Trust (WST) and the Department for International Development (DFID). I am indebted to Marzia Adil for accompanying me to different parts of Kabul, organising my interviews, and occasionally translating from Pashto to Farsi. My thanks go to Meena Baktash and Shiragha Karimi, who provided me with invaluable information, as well as to Haleh Afshar and John Rose, who made valuable comments and suggestions on an earlier version of this paper, and to Narguess Farzad for helping with the translation of terms and phrases from Farsi into English.

Notes

1   My intention was not to marginalise men, but to give prominence to women's voices in identifying their needs in the process of reconstruction in Afghanistan.
2   In the context of South Africa see Krog (2001).
3   In the context of Latin America see Johnson (1992).

References

Benjamin, J. and K. Fancy (1998) *The Gender Dimensions of Displacement: Concept Paper and Annotated Bibliography*, New York, NY: UNICEF.

Bennett, O. *et al.* (1995) *Arms to Fight, Arms to Protect: Women Speak Out About Conflict*, London: Panos Institute.

Bunch, C. and R. Carrillo (1992) *Gender Violence: A Development and Human Rights Issue*, Dublin: Atti Press.

Chambers, R. (1994) 'The origins and practice of participatory rural appraisal', *World Development* 22(7): 953–69.

Collett, P. (1996) 'Afghan women in the peace process', in L.A. Lorentzen and J. Turpin (eds.) *The Women and War Reader*, New York, NY: New York University Press.

Cooke, B. and U. Kothari (2001) *Participation: The New Tyranny?* London: Zed Books.

Jacobs, S. *et al.* (eds.) (2000) *States of Conflict: Gender, Violence and Resistance*, London: Zed Books.

Johnson, H. (1992) 'Women's empowerment and public action: experiences from Latin America', in M. Wuyts *et al.* (eds.) *Development Policy and Public Action*, Oxford: Oxford University Press.

Korten, D. (1990) *Getting to the Twenty-first Century: Voluntary Action and the Global Agenda*, Bloomfield, CT: Kumarian Press.

Krog, A. (2001) 'Gender and voice in truth and reconciliation', in Moser and Clark (eds.) (2001).

Langen, S. (2001) *Tea with Taliban*, London: BBC Television.

Lentin, R. (ed.) (1997) *Gender and Catastrophe*, London: Zed Books.

Mertus, J.A. (2000) *War's Offensive on Women: The Humanitarian Challenge in Bosnia, Kosovo and Afghanistan*, Bloomfield, CT: Kumarian Press.

Moghadam, V. (1994a) 'Building human resources and women's capabilities in Afghanistan: a retrospect and prospects', *World Development* 22(6): 859–76.

Moghadam, V. (1994b) 'Reform, revolution and reaction: the trajectory of the "women question" in Afghanistan', in V. Moghadam (ed.) *Gender and National Identity*, London: Zed Books.

Molyneux, M. (1985) 'Mobilisation without emancipation? Women's interests, the state, and revolution in Nicaragua', *Feminist Studies* 11(2): 227–54.

Moser, C. (1989) 'Gender planning in the Third World: meeting practical and strategic gender needs', *World Development* 17(11): 1799–825.

Moser, C. and F. Clark (eds.) (2001) *Victims, Perpetrators or Actors? Gender, Armed Conflict and Political Violence*, London: Zed Books.

Moser, C. and C. McIlwaine (1999) 'Participatory Urban Appraisal and its application for research on violence', *Environment and Urbanization* 11(2): 203–26.

Moser, C. and C. McIlwaine (2000) *Perceptions of Urban Violence: Participatory Appraisal Techniques*, Urban Peace Program Series, Latin America and Caribbean Region, Sustainable Development Working Paper No. 7, Washington, DC: World Bank.

Moser, C. and C. McIlwaine (2001) 'Gender and social capital in the context of political violence: community perceptions from Colombia and Guatemala', in Moser and Clark (eds.) (2001).

Narayan, D. (1997) *Voices of the Poor: Poverty and Social Capital in Tanzania*, Environmentally Sustainable Studies and Monograph Series No. 20, Washington, DC: World Bank.

Nikolic-Ristanovic, V. (1996) 'War and violence against women', in J. Turpin and L.A. Lorentzen (eds.) *The Gendered New World Order: Militarism, Development and the Environment*, New York, NY: Routledge.

Rostami Povey, E. (2001) 'Women's contestations of institutional domain in Iran', *Feminist Review Collective* 69 (Winter): 44–73.

Rostami Povey, E. (Poya, M.) (1999) *Women, Work and Islamism: Ideology and Resistance in Iran*, London: Zed Books.

Shah, S. (2001) *A Dispatches Investigation: Beneath the Veil*, London: Channel 4 Television.

Simpson, G. (1998) 'Reconstruction and reconciliation: emerging from transition', in D. Eade (ed.) *From Conflict to Peace in a Changing World*, Oxford: Oxfam GB.

Turshen, M. and C. Twagiramariya (eds.) (1998) *What Women Do in Wartime: Gender and Conflict in Africa*, London: Zed Books.

Wallace, T. (1993) 'Refugee women: their perspectives and our responses', in H. O'Connell (ed.) *Women and Conflict*, Oxford: Oxford University Press.

Wolfe, N.H. (1992) *The Present Role of Afghan Women and Children*, The Hague: Bernard Van Leer Foundation.

Part Two: Introduction
Peace and reconstruction:
agency and agencies

Deborah Eade

Part Two of this Reader brings together selected papers from other issues of *Development in Practice* and elsewhere, focusing principally on the non-governmental agency sector – national and international NGOs and local civil society organisations – and on the political agency of the 'victims' of conflict, particularly women, in shaping their societies during and after armed hostilities. We have therefore chosen contributions that illustrate some dimension of these issues, drawing on different geographical range where appropriate, in ways that resonate with and complement the articles in Part One of this volume.

Several of the contributors to Part One, most notably Lesley Abdela, Chris Corrin, and Angela Mackay, illustrate the serious limitations of externally brokered peace and reconstruction processes as well as the shortcomings of most of the aid interventions made at some point along the way. Negative media coverage of relief programmes lies at one influential end of the spectrum, and magisterial accounts such as that of Peter Uvin's (1998) analysis of failed development assistance in Rwanda at the other. These criticisms are valid and necessary. Historically, the aid community has been intermittently chastened by certain watershed experiences, the 1994 atrocities in Rwanda and their aftermath being an obvious recent example. The Biafra war in the 1960s, the tragedy of the Pol Pot regime in Cambodia in the 1970s, the war-induced famines in the Horn of Africa in the 1980s and the 'low-intensity conflict' or military dictatorships afflicting much of Latin America and the Caribbean during that same decade, the sheer brutality of 'ethnic cleansing' in the Balkans in the 1990s, and the regrettable fall-out of the 'war on terror' in countries like Afghanistan and Iraq are other memorable instances where the aid community as a whole has been obliged to review its own principles and practices, and in a sense nail certain political colours to the mast. If the problem during the Cold War was for NGOs to assert independence of government policies, the challenge now is to provide humanitarian assistance in ways that do not fuel the conflict or compromise a society's capacity to come through the crisis. Old ideas about the 'relief–reconstruction–development continuum' have been blown apart by the nature of contemporary conflict. Mark Duffield, Professor of Development, Democratisation, and Conflict at the University of Leeds and a long-standing analyst of international development assistance, uses terms such as 'liberal peace' and 'durable disorder' (in ironic contrast to the 'durable solutions' sought by the aid industry) in his critique of the growing convergence of the United Nations, NGOs, military establishments, and private companies in the 'securitisation' of international assistance (Duffield 2001). Post-development writers such as Arturo Escobar might argue that the aid agencies have come very belatedly, if at all, to see that the entire paradigm is flawed.

At the same time, it cannot be denied that unprecedented strides have been made both by official aid agencies (which are accountable to, but, we must remember, can be no better than, the governments they represent) and by NGOs (whose accountability is altogether rather fuzzy, albeit with a hard centre). Indeed, it is the whole accountability question that has most galvanised the NGO community in relation to humanitarian relief work: are NGOs more accountable to their donors and their wider domestic constituencies or to the intended beneficiaries of their interventions? Is it possible to be equally accountable to both? If so, how can 'downward accountability' be improved? What rights do beneficiaries have, and how can they exercise these rights? And how might their ways of working need to shift in order for NGOs to ensure that their relief and post-conflict interventions are as accountable to women as to men?

There are no simple 'one-stop' answers to these questions, obviously, but inter-agency standard-setting initiatives such as that of The Sphere Project (2004) and the efforts of organisations such as the Active Learning Network for Accountability and Performance in Humanitarian Action (ALNAP – **www.alnap.org**) indicate a real interest among NGOs to learn from their mistakes, improve co-ordination, and raise professional standards in humanitarian endeavour. The Sphere Project's establishment of a set of minimum standards and a code of conduct for NGO relief programmes is an excellent example of the sector policing itself, holding its members accountable to an acceptable level of performance while also providing individual NGOs with significant moral backing from their peers when they are faced with tough decisions.

Hugo Slim and Mary B. Anderson have written extensively on humanitarianism and armed conflict, and their work is characterised by an engagement in the ethical dimensions of 'on-the-ground' interventions in situations where the implications of these tough decisions are seldom clear-cut. Both of them complement their own research work with serving as advisers to a number of major relief agencies, including Oxfam America, Oxfam GB, the Red Cross Movement, and the United Nations High Commissioner for Refugees (UNHCR). Here, Slim maps out some of the definitional frameworks relating to humanitarian operations, which are just as relevant to local peace builders as to aid workers and international peacekeepers. Terms such as 'humanitarian imperative', 'neutrality', and 'impartiality' are often invoked loosely and in potentially harmful ways, while 'innocence-based solidarity' makes simplistic (and to some extent patronising) assumptions about non-combatants – in particular women, children, and infirm and elderly people. Of course, civilians will have complex loyalties especially if the conflict involves their own community. To confuse vulnerability and 'innocence', and to use the latter as a criterion by which to judge who most merits assistance, is not only crude, but also implies that to have political agency renders a person less deserving of aid. Equally problematic is to deny the political agency of an individual or group of people, which, as other contributors to this volume illustrate, happens so readily when women are regarded primarily as mothers (and so responsible for other dependants) and/or as helpless victims (and so dependent on aid). One way of avoiding moral traps of this kind, Slim argues, is for aid agencies to be guided by international humanitarian law as a basis for their action.

Anderson illustrates the ambivalence of the 'beneficiaries' of relief assistance towards their 'benefactors' – grateful for help, but critical of (and sometimes angry about) the way in which it is given. It may be better to give than to receive, but that does not make it right to make inappropriate gifts. She does not draw the demagogic conclusion that all local criticism of international assistance is right, but rather that there is a need to 'acknowledge tensions between giver and receiver as inevitable'. Two of her key recommendations – identifying areas of equality and inequality, and accepting a clear division of labour within the donor–recipient relationship – would force all parties to deal more honestly with the power relations inherent in the aid chain. Doing this, and in ways that ensure that women's interests are fully respected, would make profound demands on everyone involved and ultimately shift not only the way in which aid is delivered, but also the way in which it is conceptualised. In their article, **Martha Thompson** and **Deborah Eade**[1] describe a very different way of working, based on their experience with Salvadoran refugee and displaced populations throughout the 1980s. The role of civil society in the form of popular organisations and grassroots mobilisation during the war in El Salvador has been well documented. Here, the authors draw out some critical policy and practice lessons from how Salvadoran peasant women developed their own 'protection capacities' and leadership potential, even in the face of their aggressors. The behaviour of these women challenged conventional aid-agency assumptions about the political agency of poor and uneducated people. Time has shown how unique this experience has proved to be. While it is not suggested that any such experience could be replicated or transposed from one setting to another, the authors believe that some aspects of it could be useful to contemporary thinking about the protection of civilian populations in general.

The papers by **Jenny Pearce** and **Glenda Caine** are based on their presentations at a 1996 symposium co-hosted by the Centre for the Study of Violence and Reconciliation (CSVR) and Oxfam GB's South Africa office, entitled Building Bridges in Southern Africa: Conflict, Reconstruction, and Reconciliation in Times of Change. We include them here not for their case-study value, as the historical specificities have obviously been superseded (albeit less so than might have been wished), but because of the insights they bring to the debate. Writing about three Latin American countries that experienced prolonged civil conflict (El Salvador, Peru, and Nicaragua), Pearce contrasts the absence of war with 'positive peace', stressing that the ways in which power relations – including gender – are configured at the end of any conflict will affect post-war reconstruction and the likelihood of sustainable peace. Many of the countries experiencing actual or latent conflicts have never experienced 'development', and cannot therefore 'return to democracy' – democratic institutions need to be grounded in local realities and must therefore evolve over time. However, Pearce's experience is that external agencies tend to focus not on local capacities but on '*their* interventions (for instance, what *they* can do to articulate relief and development, what *they* can do to prevent conflict and build peace)', and that male aid professionals generally have a poor appreciation of the impact of gender relations on 'the ability of traumatised, poor, and ill-educated populations to play their full role in the post-conflict situation'. The truth of this observation is borne out by Suzanne Williams, and resonates with the experiences recounted by Corrin and Abdela.

Caine offers a brief description of peace training work undertaken in the KwaZulu Natal region of South Africa, an area with a long history of political violence in a country 'with a culture in which violence is commonly used as an acceptable method of problem-solving'. She too emphasises that sustainable peace work cannot be undertaken by 'outsiders' to the conflict, although a trusted external broker may help the antagonists to start communicating. Although Caine does not explicitly refer to gender-based aggression, violence against women in South Africa has if anything worsened in the post-apartheid era; and the practical lessons she draws are relevant to any society or social group seeking to develop non-conflictual responses to the perceived (or actual) threat of violence. These lessons are poignantly exemplified in the dialogue between **Sumaya Farhat-Naser** and **Gila Svirsky**[2], veteran feminist peace campaigners and co-founders of the Jerusalem Link for Women, an organisation comprising Bat Shalom in West Jerusalem and the Jerusalem Center for Women in East Jerusalem. Their commitment to working through their differences in order to build a culture of peace is an inspiration, especially in view of the complex political, psychological, cultural, and logistical obstacles to be faced. Both women also faced criticism from forces opposed to their efforts, and even from within their respective organisations. Establishing and maintaining trust and 'active listening' in such extreme circumstances calls for exceptional personal courage. That young Israeli and Palestinian feminists are now leading efforts to create spaces within which women from different cultural communities can come together, as described here by **Rola Hamed**, therefore deserves to be better known and to enjoy some of the protection that can derive from international attention.

The need to identify and then help women to build on their existing capacities to work for 'active peace' is highlighted by **Myriam Gervais**, writing about post-reconstruction Rwanda. Although aid agencies are undoubtedly sincere in wanting to enhance women's security (personal, economic, and socio-political), the impact of their interventions is often hampered by an inadequate understanding of the ways in which issues of poverty, gender, and security intersect. In the ultimate analysis, there is no substitute for a detailed understanding of the local situation, something which again stresses the limited role that outsiders can or should seek to play in peace building activities. Finally, **Suzanne Williams**[3] argues in her contribution that to address gender power relations in the context of a war-torn society not only entails entering a contested terrain within that society, but also among and within the various intervening agencies, including international NGOs. Drawing on her own wide-ranging experience on working on issues of gender, development, and violence within Oxfam GB, Williams uses the metaphor of the 'hard' and the 'soft' to describe different structures and management cultures that can basically co-exist in a large aid agency, but which often clash 'in the highly charged context of emergencies and post-conflict interventions, [generating] tensions over priorities and resources, value, and reward'. Her basic argument is that organisational imperatives are conceptualised and implemented in highly gendered ways, and that only a comprehensive commitment to gender equity throughout every aspect of that organisation's work will enable it really to begin to address such tensions. In other words, without this deep institutional commitment and the concomitant openness to changing their own ways of thinking and working, greater professionalisation and technical standard setting, vital though they are, will only take aid agencies so far in engendering their accountability processes. To echo Haleh Afshar's concluding comment in her introduction to Part One of this Reader, there is still some way to go before theory and practice inform each other so as to ensure that women's actual and potential contributions during war and in peace building are realised to the full.

Notes

1   This article was commissioned for a special issue of the journal *Social Development Issues* on Women in Conflict in Crisis: New Issues in an Insecure World (*Social Development Issues* 24(3): 50–8, 2002). We are grateful to the editors, Mary Ellen Kondrat, María Juliá, and Cathy Rakowski, and to the Inter-University Consortium for International Social Development, for allowing us to reproduce this article.

2   We are grateful to Zed Books for allowing us to reprint this chapter from Perry and Schenck (2001:133-54).

3   We are grateful to Lawrence & Wishart for allowing us to reprint this chapter from Cockburn and Zarkov (2002).

References

Cockburn, Cynthia and Dubravka Zarkov (eds.) (2002) *The Postwar Moment: Militaries, Masculinities and International Peacekeeping*, London: Lawrence & Wishart.

Duffield, Mark (2001) *Global Governance and the New Wars: The Merger of Development and Security*, London: Zed Books.

Perry, Susan and Celeste Schenck (eds.) (2001) *Eye to Eye: Women Practising Development Across Cultures*, London: Zed Books.

The Sphere Project (2004, revised edn.) *Humanitarian Charter and Minimum Standards in Disaster Response*, Geneva: The Sphere Project. (The English-language text of the revised edition and the 2000 edition in translation are available free of charge at www.sphereproject.org.)

Uvin, Peter (1998) *Aiding Violence: The Development Enterprise in Rwanda*, Bloomfield, CT: Kumarian Press.

Relief agencies and moral standing in war: principles of humanity, neutrality, impartiality, and solidarity[1]

Hugo Slim

In Dante's 'Inferno' there is a special place of torment reserved for those who have been neutral in this life. Their sin is so particular that they do not even merit a space in hell. Instead, they are confined to the outer part, or vestibule, of hell and separated from the rest of the damned by the river Acheron. The precise sin of this group of people is that of moral indecision and vacillation. Throughout their lives they never made a stand for something they believed. True to form, Dante inflicts upon them a torment which neatly fits their crime. They are destined to rush forever behind a banner which 'whirls with aimless speed as though it would never take a stand', while at the same time they are chased and stung by swarms of hornets (Dante 1984: Canto 3, lines 53–4).

Many relief workers probably feel that they have already experienced the particular anguish of Dante's punishment. On frequent occasions, the international humanitarian system might be accurately described by Dante's image: a great crowd of international agencies rushing frantically behind the whirling banner of concern brandished by the international community, which seldom takes a definitive moral stand and plants its banner firmly in the ground. Indeed, the urgent and relentless flapping of UN and NGO flags from thousands of fast-moving white vehicles around the world today seems uncannily reminiscent of Dante's vision of the vestibule of hell. And even if relief workers and peacekeepers have not yet experienced such hell, there are those today who might be tempted to think that such a fate should certainly await them when the day of reckoning arrives. The organisation African Rights, in particular, has severely criticised the 'neutralism' of humanitarianism and what it considers to be the absurdity of current relief-agency claims to humanitarian neutrality in political emergencies and war (African Rights 1994:24–8). Yet in classical humanitarianism, neutrality is prized as one of the four essential operational principles alongside humanity, impartiality, and independence.

So why has neutrality become a dirty word? Is it really a sin? Or do Dante and African Rights understand the word differently from conventional humanitarian practitioners? Is neutrality inevitably unprincipled, or is it in fact the operational means to highly principled ends? Is real humanitarian neutrality really impossible, when any humanitarian action inevitably plays to the advantage of one side or another? A passionate debate now rages about the moral positioning of humanitarian agencies and peacekeeping forces. And as most relief agencies and UN forces alike abandon the idea of neutrality, they are clinging with renewed vigour to the other traditional humanitarian principles of humanity and impartiality, or going beyond traditional humanitarian principles by justifying their position in terms of solidarity, or by giving more refined interpretations of impartiality.

The debate surrounding humanitarian neutrality and its fellow humanitarian principles is a debate about the moral stance or position of third parties in other people's wars. Where should an NGO, international agency, or UN force stand in a violent dispute between various groups? The issue of positioning concerns relief organisations not only at a corporate level, but also at an individual level. In order to operate in the midst of war, a relief agency needs to make its organisational position in that conflict known to the combatants. But at a personal level, it is also essential for staff morale that each individual has a strong sense of his or her individual position in relation to the prevailing violence. Playing a third-party role in a context of violence and injustice is personally taxing, and is one of the greatest challenges facing relief workers and UN soldiers in today's emergencies. The ability to do so with a sense of moral conviction and international legality is crucial to the morale of relief and development workers and also to the non-combatant civilians they seek to help.

The purpose of this paper is to explore the moral implications of the operations of relief agencies, acting as third parties in wartime. I begin by identifying the essential problem of moral stance and organisational positioning as one of locating humanitarian values within a context of organised inhumanity. In the main part of the paper I examine current usage of the terms *humanity*, *neutrality*, *impartiality*, and *solidarity* as they are used to define humanitarian positions. I then briefly consider the psychological implications for relief workers of operating as non-combatant third parties in war, emphasising the importance of clear positioning to counter what I have termed 'bystander anxiety'. Finally, I recognise that a range of different positions is both inevitable and desirable in a given conflict; but conclude by emphasising the responsibility of any third-party organisation (military or civilian) to be transparent in its position and to preserve rather than distort traditional humanitarian principles and language. I end by recommending concerted support for international humanitarian law (IHL) and its possible reform as the best way to focus the current debate about the place of humanitarianism in war.

Standing for humanitarian values

Relief agencies have problems with their identity and position in today's wars, because they are trying to do something which is intrinsically difficult: they invariably find themselves trying to represent the values of humanity and peace within societies that are currently dominated by the values of inhumanity and violence. More often than not, therefore, they are swimming against the current of that society, or certainly of its leadership. They are representatives of values that are often seen as a threat by leaders and peoples committed to violence and war. If humanitarian values are given too much consideration in situations of war or political violence, political and military leaders fear that they might undermine their followers' will to fight, or provide succour to their enemy. Nevertheless, it is part of the paradox of human nature that humanitarian values can be present in war and since time immemorial have usually co-existed with violence to some degree (see Guillermand 1994). Where there is organised violence, there is often mercy too. But the intricacies of the Geneva Conventions which were put together after World War II show how even the most united and victorious military and political leaders prefer humanitarian values to be rigidly controlled to prevent them from becoming an excessive threat to the war effort.

The task of representing humane values to various combatant parties will always place a humanitarian third party in a difficult position. In most cases, the values represented by the humanitarian will be greeted with distinct ambivalence. On the one hand, they may be recognised and even strangely cherished in some quarters of the warring parties and their societies: many humanitarians can recount a story about a gentle warrior whose co-operation was critical to saving many lives. On the other hand, they will also be treated with the utmost suspicion by crucial sections of any warring party, and perceived as a threat to the violence they are embarked upon. More cynically, but equally routinely, humanitarianism will be seized upon as something which can be abused to bolster the adversaries' own war efforts. The organisation and its individuals who dare to represent the values of humanity in war will thus usually meet a mixed response, with their values being seen simultaneously by different groups as ones to cherish, to attack, or to abuse.

While it has always been difficult to represent and position humanitarian values in war, the proliferation of relief and development agencies working in today's wars now seems to make that positioning even more difficult. One of the main reasons why humanitarian principles have been so difficult to clarify and affirm in the last five years must be that there are now so many different organisations trying to assert themselves as 'humanitarian'. The proliferation of NGOs in particular (which has been an inevitable consequence of Western donor policy in recent years) has led to wide differences in the ethical maturity and political sophistication of various organisations which are all competing to work in the same emergency. Anyone surveying the swarm of NGOs delivering primarily governmental humanitarian assistance in many of today's emergencies would be unwise to accept them all as equally principled and professional. With so many different organisations trying to establish a humanitarian position within today's wars, and with all of them using the same tired humanitarian language to do so, it is hardly surprising that the humanitarian scene has become overcrowded, its messages garbled, and its stance somewhat undignified.

So what concepts *are* relief agencies using today to distinguish their third-party, humanitarian position in war? Many of the more mature have done some hard thinking about the principles of their position and the nature of their stance in today's conflicts. But despite their commitment to such thinking, attempts at a real breakthrough in the development of an overarching principle for their position have achieved very little. To a large degree, this is because different agencies have different views on where they stand. As a result, the new NGO codes and principles still lack the kind of clarity, brevity, and irresistible persuasiveness which might impress militiamen at checkpoints or convince a beleaguered government enduring the attacks of a rebel army.[2] The established humanitarian principles and conventional language which relief agencies have traditionally used to formulate their humanitarian stance are sounding distinctly hollow, confused, and even hypocritical in the mouths of today's multitude of international civilian and military organisations which operate with a humanitarian mandate. More precise understanding and usage of these terms might make for clearer positions. In the meantime, it is perhaps small wonder that the precise meaning of words like 'impartiality' has evaporated in recent years in a world where, in the same emergency, a Red Cross nurse can use the term to describe her medical programme and a UN commander can use the same word to describe air strikes.

Humanity, neutrality, and impartiality

Relief agencies traditionally assert their humanitarian position with the three key terms of *humanity*, *neutrality*, and *impartiality*. These three guiding principles (which also herald the opening of UN General Assembly Resolution 46/182 (1991), which attempted to define humanitarian assistance in the 'new world order' after the Cold War) are of course lifted straight from the top three of the Red Cross and Red Crescent Movement's seven guiding principles as formalised in 1965.[3] Indeed, most humanitarian language which emerges from the mouths of NGOs and UN forces is in fact little more than the rebounding and frequently distorted echo of the language and principles of the Red Cross and Red Crescent Movement – an echo which, as we have seen, sounds particularly incongruous when it issues from the mouths of stridently political NGOs or heavily armed UN soldiers. Nevertheless, these three ideals are currently being actively reaffirmed in various forms in an effort to make them work again for today's civil wars, and for the new range of international third-party organisations which seek to find a role within these wars. The confusion seems to arise because different agencies are using the same language to describe different positions or no positions.

Humanity and its heresies

The first principle, that of humanity, apparently remains the least controversial, and is the principle most easily asserted by relief agencies, international politicians, and UN forces alike. However, much of the agreement on the principle of humanity seems to cluster around a somewhat heretical understanding of this principle. There are perhaps two particular heresies in play: first, a reductionist one which commodifies humanitarianism and relates it solely to material help; and second, an aggrandising one which tends towards making humanitarianism non-negotiable in war. The former is a heresy of substance (what), and the latter a heresy of approach (how).

The core of the Red Cross and Red Crescent definition of humanity is the desire '*to prevent and alleviate human suffering wherever it may be found ... to protect life and health and to ensure respect for the human being*'. Here is enshrined the classical definition of humanity. Although brief, it embodies a sense of humanity in all its fullness, showing the humanitarian quest to be much more than a purely physical pursuit aimed only at saving life. Rather, the actual meaning of humanity transcends mere physical existence to embrace 'respect for the human being'. This phrase is essential, because it extends the purview of humanitarianism to rights (such as religious freedom and fair trial) that are well beyond the simple right to life, and are clearly spelled out in the Geneva Conventions. As Pictet points out, the humanitarian ideal of the Red Cross and Red Crescent Movement actually extends to a person's 'life, liberty and happiness – in other words everything which constitutes his [*sic*] existence' (Pictet 1979:26).

The first heresy which is so evident in current usage of the principle of humanity caricatures humanitarianism as an essentially materialistic concern for physical welfare, manifested in the provision of a range of commodities such as food, water, shelter, and medicine. This commodification of humanitarianism and its subsequent reduction to a package of 'humanitarian assistance' is a serious heresy which undermines wider humanitarian values. To interpret humanitarianism as an essentially minimalist endeavour relating to simple human survival is a misreading of its first principle. The Geneva Conventions are full of civil and political rights, as well as rights relating to simple physical survival. Restricting humanitarian concerns to relief commodities precludes many other vital aspects of the Geneva Conventions that relate to Pictet's notions of liberty and happiness. Without recognising humanitarianism's concern for all types of rights, humanitarian reductionists actually minimise the rights of those they seek to help. Recognition of this heresy may well be liberating and serve to free people from a conundrum which is more imagined than real. NGOs in particular seem to have convinced themselves that a humanitarian position and a human-rights position are somehow at odds with each other. This is obviously not the case: a truly humanitarian position on the plight of civilian populations in war, as articulated in the IV Geneva Convention, is firmly positioned in the full spectrum of human rights. Tragically, much time and ink may have been wasted in recent years, trying to find a way of reconciling human rights and humanitarianism, when in fact they were never divided in the first place.

The second heresy is exemplified in some new language. Instead of the simple principle of humanity, most relief agencies have now adopted the more cumbersome (and perhaps sinister) term 'the humanitarian imperative'.[4] This is presumably in the hope that by giving the principle of humanity an imperative gloss and making it unreservedly a moral absolute, the phrase will present humanitarianism as a non-negotiable, almost genetic and biological force, so always over-riding the position of the warring factions. In addition, the humanitarian imperative usually seems to relate solely to 'humanitarian assistance' – the minimum package of relief *commodities* which donor governments are prepared to allow as emergency aid and which typifies the first heresy.

Very much in the Gallic humanitarian tradition, this second heresy gives humanitarianism a non-negotiable aspect.[5] This is at odds with the spirit of classical humanitarianism, which has always recognised that it must negotiate its place in violence, assuming the right of human beings to wage war, but seeking to limit the effects of that war with the consent of the warring parties. The Geneva Conventions recognise that warring parties have rights as well as obligations in agreeing how humanitarianism should be realised in war.[6] By implying that the rights are all on the side of the relief agencies and the victims of war, current interpretations of 'the humanitarian imperative' may optimistically (and even illegally) imply the automatic presence of relief agencies in war and undermine the very serious negotiation which needs to take place between warring leaders and humanitarians to ensure that humanitarian action is fair.

Perhaps the worst aspect of the non-negotiable heresy is that it is so unrealistic. In reality, unless assistance is delivered by force, humanitarianism will always be negotiable. While it is highly likely that altruism in its most universal form is innate to human nature and even an important aspect in the survival and evolution of all species (Geras 1995; see also Ridley 1996), there is also no doubt that it is usually in fierce competition with human traits which tend towards inhumanity, like fear, oppression, self-determination, enmity, hatred, aggression, and violence. There is, therefore, something rather simplistic and imperious about the new phrase 'the humanitarian imperative'. It displays some humanitarians' exaggerated sense of their own importance within a people's vision of their own conflict, suggesting that the new wave of humanitarian ideologues have failed to grasp that conflicting societies are usually deadly serious about their *right* to wage war. In contrast, less grandiose humanitarians who have experience of representing humanitarian values in war realise that they are usually pleading for a minority position, and one which has to be nurtured when it cannot be imposed.

Finally, it is also worth noting what might be an inconsistency rather than a heresy in the current use of the principle of humanity and its new imperative. Many relief agencies, like the politicians whom they frequently criticise, tend to be extremely selective about the various humanitarian 'imperatives' around the world. In an Orwellian fashion, it seems that all crises that threaten the lives of civilians are imperative, but some are more imperative than others. The more imperative emergencies are of course usually determined by the *Realpolitik* imperatives of relief agencies' donor governments, and by the financial or promotional imperatives of competing relief agencies. Thus behind the rhetoric there is an element of bluster and even hypocrisy when relief agencies talk about 'the humanitarian imperative'. Dropping the new term and reverting to the more extensive and more dignified original principle of *humanity* might be wise.

The temptation to abandon neutrality

Of the three classical principles which seek to underpin a humanitarian position, *neutrality* is the one from which most agencies and all military peacekeeping doctrine are in retreat. As suggested above, there is now a majority view that neutrality is either undesirable, because it is equated with being unprincipled, or is simply unachievable in practice, because relief aid is so frequently manipulated. However, the recent pariah status of neutrality in the humanitarian's lexicon seems to stem from a widespread misunderstanding of the term. As Denise Plattner has pointed out, although it is much talked about, there is no definition of neutral humanitarian assistance, and her 11 criteria go far to determine the parameters of what such a definition might encompass (Plattner 1996).

In its strict sense, humanitarian neutrality is not the neutralism of Dante and African Rights. Truly neutral relief workers and peacemakers are not indifferent, unprincipled, and vacillating creatures destined for the vestibule of hell. On the contrary, they have a determined commitment to particular ideals. They have already taken a stand, and for them neutrality is ultimately the operational means to achieve their humanitarian ideals within an environment which is essentially hostile to those ideals. For the ICRC and for other relief agencies which choose such a position, neutrality is thus a pragmatic operational posture. Far from being unprincipled or amoral, it allows them to implement their ideals, within the limits prescribed by international humanitarian law.

The Red Cross and Red Crescent definition of neutrality is enshrined in its third fundamental principle:

> *In order to continue to enjoy the confidence of all, the Movement may not take sides in hostilities or engage at any time in controversies of a political, racial, religious or ideological nature.*

Within this principle, Pictet has emphasised the important distinction between military neutrality and ideological neutrality (Pictet 1979:54–9). Being neutral means taking no part in military operations and no part in ideological battles. Drawing on the work of scholars who have defined the constituent parts of State neutrality, and on Pictet's commentary on ICRC neutrality, Plattner agrees that the three key ingredients to a neutral position are *abstention*, *prevention*, and *impartiality*. For an organisation, as for a State, 'abstention' means no involvement in military or ideological activity. 'Prevention' obliges the organisation to ensure that neither party is able to use the organisation to its advantage. 'Impartiality' requires the organisation to apply equal terms to the warring parties in its dealings with them (Plattner 1996:164). As such, Plattner concludes that 'neutrality may therefore be understood as a duty to abstain from any act which, in a conflict situation, might be interpreted as furthering the interests of one party to the conflict or jeopardising those of the other' (*ibid.*:165).

While perhaps approving this definition in theory, seasoned relief workers and peacekeepers will of course seize quickly on the word 'interpreted'. As they know only too well, in the extremely contested arena of war and political emergencies, the devil is in the interpretation of actions and events. Perception is everything and varies from faction to faction in conditions where one group's legitimate relief is seen by another group as an obvious contribution to the war effort of the enemy. African Rights is thus correct in condemning the 'tendency to believe that neutrality need only be asserted to be proved' (African Rights 1994:24). In reality it has to be proved by rigorous adherence to the principles of abstention, prevention, and impartiality, and by constant negotiation, thorough appraisal of the conditions of the respective parties, and continual recourse to the precepts of the Geneva Conventions.

Apart from the Red Cross and Red Crescent Movement, which still rigorously uphold it, few agencies still draw on the concept of neutrality to stake out their position. One determined exception is UNICEF and its Operation Lifeline in South Sudan (OLS), which has worked hard to draw up and disseminate a set of humanitarian principles. In doing so, they have firmly embraced the principle of neutrality:

> The guiding principle of Operation Lifeline is that of humanitarian neutrality – an independent status for humanitarian work beyond political or military considerations.
>
> (Levine 1995)

The many NGOs which have rejected the notion of neutrality have done so for two main reasons. First, as Plattner points out, they feel that it often imposes an unacceptable silence upon them in the face of grievous violations of human rights (Plattner 1996:169–70). What Pictet has described as the inevitable 'reserve' required of the neutral (Pictet 1979:53) is considered to be too high a price to pay for NGOs who mandate themselves as advocates of human rights and social justice. Secondly, abiding by neutrality's commitment to prevention and abstention seems increasingly unfeasible in the light of what we now know about the manipulation of relief supplies, and the fact that combatants and civilians are intrinsically mixed in today's civil wars. For example, in the same article in which UNICEF argues for neutrality, the apparent paradox of its position is made clear. Within a matter of a few column inches, it also eloquently makes the case for why such neutrality is not so simple and is perceived by many as impossible to achieve in today's wars:

> The military are not a distinct group, separated from the civilian population, but are fathers, brothers, sons frequently returning to their homes. Clearly, in such circumstances, women and children who have received aid from OLS agencies are not going to refuse to feed their own family members.
>
> (Levine 1995)

Despite these problems, UNICEF is one of the very few agencies which is trying to observe and apply the principle of neutrality in its work. But while neutrality may be right for some organisations, it is certainly not right for all of them. Some are bound to find it offensive to the mandates they give themselves. Also, as African Rights points out, the majority of organisations will find that they simply do not have the means – in terms of diplomatic and political contacts, finances or professional competence – to negotiate and secure a rigorous position of neutrality in their relief work (African Rights 1994:24). Nevertheless, these factors do not mean that neutrality in itself is not possible, nor that it is an unprincipled means of operating. In the right hands and in pursuit of the right ideals recognised in international humanitarian law, neutrality is an extremely valuable principle. Relief agencies need to decide if they are going to abide by it or not. If they are, they should ensure that they acquire the appropriate skills. If they are not, they should not discredit the principle simply on the grounds that it is at odds with their own mandate and capabilities.

Embracing impartiality

Because of their difficulties with neutrality, most NGOs have abandoned the concept and embraced its close relation, *impartiality*. In common with most other NGOs, ACORD (a European NGO consortium with extensive and considered experience of working in political emergencies and war in Africa) has determinedly reasserted the principle of impartiality over that of neutrality as the guiding ethic of its operations in war:

> *Whereas neutrality dictated that ACORD could take no position of any kind in a conflict, impartiality means upholding accepted human values irrespective of the allegiance of those involved.*
> (Jazairy 1994)

While ACORD rejects neutrality, it affirms the notion of impartiality. But it has misunderstood the principle of neutrality. For, as we have seen, neutrality may stop an organisation from taking sides (militarily or ideologically) and protect it from public criticism, but it does not prevent an organisation from having a principled position, based on firm ideals. The classical definition of impartiality, taken from the Red Cross and Red Crescent principles, is that an organisation

> *makes no discrimination as to nationality, race, religious beliefs, class or political opinions. It endeavours to relieve the suffering of individuals, being guided solely by their needs, and to give priority to the most urgent cases of distress.*

As Pictet (1979:37–43) and others have pointed out, the principle of impartiality is therefore built on the twin pillars of non-discrimination of person and proportionality of need. In other words, the similarity of all people but the differences in their needs should at all times determine the judgements of the impartial humanitarian, in the light of the objective precepts of humanitarian law.

The attraction of impartiality over neutrality for most NGOs and UN forces is that the concept permits the impartial person to be judgemental – albeit not gratuitously so, but in line with agreed values. Pictet caricatures the difference between neutrality and impartiality thus: 'the neutral man [*sic*] refuses to make a judgement, whereas the one who is impartial judges a situation in accordance with pre-established rules' (1979:53). NGO policy has pounced on the objectivity of impartiality and its potential for being judgemental. For advocacy-driven NGOs and robust peacekeepers alike, impartiality seems to offer the most scope for justifying a strategy of speaking out or shooting out, while also maintaining humanitarian values.

The Médecins Sans Frontières movement (MSF) has sought to emphasise that impartiality need not be passive or condone human-rights violations, by adhering to a more refined expression of the principle: the notion of 'active impartiality'. The active dimension of MSF's impartiality refers to the fact that they will speak out and condemn any party in a conflict which they see as breaching human rights or humanitarian law. The development of this harder interpretation of impartiality is, therefore, determinedly not neutral and abstentionist. Public criticism will be made against people or groups on the basis of what they do, but not on the basis of who they are. Impartiality in this context relates to the various factions or parties involved, but rejects the idea of abstention in the face of human-rights abuses. The idea of active impartiality might therefore be summed up as impartiality to persons, but partiality to their actions.

Leaning towards solidarity

A fourth concept is gaining increasing currency within debates about humanitarian positioning: it is that of 'solidarity'. This represents the stance of those who wish to abandon both neutrality and impartiality. African Rights and others have suggested that, in many political emergencies and wars, the notion of solidarity might be the most appropriate guiding principle around which relief agencies could align their operational position. In its paper *Humanitarianism*

Unbound, African Rights states that 'It is arguable that solidarity is the most important principle of all', adding that 'what solidarity operations have in common is a political goal shared with the people' (African Rights 1994:26, 27). The writer defines 'genuine solidarity in relief work' as including four main components:

> 1) *Human rights objectivity and the pursuit of justice. This means a commitment to pursuing an agenda based on a set of rights.*
> 2) *Consultation with and accountability to the people with whom solidarity is expressed.*
> 3) *Shared risk and suffering with the people.*
> 4) *Concrete action in support of the people and their cause. This may include providing relief and/or political or human rights lobby and advocacy.*
> (African Rights 1994:27)

The idea of solidarity obviously involves taking sides. Such a concept may be anathema to many people who give to and work for NGOs, and it is certainly in opposition to classical humanitarian principles. But in both Christian moral theology and development work based on social justice, there is an important tradition of taking sides. Albert Nolan, a Dominican veteran of the South African liberation struggle, is a leading advocate of this position:

> *In some conflicts one side is right and the other side is wrong ... In such cases a policy of seeking consensus and not taking sides would be quite wrong. Christians are not supposed to try and reconcile good and evil, justice and injustice; we are supposed to do away with evil, injustice and sin.*
> (Nolan 1984)

Such a solidarity-based approach is obviously easier when the sides are clearly drawn, when right and wrong are as distinct as night and day, and when the wronged can be easily distinguished from the wrong. But such clarity is not always the case in today's internal wars, and the principle of solidarity can seldom be applied with confidence in many conflicts. Solidarity is a principle which was right for those who backed long-established (and often non-violent) resistance movements like the civil-rights movement in the USA or the liberation movements in South Africa and Eastern Europe. It is also one which should always be actively applied in genocide as in Rwanda. But in wars like those in Somalia, Liberia, and Sierra Leone, the 'good' sides are not so clearly identifiable. At a practical level, the application of solidarity faces problems too. The tenuous nature of the chain of command in today's wars can compromise the principle of taking sides. Political and military leaders (whether intentionally or not) often have little control over those who carry out atrocities in their name, meaning that solidarity can all too easily become solidarity with excessive and uncoordinated violence.

In an attempt to avoid these pitfalls, a certain element of humanitarian discourse has adapted the notion of solidarity and claimed solidarity not with those who are 'right', but with those who are somehow regarded as 'innocent'. In this analysis (which might be called 'innocence-based solidarity'), the lowest common denominator of innocence is usually drawn along lines of sex and age. So women, children, and the elderly are perceived as 'the innocent' and as 'vulnerable groups' who merit the solidarity of relief agencies. But, as the above quotation from UNICEF makes clear, such a position is often simplistic and ill-informed. This kind of innocence-based solidarity is thus equally precarious as a general principle of humanitarian action. And Levine's lament about current humanitarian action is apt when considering the conflict between classical humanitarianism and its detractors: 'we have not worked out what it means to be neutral in a conflict yet in solidarity with all its victims' (Levine 1996). On the one hand, ICRC would claim that this is something they have worked out years ago, while African Rights would probably claim that such a position is both undesirable and impossible.

Moral stance and personal morale

Beyond the desire to clarify humanitarian principles, there is another reason why a clear sense of the moral positioning of third-party organisations in war is so important: its effect on staff morale. Being a third party to the wanton cruelty and violence in so many of today's civil wars is personally testing for individual relief workers. Even with the clearest sense of purpose, an individual can feel all the recriminations of being a bystander in the face of appalling atrocities. Experiencing the violence and destruction around them in places like Rwanda, Bosnia, and Liberia, it is usual for most relief workers to experience a gamut of emotions which range from pity and compassion through powerlessness, frustration, and fear, to anger and outright hostility to all concerned. It is common for several of these emotions to be experienced simultaneously in an individual. It seems equally common for individuals to swing from one end of the spectrum to another at different intervals. At the hostile end of the spectrum, it becomes possible to categorise a whole people as somehow deranged and sub-human.

Humanitarians seldom do anything obvious to stop the causes of the violence around them. Their impact is usually only palliative; at best they become some small beacon of alternative humane values in the midst of inhumanity. Because of this frequent inability to stop the violence around them, many humanitarians and peacekeepers have to deal with what might be termed 'bystander anxiety'.[7] It is this anxiety which perhaps underlies the concerns of NGOs in particular to be dissatisfied with classical humanitarianism and move towards notions of active impartiality and solidarity. Although not necessarily the case, public silence is feared as the hallmark of the bystander, and so advocacy becomes all-important to NGOs.[8]

In such a context, it becomes extremely important for relief workers to know where their particular organisation stands and what position it is taking as a third party. Their own personal contribution must make sense as a moral and active one within the violence around them, and such activity must be clearly explained in terms of whichever principle – neutrality, impartiality, or solidarity – their organisation has chosen to pursue. In this way, the individual can interpret his or her role within the violence beyond that of a bystander, consciously countering the invidious feelings of bystander anxiety with a definite vision and understanding of his or her position.

Behind the words

To sum up, the semantic manoeuvring around humanitarian principles which currently preoccupies humanitarian policy makers is symptomatic of the confusion which arises when so many different types of third-party organisation seek to clarify their moral position in political emergencies and war today. Not surprisingly, however, the variety of shifting positions and their mutating vocabulary create confusion, and the humanitarian community still seeks a decisive moral banner under which to go about its business. The result is that the notions of humanity, neutrality, and impartiality, which traditionally under-pinned classical humanitarianism, are being stretched or abandoned and so risk being undermined in a process in which they come to mean different things to different people.

Yet behind the wordplay there is a definite determination to preserve the old values of humanitarianism, while applying them within the byzantine politics (local and international) of today's emergencies. Most of the different attempts to reframe humanitarian principles seem to have three main ideals in common: a commitment to the principle of humanity – albeit it in a minimal form; a desire to speak out (or shoot out) in the face of human-rights abuses; and a guarantee of third-party immunity for humanitarian agencies. The current wordplay of most relief agencies shows them attempting to combine these three ideals into a single position. Relief agencies are eager to assure themselves and others that they subscribe to a morality beyond the sanctity of human life alone. However, as has been argued, such an anxiety is based on an unnecessarily minimalist interpretation of the principle of humanity. In reality, the principle of humanity as respect for the whole human person and as developed in the Geneva Conventions easily embraces the wider moral concerns of NGOs. Instead of agonising over new mission statements and giving added nuance to old principles, many relief agencies should perhaps spend more time reading the Geneva Conventions (particularly the IV Convention) and adopt them as the best possible bulwark of their position in war. It is to their shame that the number of NGOs and their staff who are familiar with the Geneva Conventions, and who refer to them in their work, is pitifully few.

With so many agencies (civilian and military) now operating in and around humanitarian programmes, a range of positions from classical neutrality to solidarity is to be expected and desired in any given emergency. But every agency is responsible for making its position clear for the sake of the credibility of the important principles involved, as well as for morale of the suffering community in question and the individual relief workers working with them. The challenge is to clarify humanitarian terms and the principles to which they refer, so preserving their legitimacy and effectiveness in war. The best way to do this is to work together with the laws and principles we have already – most notably the IV Geneva Convention – and so to concentrate our efforts on thinking how to improve what we have. Gathering round the banner of international humanitarian law in this way should bring a double boon: first, it will provide a united front and common forum for action and thinking on humanity in war; and second, by taking so principled and obvious a stand, we might just avoid the vestibule of hell.

Notes

1 This is a shortened version of a paper which also explored the moral stance of UN Peacekeeping Forces and which was published as a chapter entitled 'Positioning humanitarianism in war' in Gordon and Toase (2001).

2 See, for example, the *Code of Conduct for the Red Cross Movement and NGOs in Disaster Relief*, Geneva 1994; the Providence Principles from Brown University, 1991; and the Mohonk Criteria for Humanitarian Assistance in Complex Emergencies, World Conference on Religion and Peace, 1994.

3 The seven fundamental principles of the Red Cross and Red Crescent Movement were proclaimed by the Twentieth International Conference of the Red Cross in Vienna 1965. They are Humanity, Impartiality, Neutrality, Independence, Voluntary Service, Unity, and Universality.

4 See, for example, the *Code of Conduct, op. cit.*

5 Gallic debate on humanitarianism has tended to be particularly strident in recent decades, evolving around the notion of *'sans frontièreism'* and the *droit d'ingérence*. While such robust relief ideology has its place alongside military intervention, it lacks a certain subtlety in situations where forceful intervention is not available or not necessary and where negotiation is inevitable and desirable.

6 See for example Article 23, IV Geneva Convention.

7 In the extensive literature on the Jewish Holocaust, the word 'bystander' has emerged as one of the most damning. The particularly odious image of a bystander thus seems to make it an appropriate term to express relief workers' fears.

8 Effective action is not always to be equated with speaking out. Much can be achieved in silence. Indeed, discretion and secrecy may be the optimal strategy in many particular situations.

References

African Rights (1994) *Humanitarianism Unbound,* London: African Rights.

Dante (trans. Mark Musa) (1984) *The Divine Comedy,* 'The Inferno', Penguin Classics, London: Penguin.

Geras, Norman (1995) 'Richard Rorty and the righteous among the nations', *Journal for the Society of Applied Philosophy* 12(2).

Gordon, D.S. and F.H. Toase (eds.) (2001) *Aspects of Peacekeeping,* London: Frank Cass.

Guillermand, Jean (1994) 'The historical foundations of humanitarian action, part I: the religious influence' and 'Part II: humanism and philosophical thought', *International Review of the Red Cross* Nos. 298/299.

Jazairy, Idriss (1994) *An Expanding Role for ACORD in the Face of Wider Conflict,* London: ACORD Annual Report.

Levine, I. (1995) *Sudan: In Pursuit of Humanitarian Neutrality: Aid Under Fire,* Issues in Focus Series, No. 1, Geneva: UNDHA.

Levine, Iain (1996) 'Humanitarianism and humanity', *DHA News*, No. 19 (August), Geneva.

Nolan OP, Albert (1984) *Taking Sides,* London: Catholic Institute for International Relations.

Pictet, J. (1979) *The Fundamental Principles of the Red Cross: A Commentary,* Geneva: Henri Dunant Institute.

Plattner, D. (1996) 'ICRC neutrality and neutrality in humanitarian assistance', *International Review of the Red Cross* No. 311.

Ridley, Mat (1996) *The Origins of Virtue,* London: Viking.

Aid: a mixed blessing

Mary B. Anderson

Introduction

Over the years of providing humanitarian and development assistance, international aid agencies have become increasingly concerned about avoiding paternalism and working with, rather than for, those in need. The evolving shift in aid providers' awareness and in their programming approaches is captured in the serial re-naming, over the past decade and a half, of the people for whom aid is intended, beginning with 'victims' then 'recipients' then 'beneficiaries' then 'counterparts' and now 'participants' or, sometimes, 'clients'. Increasingly, NGOs 'partner' with local agencies (and donors require it); programmes are designed to 'build'[1] local capacity; and community 'participation' is encouraged (or, at least, talked about) in all phases of aid delivery, from planning through to evaluation.

Nonetheless, in spite of efforts to put those who receive aid at the centre of aid programming, recipients' reactions are mixed.

Mixed messages from aid recipients[2]

A crisis occurs and the television cameras focus on:

- Smiling children in a refugee camp in Kenya jostling, laughing, and joking as they press for handouts – or a stricken Kosovar mother for whom reaching the international aid agency across the border is a matter of life or death for her injured baby.

- A Turkish earthquake survivor thanking the international rescue team for freeing him from the rubble of his former home – to wailing women in Macedonia demanding more aid, crying *'There is not enough; the food is insufficient; the shelter is overcrowded; we need more or our children will die.'*

- A professor in Bosnia-Herzegovina citing statistics of his country's poverty and need and instructing the international community about its obligation to correct these conditions – to a Sierra Leonean who says, '*You save my life today but for what tomorrow? Isn't a dignified death preferable to continued life dependent on the uncertain generosity of the international community?*'

- The flood survivor in Bangladesh recounting the two crises experienced by his village, '*the first, a flood that washed away our homes; the second, international aid that turned us all into beggars*' – to the village food committee in Southern Sudan telling an international NGO to stop food distributions because '*though we need food, if we receive it, our village will be raided by militias and then we will have even less food and be even more insecure.*'

- The women in a Northeast Thailand village shrugging to express their frustration that '*... the aid agency keeps insisting we plan activities by consensus, but we're too busy for endless meetings that they call "community participation"*' – to the Guatemalan refugees in Mexico, demanding establishment of refugee committees to plan all camp activities.

Such 'voices' of aid recipients convey a complicated and mixed message to the international community of aid donors. Some demand 'more' while others say 'no more'. Some want greater involvement in the decisions and planning of assistance; others want only to get the funds or the goods and go on with their lives. Some focus on a history of inequality that obligates the international community to an active role in overcoming poverty; others believe that international assistance is always tainted by less-than-honourable motives for external control. Reactions range from heartfelt appreciation to extreme suspicion; from an attempt to get more of it to contempt for donors' wealth; from disgust at outsider control to adoption of insider control; from acceptance of outsider expertise to rejection of dependence on the delivery of aid.

How does one understand such mixed messages? How can we – the 'outsider' aid community – attend to the concerns and demands of those who receive aid, and respond thoughtfully when they don't agree with each other?

Furthermore, how should we interpret the fact that, in spite of the cacophony of difference, there is a common thread of unease or dissatisfaction among many of the comments, including even some of those who express appreciation for aid? Why is it that something *feels* wrong to many of the intended beneficiaries of aid? What can we do about this?

The issues underlying this unease do not appear solvable through improved aid techniques, better aid goods, or greater logistical efficiency. That is, they cannot be addressed through the 'stuff' of aid alone. Rather, these issues are essentially relational in nature and, thus, require a revisiting of the difficult inequality that exists, inevitably, between international givers and receivers.

Inevitable inequality

The relationship between international donor communities and the aid-providing NGOs on the one hand, and the people who, because of crises, find themselves unable to sustain or improve their lives without outside help on the other is by its nature unequal in three important dimensions.[3] First, there is an essential inequality in power that derives from the ability of one side to give because it enjoys a surplus of goods and abilities, while the other side is in need. Second, there is inequality of optionality, arising from the fact that one side can choose whether or not to give, while the other side has little or no choice about accepting aid if they are to survive. Third, inequality arises from the fact that the giving side of the relationship is primarily accountable to communities and powers outside the crisis and only secondarily, if at all, to insiders, the people who receive aid.

There is no way within the systems and structures of international aid that these three inequalities can be overcome. They are inevitable so long as some peoples are able to give while others must receive. However, the tensions inherent in the giving and receiving of aid do not have to be antagonistic and destructive. Recognising their inevitability, we may perhaps develop a process by which these tensions become dynamic and creative.

Creative tensions

What might such a process entail? Though they do not represent a full solution, I suggest here four areas for consideration and action that acknowledge tensions between giver and receiver as inevitable and accept and incorporate them to achieve healthier, more productive outcomes from aid.

Identification of areas of innate equality and inequality

A first step for addressing the giver/receiver tension is for aid donors and recipients both to reaffirm their essential human equality on the one hand, and to acknowledge openly the innate inequality in their circumstances on the other. Fundamental humanitarianism is based, in large part, on the belief that all humans, as humans, have a right to and deserve help when they face difficult circumstances. Underlying this belief is the basic tenet that, as human beings, we are bound to each other in reciprocal valuation of individual dignity and worthiness. That is, we humans are fundamentally equal to each other, at least in principle.

In fact, however, we are deeply unequal by circumstance. To pretend otherwise, or even to try to create protocols and aid structures that attempt to approximate circumstantial equality, may actually undermine the dignity, worthiness, and humanness of both giver and receiver.

When funds and goods flow in one direction and decisions about how much, when, and where such flows occur are lodged outside the community of recipients, no number of 'consultations', participatory meetings, or partnership arrangements can change these facts. Perhaps a more honest and, strange as it may sound, humble acknowledgement on the part of the donor side of the relationship of their good luck[4] in being well-off could provide a better basis for interaction with recipients (who certainly know this anyway). If we manufacture aid structures to obscure this reality or to establish a pretence of equality, a degree of honesty is lost, undermining mutual respect, genuine sympathy, the dignity of life whether poor or rich – all values which might form a healthier basis for the enterprises of aid giving and receiving.

Acceptance of and clarity about the division of labour

Second, givers and receivers of aid should accept the importance of (and define) an appropriate division of labour in their functions. Who knows most about what? Who is better prepared to take which actions? Who is capable of, or responsible for, which decisions?

This step must be based on local realities rather than idealised preconceptions or hopes. It is, of course, always true that people within a society in crisis know their society better than any outsider. However, this does not mean that insiders should assume any or all of the responsibilities for aid delivery in all situations. A valid division of labour incorporates an assessment of who has what to offer as inputs (who has what knowledge or other competence) and an assessment of likely outcomes from the interactive process (what combination will achieve the goals most effectively?).

Sometimes local knowledge (a superior input) can involve also local prejudice (distorting outcomes). For example, experience in conflict settings shows that, very often, local individuals and institutions are embroiled in the inter-group divisions that define the conflict and, thus, not likely to apportion aid impartially or fairly. Sometimes this is a result of their preferred alliances; sometimes the conscientious commitment of local people to serve all sides is subverted by the pressures applied on them by colleagues, family members, militias. In either case, it may be preferable for outsiders to assume responsibility for allocating aid.

Alternatively, in other aid settings, local structures may exist for wise and sensitive decisions about how to allocate limited aid. There may be existing systems for physically distributing aid goods or for identifying when aid is no longer needed. Where this is the case, the assumption of these responsibilities by outside aid givers only undermines existing local capacity (possibly weakening it) and wastes aid resources on the creation of unnecessary parallel systems.

A well-thought-through division of labour would, similarly, acknowledge that in virtually all international aid situations, external donors know better than local recipients the dangers of too much aid, too long. Broad experience of providing aid has educated donors and international NGOs about the dangers and downsides of aid. First-time aid recipients do not know these potential costs. A healthy division of labour between giver and receiver should acknowledge these differences in 'aid expertise'. Clarity about roles can be a vehicle for acknowledging capacities that exist within recipient communities and, thus, affirming the dignity and worthiness of recipients' humanness. It also can provide the mechanism for clarifying the genuine differences in circumstances that, unacknowledged, can lead to distrust and resentment between givers and receivers.

Defining the goal of aid as 'none needed'

Third, a re-shaping of the relationship between givers and receivers could be furthered by agreement that the sole purpose of aid is to enable people not to need it. This should be the goal of both humanitarian and development assistance, even though in both dimensions need is shaped to a greater or lesser extent by events outside the control of aid.

A corollary to this is the further acknowledgement that long-term aid relationships are often unnecessary and damaging. Short-term aid can, under many circumstances, both be effective in tiding people over a crisis and have a positive developmental impact in that it does not impede recipients' resumption of full responsibility for their own survival and welfare.

It is important, here, to distinguish between a long-term commitment of aid providers to aid recipients (entailing a full sense of continued caring for people's welfare) and long-term aid programmes. A firm commitment to long-term caring may best be realised through short-term inputs of external material assistance coupled with sustained engagement in promoting the changes in the world order that allow extreme poverty and wealth to co-exist. Not all (or even most) 'root causes' of poverty and suffering are located in the place where poverty and suffering occur.

Managing anguish and joy simultaneously

Finally, our handling of the tensions inherent in the donor–recipient relationship might be improved through more skilful and thoughtful management of the contradictions encountered daily in aid work – namely, the contradictions between the horror and anguish of suffering which prompts aid, and the importance of affirming the joy and pleasures of life if aid is to be worthwhile. In the process of helping and being helped, it is easy to focus on pain and loss. However, if life is to be preferred over death (that is, if saving lives through humanitarian assistance or helping improve the chances of sustained lives through development aid is worthwhile), then life should be, daily, enjoyed.

Philosophers and theologians have told us that suffering is not, in itself, demeaning and demoralising. However, responses to suffering can make it so. Somehow, among aid workers, there is a widely accepted sense that a frenetic pace of exhausted response is the right way to do emergency aid or, equally, that long-term, slow-and-tedious plodding is required in development aid. But suffering can be demeaned by harried efficiency or working tedium just as much as by pity or denial.

In all societies and across all societal differences, genuine friendships are possible. Everywhere there are people who are fascinating, engaging, loving, and fun. There must be some other step we can take as aid providers and aid recipients to maintain inward composure in the face of grim realities so that we allow time for talk, exchange of family lore, sitting together to rest and reflect, and doing 'recreational' things together. Mutual enjoyment should not be confined to enclaves of aid givers but must also be sought among recipients. Aid providers may be able to redress some of the innate imbalance in their relationships with recipients if they find ways to be empathetic with the latter's sad experiences and, simultaneously, affirm that life is to be enjoyed.

Our Sierra Leonean friend reminds us of this when he asks his difficult question: '*You save my life today, but for what tomorrow?*' To his query I would only add: if life is worth saving today, then it should also be liveable, worth living, today (as well as tomorrow). The processes of providing and receiving international assistance need to be re-humanised by enjoyment.

The mixed messages so honestly conveyed by the multiple and varied recipients of aid carry one clear and common text. Another great challenge – perhaps the most important of all for aid providers and recipients – is to accept both our innate human equality and our circumstantial inequality and, in the face of both, to establish relationships of mutual respect and contemporaneous enjoyment of each other. The mixed messages remind us that humanitarian and development assistance are not only about timely deliveries of needed goods (critical as these are). International aid is, fundamentally, about relationships.

Notes

1   Personally, I avoid the phrase 'capacity building' because it risks the same dangers found in earlier 'needs assessments'. That is, too often outsiders define which capacities are missing in a society and, hence, which ones they are going to 'build'. Far preferable, and emphasised years ago by my colleague, Peter Woodrow, and me is the idea of recognising the capacities that *exist* in societies and, as outsiders, supporting and building *on* these rather than assuming a capacity deficit that we, as aid providers, need to fill (Anderson and Woodrow 1989). Of course, there are other writers and thinkers (for instance, Eade 1997) who also use the idea of building capacities to refer to efforts to be responsive to local people who, specifically, request technical or other outsider help.

2   Each quotation here is based on comments made to me directly or to colleagues who have reported them to me. Before I wrote this paper, I

reviewed with several other aid workers their impressions about how recipients feel about aid. Interestingly, among us, we could think of few instances in which we had heard unambiguous praise of aid from any recipient. This is not, of course, a scientific sampling of opinions, but it seems to support my sense that messages from recipients are, at best, mixed.

3 I thank my colleague Hizkias Assefa for helping me to think through these ideas of inequality between outsiders and insiders, in a series of personal conversations.

4 The word I really want to use here is 'grace' which, I learned long ago in my Presbyterian upbringing, means 'unmerited favour'!

References

Anderson, M.B. and P.J. Woodrow (1989, new edn. 1998) *Rising from the Ashes: Development Strategies in Times of Disaster,* Boulder, CO: Lynne Rienner.

Eade, D. (1997) *Capacity Building: An Approach to People-centred Development,* Oxford: Oxfam GB.

Women and war: protection through empowerment in El Salvador[1]

Martha Thompson and Deborah Eade

The portrayal of war

The human cost of war is something with which all readers of this volume are familiar, albeit vicariously. The international media bring the images of war right into our own homes. The protagonists in these representations are almost exclusively male – soldiers, diplomats, politicians. By contrast, women are assigned one of two supporting roles: either the helpless victim caught in the crossfire, or the pillar of strength in adversity. The men do the talking and strategizing; the women suffer and struggle in the background. The implicit message of this narrative is clear. When conflict breaks out, men prosecute war to defend the homeland, while women bind the social wounds and keep the home fires burning. The statistics are well known, and may no longer have the power to shock:

> *contemporary wars are fought out not on demarcated battlefields, but in the towns, villages, and homes of ordinary people. The fact that 90 per cent of today's war casualties are civilians, and the fact that four out of five refugees and displaced persons are women and children ... are so often quoted that we hardly stop to think about what they mean.*
> (Eade 1996:5)

To these, we can add that one-fifth of humanity survives on less than a dollar a day, and that two-thirds of the world's poorest people are women, as are two-thirds of adults who cannot read and write. Women perform most of the unremunerated work in the 'hidden economy', and are disproportionately represented among the world's 'working poor', with lower average earnings than men in every country in the world, significantly so in some. It goes without saying, then, that most of those who become homeless, stateless, and penniless as a result of armed conflict are women (Eade 2001).

First published in *Social Development Issues* 24(3): 50–8 in 2002

Recent years have witnessed renewed interest in the protection of civilians in war, which parallels increasing efforts to contain war-affected populations and prevent them from crossing borders. International humanitarian law (IHL) does, however, afford protection to internally displaced people who are in 'refugee-like situations', and although there is no agency with explicit responsibility for such people, both UNHCR (United Nations High Commissioner for Refugees) and ICRC (the International Committee of the Red Cross) have played that role. Indeed, ICRC has played a leading role in both the discussion and the conceptualization of protection, which now encompasses a variety of activities formerly undertaken by human rights bodies, solidarity organizations, UN specialized agencies, humanitarian aid workers, and the ICRC itself.

In its 2001 publication (ICRC 2001), the ICRC defines the three areas of activities to strengthen protection for displaced persons:

1 **Responsive actions:** any activity that puts a stop to a specific pattern of abuse and/or alleviates its immediate effects including: information, pressuring, or dialoguing with authorities, and pursuing legal assistance.

2 **Remedial actions:** any action that restores people's dignity and ensures adequate living conditions through reparation, restitution, and rehabilitation including: pressuring authorities by public disclosure, helping bring about repatriation and resettlement, and providing direct services by being present.

3 **Environment-building actions:** any action that fosters an environment conducive to respect for the rights of individuals in accordance with the relevant bodies of law in their broadest sense. This includes any activity aimed at implementation of international law, any activity that documents human rights abuses, and humanitarian activity given that its ultimate goal is to protect people.

Frequently, these protection activities are ascribed to outside actors not to the affected population itself. However, the experiences of El Salvador in the 1980s and 1990s showed that displaced people themselves developed a whole strategy for protection based on these three types of activities long before they were articulated in the above form. Reviewing this experience can provide a new perspective, and take forward current thinking on protection issues by bringing two unique elements to the debate. First, the measures that most increased protection for civilians during the brutal 11-year civil war were developed by organized communities of civilians displaced by the conflict, whether on their own or through their relationship with international NGOs and solidarity organizations. The primary actors therefore moved from being 'war victims' to building strategies for their own protection. Second, and what we shall focus on in this chapter, is that it was Salvadoran *campesinas* (peasant women) who played a major role in building and developing these 'protection capacities' for themselves and their communities (see Eade 1991).

Nobody would suggest that standard 'protection recipes' can be replicated across vastly different cultural and political realities. But we do believe that the main ingredients of the Salvadoran experience are relevant to other settings. In particular, then, we shall look at how people usually characterized as victims and aid beneficiaries moved to influence their environment; what factors in the relationship between them and international agencies fostered their empowerment; and what made it possible for women to play such a key role.

It is well documented that women are particularly vulnerable to the depredations of war. [For an annotated bibliography of the contemporary literature, analytical, testimony-based, and policy-focused, see the Resources chapter in this volume.] All too often, however, this knowledge fails to inform humanitarian policy and practice. Existing inequalities and gender imbalances are characteristically heightened by war, as women continue in highly adverse circumstances to combine their domestic and other roles, often assuming those of absent husbands and sons as well. Basic supplies run short, normal services are disrupted or suspended, sources of income dry up, and displacement becomes the key to survival. Fear is omnipresent, both of the known, and of the unknown. Terror is a deliberate tactic of war, and includes the constant threat of attack as well as actual violence. The social fabric begins to unravel as trust is undermined. And yet, it has become an aid-agency truism that social disruption can sometimes create new opportunities for women, enabling them to break out of restrictive gender norms. Precisely because of this, it is worth looking more closely at what took place during the war in El Salvador.

The 1980–92 civil war in El Salvador

By 1980, El Salvador had some of the most dramatic social and economic inequalities in Latin America. The whole system was shored up by state violence and the brutal repression of dissent or any democratic reform. The 1980–92 civil war was the eighth armed uprising in 200 years that had torn apart this small agricultural country. It was a particularly cruel war for the civilian population. The government maintained a system of structural violence that targeted any organized opposition to the status quo. Human-rights groups estimate that of a population of five million, some 80,000 people, mainly non-combatants, were killed.

When this polarized situation exploded into civil war in 1980, the Frente Farabundo Martí para la Liberación Nacional (FMLN) had widespread support from economically marginalized groups, particularly those who had been influenced by liberation theology, as well as labor unions and peasant organizations. The military targeted all civilians it viewed as supporting the FMLN. In the cities the armed forces arrested, disappeared, tortured, and killed tens of thousands of people, professors, union organizers, healthworkers, slum dwellers, students, lawyers, and churchworkers. By 1984, the popular movement had been wiped off the streets and almost a generation of civil society leaders had been assassinated.

In the countryside, military led a brutal scorched-earth policy to depopulate the zones in the north and east of the country held by the FMLN. They razed homes, massacred entire communities, destroyed crops and livestock, and carried out 'carpet bombing'. By 1985 the FMLN-held zones were largely depopulated and one in five Salvadorans was displaced within the country or had sought refuge abroad. Those who sought refuge outside El Salvador at least had the possibility of applying for refugee assistance and protection, while the internally displaced were more vulnerable in terms of both security and livelihoods.

Yet by 1986, in spite of the war and major US military and humanitarian aid to 'win hearts and minds', groups of organized displaced within the country were beginning to agitate for the right to return. 'Repopulation', signifying organized community returns back into their places of origin in the conflict zone, became a new rallying cry within the popular lexicon. By 1988, the popular movement had reorganized and was protesting against the government; and the repopulation of the conflict zones was well underway. This recovery is doubly impressive because it happened in the very teeth of war, and was carried out by the same people who had been military targets. The repopulation movement was characterized by strong, decisive action by the 'victims' of war. They were the actors in this movement and collaborated with international agency workers in ways that enabled them to work for their own protection.

Significantly, women were at the fore of the two most audacious initiatives of this movement. It was a women's organization, the Co-Madres ('mothers of the disappeared'), which led the public recovery of the popular movement, and women were prominent in organizing the repopulation of the conflict zones. In fact, 80 per cent of the leaders of the National Coordination for Repopulation (CNR in its Spanish acronym), which spearheaded the repopulation movement into the conflict zones, were women under 30 years of age.

Women in pre-war El Salvador

The women who were prominent in the leadership of the repopulation movement and the many others who organized to confront the military in the conflict zones were people who had had always been at a disadvantage. *Campesino* culture was intensely patriarchal and *machismo* reigned in the household. Women were under the control of their husbands; they had little access to education, and the concept of women's rights was unknown. Gender roles were fixed – women gathered firewood and water, looked after the children, cooked for the household, cared for small animals, and supported men in the production of basic grains. Motherhood was women's major claim to dignity and respect, but that dignity was sentimentalized and devoid of economic rights or any legal claim.

Not surprisingly, rural women did not have high self-esteem. The absence of any strong role models for them (apart from wealthy men's wives, who are almost universally portrayed as uncaring and lacking in any compassion) deepened this lack of self-worth. In addition, El Salvador was a country of profound economic and social inequities buttressed by deep prejudices against poor people, casting them as ignorant, undeserving rabble. The exception to this general picture was the gradual incorporation of women as delegates of the word in the Christian Base Communities organized by priests who promoted liberation theology. This unique venue provided poor rural women with a chance to learn, to build a sense of self-worth through their religious faith, and to assume leadership positions.

Thus the women who became involved in building civilian protection had overcome major obstacles in order to play the significant roles that they did. The opportunity to act was also an opportunity to act politically. Every public civilian action in the counter-insurgency war was heavy with symbolism and the repopulation of the conflict zones was perhaps the most symbolic act of resistance of all. And it was pivotal in changing how the war was fought, because the military strategy depended on separating the civilian population from the FMLN and penning the FMLN up in the mountains. Furthermore, the low-intensity warfare practiced by the Salvadoran military relied upon state-sponsored violence and on terrorizing the civilian population. The repopulations were an open defiance of the armed forces and the measures the returnees took to defend themselves were a remarkable illustration of this civilian challenge – a challenge which *attacked* the very root of the fear through which the military exerted social control.

The development of protection strategies

By 1983 there were about 20,000 refugees in camps in Honduras and several thousand in 27 camps of internally displaced run by the Catholic church in El Salvador. These 'victims of war' had a unique opportunity to develop protection skills in an environment that was far from secure, but less dangerous than what they had been through. They learned how to develop responsive actions to build their own protection capacities. In doing so, they gradually became protagonists rather than victims. There were a number of specific reasons for their success – not least, a cohesive political project which had popular support, a concept of a new society, and growing external political pressure on the Salvadoran government. Nonetheless, there is a great deal to be learned from this about how aid agencies can interact with civilian populations.

Telling their stories

In their respective camps in Honduras and El Salvador, the refugees and displaced were able to tell the stories of what had happened to them to the steady stream of visiting journalists, human-rights workers, international delegations, and agency representatives. Since the conflict zones were 'no go areas', the best way to get information about them was to listen to these stories and hear the news from the most recent arrivals. The only witnesses of the many rural massacres were the survivors. And only in the church-run camps in El Salvador or the refugee camps over the border did those survivors feel safe to tell their story.

Women who had seen their houses destroyed, children hanged from eaves, men chopped up, and women bayoneted, felt the despair of abandonment. They felt that the military could do this to them with impunity because they were poor. Often, the women in the camps formed mothers' groups to find some comfort in this despair. They shared their stories of what they had seen – neighbors' children, wounded by gunfire, that they'd had to abandon because they couldn't carry them along with their own, their husbands killed, their children dying of disease or exposure as they fled. They gained comfort in sharing their experiences and the awful loneliness was somewhat alleviated as they felt each other's understanding and pain.

From telling stories to reclaiming human rights

From these mothers' groups came many of the testimonies that began to paint for the outside world a picture of what was happening in the war zones, accounts that belied what the official sources were saying about military operations there. For the refugees and the displaced, testimony first meant simply telling their stories. But in the process of doing so for various audiences, they began to understand that what had happened to them was important, and that it horrified people. As one man said: 'We began to learn about this thing that they call human rights, we wanted to hear more about it'. What they learned is that there were people around the world who believed that *campesinos* had human rights and who felt those rights had been violated. They learned that some people had no intention of letting the official version of events erase the atrocities, and that there was power in the victims' testimony.

The displaced and the refugees slowly began to understand that there was a legal framework of IHL law through which they could articulate their experiences as victims of military attacks. In the capital city San Salvador, Tutela Legal, the legal office of the Catholic Archdiocese, helped people recall dates and names – details that would turn a story into a legal denunciation. The women's groups were repositories of so many stories, and from these came our understanding of the war in the rural areas.

Once they grasped the idea of framing their experience in the context of human rights, a transformation process began. From feeling that, as victims, they had no rights and that no one cared about what happened to them, they moved to learning about and articulating their rights, and then to demanding that those rights be respected. Through the human-rights workers in El Salvador, the priests that ministered to them, and the aid-agency workers in the camps, the refugees learned about the 1997 Second Protocol of the 1949 Geneva Conventions, which delineates the rights of civilians in situations of armed conflict.

Becoming human-rights reporters

Initially, it was international workers and visiting delegations that would record the stories and translate the testimonies into denunciations of human-rights violations. Later, agencies and human-rights workers trained the refugees to take down the details needed in human-rights reporting. When people returned to the conflict zones, they were already aware that reporting human-rights violations was a way of enhancing their protection. If the military captured someone, the community leaders would send a delegation to report it to Tutela Legal, the Salvadoran Human Rights Commission, and/or America's Watch Human Rights office. This became increasingly dangerous, however, because the offices were under surveillance and the delegations were not too hard to identify.

In order to minimize the risks, the returnees began to produce written reports for the human-rights offices. At first, men seemed the obvious choice to make the long trip past the military checkpoints to take these reports to the capital. Soon, however, communities realized that they could manipulate the cultural gender stereotypes to their advantage. The military viewed women as less important and less intelligent then men and so were less likely to stop and search them. So women were increasingly chosen to carry the information, folding the report up into a tiny triangle and braiding it into their hair. With a basket of fruit balanced on her head, the courier would go through the checkpoint, humbly asking permission to go and sell her wares. Once through, she would take the bus and get the report through to the human-rights office.

Over the years, people in the conflict zones delegated community members to be human-rights workers. These individuals would visit people who had suffered military attacks and record the incident, analyze the overall situation, and later work with internationals from NGOs or church organizations based in the area to send information out by computer. Young women were often chosen for this task because they were literate, had fewer household responsibilities, and could move around more easily because the soldiers took them less seriously. This is not to say they were not vulnerable to rape or abuse if soldiers caught them alone on the road. But women found that adopting the guise of a simple *campesina* often enabled them to escape notice and blend into crowds without raising the soldiers' attention.

Organization

The refugees and the internally displaced learned a great deal about community organization during their time in the refugee camps. The lack of traditional authority figures coupled with NGO encouragement enabled them to take on new responsibilities. The preponderance of women in the camps meant they had to take on new roles. In Honduras, the refugees formed self-governing structures with refugees in charge of health, education, day-care, agriculture, sanitation, construction, and production workshops. These structures worked closely with the NGOs in the camps, allowing the refugees to develop leadership and organizational skills in a relatively protected environment. In addition, the constant pressure from the Salvadoran military together with UNHCR's presence gave real impetus to the refugees' will to defend themselves. They faced real adversity but also had recourse to an international organization whose role was to protect them, a combination that helped them develop a strong communal organization against military harassment based on a human-rights discourse. This in turn led to highly organized communities with the real capacity to carry out their own political project.

In Honduras, perhaps the most dramatic change in women's roles took place as part of the social organization of the camps. Women increasingly took on roles of leadership, gaining valuable experience, providing role models, and challenging old stereotypes. When the camps were first established there were no women section leaders, but by the time the refugees returned, women held many positions of leadership, right up to highest level. The collectivization of domestic tasks and the provision of water and firewood were what made this transformation possible (Cagan and Cagan 1991).

In the camps for the displaced in El Salvador, women got a degree of training and opportunities to take on new responsibilities and some leadership positions. These camps were overcrowded and afforded little freedom of movement. But the fact that food and water as well as childcare were provided generally freed women up for literacy classes, training, meetings etc. In 1984, the church in El Salvador decided that the overcrowded camps were inadequate and proposed incorporating the displaced in existing co-operatives and on to lands that it had purchased. Four hundred people from the various camps met and formed their own organization, the Christian Committee of the Displaced (CRIPDES). Over the next two years CRIPDES represented the displaced, negotiated with the church, and helped organize people in their new sites (Edwards and Siebentritt 1991).

When the displaced were relocated to co-operatives, the women lost ground. The co-operatives were run along traditional gender lines, and women's time became largely taken up with individual household duties. When the displaced set up their own communities, there was more funding, more collective practices were instituted, and women tended to fare better.

Despite these setbacks, CRIPDES was increasingly led by single young women without children. Many of them had spent time in the camps and had experienced military aggression firsthand, and most came from families with a history of organizing. As CRIPDES moved into the dispersed communities in the central and southern regions of El Salvador, these young women traveled by bus around the country organizing, exhorting, and building a movement.

Audacity

The strongest leaders among the young women who had cut their political teeth in CRIPDES went on to play a prominent role in the next stage of the struggle. In 1986, when few of the male labor-union or *campesino* leaders were taking prominent public positions, these young women led one of the most audacious movements of the war – the repopulation, or return to their places of origin.

This audacity was a creative response to the desperate situation of the displaced. In December 1985 and January 1986, the armed forces launched Operation Phoenix and Operation Chávez Carreno, offensives aimed at forcibly displacing civilians from war zones in four provinces. As part of this campaign, the military took over 1500 civilians off the Guazapa volcano, only 19 miles north of San Salvador. Times had changed: international pressure about the massive human-rights violations had by then produced some limited effect. The government felt that there was too much international attention focused on El Salvador to allow these civilians to be killed. So they were turned over to ICRC and many ended up in the church camps. Here they met others who had learned about framing a human-rights discourse, agency resources, and the potential and protection of church support. It proved a combustible combination. In May 1986, CRIPDES called a national conference to discuss the problems of the displaced, in particular the lack of land for their relocation and concluded that the only durable solution was return to their places of origin. They formed the CNR to facilitate a movement of organized returns to the conflict zones, in spite of the war (Thompson 1996, 1997).

There were several lessons to be gleaned from these experiences, and the refugees and displaced learned them all. They saw that reporting their testimonies had helped build a body of legitimate information about the massive violations of human rights during the war. They saw that this information could be used to build a case against the government, and that it was a key factor in increasing and maintaining the pressure that had forced the government to realize that the military could no longer act with such blanket impunity. The Guazapa incident was the first time that the government recognized it could not afford a massacre and decided instead forcibly to remove civilians from a conflict area. The major lesson drawn from this was that the rules of survival in a conflict zone might have changed for the better.

Building legitimacy for a political project

Initially neither the military nor the government took the call for repopulation seriously, Perhaps the fact that the CNR was largely led by young women made them easier to dismiss, as they are not perceived as powerful actors in a wartime situation. But these young women had done their homework. Their essential building block for creating a safer environment was to build legitimacy for the return to the conflict zones. CNR leaders insisted that the repopulation be high-profile, collective, organized events – and that these be recognized as civilian communities whose residents had the right to live in their place of origin, free from attack, detention, or removal (Edwards and Siebentritt 1991). As the repopulations gained momentum, the returnees couched their demands for return, protection, and assistance in the framework of the Second Protocol to which El Salvador was a signatory. Together with agency workers and human-rights organizations, they hammered out the main tenets of their rights as returnees (Thompson 1995:129):

- a right to be in their places of origin, and carry out daily life. This included the right not to be bombed or militarily harassed.

- a right to access to the supplies and materials they needed to carry out their daily lives (therefore the military checkpoints were not acceptable).

- a right to humanitarian aid from NGOs and international agencies, who therefore had right of access.

The refugees in Honduras had no intention of returning only to become internal refugees (Weiss-Fagan and Yudelman 2001). They used the above arguments in 1987, 1988, and 1989 in order to justify their collective repatriations to the conflict zones. If the victims of war can claim legitimacy under international law in establishing human-rights benchmarks against which any violations can be measured, they can thereby enlist allies to advocate for them. The repopulated communities did exactly this. The Catholic, Episcopal, and Lutheran churches in El Salvador provided funds and ministry to them in the conflict zones. National NGOs and the national popular movement also supported the repopulations with their presence, solidarity, and project assistance. Because the repopulations were based on an IHL discourse, these outside groups could legitimately claim that they had a mandate to work with them. Ten international agencies in El Salvador developed their work on this basis. Founded on a relationship of mutual trust and respect, the agencies and the communities developed complementary roles in constructing protection. The agencies provided funding, presence, and projects, but any advocacy work was done in conjunction with the communities. They employed a person to do investigation and reporting on violations of human rights and problems with humanitarian work in the repopulations (Thompson 1997). That information along with analysis and recommended action was sent on a regular basis to a network of agency and human-rights organizations in North America and Europe.

Building visibility

The major massacres had taken place hidden away from international eyes and the cameras and notebooks of the press. However, returnees were clear that they had to build a safer environment if they were going to return to the conflict zones while the war was still on. They had to reduce the military's sense of impunity to kill and torture people in these areas. Once they established their legitimate right to return, they had to increase the political cost of any military attacks against returnees. That meant raising the visibility of the communities.

The first CNR caravan of buses that carried the displaced back to Chalatenango in July 1986 arrived at the army checkpoints accompanied by a lively medley of journalists, church leaders, humanitarian NGOs, and solidarity delegations. Bewildered by this bold move, the military actually let them past, up the dirt roads into the weed-grown ghost town of San José de Las Flores. All the repopulations followed suit with highly visible caravans accompanying people back to their homes, making it very clear that these communities were in the public eye. The church and the humanitarian agencies demonstrated that they intended to have access to them, and internationals linked to the agencies were placed in each community to establish a visible international presence. The communities themselves conducted a program of communication outreach, cultivating relationships with journalists, embassy representatives, and human-rights groups. Meanwhile, the agencies sought official funding, bringing in diplomatic representatives when the communities were attacked or projects destroyed.

The communities were also helped to send their human-rights reports out to an international rapid-response network of individuals who had agreed to do advocacy on their behalf. These individuals would send telegrams, faxes, e-mails, or letters to the President, the head of the military, and the military barracks responsible for those specific violations – and this increased visibility helped the protection effort in very tangible ways. A community leader from Morazán recalls:

'After I was in my cell for two days, they took me to see the colonel. He was very angry, throwing some papers at me, "Who do you know in the USA?" he was shouting. "How is it that all these people know you are captured? They are sending these faxes here." He was very angry at me, but after four days he let me go; he said that they were making too much fuss.'
(Thompson 1997:53)

Collective action for access

By 1990, there were 94 repopulated communities in northern Morazán and northern Chalatenango. Access was the key factor for their survival. The communities needed to get materials and supplies past the military checkpoints and they needed to ensure that outsiders could visit them in order to guarantee their visibility.

An early struggle on the issue of access was won by women in Morazán (Thompson 1996:329). The church had sent two trucks of dried milk for children in the war zone but the military wouldn't let the trucks out of the provincial capital, San Francisco Gotera. Several mothers' associations got together and sent a delegation on five separate occasions to make the seven-hour trek down to the military barracks to request the milk. Unexpectedly, after the fifth visit, the colonel gave in and let the trucks through. The women claimed their legitimacy as mothers and quietly insisted on their right as mothers to feed their children, again choosing to use a cultural gender stereotype to their advantage.

Women were extremely effective in persuading soldiers to grant access and were chosen to intercede for that reason. Men went along but it was often the women who did the talking. Esperanza, a leader from one of the Chalatenango communities, would accompany trucks of supplies up to the conflict zones and argue them through the checkpoints well into her eighth month of pregnancy.

Women also used a gender stereotype to confront military incursions into the communities. Women and children would quickly surround the soldiers, and the women would talk to them as mothers and grandmothers: 'How can you take action against us, we could be your mother or your grandmother. You are peasants like us, so why do you try and hurt us? Would you do this to your sister, your mother?' Salvadoran custom has it that it is unmanly to strike a woman with a child in her arms. In some of the testimonies of the massacres, the survivors would repeat unbelievingly that 'they would even shoot women with children in their arms', an unusual spin on Susan McKay's 'womenandchildren' nexus (cited in Karam 2001). Some recounted that the military would yell at the women to put the children down so they could shoot them. This image of a mother with a child in her arms is a powerful one in El Salvador and the women in the repopulations would constantly use it to plead with the soldiers, to ask that they leave them alone, to rebuke them for harming community members. They chose the one powerful image of women in their society to protect themselves and their communities.

What enabled women to play such a major role?

Almost all of the women who played leadership roles in the repopulation movement had spent some time in the refugee camps in Honduras. This experience gave them tools to address some of the triple obstacles they faced as poor peasant women.

- As we have seen, the mothers formed mutual support groups where they could share their stories, take comfort from each other, and reflect on what had happened to them in terms of justice and rights. This broke down tendencies to isolation and despair. When delegations started coming to hear their testimonies, the women learned that their experiences were important, and this in turn began a process of reaffirming their self-worth.

- In the camps, particularly in Honduras, women had the means and opportunity to develop leadership and acquire new skills, including literacy. They were able to take advantage of the training and education offered because the domestic burden was reduced by simple technology and collectivization. Firewood and water were provided, and they organized communal childcare. Health and education were free. In one refugee camp, communal kitchens provided food for everyone. Although the situation to which they returned provided less practical support for women, they still had childcare, water close by, community corn mills, food for the vulnerable population, and health and education facilities. These factors reduced some of the class obstacles that had always kept women back. In the camps, women outnumbered men, because women and children had been sent to the camps for their protection. But this gender imbalance created the space and opportunity for women to change their conventional gender roles, as the absence of traditional authority figures removed some of the cultural constraints on their active participation in public life. Once women took on more responsibilities and more leadership roles, they became new role models for other women.

- The young women who led the CNR drew a great deal of strength from each other and their similar status as single childless women who nonetheless had a strong community. They were able to discuss the merits of having children, getting married, etc. with each other and figure out what would be best for them. These women were extraordinary role models for other young women who saw them up on the platforms of rallies, rebuking the military, being defiant. Their lack of family responsibilities and their political commitment gave them both freedom and a social structure. Although most of them were held in military detention at one time or another, and some were tortured and raped, they continued their work.

- Women took strength from collective action and from playing an active part in a wider political project. This community strength was palpable. It enabled women to shake off the image of victim while at the same time their sense of belonging helped to give sense and meaning to their suffering. Women saw that by working together to confront the armed forces, they actually made advances. This was not a linear journey. Sometimes they were successful and sometimes the soldiers ended up achieving what they set out to do, capturing someone or refusing to let goods through the checkpoints. They did not win all the time, but enough to see progress, and they drew strength from each victory.

- Women were shrewd in exploiting the cultural prejudice that women were not as intelligent as men and so were not watched so closely as men were.

- They were able to build on and also exploit the only source of dignity poor women had in El Salvador, motherhood. They used it to protect themselves, justify their defiant actions, and pressure young soldiers.

- As people strengthened their capacity to protect themselves, they also made it more possible for the wider community to participate in creating that protection.

Conventional understandings of conflict pay rather scant attention to grassroots political agency, to the capacity of ordinary people to act for the common good in pursuit of what they consider to be a just society. We hear much more about civilians as innocent and helpless victims, or even as cynical and manipulative aid-grabbers, than we do about their acts of courage, their capacity to bring about and respond to positive change, or their own ideas about how to build a new society. To quote Jenny Pearce

> ... a real appreciation of how gender relations affect the ability of poor
> and powerless women to play their full role in the post-conflict situation
> (as opposed to a knowledge of the discourse) is essential. In my experience,
> few of the professional men involved in external assistance programmes ...
> have that real appreciation ...
> (Pearce 1998:85)

Victims of society, or social actors? A concluding reflection

Women frequently *are* victims of violence, of gender-inequitable public policies, and of discrimination. To take but one example, one in two women in the world have experienced some form of male violence, usually in the home. This so-called 'domestic' or 'culturally condoned' violence remains largely invisible: too mundane, too shameful, or too frightening for the survivors to talk about in public; and too private or intimate for outsiders to get involved (Pickup 2001). But to regard women simply as victims of patriarchal social forces, never able to challenge and overcome them, would be to wrong them – us – further: there is a critical difference between *experiencing* injustice, and being *defined by* one's victimhood.

The use of rape as an instrument of war seeks to undermine the victim's personal and social identity and the integrity of her person, by torturing and humiliating her. The practice of 'political disappearance', used extensively throughout Latin America, seeks to terrify and paralyze the victims' families, their communities, and everyone known to them. Both mechanisms are immensely effective in sowing terror and a sense of moral chaos. But, what is truly remarkable is the way in which – as we have shown – the intended victims can together grow through such brutality, and find the strength to denounce and fight against it. That Pinochet came as close as he did to facing trial for atrocities committed under his dictatorship, for instance, owes more to the resolve and courage of human-rights groups and families of the disappeared than it does to international law. That rape is now formally recognized as a crime of gender in indictments of suspected war criminals owes more to the collective bravery of women in speaking out than it does to the judicial system. Having once broken the silence, survivors of rape may well move on to question the prevalence of male violence against women *outside* the context of war, and so to challenge gender–power relations within their own societies. Similarly, having once lost their fear, Salvadoran *campesinos* were able to challenge the structural violence that had oppressed them for generations, and to develop their own protection capacities. The real question, in both cases, is whether the shift from victim to social actor will also give women the capacity to take their new-found confidence from the conflict to the development agenda, and whether international agencies are ready to help them to do so.

Notes

1   Disclaimer: this paper is based on the authors' extensive experience in Central America and has been shaped by their collaboration with agency colleagues and by their own involvement in local organizations throughout the region. The views and interpretations expressed are, however, those of the authors alone and should not be attributed to any agency for which they have worked.

This article was commissioned for a special issue of the journal *Social Development Issues* on Women in Conflict in Crisis: New Issues in an Insecure World (*Social Development Issues* 24(3): 50–8, 2002). We are grateful to the editors, Mary Ellen Kondrat, María Juliá, and Cathy Rakowski, and to the Inter-University Consortium for International Social Development, for allowing us to reproduce this article.

References

Cagan, Beth and Steve Cagan (1991) *This Promised Land, El Salvador*, New Brunswick, NJ and London: Rutgers University Press.

Eade, Deborah (ed.) (1996) Editor's preface to *Development in States of War*, Oxford: Oxfam GB.

Eade, Deborah (1997) *Capacity Building: An Approach to People-centred Development*, Oxford: Oxfam GB.

Eade, Deborah (2001) 'Mujeres y Conflictos Armados', *Papeles de Cuestiones Internacionales*, Número 73, Invierno:15–22.

Edwards, Beatrice and Gretta Tovar Siebentritt (1991) *Places of Origin*, Boulder, CO and London: Lynne Rienner Publishers.

ICRC (2001) *Strengthening Protection in War: A Search for Professional Standards*, Geneva: ICRC.

Karam, Azza (2001) 'Women in war and peace-building: the roads traversed, the challenges ahead', *International Feminist Journal of Politics* 3(1): 2–25.

Pearce, Jenny (1998) 'Sustainable peace-building in the South: experiences from Latin America', in Deborah Eade (ed.) *From Conflict to Peace in a Changing World: Social Reconstruction in Times of Transition*, Oxford: Oxfam GB.

Pickup, Francine, with Suzanne Williams and Caroline Sweetman (2001) *Ending Violence Against Women: A Challenge for Development and Humanitarian Work*, Oxford: Oxfam GB.

Thompson, Martha (1995) 'Repopulated communities in El Salvador', in Minor Sinclair (ed.) *New Politics of Survival: Grassroots Movements in Central America*, New York, NY: Monthly Review Press.

Thompson, Martha (1996) 'Empowerment and survival: humanitarian work in civil conflict (part 1)', *Development in Practice* 6(4): 324–33.

Thompson, Martha (1997) 'Empowerment and survival: humanitarian work in civil conflict (part 2)', *Development in Practice* 7(1): 50–8.

Thompson, Martha (1999) 'Gender in times of war', in Fenella Porter, Ines Smyth, and Caroline Sweetman (eds.) *Gender Works: Oxfam Experience in Policy and Practice*, Oxford: Oxfam GB.

Weiss-Fagan, Patricia and Sally Yudelman (2001) 'El Salvador and Guatemala: refugee camp and repatriation experiences', in Krishna Kumar (ed.) *Women and Civil War*, Boulder, CO and London: Lynne Rienner: 79–95.

Sustainable peace building in the South: experiences from Latin America

Jenny Pearce

Introduction: contextualising conflict

The 'peace industry' has grown enormously in the wake of the Cold War. The UN system, government and non-government aid programmes, and new academic research have focused their attentions on the complex and very violent internal wars which seem to have characterised the immediate post-Cold War era. The only area of overseas aid which has grown in recent years is that directed at disaster relief and peacekeeping. According to the World Debt Tables 1996, aid levels in 1995 were 13 per cent lower than those recorded in 1991. Aid for disaster relief and peacekeeping, however, had more than doubled from US$2.5bn in 1990 to US$6bn 1994–5 (Ridell 1996).

A new terminology has emerged. The UN Research Institute for Social Development (UNRISD) has focused its attentions on 'war-torn societies'; the United Nations has created a distinct group of conflicts, which it calls 'complex political emergencies'.[1] A new range of issues has come to preoccupy official and non-government donor agencies, such as the relationship of relief to development; peace making and peace building; the role of the military in humanitarian work; post-war reconstruction; and conflict prevention.

Attempts to generate universally applicable formulas collapse, however, when confronted by the huge range and complexity of the actual situations involved. 'Conflict' is not a very useful analytical category at all. Nor is it unequivocally negative: one of the conflicts examined in this paper was considered positive by a wide spectrum of international opinion and humanitarian agencies.

Much of the present concern with complex internal conflicts is in fact limited to certain recent and exceptionally violent conflicts that have attracted considerable media attention, notably former Yugoslavia,

 First published in *Development in Practice* 7(4): 438–55 in 1997

Central Africa, West Africa, and the Horn of Africa. Political imperatives and resource constraints place these major 'fires' at the top of the conflict-intervention agenda. The media tend to focus on these, making them real to millions of households, and in turn forcing politicians to respond somehow.[2] One could almost say that, whether media-determined or not, there is a threshold of what is not politically acceptable at the international or national level, and crossing it will provoke a response. Public and élite opinion tolerates 25,000 violent deaths in Colombia in 1995, but not the 800,000 that took place in Rwanda in 1994. Long-term conflicts with high accumulative death tolls (such as Guatemala, where between 1961 and 1997 an estimated 150,000, mostly poor indigenous peasants, were killed and some 45,000 'disappeared') attract much less attention than the massacre of thousands in a short period of time. An analogy might be the identification of the AIDS virus. The high loss of life resulting from the virus is appalling, but many more millions in the South have died and continue to die through avoidable illnesses such as diarrhoea, TB, and measles.

There is both a terrible reality to, and understandable preoccupation with, complex contemporary conflicts. At the same time, the focus on these distorts the real world, its many forms of violence, and the historic and developmental crises from which these emerge.

Non-government organisations (NGOs) concerned with longer-term development, for instance, find that it is the emergencies which raise the funds. The media-encouraged (or media-driven) public need for a 'quick fix', a 'result' commensurate with their donations, channels attention into certain kinds of operation and short-term vision. No cynicism is implied here. The desire to save lives is palpable. However, the logic of contemporary discourses on conflict is to extract the immediate and urgent from the long-term social realities in which they are embedded. The 'complex political emergency' becomes a phenomenon in its own right, requiring its own explanations, responses, and expertise.

It is not dissimilar to the debate on 'famine'. The image of mass starvation that shook the world in the mid-1980s similarly led policy makers and much of the academic community to put aside the many studies of rural livelihoods and their macro-level environment. The words of my colleague, Donna Pankhurst, in her review of the literature on famine, could be used with respect to the 'complex political emergency':

> *Famine came to be seen as something separate and detached from the rest of history, requiring new explanations, which was reflected in the number of texts and commentaries on the subject ... Where famine is seen as the outcome and end result of many factors which make people poor and make them vulnerable to changes in their systems of production and reproduction (such as drought and war), then we can avoid seeking solutions to famine, or plans to ensure its prevention separately from all other analysis of how people become so vulnerable.*

(Pankhurst 1989:513)

The separation between the emergency and developmental wings of Northern agencies intervening in the South further encourages the decontextualising of conflict. The divide often reflects institutional separations (and sometimes rivalries): for instance, at the international level between United Nations Development Programme (UNDP) and United Nations High Commissioner for Refugees (UNHCR); at the interagency level between agencies concerned with refugees and those concerned with development; and at the intra-agency level between the development and emergency departments within NGOs such as Oxfam GB. Increasingly, 'emergencies' become the headline-grabbing, fundraising core of international assistance, as opposed to 'development', which is a more complicated process to explain, and beset with failures rather than clear successes. While individuals move between these various agencies and gain relevant and important experience of the connections between their activities, institutional dynamics often prevent the learning from these experiences at the institutional level. Time for reflection, analysis, discussion, and systematising of experiences can be seen as an indulgence in the hectic and emotive world of relief and development.

But while the idea of a continuum between emergency relief and development, with clear cut-off points between the end of one phase and the beginning of the next, may be institutionally useful, in my experience it is a very poor way to conceptualise reality.[3] Most of the regions beset by conflict in the South never had 'development'; indeed, such conflicts often have their epicentre in the most peripheral regions of countries where development has been uneven, if at all. Failure to understand the socio-economic context of conflict seriously weakens the emergency effort, as well as the prospects for post-conflict peace building.[4] There is a huge difference between peacebuilding in former Yugoslavia, for example, where there was a relatively highly skilled and educated population and level of economic development before the war, and much of Africa.

The reality of the world today, and notably in its southern hemisphere, is that there is a spectrum of violent situations. There are the exceptionally violent conflagrations already mentioned, but there is a range of others. For instance, besides many protracted conflicts (such as Afghanistan, Sri Lanka, Colombia, or Angola), there are conflicts in a fragile transitionary phase from long-term conflict to peace (as in Guatemala, where the Peace Agreement was signed on 29 December 1996), conflicts which have formally ended but where social problems continue to threaten long-term peace (as in El Salvador or Mozambique), and situations that simmer on the edge of major conflict (as in Burundi).

The number of potential conflicts is great. Today's developmental crisis may be tomorrow's violent conflict; contemporary 'emergencies' all express deep developmental, social, and political crises. As Adams and Bradbury point out,

> In 1993, when the UN designated 26 conflict-generated emergencies as 'complex', there were over 80 other violent conflicts recorded. In many countries not at war, violence and insecurity are daily realities in the private and public lives of many women, children and ethnic and religious minorities, with profound consequences for their physical, psychological, and material well-being. Insecurity and violence are development issues that have received little serious attention from the UN, governmental agencies, and NGOs working for poverty alleviation and justice.
> (Adams and Bradbury 1994:36)

There is an urgent need to build up a body of authoritative knowledge about this range of conflicts and the social, economic, and political processes from which they erupt. We need to improve our conceptual tools for understanding them and their outcomes. In particular, we need to root conflict analysis, emergency intervention, and peace building within specific socio-historical contexts. Conflicts have a social history: they are not abstract categories. Peace building has a political economy. It also depends critically on human resources: most people will have been negatively affected by personal experience of violence, loss, and destruction, but also positively shaped by courage, new skills, and coping strategies. Peace building should not become a set of abstract principles, unless they derive from careful study of a number of cases, take into account the range of contingent factors which affect post-war environment, and are then continuously revised in the light of experience.

Building a body of knowledge: the contribution of Latin America and Southern Africa

The recent internal wars of Latin America and those of Southern Africa are examples of conflicts that are not considered to be 'complex political emergencies'. These conflicts have disappeared from the headlines, but they have nevertheless had a devastating impact on their respective countries. Peace building is taking place in a problematic macro-level environment in both regions.

The international dimension to these conflicts contrasts them with more recent ones. They were all in a sense 'Cold War' conflicts; the Peruvian conflict reflected Cold War ideologies, but did not involve the superpowers in the way that Central America did. But in fact the international influences only exacerbated and prolonged what were essentially internal conflicts. Apart from the notable exceptions of Angola and Colombia, these largely came to an end in the last phase of the Cold War or in its immediate wake. Guatemala has been the most prolonged of the conflicts and of the peace processes, with an agreement signed only at the end of 1996. As the first examples of peace settlements with international supervision, they have been used as models of post-war reconstruction.

Long-term peace building is the responsibility of local people, many of whom have been involved in the war in different ways: some as victims/survivors, some as protagonists, and some as relief workers and peace builders. We need to understand these processes of local 'peace building from below' and to learn what is and what is not effective.[5] But we also need to understand the factors operating at a broader level, including the external interventions, which facilitate or hinder local capacity to reconstruct societies from the devastation of war.

This article arises from my contribution to the Oxfam/CSVR Symposium, in which I described recent Latin American experiences of conflict and peace building. It looks comparatively (and very schematically in such a short article) at two regions of conflict in Latin America: Central America (Nicaragua and El Salvador) and the Andes (Peru). The comparative method is used to draw out differences as well as similarities. It focuses on these countries because they are all in the post-war reconstruction phase. It is based on four years of research and fieldwork in most of the areas of conflict in Latin America except Chiapas in Mexico, with a particular focus on the problem of internal displacement.

The article begins with an analysis of each conflict, using a socio-historical approach. It subsequently tries to identify the critical social changes which took place as a result of conflict and how the humanitarian intervention responded to them. How did people cope with and survive the war, and what skills and capacities might they bring to the peace? Finally, it asks to what extent these local capacities have been able to influence the post-war situation and prospects for long-term and sustainable peace building.

Conflict analysis

Violent conflicts appear to be cataclysmic events, but they are in fact the result of processes that have developed over time. They are rooted in some way in the interactions between identities of class, ethnicity, and sometimes religion (gender inequalities have not yet led to open warfare on gender lines!), and structural socio-economic factors. These identities are channelled, articulated, and politicised through the presence of some catalyst, and conflict is triggered by political acts or action of some kind.

The identities of any individual or subject are, as the postmodernists have taught us, multiple; they are neither fixed nor essential. In the conflicts examined below, for instance, most women have tended to suppress or play down their gender-related identity and concerns in favour of a sense of belonging based on class, ethnicity, or nationality, which cuts across gender; although gender-awareness has at the same time often grown stronger in the course of the war itself.[6] A vital question is why at any given moment one identity appears to predominate over others and even provides a reason for taking up arms. There is no automatic reason why any of these identities should result in conflict. Conflict analysis needs to understand how historically rooted injustices, exclusions, inequalities, and rivalries that exist in all societies turn into violent internal war in some.

Central America: Nicaragua and El Salvador

Long before the civil wars that tore this region apart in the 1980s, its socio-economic and political structures had developed along particularly exclusionary and socially divisive lines.

Common to both countries was the concentration of economic and political power in the hands of a mostly white or *mestizo* (mixed white and Indian) élite. Only a small, politically weak, professional middle class lay between the mass of the peasant population and the urban poor people. The structural inequalities resulted in clear class cleavages in El Salvador (in the case of neighbouring Guatemala they were class and ethnic cleavages). In Nicaragua, however, class divisions were complicated by the fact that the élite itself was divided, with one dynasty concentrating power and wealth at the level of the State and alienating other sectors of the élite.

There were also significant spatial or geographical patterns to the deep social divisions in the two countries. In El Salvador, departments such as Chalatenango, Cabañas, and Morazán were the poorest, most ecologically damaged, and agriculturally unsustainable regions. Poor, land-hungry peasants struggled to sustain a fragile, vulnerable livelihood in these departments, which later constituted core regions of the conflict. In Nicaragua, there was also a geographic and ethnic divide between the Pacific and Atlantic regions of the country. The social structures of the former did not reproduce themselves in the latter, where indigenous Miskito and Sumo peoples had come under the influence of Britain and the Moravian Church, and had little communication or relationship with the Spanish-speaking Catholic population of the Pacific region.

More than any other structural inequality, the role of land distribution and use in the unfolding conflicts was probably the most significant. Inability to sustain the peasant economy on the amount and quality of land available to the poor majority was a core issue. Economic growth was nevertheless facilitated by the relationship between the agro-export and peasant economies: unable to live on the available land all the year round, peasants had to migrate and sell their labour cheaply at harvest time on the agro-export estates, in order to earn some cash to support themselves for the full year. The problem became ever more acute with population growth and the expansion of agro-export crops and concomitant expulsion of peasants from their land. The gravest situation was found in the smallest, most densely populated country, El Salvador.

Many dispossessed people headed for urban areas, where they would once again end up on the margins of society, with relatively few gaining jobs in the small manufacturing sector. In Nicaragua, where there were still unsettled agricultural areas, colonisation schemes banished some of the land-hungry to remote areas in the 1960s and 1970s, where poor infrastructure and State neglect resulted in a difficult struggle for survival. Nueva Guinea in Nicaragua would later become one of the conflict-ridden regions of that country, for instance (the Ixcán in Guatemala would be another example of a zone of colonisation in Central America which subsequently became a centre of conflict). In Nueva Guinea, many peasants remained politically tied to *Somocismo* in gratitude for the former dictator's land grants, and this made them a fertile recruiting ground for the anti-Sandinista forces in the 1980s. Chalatenango in El Salvador was an area of unplanned colonisation. When thousands were expelled from the coastal regions to make way for cotton-growing in the 1950s, and thousands more were driven from their small subsistence plots on the coffee estates, they headed for the regions of little interest to the agro-exporters. In Chalatenango it was cattle ranching, not agro-exports, which predominated, and some land was available for rent.

The Andes: Peru

In Peru, class and ethnic identity overlapped in the highland departments of Ayacucho, Huancavelica, and Apurimac. These represented the poorest regions of the country and the epicentres of the conflict that erupted in the early 1980s.

Populations of alpaca herders and subsistence farmers and sharecroppers, some of whom paid labour dues up until the late 1970s to local landowners, lived in remote and desolate altitudes. The State showed little interest in the contribution that the region might make to the national economy, except insofar as the land reform which finally gave the peasants title to land in the late 1970s was aimed also at forcing expropriated landowners to invest their capital elsewhere. Ethnic identity among the peasants was culturally strong, with most still speaking primarily Quechua. Many women spoke no Spanish at all, and many men did so with difficulty. The problem of communicating with the wider Peru was an isolating factor, exacerbated by widespread racism towards the 'Indian'. Ethnicity was not an identity which the peasants and herders themselves valued or affirmed. Any action in the wider world taken by these people reflected their socio-economic position and not their ethnic identity; examples are the peasant movements which did emerge in the wake of the Velasco government's efforts to mobilise them 'from above' in the early 1970s.

In the valleys, such as that around Huanta in Ayacucho, where larger landowners and better-off peasants lived, the population was mostly *mestizo*, and strongly rejected the 'Indian' influence within it, although most spoke Quechua as well as Spanish. Nevertheless, they would never be accepted into the same social élite as the Lima-based bourgeoisie. The frustrations of a generation of sons and daughters of peasants on medium-sized farms, with educational opportunities but few professional or social ones, would play a major role in the subsequent conflict.[7]

Catalysts of war

None of the conditions described leads invariably to war and/or violent conflict. Many parts of the world are characterised by deep class and ethnic divisions and a highly exclusionary distribution of political and economic power corresponding to them. Often these divisions, like the ones we are exploring, rest on a great deal of threatened or actual violence. The status quo is defended through a variety of coercive mechanisms from national to private armed force. Some writers have even identified 'structural violence' to describe situations of violence embedded in social relations but which do not manifest themselves in armed conflict between the parties (Galtung 1990).

Affirming identity does not necessarily lead to conflict.[8] But there are situations where identity is mobilised in such a way as to challenge another social group or the State. It is the character of these catalysing factors which is critical to the analysis of conflict; they introduce new elements into an ongoing situation, and transform perceptions about the legitimacy of that situation and what can be done to change it.

Central America: El Salvador and Nicaragua

In **El Salvador** the catalysts consisted firstly of the radical Church and secondly of left-wing political movements. The fact that the Central American civil wars originated in the 1960s and 1970s meant that they were heavily influenced by the ideological currents that on the left made class an over-arching identity which could bring others, such as gender and ethnicity, under its umbrella. This produced a powerful mobilising tool to pitch against a State which also organised itself essentially around the interests of one class. A peasant movement began to emerge in the poorest zones of the country in the 1970s, linking up with other popular organisations in the urban areas, and articulated politically by the guerrilla movements that formed the Frente Farabundo Martí de Liberación Nacional (FMLN) in 1980. The class-based nature of this movement was a source of its initial strength, but it provoked a stronger class solidarity among the Salvadorean oligarchy who controlled the State and could call upon the armed forces, and ultimately the US government, for support.

In **Nicaragua** the success of the Sandinistas in overthrowing the Somocista dictatorship triggered the relentless hostility of the US Administration to what it perceived to be a revolutionary pro-Soviet government. While the revolution against Somoza had attracted a multi-class alliance, this did not survive the assumption of power by the Sandinistas, although the new government attempted to preserve it. Those who opposed the focus on social distribution and popular participation of the Sandinista government were the catalysts – with US backing – of an armed movement to overthrow it.

This armed movement was able to exploit the social discontent among sectors of the peasantry alienated by the Sandinistas' approach to the agrarian question. It also managed to mobilise the ethnic particularities of the Atlantic Coast communities, which were deeply disaffected by the Sandinistas' ill-conceived initial approach to a region used to virtual autonomy from Managua.

The counter-revolutionary movement grew with external support, but nevertheless exploited many internal social tensions and class and ethnic identities to bring down the first State in Nicaragua's history that proposed to base itself on the 'logic of the majority'. The historic weakness of a State which had developed around a dynastic dictatorship could not be overcome very rapidly, however, and certainly not with sufficient speed to deal adequately with the social contradictions exposed by the overthrow of the old order.

The Andes: Peru

In **Peru**, the catalyst was a movement which emerged with a messianic Maoist vision, which it attempted to apply to the most impoverished regions of the Andes. *Sendero Luminoso* ('Shining Path') set out to mobilise the peasants in a struggle against feudalism and capitalism. It exploited the abandonment of these regions by the State, an abandonment reaffirmed by the application of the agrarian reform to the Ayacucho region in the late 1970s. This gave peasant communities their land and freed them from servitude. But almost no other support was given to peasants struggling with an inhospitable terrain and lack of infrastructure to connect them either physically or socially to the rest of the country.

Indigenous communities responded initially to *Sendero* because the movement filled a virtual power vacuum in the area and sought to give them a wider vision of their role, although it made violence a means for them to achieve recognition, status, and survival. *Sendero* had little interest in their ethnicity, much more in their class identity. Indeed, it was *Sendero*'s disrespect for their traditions and community structure which, among other factors, led the indigenous people to turn against the guerrilla movement. The imposition of a revolutionary committee structure, for instance, on the time-honoured community structure, and the killing of community elders and Presidents, were two such. But repudiation of *Sendero* was not enough to save the peasants from the vengeance of the Peruvian army. Peasants were killed in their thousands, either by *Sendero* for betraying them, or by the army for having given support to the guerrillas.

Similarities and differences

In analysing these three conflicts, some common threads are apparent amid many differences. A significant similarity is the way in which social marginalisation and exclusion could be mobilised by political forces in very divergent ways. In **El Salvador**, the popular movement of the 1970s was strong enough to create a social dynamic of its own. While it was closely linked to the political force that would lead it into conflict, there is sufficient evidence that a conscious movement of poor people had emerged and chosen a revolutionary option. This would be a very important factor in determining the way in which the conflict took shape, and the humanitarian responses to it. Much support was channelled to the popular organisations and people's initiatives in this conflict. Only the USA and its agencies chose to put all their efforts into shoring up the Salvadorean State, both militarily and politically.

In **Nicaragua**, although the Sandinistas emerged from a multi-class alliance with strong backing from the urban poor, intellectuals, and significant sectors of the peasantry, they were not able to generate a national following behind their modernising and transforming governmental project. There was little history of popular organising before the revolution, and the lack of consciousness was apparent in the ability of external forces to mobilise social and political discontent around an anti-government initiative. However, the fact that the Sandinista State was committed to a socially radical and nationalist agenda would also influence the international humanitarian response to the conflict. A great deal of international support was channelled through the Sandinista State.

In **Peru**, social sectors isolated and neglected by a State with very little interest in the subsistence agriculture of the Andean highlands were mobilised by an ideologically rigid armed group. Although many abandoned this allegiance, they were already exposed to army revenge. It was only when subsequently the army began to arm them, and peasant militia were created, that the peasants gained a real protagonism of their own in this conflict. That protagonism has provided the basis for a humanitarian response now that the war has come to a kind of ending.

The impact of conflict

The particular character of each of these conflicts had a profound impact on their societies. Men and women changed their roles as they do in all wars; they may be victims of terrible things, but they also have to cope with the situation. Men tend to carry the guns and lead movements, while family survival comes to depend on women alone. Social and political change and economic destruction, unevenly spread and experienced, all characterise conflict. Only a careful analysis of this can provide the tools for understanding the challenges of peace, and in particular enable peace-building strategies to harness the positive energies and capacities developed to cope with and survive the conflict.

Central America: El Salvador and Nicaragua

In **El Salvador**, observers close to the popular sectors identified an impressive level of organisation among the most illiterate and marginalised social groups. An estimated 500,000 people were displaced inside the country by the war (10 per cent of the population), over 70,000 people were killed, and an estimated 68 per cent of the population was living below the poverty line in 1990 (CEPAL 1990). But there is no doubt that the population most affected by army bombardment, State terror, and counter-insurgency showed an extraordinary protagonism at key moments.

In the zones of guerrilla control, they established their own local governments and developed creative and courageous responses to the destruction and danger around them. In the refugee camps, they organised workshops and training; and, when the moment was appropriate for them (and in opposition to the wishes of international agencies such as UNHCR), they asserted their right to return in the manner they wished – openly. In the returned communities which were set up within the zones of conflict, they challenged the army through peaceful resistance to efforts to dislodge them from the civilian space they had won.

These activities opened up a political and civil space in the country, and enabled the popular movement to start re-grouping from 1986 onwards. Local NGOs were able to establish themselves and channel funds to the war-affected populations. While the guerrilla movements maintained political and military leadership, it was this grassroots organising that held people together in the face of relentless government repression, largely financed by the USA.

These capacities of the population had a big impact on international humanitarian NGOs. There was an understanding that an historic struggle was at stake for social and economic change in favour of the poorest people. The humanitarian support from these NGOs was not neutral, but value-driven, and very much based on respect for the political options of the 'victims/protagonists' of the war. These international NGOs accompanied the popular organisations, lobbied their own governments to challenge the US role in the country, and provided an international umbrella of protection (Thompson 1996).

In El Salvador, therefore, the history of the conflict is the history also of a social *and* political process, in which mostly illiterate or semi-literate men and women participated in a prolonged struggle to bring about a fundamental transformation of their society. This they ultimately failed to do, however. But that population had gained an experience of protagonism that should have enabled them at least to influence the peace.

In **Nicaragua**, the conflict unfolded in a context where the State under the Sandinistas was itself the protagonist for a project of social change. The lack of tradition of independent popular organising, the weakness of political parties, and the culture of exclusion had to be addressed in order to mobilise support. At the same time, however, the Sandinistas had to channel that support into their national project, which included an alliance with the private sector. The Sandinistas did generate an enthusiastic following among a significant sector of the population. Many international NGOs, and Western as well as East European governments, gave the State strong support for what was seen as an historic opportunity for people-centred development. Humanitarian assistance during the war in Nicaragua encompassed a great deal of solidarity and political support for the project of the Sandinista State.

The military response organised by the USA and its local allies both undermined the social dimensions of the Sandinista project and exacerbated its contradictions. The Sandinistas were attempting to persuade the private sector to accept a loss of political power in exchange for retaining considerable economic power. Popular mobilising became increasingly organised around the defence of the revolution and support for the Frente Sandinista de Liberación Nacional (FSLN), weakening its capacity to generate autonomous and sustainable social action. In the conflict zones, the logic of war replaced the logic of the social processes.

The conflict in Nicaragua divided the majority population of poor peasants and indigenous peoples. It had high human, social, and economic costs for an already impoverished country; but it also contributed to the premature collapse of an attempt, however flawed, to harness popular energies into modernising the country and State.

The Andes: Peru

In **Peru**, the impact of the war was felt primarily in the three Andean departments referred to above.[9] An estimated 600,000 people were displaced within Peru during the conflict, 80 per cent of them from these departments, which also accounted for many of the 25,000 dead. However, the responses to the conflict among the population also demonstrated how 'victims' can also be 'actors', developing capacities to cope with the most barbaric and traumatic circumstances.

The conflict forced people to choose between fleeing the zone of conflict, dying at the hands of *Sendero* or the army, or staying and offering armed resistance. Many fled, either following historic migratory patterns and heading for Lima, or settling in the nearest urban centre. But, unlike historic migrations, these were not planned population movements, but forced expulsions.

Unprepared and often traumatised, the displaced ended up on the periphery of towns and cities where they did not even speak the language. Many were widows or women left to cope with the children (including many orphans) alone, because their husbands had stayed to fight. Many displaced men were even less able to adapt from peasant life to urban environments, and found it more difficult to find work than the women, who could at least do domestic work. Nevertheless, the experience of urban life had a profound effect on these displaced people. Despite often appalling living conditions, the possibility of some schooling for their children and the experience of modern communications and urban social life have changed the expectations and aspirations of significant groups of Andean peasants.

Others stayed to resist, in some regions managing to preserve the community structure, but in others forced to move from isolated rural dwellings into virtual camps, from where they would venture out to farm their distant plots or to fight *Sendero*. It is the ill-armed peasant militia or *rondas*, rather than the army, which many believe to be responsible for the defeat of *Sendero* in the Andes.[10] This has given *ronderos* a sense of self-worth that was historically denied them.

The humanitarian assistance to the population affected by this war was very limited. Peru did not attract the international attention paid to the Central American wars, and *Sendero*'s hostility to international aid made it very dangerous to work in the war zones, although some agencies such as Oxfam GB managed to maintain a flow of aid. Only with the capture of *Sendero*'s leader in 1992 and the virtual – though not complete – defeat of *Sendero* have the dimensions of the crisis affecting the displaced population become apparent.

The problem of sustainable peace building

The impact of war was devastating for all three countries examined above. But social changes did take place, with some positive implications in terms of new capacities, skills, and expectations among the populations. These capacities are easily eroded in peacetime, as is well known in the case of women who take new public roles during wartime and return to private domestic ones subsequently. Indeed, the 'gendered' nature of peace agreements reflects this (Pankhurst and Pearce 1997). Fundamentally, however, the problem is that most peace agreements do not even purport to encompass or reflect social changes. They are political deals.

The discussion of peace building is frequently confused by the different ways in which the term 'peace' is used. Some define it negatively as the 'absence of war'; others invest it with a positive content too: ultimately the 'peaceful' society is one in which there are no causes for violence and conflict. The mechanisms for achieving this and its precise content are much debated, and the debate centres around the concepts of justice, equality, liberty, and democracy. The debate about positive peace draws our attention to the apparently obvious: that the absence of war does not necessarily mean the absence of violence in a society, and it certainly does not mean an end to conflict. Socio-economic inequality, unequal gender relations, political exclusion, and racism are just some of the factors that fuel social and political violence in any society. For some, therefore, a sustainable peace is only meaningful and possible if steps are made to deal with these fundamental problems. Others prefer to focus on the immediately achievable, the by-no-means-simple task of bringing parties to armed conflict into a negotiation which will at least allow for the 'management' of the conflict, or a decision by the parties not to pursue their differences through violence.

How can these two approaches be married? In practice, of course, a peace agreement may not deal with all the underlying causes of the conflict, but it might open up a political space to deal with them in another way. The problem arises if the peace agreement is treated as an 'ending' to something, rather than a 'beginning' in which the parties to conflict have formally agreed to address their differences in non-violent ways.

The process of peace building – and it is by nature a protracted and complex one – will depend on the prospects for reconciling fundamental, often structurally embedded, differences through peaceful means. Given that conflicts are about attempts to change power relations in some way, their outcome will create an environment which negatively or positively affects this. The historical outcome of the conflict and the political economy in which the peace-building process takes place are critical factors for societies emerging from internal war. The conflict will have changed something in the society. But *to what extent* will these changes allow for the emergence of new social practices, the construction of accountable and representative government institutions, and inclusive economic processes? To what extent will the rule of law be legitimised, so allowing alternative means to violence for the redress of grievances, and the protection of the basic rights of all the population? Will the cessation of armed conflict enable the victims of violence to write their history freely, and to deal with the trauma of bereavement? If the changes do not facilitate these things sufficiently, the ending of the conflict will simply bequeath a legacy of frustration and resentment to another generation.

'Peace building' cannot be seriously discussed in the abstract, because armed conflicts end in so many different ways and offer such different possibilities. The social history of the pre-conflict period must be related to the political economy of the post-conflict context. If the reasons why people took up arms have not been addressed and there are no means of articulating them politically, how will they manifest themselves in the peace? Demoralisation and exhaustion may depoliticise aspirations and atomise individuals into seeking private solutions, giving the illusion of a 'stable peace'. But this will not be a society that has dealt with its past. In the short term, people are relieved that war is over, but the legacy of violence will imprint itself on the society and express itself somehow, in inter-personal relations, in levels of domestic violence, on children and, quite probably, eventually in the political arena once again.

The issue of 'impunity', truth, justice, and reconciliation remains one of the most problematic issues in the aftermath of conflict. In reality, most peace agreements are compromises or defeats/ victories, rather than a joint attempt to redress the grievances of the past in order to build something new. The question of what is done to bring to justice perpetrators of extreme violence goes to the heart of the nature of the peace agreement and the power relationships it expresses as the conflict ends. Guatemala, for instance, is now beginning its transition to peace, following the signing of an accord. However that accord was made possible by an agreement to an amnesty that protected the guerrillas from prosecution for political violence but also, far more significantly in terms of the scale of the violence they used, exonerated the army of responsibility for the mass and cruel violence it perpetrated against indigenous people and opposition groups. What kind of peace will emerge in Guatemala, where the rule of law has been practised so partially?

Realistic peace building

Realistic peace building must confront the flawed foundations of the peace agreement. It must take into account the power relations, persistent exclusions, and the social implications of the post-war political economy. The case studies below suggest that the most important steps towards a sustainable peace are those which foster and strengthen local capacity to deal with the past, to engage with the present, and to shape the future in ways which do not exclude, oppress, or divide.

Central America: El Salvador and Nicaragua

El Salvador has been acclaimed as achieving one of the most 'successful' peace agreements. There are undoubtedly many significant features of the Salvadorean peace negotiations. But, in 1995, there were more killings each day through criminal violence than during the war.[11] Questions of land, poverty, and marginalisation are as much a concern as before the war. The difference is that the ability of previous leaders to articulate excluded groups politically is much diminished.

The protracted conflict wore people down; while the guerrilla movement remained militarily powerful, it was clear that they could not take power through arms. Sectors of the oligarchy meanwhile had also understood that they could not defeat the movement militarily. The price of peace would be to broaden the basis for political participation in the country, and this became acceptable to a sufficient sector. Meanwhile, the Cold War was ending and the USA was seeking to extricate itself from its military commitments.

Many other factors influenced the peace, but it is important to note that, in the end, and despite the mobilisation of civilian groups in favour of peace (through initiatives such as the *Debate Nacional*), it was negotiated between the élites of both sides of the war.[12] While the 'victims/ protagonists' had high expectations of the outcome, the war did not transform the socio-economic basis of power in the society. It opened a political space for civilian government and free, contested elections, and most notably allowed for the political participation of the former guerrilla leaders. The international presence played a major role in guaranteeing the transition from war to peace.

International pressure ensured that local NGOs were given the space to participate in discussions about the post-conflict resettlement and reconstruction programmes, through what was called the CIREFCA (International Conference for Central American Refugees) process. But most of these NGOs had emerged during the war, closely tied to the FMLN and ill-prepared for the tasks of post-war reconstruction or working with people in a non-instrumentalist way. The popular sectors, despite their protagonism in the war, found it hard to adapt to the new discourse of electoral politics which relegated them to the role of voters, with little space to retain their political engagement. The demoralisation that resulted brought with it the dissipation of that creativity, courage, and energy with which people had responded to the revolutionary war.

The failure to transform the Salvadorean State would also have profound implications for the peace. A State that had historically served only one sector of society, and was very much weakened by the war, was in a poor condition to lead the post-war reconstruction; but above all it still fundamentally reflected the pre-war class structure. Issues such as the rule of law, accountability, and effective administration remain unsolved in El Salvador, although there has been a concerted international effort to address them and to support the modernising social and political forces. While these dominated the governing right-wing ARENA party (as they did under President Cristiani, 1989–94), there were some prospects for progress. But his successor, Calderón Sol, proved ill-equipped to take the country forward. It is telling that the most searching analysis of the post-war reconstruction effort in El Salvador has drawn attention to the limitations of external post-war assistance where the national government lacks the political will to collaborate:

> External assistance has played a critical role in El Salvador's peace process. Grants and loans from bilateral and multilateral agencies have been the main source of finance for many programs mandated by the Peace Accords, including the land transfer program, the reintegration of ex-combatants, poverty alleviation programs and infrastructure projects. External assistance actors have also influenced the political momentum of the peace process. Aid has affected not only the balance of payments, but also the balance of power. Aid can be an important complement to limited domestic resources. It can, however, also become a substitute for them ... This dilemma has been clearly apparent in El Salvador. External assistance unquestionably has contributed greatly to post-war reconstruction and to the consolidation of peace. But external assistance actors have been less successful in prompting the government to mobilize greater domestic resources to finance peace programs. Indeed, virtually no internal fiscal reforms were undertaken specifically with a view to financing the peace.[13]
> (Boyce 1995:1201)

The inability of former guerrilla leaders to provide political leadership to their supporters for the new agendas of the peace has had a very negative impact on the popular movement and its ability to influence that peace. There are some examples of successful interactions between NGOs and international agencies in the reconstruction, and some efforts to build accountable municipal governments, but they are relatively few and still not part of a systematic *government* project.[14] And while international agencies have stressed 'participation' in their interventions, time and attention must be invested in helping traumatised, impoverished, semi-literate populations to recover from war and respond to the often technocratic visions of professional external actors.

There is no plan to incorporate the former war zones into a national development plan. They are left to the projects of international financial agencies and international NGOs. Many of the urban and rural poor people of El Salvador subsist on dollar remittances from relatives in the USA, rather than on their own productive capacity. The survival mentality today contrasts strongly with the creative mobilisations of the war period. Outstanding tensions over land and the future of demobilised ex-combatants continue to threaten the prospects for peace: the disaffection of the latter has already led to more than one violent incident.

In **Nicaragua**, the counter-revolutionary army was ultimately defeated militarily, but not politically – the reverse of the situation in El Salvador. The electoral defeat of the Sandinistas in 1990, just after the formal signing of the peace agreement, meant that the process of peace building would take place without the commitment of a 'progressive' State. At the popular level, the legacy of Sandinista organising had left its mark, and there was much greater capacity to defend popular interests than otherwise. But much of this was still led and organised by the Sandinistas, now fighting to regain political power through electoral means.

The most vigorous and independent voices, many observers noted, were from the women's organisations that throughout the Sandinista period had defended both the revolution and also, increasingly, their gender interests. The other group that would emerge in the early years of the peace were the demobilised soldiers, peasants from both sides of the war who now identified common interests and who felt betrayed by their leaderships. The Foundation of Ex-combatants included former members of both the Sandinista and the counter-revolutionary or *contra* armies.

The Sandinistas had not had the time or resources, particularly after the economy was put on a war footing, to modernise the State apparatus. The State they bequeathed was still prone to corruption and bureaucratism, tendencies enhanced by the weakness of the new Chamorro government. The government's main concern was to transform the macro-level policy environment from a State-led to a market-driven one. It was not concerned with systematic post-war peace building. While the international financial community did contribute funds for this purpose, the lack of local capacity to administer them proved a major obstacle. Local NGO capacity was much weaker than in El Salvador. The Sandinista State had tended to dominate the associational sphere. While new NGOs emerged with the electoral defeat of the FSLN, they still mostly lacked the capacity and experience to make proposals relevant to the new conditions. A study of the search for peace and consensus in Nicaragua in the five years after the 1990 peace agreement concluded:

> As a direct result of civil war fought within the context of the cold war, Nicaragua's peace process has been beset since 1990 by a sometimes violent array of conflicts over land, over economic policy and division of resources, over institutional power, and over quotas of power within and between a political class with many small parties and factions. For common citizens it has been a bewildering and dispiriting political scene they have viewed from an unsteady economic terrain which has deteriorated an already poor living standard.
> (Dye et al. 1995)

Again, the picture is not entirely negative. There have been some interesting local experiences. One of these is Nueva Guinea, where the Protestant Church had been very influential during the war in brokering peace between the *contras* and the Sandinista army. While it continued these efforts in the wake of the peace agreements, supported by international NGOs, these were continuously undermined by the economic marginalisation of the region. With little State investment in infrastructure and development, it is left to international and local NGOs and, in the case of Nueva Guinea, the peasant union, UNAG, to develop and implement projects. But often they do so with conflicting rather than common agendas. This tendency is sometimes fuelled by the increasing scarcity of funds and, therefore, competition among various organisations as Nicaragua moves from being a country of concern to the international community to one where 'peace' has been restored.

The situation is worsened by the neo-liberal national policy environment. A key ingredient of the peace building in the zone, to encourage what have been mostly *contra*-supporting communities to accept Sandinistas into their midst, is economic reconstruction and improvement in the living standards of the people. The peasants in the zone, however, are moving desperately from crop to crop, as trade liberalisation brings in cheaper staples from neighbouring Costa Rica. As a new crop is tested for its market potential, so communities all turn to it, and the price collapses. The resolution of these problems is critical to the sustainability of long-term peace in a region where poor people in very recent memory took up arms against each other.

The Andes: Peru

In **Peru**, the war has never been formally brought to an end, and the State has felt no compulsion to invest in the reconstruction of the war-torn regions. Political parties have been much weakened in Peru over the last decade, in particular on the left. This has adversely affected Peru's historically strong non-government and popular organisations, which were mostly linked to the parties. President Fujimori has claimed the credit for the victory over *Sendero* and has used this to launch his programme of economic modernisation. This does not include the Andean highlands, which according to the Peruvian anthropologist, Carlos Monge, are still seen by the government as *un gran comedor popular* (a big soup kitchen).[15] In other words, while efficiency, competition, and the free market are the agenda for the productive coastal export zone, the Andean highlands are still viewed as an unproductive region where State paternalism is the only economic hope.

As international and local NGOs struggle to develop an agenda for post-war reconstruction in the face of government indifference, so also their conceptions of what this should mean differ widely and often conflict with each other.[16] Technically competent NGOs lack sensitivity to the social dimensions of rebuilding communities devastated by violence and bereavement. The men who head the NGOs, for instance, do not know how to build on the capacities demonstrated by the women during the war years.

In El Salvador a highly politicised popular movement and NGO community found it hard to make the transition to a new role in the peace. In Nicaragua, the Sandinista State had not encouraged independent organising, and therefore the NGO and popular sectors were too weak to take full advantage of the post-war situation. In Peru, however, one of the most interesting developments is that of the organisational capacity of the displaced communities seeking support for a return programme or for permanent settlement in their places of refuge. With a new sense of protagonism inherited from their role in the war, these communities, particularly in the Ayacucho area, are embarking on an important attempt to influence the reconstruction programmes in the region. Their capacity to do so will greatly depend on the dynamics of their evolving relationships with the State and with the local and international non-government agencies that are currently supporting them.

Conclusion

This article has emphasised that 'conflict' should not be treated as an asocial, ahistorical category; nor should peace building be understood without reference to the way in which power relationships have been reconfigured at the end of the conflict, and the nature of their impact on the political economy of post-war reconstruction.

At one level, these may seem very obvious points. However, a great deal of the debate on 'conflict', 'conflict prevention', and 'peace building' appears to treat them as if they have a reality of their own, divorced from their social context. The external agencies concerned with peace seem increasingly to focus the debate on *their* interventions (for instance, what *they* can do to articulate relief and development, what *they* can do to prevent conflict and build peace), and much less on the dynamic of *local* capacities and how they can shape the future prospects for peace building. And where the discourse does focus on them, the practice of supporting the efforts of traumatised, poor, and ill-educated populations to rebuild their lives is often insensitive and reflects unrealistic expectations of rapid results and achievements. For example, a real appreciation of how gender relations affect the ability of poor and powerless women to play their full role in the post-conflict situation (as opposed to a knowledge of the correct *discourse*) is essential. In my experience, few of the professional men involved in external assistance programmes have that real appreciation, and repeated gender-training workshops help only partly.

Latin America offers some useful case studies of conflicts that have tended to be forgotten as international concern looks to the newly defined category of conflicts: the 'complex political emergency'. The Latin American examples, which are now in their post-war reconstruction phase, do nevertheless suggest some important topics that are worth exploring for their relevance to other conflicts and peace-building processes in the South.

The relationship between identity and structure is one such topic, which is critical to the analysis of conflict and for assessing the prospects for a sustainable peace. The case studies reveal the importance of understanding the process of identity mobilisation in conflict, whether there is an 'empowering mobilisation', a 'manipulated mobilisation' (that is, one which seeks to manipulate exclusions for a political project which expresses the power rivalries of élites and leaders), or an 'affirmative mobilisation'.

In El Salvador, conscious movements emerged, linked by class interests, initially with the help of the radical Church, creating strong and combative popular organisations. This empowering mobilisation enabled ordinary peasants and workers to play an extraordinary role during the war, which was widely recognised by humanitarian agencies. These movements, which were closely tied to political leaderships during the war, have mostly, however, been unable effectively to influence the peace. Their leaders saw them in peace-time as a source of electoral support, not as a human resource for long-term peace building. The rural and urban poor people of El Salvador had demonstrated in the zones under guerrilla control, in the refugee camps and returned communities, their capacity for organisation and their readiness to learn new skills. But these have mostly not been harnessed for the peace.

In Nicaragua, poor peasants and ethnic groups were mobilised behind a counter-revolutionary project which was essentially about élites regaining political power and the USA regaining influence in the country. But the Sandinistas also mobilised 'from above' around their own agenda for government in an historical context of weak associational life, a tendency exacerbated by the demands of war. The reconstruction effort was weakened by expectations among the population that the State or external agencies would provide solutions to their problems.

In Peru, there are signs that indigenous peasants have gained a sense of self-worth which could be the basis for an 'affirmative' identity for the peace. Indigenous women are potentially able to use their experiences during the war to play significant roles in the reconstruction of their communities. In this case, there is no 'mobilisation' around these identities, but a sense of self-value and a new sense of 'rights', which has emerged in the course of the conflict and which could be supported by humanitarian efforts in the post-war situation.

A second topic to highlight is the role of the State. In all three countries, the incapacity or unwillingness of the post-conflict State actively to promote the conditions for peace building has seriously weakened the process. The three countries share a history of socially exclusionary, coercive, corrupt, and unaccountable States. The historic outcome of the conflicts in El Salvador and Nicaragua has placed the issue of State modernisation and legitimacy on the agenda, but has not brought about the shift in social and economic power which could force it through. Renewed polarisation into armed groups is unlikely, but the poverty and exclusion that led to war in the first place now fuel the non-political criminal violence of the desperate. In Peru, the historic outcome of the war has been to strengthen the modernising impetus of the State, albeit under the authoritarian leadership of President Fujimori. But here, too, the distribution of social and economic power remains unchanged, despite the modernisation process afoot. It is too soon to judge the capacity of the victims of the war to claim State recognition that they bore the brunt of army and *Sendero* violence, as well as their rights as citizens in a country that has barely accepted its indigenous population in this way.

A third topic is the role of NGOs. There is much concern among the international community to build up local NGO capacity in the wake of war. This is not so much a recognition of the need to strengthen long-term, sustainable local peace-building capacity, as has been argued here. It is more about the macro-economic agenda of the international financial community, where NGOs are now seen as service-providers preferable to bureaucratic and corrupt States.

However, NGOs are not *necessarily* preferable to an effective, competent, and accountable State. And in order to enhance the capacity of NGOs to take on these new roles, the comparative advantages of NGOs – their cost effectiveness, their closeness to beneficiaries, their lack of bureaucracy, etc. – often diminish. The NGOs in the three countries we have looked at are fragile institutions. To what extent will more sustainable peace processes be fostered by 'scaling-up' these organisations to carry out poverty-alleviation functions in the absence of State programmes? Experience from all three cases suggests that what is needed is indeed more effective NGOs, but ones that remain close to the marginal social groups caught up in the conflict, that can support, not substitute for, *their* efforts to articulate their needs better, to organise more effectively; NGOs which can assist them to make better use of the reconstruction funds available from international agencies, which can facilitate inter-community reconciliation, and so on.

Last, but by no means least, there is the topic of the post-war economy, and in particular the challenges of growth and equity which are both so critical to a sustainable peace. The main conflict areas of all three countries are characterised by their peripheral status in their national economies. The wars did not change that status. On the contrary, they further devastated and decapitalised them. While international institutions have poured money into these regions in the wake of war, in particular into El Salvador, there is no substitute for a national plan of socio-economic development that includes these regions.

However, these very same international financial institutions also promote the economic model of greater integration into the world economy on the basis of comparative advantage and a market-led approach to development. The export sectors are owned by the country's élites, and the main challenge for the national economy is to encourage greater efficiency, diversification, and competitiveness in these sectors. There is real concern among the international financial institutions about the inequitable distribution of wealth in these war-torn countries, and much emphasis on how to build capacity to redress this imbalance and make the State more accountable and democratic. But in societies recovering from war, where the majority of the population lack basic services and minimal education, where bereavement and destruction have characterised their recent lives, their capacity to influence the State has to be nurtured and encouraged over time.

We return to the argument that if peace is not limited conceptually to 'the absence of war', then peace building is a prolonged process which must incorporate concerns for development, justice, and equality. Emergencies are dramatic moments which affect public and political opinion and are capable of raising considerable economic solidarity. However, a serious commitment to peace requires much more than the rapid response to such emergencies. It requires an understanding of the historic social dislocations and divisions which, in the South in particular, have been exacerbated by external powers, poverty, and repressive exclusionary States. It also requires an honest appraisal of the impact of wars and their endings in particular cases. From what reality does the peace-building process begin?

It is likely that historic divisions have been only partly reconfigured, if at all, by the conflict, while economic destruction has further diminished the limited material capital of the society. But even a massive injection of dollars offers no guarantee for long-term peace building. An interim approach is sensitively and systematically to support the efforts of local people attempting to rebuild lives and livelihoods. Learning from their experiences and building on their capacities, rather than introducing quick-fix solutions dreamt up by outsiders, may be a longer path to peace, but a more sustainable one.

Notes

1 ' … the term "complex emergency" was coined in the United Nations to describe those major crises, which have indeed proliferated since 1989, that require a "system-wide response": a combination of military intervention, peace-keeping efforts, relief programmes, high-level diplomacy, and so on. In other words, the complexity refers to the "multi-mandate" nature of the international response as well as to the multi-causal nature of the emergency' (Deborah Eade: Preface to Martin and Alvarez 1996).

2 The relationship of the media to conflict has been explored in Minear *et al.* (1996).

3 Many fieldworkers recount anecdotes which reflect the artificial distinctions made by some donor agencies and governments. A former Oxfam fieldworker in Central America, for example, recalls how the Overseas Development Administration's distinction between relief and rehabilitation during the conflict of the 1980s meant that it was possible to secure emergency co-funding for housing materials for Salvadorean refugees returning from Honduras, but not to reconstruct their homes once there (unless they were bombed). The same nails and roofing sheets could be classified as 'relief' or 'development', involving distinct budget lines and grant processes.

4 Mary B. Anderson suggests that humanitarian intervention which is intended to provide relief to victims of war or to support the capacities of people to achieve economic and social development often ends up 'reinforcing or exacerbating conflict in the area where aid is given' (Anderson:2).

5 The Bradford University Department of Peace Studies is engaged in a collaborative research project on 'peace building from below', aiming to identify its contradictions as well as its potential for long-term peace-building.

6 The extent to which women have kept alive their concerns about gender has often been underestimated or simply ignored. A growing body of literature and testimony is now focusing on women's experiences of and perceptions of their role in conflict and war (e.g. Hooks 1991; Smith-Ayala 1991). That women experience war in ways that reflect gender-determined relations of power is beginning to be documented. The systematic rape of Bosnian women as part of a strategy of war caught the headlines, but rape is increasingly understood to be a strategy of war over the centuries. The extent to which women experience violence in their daily lives in contexts that the world has not yet recognised as a 'conflict' situation is also only recently being acknowledged. The 1995 UNDP Human Development Report (UNDP 1995:7), for instance, reported that two-thirds of married women in countries as varied as Mexico and Papua New Guinea experience domestic violence, one woman in six worldwide is raped at least once in her lifetime, and over half of all murders of women in countries ranging from Brazil to Bangladesh are committed by husbands or partners.

7 The history of this process is only now being seriously researched. An important example is Coronel (1996).

8 The concept of 'affirmative ethnicity' was raised at the Johannesburg Symposium, and emphasises the

positive dimensions of awareness of one's difference or specialness, such as a sense of self-worth. There is no implicit or inevitable translation of such affirmation into the denigration of others or into actual conflict with others. Why this happens and when has to be researched.

9 The war did of course have a national dimension, particularly after *Sendero* had partially shifted its theatre to Lima. The jungle areas were also badly affected by the war, though the extent is less known, given the isolation of the region and the fact that *Sendero* still operates there.

10 The controversial role of the *rondas* is explored in Degregori *et al.* (1996).

11 The Human Rights Office of the Central American University (UCA) in El Salvador estimates that crime figures for 1995 included 24 murders and 500 robberies or muggings a day.

12 Geraldine McDonald conducted a series of interviews in 1993 for her PhD research in the Department of Peace Studies, University of Bradford (McDonald 1996). In assessing the impact of the popular sectors on the Salvadorean peace process, she records her interview with Salvador Samayoa of the FMLN: 'Salvador Samayoa explains that the FMLN argued for the establishment of a participatory mechanism for social sectors in the Geneva agreement as a means of improving the balance of forces in its favour. The "consultation" of so-called social sectors was in reality a means for both sides to gain legitimacy for their positions at the negotiating table. These organisations didn't exist autonomously. We knew that their entire social base was made up of FMLN supporters. They received political lines from us, we organised them, but we did it

clandestinely ... this was a game we had to play and the government played it too ... Who accepted that the *Instituto de Libertad y Democracia* (Institute for Freedom and Democracy) was autonomous? Nobody did, and yet we still had to pretend that it was. In fact it was an organism of the right, of the ARENA party and it was at the service of the government' (G. McDonald's translation, from the draft thesis chapter, 'Elite-led negotiations in El Salvador: perpetuating the legacy of exclusion', McDonald 1996).

13 The potential contradiction had been noticed for some time by international NGO workers with long experience in the country. Pauline Martin and Francisco Alvarez noted in 1992 that 'the National Reconstruction Plan of the Salvadorean government does not in our view inspire much hope that it has the will or the ability to go beyond party-political interests to build a broad-based consensus around rebuilding the country' (Martin and Alvarez 1996:58).

14 The reconstruction processes taking place at local, municipal level are beginning to be documented. Even where there are FMLN mayors, however, many difficulties remain. See for example Lungo (1995).

15 Interview with the author in Lima, May 1996.

16 For instance, there is a debate between the 'modernisers' and the so-called *Andinistas,* who aim to preserve something of the indigenous skills and way of life. These comments are based on the author's discussions with local NGOs, academics, government officials, and the displaced and returned communities of the Ayacucho and Huancavelica areas in 1993 and 1996.

References

Adams, M. and M. Bradbury (1994) *Conflict and Development: Organisational Adaptation in Conflict Situations,* Oxfam Discussion Paper 4, Oxford: Oxfam GB.

Anderson, Mary B. 'International Assistance and Conflict: An Exploration of Negative Impacts', unpublished mimeo.

Boyce, James K. (1995) 'External assistance and the peace process in El Salvador', *World Development* 23(12): 1201.

CEPAL (1990) *El Salvador: El Estado de la Pobreza y Lineamientos de Política para Afrontarla,* Santiago: CEPAL.

Coronel, José (1996) 'Violencia politica y respuestas campesinas en Huanta', in Degregori *et al.* (1996).

Degregori, Carlos Ivan *et al.* (1996) *Las Rondas Campesinas y la Derrota de Sendero Luminoso,* Lima: IEP Ediciones.

Dye, David *et al.* (1995) *Contesting Everything, Winning Nothing: The Search for Consensus in Nicaragua 1990–1995,* Cambridge, MA: Hemisphere Initiatives.

Galtung, J. (1990) 'Cultural violence', *Journal of Peace Research* 27(3): 291–305.

Hooks, Margaret (1991) *Guatemalan Women Speak,* London: CIIR.

Lungo, M. (1995) 'FMLN mayors in 15 towns', *NACLA: Introduction to Hope: The Left in Local Politics* XXIX(1): 33–7.

McDonald, G. (1996) 'A Comparative Analysis of Peace-building from "Below" in Colombia and El Salvador', mimeo.

Martin, Pauline and Francisco Alvarez (1996) *Development in States of War,* Oxford: Oxfam GB.

Minear, L., C. Scott, and T.G. Weiss (1996) *The News Media, Civil War and Humanitarian Action,* Boulder, CO: Lynne Rienner.

Pankhurst, D. (1989) 'Review article: poverty and food – contemporary questions', *Journal of International Development* 1(4): 513.

Pankhurst, D. and J. Pearce (1997) 'Engendering conflict analysis', in H. Afshar (ed.) *Women and Empowerment,* London: Routledge.

Ridell, R. (1996) 'Trends in International Cooperation', London: ODI, mimeo.

Smith-Ayala, Emilie (1991) *The Granddaughters of Ixmucané: Guatemalan Women Speak,* Toronto: Women's Press.

Thompson, M. (1996) 'Empowerment and survival: humanitarian work in civil conflict' (part I), *Development in Practice* 6(4): 324–33.

UNDP (1995) *Human Development Report.*

Training for peace

Glenda Caine

After 300 years of colonialism, South Africa began its transition to democracy in April 1994. Among the legacies of the past are fractured communities that are out of touch with their cultures and traditions, shattered family structures, and a deep-rooted history of division. On top of this, South Africa also has been left with a culture in which violence is commonly used as an acceptable method of problem solving.

It is within the constraints of this environment that the Independent Projects Trust (IPT), an NGO, offers training in conflict-resolution skills. This training is delivered throughout the region of KwaZulu Natal and focuses on structures such as the following:

- South African Police Services and Community Police Forums
- School Boards, including Management Committees, principals, teachers, and pupils
- women's groups
- political parties
- traditional structures and grassroots leadership in rural areas.

In this paper, we focus on our work with traditional structures in rural areas.

Background

The province of KwaZulu Natal is situated on the eastern seaboard of South Africa, and is bordered by Mozambique in the north and the former Transkei in the south. It occupies approximately one-tenth of South Africa's land mass and has a population of about 9.4 million. The region is characterised by hilly terrain, and the northern-most reaches are remote and often inaccessible by road. A large portion of the province is rural, and the IPT has three offices in these areas:

Port Shepstone in the south, Ulundi in the far north, and Empangeni in the north. The organisation's head office is in Durban, which is the urban centre of KwaZulu Natal.

Most people in the region are Zulu speakers, and it is the second most densely populated region after Gauteng. Although there is significant economic development, this is largely concentrated round the port of Durban and the Richards Bay and Empangeni area. Important crops are sugar and citrus, but the associated activities do not generate enough employment, and it is estimated that the unemployment rate in rural KwaZulu is as high as 70 per cent. Some 46 per cent of all households depend on remittances from male family members who work as contract labourers on the mines and in the industries of Gauteng. The continuation of this system of migrant labour exacerbates the spread of HIV/AIDS: the region has the highest rate of infection in South Africa, as high as 40 per cent in some rural areas.

Infrastructure is – at best – rudimentary, with little or no provision of running water, or access to electric power outside the urban areas. The average monthly per capita income is R210, while the household subsistence income is estimated at R900 per month. Approximately one million children do not attend school.

KwaZulu Natal has a history of political violence which dates back to the 1980s and frequently threatens to undermine the stability of the new dispensation. At risk of over-simplifying things, it can be said to have arisen from the mid-1980s, when the Inkatha Freedom Party (IFP) sought to consolidate its influence in the province, against the growing support for Congress of South African Trade Unions (COSATU) and the United Democratic Front (UDF), both aligned with the African National Congress (ANC). The IFP also threw its weight behind the effort of the National Party to crush the Mass Democratic Movements, a factor which had a long-term negative effect on relationships in the region.

The rural areas of KwaZulu Natal are dominated by traditional structures. This is a system of chiefs (*amakhosi*) and headmen (*indunas*) who exert a major influence over rural life. The rural areas are generally controlled by the IFP, and the urban areas by the ANC. There is continuing tension between the political parties in the province, which is likely to increase as the second general election approaches in 1999.

It is against this backdrop that the IPT trains in rural areas and gives community workers the skills to help their own communities to handle disputes in an effective and peaceful manner.

Definition of community-based peace workers

Rural areas in KwaZulu Natal have been scarred by years of deprivation, and then further damaged by internecine violence. It is critical that we begin to build peace mechanisms into community structures. Little development takes place where there is war and, left unchecked, communities then enter a downward spiral from which there is little hope of return.

The successful peace structures in this region have generally had spontaneous origins, and have often comprised two-person teams, one from each of the combatant groups – for instance the ANC and IFP. These are the types of structure that have the most chance of success in terms of a sustainable peace.

A spokesperson for one of the longest-surviving peace structures in this region gave the following qualities as essential for aspiring peace workers and a successful process:

- fear of God
- honesty
- 'knowing the opposition', understanding and accepting them
- a willingness to 'take it slowly' and handle setbacks
- both parties must be fearless and committed enough to appear in public together
- neutral zones must be identified for joint meetings
- hard-liners may be elected into office, and should be kept in the process and visible at all times
- peace must have a high value for both parties
- small peace cells must be active throughout the community and able to react to crises.

Peace workers at the grassroots level face unique problems. They will be beset by daily challenges, and their constituency – which is usually at the bottom of the pile in the struggle for food, water, and shelter – is often sustained by the violence. This violence may also serve the needs of middle leadership, because it draws the focus from them and any failure on their part to deliver services. Thus peace workers battle continually against adversity. They need to be brave and have a deep commitment which will sustain them through the failures which characterise this type of work.

Training community-based workers and strengthening existing social structures

The type of training and skills transfer in which we are involved is long term, tedious, and difficult to measure. Both the training and funding agencies must have a realistic picture of these difficulties.

We have had some success in training for changing attitudes. For this we concentrate on the following modules:

- communication: effective skills, including active listening skills
- assertiveness: in a country where confrontation is the norm, assertiveness is a vital component for changing attitudes
- problem-solving skills
- co-operative behaviour and consensus-building.

There are certain steps that it is helpful to follow. Firstly, it is essential to work with both sets of combatants, in order to give each group an equal opportunity to provide community trainers. Secondly, the training organisation must be accepted as impartial and trusted by all the groups involved. Openness and integrity on the part of the training agency are imperative.

Our strategy at IPT is to meet with each party to conflict and share our plan, which is to provide training services which will foster skills and assist the parties to manage a changing and stressful environment. Having done that, we work with as many key players at grassroots level as possible, and draw these from all interest groups in the community, such as women's groups, youth, development committees, and so on. The provision of this skills training serves a two-fold purpose, since it also strengthens community ties for people to begin to work together, to realise that they share a common vision and purpose, and start to interact with each other on issues of concern to the community.

What does and does not work?

Where a community has some structures of its own, and has not been too depleted by violence and poverty, it is often possible to enable and support structures which will contribute to peace making in the area. It is, however, impossible to do so without some of the following:

- a spontaneous desire for peace among the people at grassroots level
- strong leadership from both sides of the conflict to carry the process forward

- some external support
- hope of real change and transformation in the community, through the provision of jobs and infrastructure, which will assist in creating new psychological attitudes
- grassroots and middle leadership who support the process
- media which are prepared to play a constructive role.

In conclusion, our experience is that this type of work is never easy and there are no 'quick fixes'. Long-term commitment and dedication are needed. No 'outsider', such as a training organisation, can bring peace: this has to start in the hearts and minds of the affected community.

Making peace as development practice

Sumaya Farhat-Naser and Gila Svirsky

Peace-making is the ultimate site for development in that it works towards building a stable environment in which to construct a better life for future generations. The contributors to this chapter – one Israeli, one Palestinian – live in the same country, and have been associates and partners in this struggle for ten years. Yet they still cannot go out to a restaurant together, or invite one another home for a cup of coffee. Only on a recent trip to Rwanda, where they served as peace mediators, were they finally able to live their friendship openly on neutral ground. These two women are co-founders of the Jerusalem Link for Women, a peace movement split in two, ... between the Israeli Bat Shalom and the Palestinian Jerusalem Center for Women. Through educational programmes, training seminars, non-violent demonstrations, mediation, e-mail exchanges, and interviews such as the one they conducted with us to produce this chapter, they proffer strategies for developing trust, developing relationships, and negotiating difference in the most extreme of political circumstances.

Susan Perry and Celeste Schenck (eds.) *Eye to Eye: Women Practising Development Across Cultures*

Dialogue in the war zone: Israeli and Palestinian women for peace

Gila Svirsky: Sumaya always begins.

Sumaya Farhat-Naser: We have always had women and men who try to talk to each other, who crossed the barriers to speak to each other and do something for peace. But until 1992 it was forbidden to meet as politicians or to represent political positions. It was forbidden to talk to the other side – on both sides – because speaking with the enemy

First published in Susan Perry and Celeste Schenck (eds.) (2001) *Eye to Eye:*

272   *Women Practising Development Across Cultures*

was treason, a form of recognizing the enemy, and so both the PLO and the Israeli government forbade it. But there were always groups of women, individuals who met. I remember in 1986 we met for the first time, six Israeli and six Palestinian women, to develop a programme on how to continue to work with each other. These meetings continued, hidden and informal for several years.

In 1989 a group of Palestinian and Israeli women were invited to Brussels by the Jewish Cultural Centre, which hosted a joint meeting. That meeting was a secret one during which the women worked together to form political principles and create a framework for our joint work. It was necessary to have political guidelines.

These guidelines guaranteed political protection for both sides, because these meetings were forbidden and we wanted to show our people that we were meeting for something that was good for both sides. We formulated principles such as the recognition of national and political rights, the recognition of the PLO, and our stand against violence.

In 1992 a second meeting was held, again in Brussels, because it was too difficult between 1989 and 1992 to continue meeting in Jerusalem because of the *intifada*. Our second meeting was entitled Give Peace a Chance, and we worked out amended principles. The event was extremely important, because four women who were elected to the Israeli legislature came to Brussels in their official capacity as parliamentarians. That made us realize that we had to include Palestinian women who were also elected officials, and so ten women from the Tunisian legislature came. Thus it was a meeting not only of women at the grassroots level, but also of responsible women in politics on both sides. This forced people on both sides to speak about the fact that it was illegal for politicians from either side to meet. We were happy to note that several months later this type of legislation was invalidated on both sides.

We presented our ideas in Brussels at a press conference. We emphasized that we had to work together as part of a joint venture for peace. We recognized that our main enemy in the current situation was false or inadequate knowledge about one another. There was so much fear and mistrust rooted in misinformation, and the fact that we were kept apart by political barriers and exclusive ideologies that conditioned our peoples to remain separated. The Occupation policy and policies fostering animosity caused these fears, and the belief that we could only be enemies.

What we were trying to do was to encourage both sides to view one another as partners, having parity in everything – equal rights; the right of both peoples to live in peace, dignity, and security; and accepting the notion that we both belong to this piece of land. It belongs to us both as two states for two peoples.

- We believe that Jerusalem belongs to both, as an open city that can serve as two capitals for two states.

- We reject all kinds of violence.

- We have not only the right but the obligation to involve ourselves in politics, to shape our political future constructively, and to influence the formation of a civic, democratic society in both nations. We want to see ourselves as one front working for peace for the benefit of both sides.

Those are the main principles that we have been working for, ever since.

Now, practically speaking, we received support from the European Union to establish two centres in Jerusalem – Bat Shalom for Israeli women and the Jerusalem Center for Palestinian Women (JCW). Together both centres comprise the Jerusalem Link. It was meant that these two centres should be in this same city. It would have been a serious error to have only one centre, because we have an asymmetrical situation.

On one side is an established, 50-year-old state with a well-organized, highly developed structure, all the attributes and infrastructure of a state. This includes a high level of educational, technical, and economic development. And on the other side, we have a society that has been plagued by the 30-year revolution and Occupation, and is totally destroyed, yet is on its way to beginning its dream of becoming a state. This asymmetrical situation means that the women of the Jerusalem Center must deal with much more difficult and very different problems than those faced by Bat Shalom. The Israeli women also face an unbelievably complex situation and difficulties that they have to deal with differently. And so we need these two separate centres.

This also demonstrates that both sides want to achieve independence and freedom, and do not want to distort themselves to accommodate the other. We wish to retain our political and cultural identity. Therefore it is important that we should be able to stand in front of each other and look into the other's eyes knowing that we are different, and simply respect that each side is different.

Bat Shalom is located in West Jerusalem for the Israeli women and the Jerusalem Center is in East Jerusalem for the Palestinian women. Each centre has its independent programmes that comply with the immediate needs of its own society. We also have joint programmes that address the political situation, and empower women for political activity. We discuss political principles, and are aligned with the negotiations and the Peace Process. We are committed to the Peace Process and the international covenants, laws, and references for this Peace Process. Together, we address the problem of human rights, especially in Jerusalem. We make joint statements concerning what is happening; for example, if a terrorist attack takes place, irrespective of who did what against whom, we issue a joint statement condemning the event, which points out responsibility for this action and takes a stand on the event. This is very important in terms of public education for peace. As a women's organization, we are also members of the Palestinian Women's Association, and we are very involved in educating women about democracy and human rights.

So we are forced to work and struggle on different levels. We work internally for the development of a civic, democratic society, and in doing this we are very much in confrontation with the whole political and legal system, because we are trying to promote a Palestinian legal system. As women we also have to fight for our women's rights together with other women. We have Palestinian–Palestinian dialogue on the Old City of Jerusalem, where Palestinian women – Christian and Muslim, as well as Christians from different churches – come together to talk about their problems and present their own visions for society. We have civic education for the women of the Old City. The Old City was neglected for such a long time. Palestinians were not allowed to present any sort of developmental plans there, nor was the Old City part of any Israeli development plan. Consequently, there is a lot to do.

We also have a dialogue between Palestinian women from the West Bank and Palestinian women with Israeli passports from Galilee. The main theme is the idea of national identity. Both groups are Palestinian, on the one hand, in their culture, religion, and emotions; but on the other hand, one group has Israeli passports and has gone much further in terms of exposure to Israeli society and their way of life. Therefore we have to recognize our connection to these women from Galilee, and analyze our triangular relationship. How do we make peace work, have a vision for co-existence with dignity for all parties?

The core of our work is our third dialogue programme called Women Making Peace, which provides training for dialogue between Israeli and Palestinian women. This is the most difficult programme, because many people on both sides want to meet, and are eager to do so. But it is not enough to have good intentions and a desire to meet. A suitable infrastructure must be in place. When we have lived 50 years knowing each other only as enemies, with pain and bitter experience very much alive on the Palestinian side, it is very difficult to say 'Let's sit together and hug.' We can't hug. Without proper training, women on both sides think, 'Now we can come together, and I will show them what I have experienced.' Yet everyone has, in the back of her mind, the idea either of defending herself or of attacking the other. After just two sentences, the whole discussion explodes: 'You see, they are so bad. I don't want to see them again. I knew that it was no use meeting with them. I knew that they were terrible.'

To prevent this from happening, we conduct dialogue training. We train both groups, independently, about how to meet, how to learn to respect one another's vision, how to know that there are at least two versions, not one, to every story. Although meeting together is painful, we must learn to bear this pain, to defend ourselves from feeling this pain, and learn how to cross this painful stage. We must address our fears, speak our hopes and visions aloud. But to do this, we must also lay the groundwork by training women in political analysis, teaching them to analyze the information around us. What is going on behind the scenes; what does it mean to speak about refugees, borders, Jerusalem? How do these issues affect one side or the other?

When both sides feel that they are prepared to look into the eyes of the other with respect, to heal, to listen, to understand how to contribute to a logical discussion, to be sensitive in wording, in attitude, then the groups can meet and begin working together. The aim is not to learn to drink coffee together. Anyone can drink coffee together. The aim is to discuss political issues, very difficult political issues, and to come out of these discussions with a consensus that is good for both sides. This is the aim for this dialogue programme that caters to young women, old women, and target groups such as students and policewomen.

Gila: I'm really going to miss hearing these speeches. I'm always inspired by them.

At the same time, I'm always struck by how the approaches of each side are different. The work of Bat Shalom is also different from the other peace movements in Israel.

First, perhaps I can capture the difference between us by saying that the Israeli women come to dialogue with Palestinian women so that they can sleep better at night. They can assuage their guilty feelings about being in the camp of the oppressors. On the other hand, Palestinian women come to the dialogue group to prevent the Israeli women from sleeping well at night. I think that pretty much captures the different stances that each side takes. We have had dialogue work for about three years now. We have had some very difficult times in the groups, and also some superficial times in the groups. The dialogue work is always marked by the determination of the Palestinian side to get to the political issues, to talk about what Israel is doing wrong, and to have the Israeli women understand that they must pressure their government to change things. Whereas the Israeli women come because they want to be friends with the Palestinian women. They want to drink coffee, they want to talk about their children and about good books they've read. They acknowledge the faults of the Israeli government but, at the same time, they want to get past it. But the Palestinians are not past it.

The Oslo Declaration of Principles – and the famous handshake on the White House lawn –happened in September 1993, but there is no peace. There has not been an end to the Occupation. In some ways, in fact, the Occupation has got worse. Although Israelis in general – especially the Left – recognize that we are a long way away from the final peace agreement, many people think that peace is in the bag. All we have to do now is work out the details.

But peace is not yet in the bag. On both sides, it's our task to clarify to our respective societies that not only are some things worse, but some very, very painful decisions will have to be taken – on both sides – for peace really to be in our pockets. Our job in Bat Shalom is to prepare Israeli society for some of those painful concessions. Bat Shalom serves a different function in Israeli society from the other Israeli peace organizations. It's not only because we're women, but I think being women has a lot to do with it. The principles that we signed jointly with the JCW were much more progressive – in fact, radical – principles than had been signed previously by any joint gathering of Palestinian and Israeli peace advocates. They were way ahead of their time. Some of the statements made in those principles are matters of consensus in Israel today, but some of those statements remain on the radical fringe, and it will take a few years before we move towards them.

Let me give you a couple of examples. Sumaya mentioned them in the Palestinian context. Let me present them in the Israeli context.

The first statement is that there must be a Palestinian state side by side with an Israeli state. This principle was considered anathema to the Israeli public when we first began to talk about it. It was beyond the pale. We spoke of it without going into detail. We are now ten years past our initial dialogue groups, and we can look with gratification at public opinion in Israel and say that it has moved a long way on this subject. Today, 60 per cent of Jewish Israelis believe that Palestinians have a right to a state of their own, side by side with the state of Israel. Sixty per cent! Ten years ago, it was less than 20 per cent. An additional 10 per cent of Jewish Israelis believe that while the Palestinians may not have a right to a state, this state is inevitable. Which means that 70 per cent of the Israeli Jewish public believes that there is a state around the corner and the great majority feel that it is justified. This is an *enormous* stride forward.

A second joint principle, which is not yet acceptable to the Israeli public, is that the city of Jerusalem must be a shared capital. If you ask Israelis today what they think about Jerusalem as a shared capital, 80 per cent will tell you that Jerusalem must be the exclusive capital of Israel. An additional 15 per cent have creative ideas about how to go about solving the problem of joint claims to the capital. Only 5 per cent accept the solution which the Jerusalem Link supports: the concept that Jerusalem must be a shared capital, in united and shared sovereignty – part of the city will be the capital of Israel and part of it will be the capital of Palestine. That is still a principle on which we are way out on a limb compared to the rest of Israeli society.

I'd also like to point out something that Sumaya mentioned in passing and for which the JCW deserves enormous credit: their courageous position on the rejection of violence as a political strategy. For the Palestinians that meant condemning all forms of Palestinian violence, even at a time when the Palestinians had very few other tools to make their claims or focus world attention on the injustice done to them. Nevertheless, the Palestinian women's centre said 'No' to violence. For us Israelis, condemning Israeli violence means condemning the Israeli army for its acts of state terrorism. This includes using live ammunition to control demonstrations, grabbing land by force, destroying homes, and even denying Palestinians their fair share of drinking water. These are all forms of state terrorism used against a weak civilian population, and we condemn them even though they happen under the auspices of a legally elected government. We regard this as a form of terrorism; condemning it was our own courageous contribution to the principle of non-violence.

I'd like to talk about the ways in which the women's peace work at Bat Shalom is different from the type of peace work that takes place in the rest of the Israeli peace movement. First of all the mainstream peace movement in Israel, the mixed-gender movement, is very conservative. It looks at the issues and asks itself: will the security of Israel be strengthened? Security is the ultimate criterion for them. It looks at any of the proposed solutions or political accommodations and asks: what are the security safeguards? What's in it for Israel?

We believe that this turns the question on its head. It's our belief that a peace agreement holds the best – indeed the only – hope of security. A peace that is acceptable to both sides is the only way to achieve security for Israelis, as well as Palestinians.

Our methods are different, our goals are different, and our vision of peace is different. The mixed-gender peace movement in Israel seeks a peace of mutual deterrence. This would include closing the border, locking the door, and throwing away the key. No more Palestinians mixing with Israelis. They want limits set on the extent to which the Palestinian side can arm itself – no tanks, no warplanes, no artillery. I'd like to set those same limits on Israeli society. I'm not arguing for tanks on the Palestinian side but for banishing tanks from the Israeli side as well.

The difference is that while the mixed-gender Israeli peace camp argues for mutual deterrence, the Bat Shalom women argue for a culture of peace and mutual co-operation. We argue for a future in which our destinies are intertwined, in which we have economic, cultural, and recreational co-operation – in sport, in fashion, in business, whatever. Our economies should have some integration, while at the same time maintaining the independence of both states.

I argue forcefully for the economic integration of both communities because of the terrible disparity between the two economies. The per capita GDP in Palestine is approximately $1600 per year. The parallel figure in Israel is $16,500. That's ten times more. Israel's per capita GDP is roughly the same as that of Italy and Spain, modern European countries. Palestine's economy is Third World. This enormous disparity between Palestine and Israel fosters instability between our two societies. And we have learned from history that you cannot have two neighbouring societies with such a huge economic gap between them and expect political stability. There will always be volatility unless there is some parity. So we in the women's peace movement argue for a shared future.

There are also important differences in our activities. In the women's peace movement, we do different sorts of things. The mixed movement embraces the 'big bang' theory of organizing. It has a big rally where a hundred thousand people show up, hug each other, and then all go home again until the next rally six months later.

The women's peace movement has consistently advocated ongoing peace activities – ongoing in every way possible, using every strategy imaginable to build bridges between our societies and to educate Israelis about the importance of peace. For example, in addition to the dialogue groups that have already been mentioned, the Israeli women make condolence calls to some Palestinian families when a family member has been killed by the Israeli authorities. Conversely, the Palestinians do the same thing on our side by visiting – where they would be welcome – families of Israelis who have been killed by terrorism.

We have public education activities. We run seminars and open-panel discussions. We have our own newspaper, and we pay for advertisements in national media to air our views. We had a meeting just last week to begin our analysis of a very difficult issue: the refugee problem. How can we resolve the problem of almost a million Palestinian refugees created by the 1948 war, who have now grown into a population of several million? We have begun this series of meetings to come up with a solution that makes sense.

Finally, Bat Shalom women have been physically courageous in their activities, in a way that the mixed peace movement has not yet begun to dream of. Bat Shalom is willing to engage in civil disobedience. We're willing to break the law if we believe it to be an unjust law. We act in the spirit of Mahatma Gandhi, who said that non-co-operation with evil is a sacred duty. We believe that very strongly. A case in point is the demolition of homes that has taken place over the last few years. Over 5000 Palestinian homes have been destroyed by the Israeli authorities under the pretext that they were illegally constructed, but in reality this is an effort to move Palestinians out of areas that Israel wishes to claim as its own.

The Israeli women of Bat Shalom have joined Palestinian protests, thrown themselves in front of the bulldozers together with our Palestinian sisters and brothers, defied laws, pushed past soldiers, put ourselves on the line because we know that non-co-operation with evil is a sacred duty. The consensus-driven peace movement in Israel would never participate in this way, and has shunned these activities of ours. We act in conjunction with a few men who have the same take on the politics of the region as we do, and we appreciate their presence. The women's peace group in Israel has taken leadership within Israel in terms of its courage, its progressive political beliefs, and its feminist vision of peace – not just an end to the belligerence, but peace with dignity and co-operation on both sides.

Sumaya: We Palestinian women in the Jerusalem Center have many difficulties convincing our people that this joint work is fruitful, and that we must go on with it. We have these difficulties because we work openly with Israeli women, and are stamped as a joint venture. For example, the Palestinian network association for NGOs in Palestine has refused us membership because we work with Israelis. However, because we are already stigmatized, in a sense this gives us the freedom to dare to do things that others cannot do. This is a strength in itself. We have taken small steps towards success in showing people that it is possible to reach consensus with the other side. First we have to persuade the Israeli side that we have rights, and then we must convince our own people that some Israelis are willing to recognize our rights. We try to see these small steps as something big in order to encourage ourselves, to defy the despair and disappointment we sometimes feel.

We always have the feeling that we are in a state of alarm. We have to be careful not to make political mistakes, so that we can show our people that we are keen to protect our rights and do not want to give anything up, that we never compromise. This is very tiring, and a great pressure. We have a concept in Palestine called 'normalization'. Normalization means the establishment of normal relations with the Israelis. This is strongly rejected – people say: how dare you try to make something normal in a situation where nothing is normal? We are *still* under occupation; they are *still* the occupiers. They are *still* taking land away, they are *still* restricting our movements, destroying our houses, detaining our people, depriving us of our rights, and so forth.

We have to be very careful to avoid being pushed into that corner of normalization. Normalization can be something great, the fulfillment of living together in peace. But we are not there yet. We always have to persuade or to ask our Israeli partners to understand that we cannot do many things we wish to do because we are afraid of being accused of normalizing relations. For example, meeting in a restaurant and eating together, or visiting each other at home. We cannot do it. We are afraid of it. We become vulnerable, unprotected, if we do it. On the other hand, we know very well that if we do do these things, we will become much closer to each other. The process of understanding and making a relationship will be greatly enhanced. So it's always one step forward, two back, then perhaps try another step forward. That is what we must do in this very sensitive situation. So working for peace in Palestine is very, very difficult. We must always defend why we do it. We must always consult people. We must always fear for our safety. We must be very cautious, and involve both people on the ground and people in decision-making positions so that they can give their seal of approval. We are so pleased to see that officials are now using the same phrases, the same words, we used three or four years ago. We say things today, knowing that in a few years officials will say them. This is our contribution.

Gila: On the Israeli side, the media have completely ignored us until recently, and I think this is part of the general syndrome of marginalizing women's activities. When we stood in the Women in Black vigil for many, many years, we were covered by every major international news network. We were on CNN, the BBC, all the major networks, and had a segment on *Sixty Minutes* in the US, but in Israel we never made it into the newspapers until the fifth year of our vigil. By and large, the Israeli media ignore women's work.

Sumaya: The majority of our people don't yet see the importance of the work we are doing. We see that our work together is preparing the ground for the people who will build peace together when the peace settlements are achieved. But our people still have difficulty believing that the Israeli government wants peace with us. They are reluctant to believe that our work is necessary. I myself hesitate to go to the media to say I am doing wonderful things in Israel. It can provoke a backlash, backfire on us and hurt our work. Our strategy to let people know about us is to work with groups of women, girls, boys, who participate in our courses. Every year we have five or six hundred participants in our courses. We are afraid of being attacked if the media turn their lens on us. Abroad, in Europe or the States, the media are interested in knowing about us, and academics in particular are interested. They do research on us. Journalists, on the other hand, want action, and they love to show violence, bloodshed. But our work, moderate work, is measured in small steps. There are no immediate results. We make dialogue groups; it takes time. How can this be covered by a journalist? When there is a violent act, the whole world knows about it in ten seconds. We must learn how to use the media better; we must become better skilled at presenting our words, our ideas, our message. How to make coalitions. To seek assistance. We need to work on this.

We also need to work on fostering economic development, but unfortunately that kind of development is inevitably linked with the official political system. In Palestine, any co-operation with Israelis, especially economic, must be via the official political establishment. There is an undefined relationship between NGOs and the Palestinian authority, officials, administration. We are working on that. But again, I have received several letters from Israeli businesswomen and organizers who are seeking connections with Palestinian business-women. They met several times just for discussion, but nothing came out of it because Palestinian women feared normalizing relations with Israelis. 'I don't need to do this', says the Palestinian woman to herself; 'my business is doing well. I must wait until this co-operation is fully accepted, not just ten per cent.' Except those who are in the Palestinian Authority. They have good relations; they work together. Especially the businessmen, who have the power. The women feel that it is forbidden as soon as they begin, because of the patriarchal structure, the authority of men. Men maintain the difference between business and politics. We don't think this is correct.

Gila: Yes, this is terrible. People who were once involved in the worst forms of oppression against the Palestinians are today businessmen making money from the connections they had as perpetrators of torture, or demolishers of homes, or agents in the secret-service organizations. Some of these Israelis are making money today through partnerships with some corrupt politicians in the Palestinian Authority, as well.

Editors: How does the Jerusalem Link work out its differences? What sorts of skills have you developed over the years for mediating conflict? Do you have anything formal in place? [Sighs from both Sumaya and Gila.]

Gila: That's a hard question. Well, sometimes we ignore the differences. [Laughter on all sides.] If there's a difference of opinion, such as we had for a long while about what we mean when we speak of sharing Jerusalem – what kind of model we have for the city – I think we agree not to talk about it. Wouldn't you say so, Sumaya?

Sumaya: Yes. But I have to tell you: I have been the spokesperson for the Center for more than two years now. Before that, I was on the Board of Trustees; I was a co-founder. In these years, we always had disputes. And always there is some sense of suspicion. Do they really mean what they say? There have always been issues we have not dared to speak of. But even as a responsible person, I tended until now to ignore these things, and sweep the disputes under the table. But now I am at a new stage. I have a new project with the former director of Bat Shalom in which we are trying something I suggested. We try to talk about our differences, and to address them now. You need a certain degree of maturity in order to face these disputes. So I decided to write an article about our differences in which I say why I had quarrels with Bat Shalom on this issue or that. I wrote about 50 pages, addressing 12 disputes in this single document. These were the things we couldn't talk about. Whenever we started, we quarrelled again. So I thought it would be more effective to write about them, to write about things we can't say face to face. Now that we have started, I give the article to my colleague, and she answers in writing from her point of view. Afterwards we might meet together to say: 'Isn't it too bad we quarrelled; how crazy we were.' Or we can say: 'I had not realized what you meant.' We also saw, through this process, that it is possible to solve problems once and for all. We are working on it right now; we already have 60 shared pages. For example, she was very upset with me because I write exactly as I speak, enumerating my political points: one, two, three, four. I ignored the fact that we had worked together for so long. I called her 'the Israeli' or 'the co-ordinator.' I never used her name, Daphne, or 'my friend'. And I responded: 'How can you expect me, after just two years, to say that you are my friend? You are not yet my friend. It is not that easy, especially if I am representing an official political stance in my work with you. I am afraid of being accused of normalization. You are asking me to behave as if I am living and enjoying a state of law in Israel, with all the reassurances that go with that.'

Through this writing we are trying to promote understanding. Through this writing I introduce my culture, my thinking, my behaviour, in the context of the culture and the education I had at home in the street. It is a very important process that can be followed in conflict management.

I also have many things to write to Gila – about our disputes, and problems, and difficulties with her. These are completely different from the difficulties I had with Daphne. It is so interesting. I hope this process continues.

Editors: Could you talk about the difficulties you face today?

Gila: Allow me to begin. The Jerusalem Link recently voted to change its founding principles. To be more honest, actually the Palestinians came to the Israeli side and said they had to have the principles changed. I liked the old principles because they were a broad, general vision of what peace should be. The Palestinians wanted the principles to be more specific. When we went over them point by point, the recommended changes turned out to be ones with which I found it hard to agree. Ultimately I resigned from the directorship of Bat Shalom over this. I don't want to go into great detail here over these principles, but the general dynamic was that the Palestinians would ask for a particular change and the Israelis would immediately concede. I would raise my hand and say: this is not acceptable to me; it's too extreme. Then the Israelis would say: it's OK, the Palestinians need it for their purposes; it's no big deal for us. And I would say: but it's a big deal for me. But I was in the minority at that meeting. Eventually the principles approved at that meeting were taken to the wider membership of Bat Shalom, and it became evident that there were many women in Bat Shalom who felt that they could not live with the new principles. There were a number of resignations as a result.

This is a really fine example of a poorly handled dynamic. The situation was not set up to allow for discussion, or even for the existence of a safe space for those who disagree to express their point of view. I said earlier that often we handle conflict by not talking about things. This was different. This was a situation in which the Palestinians said: 'We need this', so the Israelis, after so many years of being the oppressor, felt that they could not disagree with what the Palestinians were asking for. I think that in America in debates over race relations this is called 'white guilt'. We felt unable to make legitimate counter-proposals. In separate meetings, the Israelis spoke of bringing to the Palestinians some suggestions for compromise wording, and we did. But as soon as each suggestion was raised, there was initial resistance on the part of some Palestinian women – the younger, more extremist ones – so the Israelis immediately backed down without a full discussion. I blame the Israelis for not being more honest, more open.

Instead, we were constantly backing down against real or even imagined Palestinian objections. There was no real engagement on those issues. To this day, the matter of the principles has not been resolved.

Maybe an example will help. Both sides knew that we had to make a statement about how to resolve the problem of several million Palestinian refugees created by the war of 1948 – Palestinians who once lived in areas that are now Israel. The Palestinian side proposed a wording that included the sentence: 'This solution must honour the right of return of the Palestinian refugees in accordance with UN Resolution 194.' In my opinion, this resolution – passed 52 years ago, in 1948 – is outdated today. It would give Palestinian refugees the right to return to their former homes in Israel, thereby evicting Israeli families and compounding one injustice with another. Even my very mild suggestion that we say 'in the spirit of UN Resolution 191' rather than 'in accordance' with it was rejected. And the Israeli side did not stand up for this revision, even though many Bat Shalom members cannot live with the wording as it now stands.

I hope that following this turbulent period there will be engagement on the issues and frank discussions about what the problems are, what solutions would be agreeable to both sides. Final-status peace talks are being launched, and I want the Israeli women's peace movement to come to the Israeli politicians not with an untenable 52-year-old position, but with viable, rational proposals for resolving the issues in contention.

Sumaya: For us, the Palestinians, it was very necessary that we re-evaluate and amend our principles to include certain details of the Final-Status Negotiations. We have received more and more pressure from our society to the effect that working with the Israelis is useless. But we are very clear. We want to work with you. And we push for our joint work. First, we want to show our people that we are working on very sensitive issues, and working together with the Israelis, preparing the ground for those who are the negotiators and for those who are on the street to understand what is going on in the negotiations. Second, we feel that we have been misled by the Israeli government so many times over the past years of the peace process. The agreements that were signed went back on those written before, and each time fewer rights were given to us than in the previous agreement. The feeling was that the Israelis are cheating us. You can't trust agreements with them. We have nothing to revert to.

We need a very clear reference for our work together. We feel that our legitimacy comes from the Oslo and UN resolutions, for example. We feel that we need to be much more specific, so that we can count on some rights. It is important to us that the basis for the two states be the borders as they were on 4 June 1967, before the war broke out. Why should we now make concessions before we begin to negotiate? In any negotiation, both sides must make compromises. Why should we in the Jerusalem Link begin with a compromise that benefits the Israeli side? This is how our side viewed it. The re-evaluation of our declaration was a kind of self-protection, self-defence in our society, but also to initiate the discussions that we hope will begin. We wanted to include specifics – the refugees, the settlements, Jerusalem. We also thought the weakness of the Oslo agreements were that they did not address the problems of the Palestinians, yet they claimed that they had brought peace discussions to the final stages. We felt that we did not get even a small part of the rights to which we were entitled in the previous agreements. Thus we cannot go to the final negotiations with only 8 per cent of the land – if earlier agreements had been honoured, we would enter the Final-Status Negotiations with 30 per cent of the land.

This is to show you the immediate and critical necessity for re-evaluating and amending our principles, from our point of view. I must say frankly that it was a shock to see that this produced such turbulence in Bat Shalom, and that its director – Gila – quit. We were very surprised by this. Nobody could believe it. We worked together; we expected her to understand. How could she work with us and not share our vision of our rights? How can any individual be against the UN resolutions? She can afford to say it because everything is settled in her state, and its legitimacy is based on UN resolutions. But we are now struggling so that those same resolutions should be applied to us, and nobody can tell us they shouldn't. It was a very important discussion. The problem is that there was no room for discussion. What Gila says is right. We wanted to amend things. But they gave up immediately, so as not to have a dispute and to show they can work with us. Let's show that we get along together. So we hid our disputes and real messages again.

Letter

Gila to Sumaya

Dear Sumaya

This dialogue with you, like the many we have had in the past, has been marked by openness, honesty, and an empathetic listening, even where we disagree. I have had the feeling at all times of speaking as equals, without holding back difficult words, without making 'discounts' for the differences between us.

And yet I have also been painfully aware of the need you have to maintain distance – what the Palestinians refer to as preventing 'normalization'. Even though this has continued to sadden me, as I have longed for a 'normal' and close friendship with you, someone with whom I share so much and feel so warm towards, I know and understand that you cannot allow this to happen under the rules that you have agreed to live by. Distance is a political statement of your own, as well as protection for you against those who attack your efforts at reconciliation. I know that you need to protect yourself and your family from those voices and acts of criticism, but I ache to think how politics can come between people.

Another ache I have is the thought that you and your colleagues on the Palestinian side have not been able to understand or appreciate my decision to resign as director of Bat Shalom, based on my objection to the new principles that the Jerusalem Link adopted. You were 'shocked', you note in the interview. I do feel the need to try again to explain. Not just as someone who might have been your friend in a world that was more just, but as one who continues to be a political ally in our common cause.

Let me say at the outset that I was in complete agreement with the previous Jerusalem Link declaration. That document reflected the principles common to us all – the shared yearning of Israeli and Palestinian women for a just and enduring peace in the Middle East.

The new document, however, although it may be a suitable state-ment for the Palestinian side of the Jerusalem Link, does not take into consideration Israeli needs. Some of the new principles adopted are not fair to the Israeli side, in my opinion, and will alienate Bat Shalom from even the progressive elements of Israeli society that we have worked so hard to nurture and expand, including many of its own members. These new principles will weaken Bat Shalom's ability to influence political opinion, and hence political decision making, inside Israel.

Some of the new principles return us to old conflicts, rather than lead us to new and creative solutions, to a healing of the old pain. In my opinion, the following three principles advocate positions from an earlier era, which are no longer tenable:

- Principle 1 calls for 'establishment of a Palestinian state alongside Israel on the June 4, 1967 boundaries'. Calling for these borders without acknowledging the inevitability of 'adjustments agreed upon by both sides' is unrealistic. I had proposed that at the very least we insert the words 'based on' the June 4, 1967 boundaries, suggesting that amendments can be made, but this formulation was rejected.

- Principle 6 calls for solving the Palestinian refugee problem 'in accordance with UN Resolution 194'. This resolution – passed more than 50 years ago, in 1948 – is outdated and irrelevant today. For example, it would give Palestinian refugees the right to return to their former homes in Israel, thereby evicting Israeli families and compounding one injustice with another. I do believe that a just solution for the Palestinian refugee problem must include the Palestinian right of return to the area that is now Israel – for those who so choose – but I cannot agree that Israelis who currently live in these homes must now be turned into refugees.

- Finally, principle 4 notes that the permanent-settlement negotiations must resume without delay (with which I certainly agree), but then adds: 'the terms of reference being all relevant UN resolutions ... '. I think it is absurd to invoke the 2000 pages of UN resolutions that have been enacted since 1948 as the 'terms of reference' without a thorough reading and review of their applicability to contemporary times. Indeed, many of these resolutions foment anger and divisiveness, rather than offer constructive solutions. The previous Jerusalem Link declaration correctly referred only to Resolutions 242 and 338, which are still the key and relevant resolutions, and did not resurrect old hurts.

These were my three main objections, and they were key matters of principle for me. You yourself saw that at the meeting where the Palestinians raised these proposals the Israelis were fearful of expressing their uneasiness with them. You saw the dynamic that was created – of going along with whatever the Palestinians said. I was the only one who consistently found the voice to speak honestly, and that is because I spoke as an equal with you, having had years of frank and fruitful dialogue. It seemed to me that the other Israelis spoke out of 'white guilt' – shame over the years of oppression by Israelis of Palestinians. The Israeli discomfort with the principles became evident only when we met separately as Bat Shalom.

Sumaya, my disappointment was with the Bat Shalom board, which consented to these principles without making any effort at all to create a statement that would be fair and relevant to our side as well as yours. Those few on the Israeli side who pushed for the new principles acted in utter disregard of the negative implications for Bat Shalom. Although their primary motivation was to provide the Palestinian side with a document that they felt was necessary for Palestinian needs, in my opinion the damage rendered to Bat Shalom will ultimately harm the Jerusalem Link.

It seems that the honesty that you and I have had as directors of the Jerusalem Link has not filtered down to our respective organizations. Perhaps because they have not had the ongoing contact with each other, as you and I have had.

This matter of the new principles and my resignation as a result often evokes in my mind the words of the Lebanese writer Kahlil Gibran: 'When your friend speaks his mind you fear not the "nay" in your own mind, nor do you withhold the "ay".'

Dear and trusted colleague, thank you for your ongoing co-operation throughout our work together. I hope that the day will come when concerns over 'normalization' and ideology will no longer prevent us from actually becoming friends.

Sincerely,
Gila Svirsky
29 January 2000

Letter

Sumaya to Gila

Dear Gila

Thank you very much for your kind words and sincere feelings in describing the relations between us, which have developed through our sensitive and hard work, the joint management of conflicts, and the growing process of our personal maturity – perceiving, learning, and ultimately acknowledging each other's positions. We have become very close, and while we share almost the same feelings, attitudes, and perceptions about many points, we also have our differences – which is normal and correct – derived from our respect for the identity and uniqueness of each. Opening up and expressing our common concerns and aspirations has helped us both to understand the importance of circumstances and context when searching for solutions. The willingness to put oneself in the place of the other has made it possible sometimes to reach consensus on difficult issues. When we fail to reach consensus, it has sometimes been because of insufficient time and also an unwillingness to have intensive and comprehensive discussions. Even though we know the importance of having a frank and thorough discussion, we often avoid it because we fear confrontation. We would rather conform than confront.

Thank you, Gila, for understanding the complex issue of 'normalizing relations', which will exist as long as our peoples consider each other the enemy. Political reconciliation must precede social reconciliation. When it does, then it will be easier to meet, work jointly, and plan for a common future. But as long as one side is politically, economically, and ideologically taking advantage of the other, peace work is perceived by the majority to be not just nonsense, but also dangerous. Based on their daily experience my people believe that Israel is fulfilling Zionist ideology by acquiring as much Palestinian land as possible by force and illegal means and aims to control our people forever. They see Israel as engaged in a process of dictating rather than negotiating. In peace both sides must win; in war both lose although the loss of one side is greater than that of the other.

Why do I write all this to you? I know your thoughts, attitudes, humanity, and desire for justice. I also know your political stand and, based on personal discussions, I understood your motives for resigning. But this does not make up for the sad feeling I have in losing you as a trusted colleague and partner. I highly respect and value your thought and character. What shocked me was your quick resignation, your setting of priorities while dealing with the matter. We are both aware of the difficulties in each centre. It had always been a relief to relate, compare, and share these problems. I have the feeling that both our boards did not discuss the principles thoroughly, bringing dissatisfaction and new conflicts. Addressing disputes is the basis of our efforts to reach reconciliation. And yet we are still at the starting point, and must develop this as a valued culture to guide our behaviour.

I understand your concerns about borders, refugees, and UN resolutions. This is not only a matter of principle, but also a matter of trying to convince each other. The UN resolutions are the only legal documents that Palestinians have to protect our rights. We cannot drop these resolutions before even beginning to negotiate, or receiving a sign from your side that you are prepared to acknowledge responsibility and admit guilt. I know you are far from thinking about these issues, but I feel that it is my responsibility to address the linkage between responsibility and guilt, and thus open the door to compromise. This is the basis for the first step in reconciliation. I understand your concern about not wanting to evict Israelis from the homes they now live in, the Palestinian homes from which the owners were forced to evacuate and become refugees. First admit the injustice that was committed and recognize the rights of the Palestinian refugees, so we can then find options for solving the problem. Your fear of seeing your people become refugees is respected and understood only if you prevent the creation of refugees on the Palestinian side. We two peoples have the same values! What an appreciative reaction and feeling of relief spread among my people when they read about the Israeli researcher who published an acknowledgement of the massacre of Tantura, a village near Haifa, where 200 Palestinian people were killed in 1948, and the village was destroyed. Such forms of acknowledgement open the heart and mind to rethink, reconsider, and search for solutions.

I have interest and desire to continue this dialogue with you on political issues and on a social and personal level. I feel enriched by it. The obstacle is only the accumulation of work in the office and at home. I am sure we will do it, and I am very happy to know that you will always be there to share our concern and participate in our joint mission.

Dear and trusted colleague, I also thank you for your ongoing co-operation and because I have learned a lot from you. I hope that the barriers preventing us from becoming close friends will diminish. There are not only physical walls set by law, but the psychological barriers are also still thick and diverse. On your side, you can work for peace and be proud; you will be admired and encouraged by most, even though some will reject you. On our side, my work for peace is perceived by most people with doubt, question marks, accusations, and sometimes a sense of shame. Sometimes we have to hide from or avoid public meetings and events. My work is not only difficult and sensitive, but could turn unappreciated and even dangerous.

Most painful to me is that I consider my work very important, necessary and vital for our joint survival. I believe in that, and this is what keeps me strong and gives me the strength to continue and start again and again. The main source for my strength and courage is knowing that there are hundreds of wonderful women and men on both sides who share my vision and work sincerely and with commitment. I hope that these people on both sides will become one front that grows and grows into thousands and millions. I not only hope, but I do believe that we will make it.

Sincerely,
Sumaya Farhat-Naser
3 February 2000

Acknowledgement

This chapter is reproduced with permission from *Eye to Eye: Women Practising Development Across Cultures*, edited by Susan Perry and Celeste Schenck, published in London and New York by Zed Books in 2001.

Building bridges for peace

Rola Hamed

There are always some essential points and distinctions to be made in any discussion about the Israeli–Palestinian conflict, but in this short essay I will focus on questions about Israeli and Palestinian identities, and highlight the situation of Palestinians inside Israel (those who remained in their land and became Israeli citizens), especially after the second *intifada*. The second part of the essay offers a brief description of a feminist peace organisation, Bat Shalom, on whose Board I serve in my capacity as a Palestinian from Israel, and its partnership with a similar Palestinian organisation, the Jerusalem Center for Women, and their co-ordinating body – Jerusalem Link.

Questions of identity

The concept of identity encompasses various cultural components: language, religion, customs, traditions, symbols, and history. A history of suffering and the need for a homeland are the most dominant aspects of both the Palestinian and the Israeli identities. The legitimacy of and international support for both nations are very much based on the homelessness of the Palestinians on the one hand, and of the holocaust and its survivors on the other. In both cases, we see a nationalist ethos cultivated through stories of noble fighters who gave their lives for the nation, and of young people who devote their lives to building that nation.

Another important aspect of both identities is the diaspora. The Palestinian refugees and the Jews in Israel represent only a minority of their nations, and both peoples justify the 'return' of the diaspora. The Zionists would like all Jews to come to Israel and be a part of the Jewish homeland, while the Palestinians fight for the return of their people who have twice been expelled from their homes and villages, first in 1948 and again in 1967.

I would argue that both the Palestinian and the Israeli 'imagined communities' are stepping-stones on the way for the Palestinians and Israelis to co-exist: the Israeli connection to the Jewish diaspora and the 'law of return', which aims to keep a Jewish majority inside Israel, and the Palestinian refugees' right to return, something which is unlikely to be accepted by the people and government of Israel in the coming decades.

Palestinian women in Israel

As for my own identity, I started my political life in 1982 at the age of 10, when I participated with my grandmother in demonstrations against the war in Lebanon in my home city of Nazareth, and we faced police violence with our own bodies. As a child I would recall this event as if it had happened only the day before. Ever since then I have been active in many organisations working for peace and co-existence, and a member of the Arab Students Committees both at school and later at university. Maybe my self-confidence and ability to be who I am derives from being born into a political family and enjoying my parents' full support to go my own way and to hold my own beliefs, and their encouragement always to do my best.

My experience in peace and feminist organisations over 20 years proves that Israeli and Palestinian women can speak out with one voice and share the same vision for our common future. We can protest against the Israeli occupation, show support and solidarity with Palestinian and Israeli mothers, sisters, and daughters, with the families of victims from both sides, and with each other as individuals. We are struggling for peace and for the equality of all women and especially for the equal rights of Palestinian women from poor neighbourhoods in Israel. I believe that our organisation's joint Jewish–Arab structure helps us to see that women on both sides have the same problems and the same future.

All the same, Palestinian Arab women in Israel do face particular problems, which is why I joined with 14 activists both from women's organisations and from the universities in founding the Council for Palestinian Women in Israel in order to bring women's voice into the public sphere especially after the last *intifada* and the uprising of the Arab population inside Israel. This council is a nationwide women's voluntary organisation that seeks to raise public awareness of Palestinian women's issues.

Working for peace – Jerusalem Link

Palestinian women in Israel have been and continue to be actively involved in peace organisations. During the first *intifada* many of us participated in Women in Black, a national organisation that held a weekly vigil in towns and cities throughout Israel's occupation of the West Bank and Gaza. Today, some Palestinian women are members of the Jerusalem Link, a co-ordinating body established in 1994 in Brussels between two independent women's organisations – Bat Shalom on the Israeli side, based in West Jerusalem, and the Jerusalem Center for Women on the Palestinian side, based in East Jerusalem. The Jerusalem Link was the outcome of an ongoing dialogue between members of the two organisations dating back to 1989. Both organisations share a set of political principles, which serve as the foundation for a co-operative model of co-existence between our respective peoples. The Jerusalem Link mobilises Palestinian and Jewish women to contribute in various ways to the peace process, runs leadership seminars, and helps women to run for elected office.

The two feminist peace organisations which collaborate under the umbrella of the Link are autonomous and take their own national constituency as their primary responsibility – but together we promote a joint vision of a just peace, democracy, human rights, and women's leadership. Mandated to advocate for peace and justice between Israel and Palestine, we believe that a viable solution of the conflict between our two peoples must be based on recognition of the right of the Palestinian people to self-determination and an independent state alongside the state of Israel, with Jerusalem as the capital of both states, and a final settlement of all relevant issues based on international law.

The two organisations don't agree on everything – differing, in particular, on the critical issue of the right of Palestinian refugees displaced in 1948 to return to their homes – but we have not allowed this to prevent our close collaboration over the last decade. The urgency of our mission today springs from two years of escalating violence since the outbreak of the second *intifada*, during which time we have witnessed in ever more devastating detail the catastrophic effect of war on women in particular. Our organisations are therefore launching an international initiative to stop the violence immediately. We are insisting that all negotiating teams include at least 50 per cent women – in the Israeli and Palestinian leadership, in the UN teams, and among representatives of all governments involved in attempts to resolve this conflict.

The Jerusalem Link is based on the following principles:

We, Palestinian and Israeli women, united in a joint effort to bring about a just, comprehensive, and lasting peace between our two peoples, affirm our commitment to working together, within the framework of The Jerusalem Link, for the rapid realisation of our common vision of peace. This effort is based on the following principles.

1 Recognition of the right to self-determination of both peoples in the land, through the establishment of a Palestinian state alongside Israel on the 4 June 1967 boundaries.

2 The whole city of Jerusalem constitutes two capitals for two states.

3 The Oslo Declaration of Principles, signed on 13 September 1993, and all subsequent agreements must be implemented immediately and in their entirety.

4 The permanent settlement negotiations must resume without any delays on the basis of the agreed agenda of the Declaration of Principles, the terms of reference being all relevant UN resolutions, including 242 and 338.

5 It is our conviction that all Israeli settlements in the Palestinian territories occupied in 1967 are illegal, as stipulated by international law, and violate the requirements for peace.

6 Palestinian: Israel accepts its moral, legal, political, and economic responsibility for the plight of Palestinian refugees and thus must accept the right of return according to relevant UN resolutions.

   Israeli: Israel's recognition of its responsibility in the creation of the Palestinian refugees in 1948 is a prerequisite to finding a just and lasting resolution of the refugee problem in accordance with relevant UN resolutions.

7 Respect for international conventions, charters, and laws and the active involvement of the international community in the peace process are crucial to its success.

8 The realisation of political peace will pave the way for mutual understanding and trust, genuine security, and constructive co-operation on the basis of equality and respect for the national and human rights of both peoples.

9 Women must be central partners in the peace process. Their active and equal participation in decision making and negotiations is crucial to the fulfilment of a just and viable peace.

10 We women are committed to a peaceful solution of our conflict, also as a means for the promotion of democratic and non-violent norms and the enhancement of civil society.

11 A peaceful solution of the Palestinian–Israeli conflict and Israeli withdrawal from all occupied Arab territory, including Lebanon and Syria, are prerequisites for a just and comprehensive peace. This will pave the way for a Middle East characterised by good neighbourly relations and regional co-operation.

We have also come up with another mechanism, a proposed international 'women's commission', which would be formally attached as an advisory panel to any Middle East peace negotiations, not merely the 'road map', should it survive the current crisis. The commission, made up of Palestinian, Israeli, and international women peace makers, would have a specific mandate to review all documents in the light of the impact they would have on women, children, and normal, non-military society.

The key plank to this proposal is a UN resolution 1325, which was passed in 2001 and which commits member states to promote the 'equal participation and full involvement' of women in peace processes, and 'the need to increase their role in decision making'. It was the first UN resolution ever to address the specific impact of war on women, and was passed unanimously. The Italian government (which holds the EU presidency at the time of writing) has given its support to the women's proposal, which also has the full backing of UN Secretary General Kofi Annan. And in September 2003, Baroness Symons, Minister of State at the Foreign Office in London, pledged the support of the British government in seeking to bring the commission into effect.

Palestinian women in these peace organisations have the opportunity to prove themselves in leadership positions, to participate in decision-making processes, and to attend and present papers in national and international conferences. And while most Israeli peace groups cancelled their activities during October 2002, for fear of being branded 'unpatriotic', the women at *Sukkat HaShalom* (the peace tent) stood up for their beliefs and continued to organise protest rallies and vigils, pay condolence calls to the families of victims, and monitor human rights abuses and discrimination. (For more information about their work at this time, visit **www.batshalom.org/english/activism/program_sukkat.html** (accessed 25 September 2003.)

A parallel initiative is that of the women's peace forum organised by the North Office of Bat Shalom. This was formed by Jewish and Arab women who, as the peace process advanced, sought a better dialogue with the Palestinians of the occupied territories. Some members of the former Women's Network for Peace (now Bat Shalom) and Women in Black came to the conclusion that true peace should begin at home, with peace and understanding between close neighbours along the pre-1967 borders. We were all active in the

Women's Network for Peace and lived within the region that extends from Nazareth through the Jezareel and Beit Sha'an Valleys, up to Meggido county and Menashe Hills.

Arabs and Jews within Israel do not really know each other; they do not mix, and they live their personal and communal lives one beside the other, without any real contact between them. We felt that in order to make peace a reality, we should strive to truly know one another, our way of life, our beliefs, and hopes; and that we should promote understanding through equality, openness, and mutual tolerance.

All the women activists also go out to work and so carry the double responsibility of a career and family. They found it too demanding to participate in activities organised in Jerusalem or Tel Aviv. So the local branch of Bat Shalom provided a meeting place for them and for other women in this part of the country, who would otherwise have been completely beyond our reach.

The forum meets every 4–6 weeks, to discuss political and social issues, to decide on policies, and plan activities for women in the region. Meetings are open to everyone wanting to join. It was decided to focus on the broader issues of justice and human rights, and the end of occupation and of the oppression and discrimination against Palestinians in the occupied territories and against Palestinian citizens of Israel. Other priorities included women's rights and women's leadership. We have worked together now for many years in long-term projects and leadership workshops and also bi-national, open events held every 2–3 months, the venue alternating between a Jewish kibbutz or an Arab village or city. As this office is a branch of Bat Shalom, it also participates in activities in the wider national context, such as rallies, demonstrations, publishing newspaper ads, and so on.

Our goal is to promote political, social, and cultural activities for women, in which we strive to work together to empower women in each community and learn to work together, developing partnership and offering mutual support in order to reduce the mistrust of 'the other's' motives. The local atmosphere and the opportunity for a more informal meeting, often at short notice, encourages women from rural and traditional environments to voice their support for the process of peace and normalisation.

Resolving identity-based conflicts

Conflicts that are based upon or involve questions of identity are the most complicated ones to resolve, because an individual's identity is so fundamental to that person. In addition, because we live in a patriarchal male-chauvinist world which does not 'know' a non-violent way of solving conflicts, it may sometimes seem impossible to resolve them in peaceful ways. The only way to resolve 'identity conflicts' in the contemporary world appears to be by violent wars with great loss of life such as in Bosnia or Northern Ireland, or in the case of the Israeli–Palestinian conflict. I do not believe that the number of 'identity conflicts' will necessarily diminish in the future, given that we are seeing the creation of new and distinctive identities around the world. However, if we are committed to resolving conflicts in a non-violent way, I would suggest two approaches:

- *Crossing ethnic boundaries* by bridging different identities through similar sub-groups, based on gender, social class, sexual identity, people with disabilities, etc.
- *Decentralising power* by undertaking alternative activities which aim to make politics irrelevant and creating a new form of a dialogue between the different groups.

I am aware that these two kinds of approach do exist in situations of conflict but their influence and effectiveness is as yet too limited. But I never lose my hope and dream that we might, in the words of the John Lennon song, *'imagine all the people living life in peace … you may say I am a dreamer … but I am not the only one'*.

We Israeli and Palestinian members of women's peace organisations want to share the resources of this land and its holy places, believing that the area can be shared between two independent and equal nations. Israel should not rule the lives of Palestinians, and neither Palestine nor Israel should believe that peace can ever be won through violence and force.

Human security and reconstruction efforts in Rwanda:

impact on the lives of women

Myriam Gervais

Introduction

Reconstruction efforts supported by funding agencies seek to create conditions of sustained peace in post-conflict societies. In deadly civil conflicts, in which organised violence stigmatises members of the affected society, the struggle against insecurity in all its manifestations during the reconstruction phase is thus an essential condition for peace.

Since intra-state conflicts are often the result of structural problems, their resolution calls for the identification of corrective measures that are capable of influencing the sources of insecurity. Basically, then, interventions should not only seek to rebuild social infrastructures and rehabilitate the state, but must also support reforms that will resolve political, ethnic, and socio-economic tensions. For that very reason, promoting human security in post-conflict societies means taking specific actions that support a safe environment, social harmony, equal status, and equitable access to resources and to the decision-making process (Gervais 2002b:13–17). And at the intersection of these actions, one would place an intervention framework focusing on security problems that concern women.

Worldwide evidence of increased gender-based violence in civil strife and armed conflict (Human Rights Watch 1996; Lindsey 2001), and of the severe consequences on women of such conflict (Manchanda 2001; Turshen and Twagiramariya 1998), underlines the duty to address these issues by sustained actions that meet women's security needs in post-conflict conditions. In fact, gender-based violence still remains high during reconstruction periods, proving that peace is not enough to ensure women's security. In many cases, women are also confronted with radically changed realities: they have to assume new roles and new responsibilities at the family and community levels, and in so doing they are more susceptible to new forms of insecurity. As a result, it seems pertinent to question how development agencies have approached and sought to mitigate these security concerns. How do reconstruction efforts carried out or supported by funding agencies address issues of safety and security in the lives of women and girls? Do their actions or projects make a concrete difference to women's security? What can we learn in terms of strategies and approaches?

In recent years, UN institutions and bilateral donors have in many ways supported peace activists, human-rights advocacy groups, and grassroots community activists in their efforts to improve their ability to build peace in post-conflict societies (UNDP 2002). At the same time, NGOs are increasingly taking voluntary initiatives, promoting and implementing programmes that help build and consolidate peace in these societies (International Alert 1998; Leonhardt *et al.* 2002). Efforts have also been made to 'engender' government programmes with technical assistance from development agencies (Zucherman 2002).

Focusing on Rwanda, this paper examines a sample of initiatives and tries to evaluate how pertinent the interventions sponsored by aid agencies that seek to meet the security needs of women have been. It also tries to identify lessons for future actions assisting post-conflict populations. In doing this, I have used three indicators to assess efforts to establish a more secure environment for women. If appropriately defined in accordance with the Rwandan context, personal security, economic security, and socio-political security are indicators that may be used to reveal the effects or impacts of these actions on women's security.

The research used in this paper focused on initiatives included in socio-economic development projects funded by the Canadian International Development Agency (CIDA) and implemented by Canadian NGOs (Oxfam-Québec, CARE-Canada, and Development and Peace). These projects are found in different regions of Rwanda (in the provinces of rural Kigali, Umutara, Gitarama, and Butare), and their beneficiary populations are mainly women, including survivors of the genocide, and returned refugees of 1994 as well as refugees from camps in the DRC and Tanzania. In addition, this study also assesses the effects of initiatives carried out by women's organisations or collectives. The information and data used here were gathered during several visits to Rwanda in 2001 and 2002, including project visits, and were collected from Canadian NGOs acting as implementing agencies, as well as through a review of official documents and documentation produced by local NGOs, and meetings with government officials and local elected representatives, as well as heads and members of associations.

The case of Rwanda

In the aftermath of the 1994 Rwandan war and genocide, aid programmes were concentrated on reconciliation activities, rehabilitation of the legal system, and economic and social recovery. Over and above the funding from international financial institutions and bilateral organisations, external aid was mainly offered by UN agencies (WFP, UNHCR, and UNICEF) and by foreign NGOs that seek to involve beneficiary populations directly. These interventions sought to counter the consequences of war and genocide by providing help to displaced persons, food aid, reconstruction of infrastructure, services for genocide orphans, institutional support to local NGOs, and reconciliation projects.

Although about 96 per cent of the state's investment budget was financed by external aid, a significant characteristic of this aid has been the importance of NGO assistance after the genocide. This contribution represented 7–10 per cent of all the aid received by Rwanda between 1995 and 2000 (Gervais 2002c:6–7). Indeed, many NGOs have provided indirect support to the state budget by funding the construction of local social infrastructure (schools, health centres, water-supply systems, etc.). In post-reconstruction Rwanda, NGOs mobilised an important means to initiate changes in local communities in terms of resource management for reconciliation and governance.

Before looking at the selected interventions, it may be appropriate to offer a general overview of the context in which these were set in order to shed light on how the lives of women have been affected by war and genocide.

Post-genocide situation

With the slaughter of more than a half million individuals and unprecedented population movements, the genocide of 1994 had the effect of irremediably transforming Rwandan society, and the country was forced to confront the consequences of organised violence and the loss of a significant part of its human and economic capital.

Rwanda's agriculture-based economy was completely destroyed by the war, forcing most of its population to live in a state of extreme precariousness. The food shortages caused by the destruction of crops and the severe reduction in cultivated land was aggravated by the inability of many households to obtain the labour they needed. In 1996, 34 per cent of families – with an average of six to seven young dependants – were headed by widows, unmarried women, and wives of prisoners suspected of genocide (Ministry of Gender and Women in Development 2000:2). This reflects the fundamental changes that took place in the demographic structure of Rwanda, where, even today, 64 per cent of the labour force in basic production is female. Burdened with increased responsibilities (heads of household or farms, economic actors), women had to adapt to these new roles in a particularly restrictive context. For instance, a study carried out on violence against women in Rwanda revealed that 80 per cent of victims surveyed showed signs of trauma and 66 per cent of them were HIV-positive (AVEGA 1999:24–6). Indeed, it is estimated that 250,000 women were raped during the war and the genocide, between 1990 and 1994 (Muganza 2002). In addition to obstacles arising from the conflict and genocide, Rwandan women and girls have to deal with deeply patriarchal forms of social organisation.

Initiatives for women during the reconstruction period

A look at the projects undertaken in Rwanda during the reconstruction period reveals that there were two types of initiatives aimed at supporting women's efforts to react to the upheavals caused by conflict and genocide: the formation of solidarity groups and production associations, and the establishment of advocacy groups and women's collectives.

Since 1995, women have joined together in associations averaging 15 to 20 members, either spontaneously or at the behest of charitable organisations and NGOs, to cultivate collective fields or to carry out income-generating activities. The main motivation for these associations is to ensure the economic survival of their members. With financial support from international NGOs and bilateral or multilateral donors, various associations have also sprung up with the mission of defending the strategic interests of women: representations to government to have discriminatory laws reviewed and activism in favour of more equitable representation of women in political life. These associations have also taken on the task of providing legal and medical assistance services, forming groups to assist survivors, and providing business advice.

As mentioned previously, gender-based violence, the depth of extreme poverty, and non-egalitarian customary practices and discriminatory laws were among the main challenges faced in the aftermath of the conflict and genocide by the majority of Rwandan women. In an attempt to reveal the effects or impacts of aid-agency interventions on women's security, indicators such as personal security, economic security, and socio-political security were created and used as methodological reference marks.

Personal security

In order for the physical or personal security of Rwandan women to be guaranteed or formalised, they must be protected both legally and socially from threats and acts of aggression.

Since 1994, organised violence against women has been curbed and legal measures have been instituted to punish acts of sexual violence, thus ending the *de facto* impunity that prevailed in Rwanda. Very few perpetrators of acts of sexual violence committed during the war and genocide of 1994 have been brought to justice, however, despite the large number of cases identified (Joseph 2000:47). Most recent statistics show, nevertheless, that the courts are currently processing at least 600 rape complaints and that guilty verdicts are increasingly frequent (Muganza 2002). The government has set up – albeit belatedly – a programme for training health officials, police, and *gacaca* (traditional village-based) judges to help women who were victims of violence during the genocide.

An awareness campaign was undertaken to raise consciousness regarding the severity of sexual violence in Rwanda, a society still heavily characterised by various forms of violence against women. According to provincial sources, six rapes took place in February 2002 in the district of Gabiro alone. In a school in Kigali, a survey revealed that 60 per cent of girls had been raped. Thus, on International Women's Day, the Public Service and Labour Minister made it clear in a speech she made to a crowd gathered in Murambi, a small city in the north-east of the country, that violence against women is no longer allowed in Rwanda and that severe punishment would be administered against rapists in the future (Kayetesi 2002). Nevertheless, data show that violence of a sexual nature in Rwanda is far from decreasing. Compared to other sub-Saharan African countries, girls have access to relatively equal education. The school attendance rate is identical for boys and girls at the elementary level and higher for girls at the secondary level. However, the survey also revealed that sexual harassment by staff is a problem that girls face in secondary schools throughout the entire country (Ministry of Finance and Economic Planning 2001:31).

There remains a feeling of insecurity in the daily lives of women and girls. Following the genocide, many young adults aged between 13 and 20 years found themselves as heads of family and had to take charge of much younger children. According to the first available national statistics, these comprised 13 per cent of Rwandan families in 1996. Over time, their number has decreased somewhat (Ministry of Finance and Economic Planning 2002:2) but the ravages of HIV/AIDS seem to be perpetuating the situation. In a study aimed at learning about the conditions in which these young heads of household live, interviews conducted with a sample that covered the entire country led to the conclusion that their rights are regularly disregarded and their health and education needs ignored by the community (ACORD 2001:26). Given the rarity or shortage of land and Rwanda's particularly severe overpopulation, the property these youngsters inherited from their parents is coveted by other members of their families, or even by strangers. Moreover, with communities torn apart by war and genocide, traditional support mechanisms no longer operate. In addition, it is conventionally considered unacceptable for women to inherit from their families. Since girls who are heads of family enjoy no protection, they live in a climate of permanent insecurity and are vulnerable to attempts at intimidation and sexual assault, particularly at night. For a while, actions by charitable organisations and local and international NGOs allowed material assistance to be provided to these orphans, but the security and rights problems have not been given any special attention. This feeling of insecurity is also shared by other women, as indicated by the results of national consultations carried out as part of the poverty-reduction strategy development process (Ministry of Finance and Economic Planning 2001:37).

Many survivors of the genocide had their homes pillaged or destroyed during the struggle. It was estimated at the time that 2 million people were homeless, including more than half a million deemed to be vulnerable (Ministère du Plan 1996). In 1996, the massive return of repatriates from camps in the DRC and Tanzania raised fears of an increase in violent incidents between these returning owners and new home occupants. To lessen or eliminate this threat, donors funded home-construction projects, considered to be an indispensable condition for stability in the country and the security of the people.

Through its partner agencies, CIDA was the main bilateral funder of this displaced persons resettlement and reintegration programme. With the collaboration of local people, Canadian NGOs, such as Development and Peace in the provinces of Butare and Gitarama and Oxfam-Québec in the provinces of Byumba and Rural Kigali, built houses in various parts of the country and tended to the most needy. Widowed heads of household made up 35 per cent of beneficiaries of the programme funded by Canada (Bureau d'Appui à la Coopération Canadienne 2000:14). Before this, house building was the domain of men, who alone held title to property. By giving priority to the most vulnerable and by making this a condition for funding, NGO projects promoted the taking into account of women's needs in housing programmes. In many cases, women signed individual contracts recognised by communal authorities. The signing of a contract between a woman, the local authority, and the NGO in fact brought about a major change: women and girls were recognised as owners of their homes. These programmes also contributed to the recognition of the right of women and girls to hold property, and gave legitimacy to their role as heads of family.

Economic security

The economic security of Rwandan women is guaranteed only when they can satisfy their own basic needs and those of their dependants as economic producers and actors. With over 90 per cent of the population dependent on agriculture, access to the means of production is an essential condition for economic survival and a source of a minimum income. Although their participation on farms was indispensable, in the past, the role of women as producers was misunderstood or ignored by the state, by society, and by development projects. Traditionally, men owned the land and women could not inherit or own it: marriage remained the main route for women to gain access to land. Following the genocide, one of the challenges for female heads of household was to secure a cultivable plot of land in order to ensure their family's subsistence. One frequently observed way of doing this was to join an associative group.

After 1995, many associative or solidarity groups were created or promoted by international or local NGOs. Supported by an NGO, these associations were able to obtain authorisation from local authorities to cultivate communal land, land left fallow by its owner, or lowland land and marshes in the public domain. Marshland rehabilitation and the development of radical terraces – with funding from NGO projects –

allowed land that had until then been unusable to be exploited. For example, Oxfam-Québec supports 44 women's associations and 250 mixed associations with almost 4000 women members in the province of Rural Kigali (Gervais 2002a:14). As part of its activities, Oxfam-Québec, in co-operation with the associations it supports, has developed productive terraces on hillsides and transformed lowlands into cultivable land. In the project zone, these lands are cultivated by associations that share in the harvest.

Development of these lands by solidarity groups benefits their members, who see the precariousness of their situation lessened by being able to secure their basic needs and by providing, in many cases, a surplus to be sold in the market-place. But, so far, these groups only have the usufruct of these lands that their work helped make cultivable. The marshes belong to the Rwandan government and the situation regarding the lowlands is confusing and controversial. The associations and NGOs have invested in equipment and labour to make these lands cultivable but, for the time being, the associations' rights to these lands are in no way guaranteed and it is very possible that some associations might be dispossessed in favour of other groups or individuals (Gervais 2003:31). Also, this property question remains delicate and could mortgage the future of these associations by jeopardising their source of income, particularly in places where many people are landless. Moreover, for many women, the only way to have access to land is to belong to an association, which makes them highly dependent on those associations to ensure a minimum income.

In partnership with Development and Peace, the Irish NGO Trócaire supports the Conseil Consultatif des Femmes Commune de Musambira (Musambira Women's Advisory Council - COCOF), founded in 1995 in the province of Gitarama in the south of Rwanda. COCOF currently has more than 2000 women members in 91 socio-economic associations. This organisation, developed with technical assistance from Trócaire, has been granting credit to its members at an interest of 2.5 per cent per month, with a credit-recovery rate of 97 per cent (COCOF 2001). The relatively productive nature of the COCOF credit system is an indication that its members are now able to carry out more lucrative economic activities.

The statements of association members in various regions of the country (Gervais 2003) regarding their greater ability to pay education costs and to buy medicines, as well as the disappearance of cases of severe malnutrition in certain regions, suggest that most women have passed the survival and bare-subsistence levels and that their standard of living is improving somewhat. However, the financial security of female agricultural producers remains fragile because of the vulnerability of their activity to climatic conditions, land productivity, and marketing difficulties.

Socio-political security

The socio-political security of women in Rwanda can only become a reality if the society to which they belong respects women's rights and allows women to exercise them. To determine whether there has been a noticeable change in this direction, it is worth looking at the legal framework, the place occupied by women in their communities, and their level of involvement in and control over household decision making.

In Rwandan society, a set of discriminatory laws sanctioned non-egalitarian customary practices in legal, matrimonial, and hereditary matters. Also, after the genocide, women who were widowed and young orphaned girls could not inherit their husbands' or fathers' property. Women's associations such as the Forum for Women Members of Parliament in Rwanda, the Pro-Women Collective, and the Association for the Defence of Women's and Children's Rights (HAGURUKA) successfully fought to have a law passed on the matrimonial system and inheritance rights based on the principle of equality of the sexes. Formal recognition of equal access to resources provided the first legal framework for the protection of the rights of married women and orphaned girls (Ministry of Gender and Women in Development 2000:4). HAGURUKA notes that the inheritance law is starting to be applied and complaints in this area are decreasing. However, about 60 per cent of households are, in the eyes of the law, considered to be common-law unions (Ministère des Terres, de la Réinstallation et de la Protection de l'Environnement 2001:25–7). In other words, many marriages are informal.

Most unions are not registered at the district level due to people's inability to afford related expenses such as legal fees and dowry (Gervais 2003:15). Rwandan law recognises only monogamous marriages celebrated before a civil status officer. Women living in common-law marriages and single women with children constitute a significant part of the population, but their rights are not protected by the new law. Moreover, this law leaves a legal vacuum regarding how land is distributed among heirs from the same family. Until the new land law promised by the government (Ministry of Finance and Economic

Planning 2001:60–1) actually materialises, nothing prevents unfair practices against women when sharing land rights. A first land bill was removed from the parliamentary agenda because of strong objections from some quarters of society.

By promoting a participatory process, projects implemented by international and local NGOs have made it possible for women to get involved in decision making within the associations being supported. Through training and awareness activities, some of these projects have encouraged women's access to decision-making positions within their associations. For example, in the 250 mixed associations supported by Oxfam-Québec, 50 per cent of members sitting on decision-making bodies are women (Gervais 2002a:17). At general meetings of productive associations, it is no longer rare to see female members express and defend their points of view. Such behaviour seems to be becoming more and more socially acceptable. This greater role of women in their community is also evident in their greater involvement in local affairs.

The decentralisation policy adopted by the government involves transferring responsibilities previously allocated to the provinces to the district level. This means that districts are now the main level of power, with the provincial level of government assuming the role of supporter of the central government and local jurisdictions (Gervais 2002c; Ministère de l'Administration Locale et des Affaires Sociales 2000). This reform took effect in March 2001 with general elections in all 106 districts, in which women raised their representation above 25 per cent of elected seats at the district, sector, and cell levels. In this context, the election of six female mayors is quite significant, as it is the first time Rwandan women have been able to take on the responsibilities of elected office through an open democratic process. Moreover, the presence of women in the cabinet – numbering five ministers out of a total of 26 – was strengthened in 2002. This has been an overall improvement in the conditions that were prevalent until 2001, when women's political representation was virtually non-existent.

Nevertheless, competition for the allocation of cultivable plots of land on living sites grouped within new settlement zones – the solution proposed by the government to accommodate new arrivals – shows that the transformation of the decision-making process within communities is variable. It is not rare to see female heads of household being allocated land that is infertile or located far away from where they live. And the involvement of women in household decision-making processes appears to have generated little concrete progress.

According to a socio-economic study carried out in three districts in the northeast of the country, home to a CARE development project for women and councils aimed at capacity building, skills development, and material inputs, the inequitable sharing of household income and resources to the detriment of women is still commonplace (Ndahimana *et al.* 2001:39). Traditionally, it is men who manage assets, with women having free access only to crops produced near the home. In recent years, the involvement of women in associations is more tolerated by men because, since the end of the period of emergency, aid has been directed to strengthening associations and is no longer paid directly to beneficiaries. Members of women's associations in the same region that are also helped by CARE say that their husbands are more favourable to their belonging to an association, but that within the household the status quo remains (Gervais 2002a:30). Thus, it is still a common practice for male heads of families to control income from work on plots belonging to associations.

Evaluating the impact of these initiatives

Physical assaults on women have diminished significantly since 1994, but the level of sexual violence in Rwandan society remains alarming. The strengthening of the criminal code and awareness campaigns show, however, that violence against women is becoming less acceptable.

Through their associations, women have gained access to means of production that have allowed them to improve their living conditions – with a majority of them having actually managed to get beyond the survival and subsistence stages. But considering the link between poverty and women's ability to exercise their rights, progress in achieving women's economic security must be supported by donors and NGOs in ways that adopt a more long-term perspective.

Democracy within associations is helping to eliminate various forms of discrimination by promoting the election of candidates based on new criteria such as competence. And, in this sense, productive associations constitute a platform that allows women to exercise their rights within their community. However, the changes observed at this level seem to have had little impact on relations between men and women within family units.

The initiatives carried out within the context of reconstruction programmes in Rwanda have thus brought about changes that have had a positive impact on the security of women and girls. But, given the exceptional nature of the reference point – the genocide of 1994 –

it is too early for a final verdict on the permanence of these effects. Meanwhile, access to resources remains a vital challenge in Rwanda and a real source of tension between men and women. In sum, the achievements of recent years in terms of strengthening human security remain fragile and must be consolidated.

Conclusion

An impact analysis of selected initiatives conducted by intervening agencies in Rwanda during the reconstruction period highlights the complexity of safety and security issues in the lives of women.

Although practices varied widely among organisations and donors, these initiatives have helped to create a safer environment for women. However, specific strategies focusing on women's and girls' security would better benefit them if they were more consistently planned so as to take into consideration other crucial issues. In fact, some initiatives did not have the anticipated results because they were not designed on the basis of an understanding of the ways in which issues of poverty, gender, and security intersect. For instance, the level of violence against women *post facto* and the very slow process of change to bring about greater gender equality within family units and communities should stimulate donors and NGOs to devote more attention to the impact of their initiatives on men and women, and to develop strategies to reduce the sources of tension. Furthermore, while most projects or activities are operating at the micro-level, the complexity of safety and security issues calls for focusing far more on ways of strengthening relationships both between these interventions and other actions at the regional and national levels, and with proposed sectoral policies.

Acknowledgement

The author would like to acknowledge the Gender and Human Security Issues Action-research programme, conducted by the Centre for Developing-Area Studies at McGill University and the Women's Centre of Montreal and funded by the Social Sciences and Humanities Research Council of Canada, for its support of this research.

References

ACORD (Agency for Co-operation and Research in Development) (2001) *The Situation of Child Heads of Households in Rwanda: A Significant Challenge,* Kigali: ACORD.

AVEGA (Association of Widows of the Genocide) (1999) *Survey on Violence Against Women in Rwanda,* Kigali: AVEGA.

Bureau d'Appui à la Coopération Canadienne (2000) 'Synthèse des Réalisations, Projets Habitats Financés par le Canada au Rwanda, 1997–1999', unpublished report, Kigali: Bureau d'Appui à la Coopération Canadienne.

COCOF (2001) 'Stratégie d'Amélioration des Conditions Socio-économiques de la Femme en Commune de Musambira. Plan d'Activités 2000–2001', unpublished report, Musambira, Rwanda: COCOF.

Gervais, Myriam (2002a) 'Groupe de Projets de Développement Communautaire en Appui aux Populations Relocalisées au Rwanda. Rapport de la Deuxième Mission de Suivi', unpublished report, Hull: CIDA.

Gervais, Myriam (2002b) 'Sécurité Humaine: une Approche Centrée sur les Problèmes Structurels', CDAS Discussion Paper No. 94, Montreal: McGill University, Centre for Developing-Area Studies.

Gervais, Myriam (2002c) 'Lutte Contre la Pauvreté, Décentralisation et Projets de Développement au Rwanda', paper presented at the Conference on Réformes Institution-nelles, Stratégies de Lutte Contre la Pauvreté et Espaces Politiques, UQAM/Centre d'Études sur le Droit International et la Mondialisation, Montreal, 10 May 2002.

Gervais, Myriam (2003) 'Groupe de Projets de Développement Communautaire en Appui aux Populations Relocalisées au Rwanda. Rapport de la Troisième Mission de Suivi', unpublished report, Hull: CIDA.

Human Rights Watch/Africa (1996) *Shattered Lives: Sexual Violence During the Rwandan Genocide and its Aftermath,* London: Human Rights Watch.

International Alert (1998) *Training of Trainers on Gender and Conflict Transformation. Capacity Building for Women's Peace Movements in Burundi,* Conference Report, London: International Alert.

Joseph, Kerline (2000) 'L'Importance d'une Justice Face aux Crimes Sexuels Commis à l'Égard des Femmes en Période de Conflits Armés: le Cas du Rwanda', unpublished master's thesis, Montreal: UQAM.

Kayetesi, Zayinaba Sylvie (2002) speech of the Minister of Public Service and Labour for the International Women's Day, Murambi, Rwanda, 8 March.

Leonhardt, Manuela, Patricia Ardon, Njeri Karuru, and Andrew Sherriff (2002) *Peace and Conflict Impact Assessment (PCIA) and NGO Peacebuilding – Experiences from Kenya and Guatemala,* London: International Alert.

Lindsey, Charlotte (2001) *ICRC Study of the Impact of Armed Conflict on Women,* Geneva: ICRC.

Manchanda, Rita (ed.) (2001) *Women, War and Peace in South Asia: Beyond Victimhood to Agency,* New Delhi: Sage Publications.

Ministère de l'Administration Locale et des Affaires Sociales (2000) *Politique Nationale de Décentralisation,* Kigali: Imprimerie Nationale du Rwanda.

Ministère des Terres, de la Réinstallation et de la Protection de l'Environnement (2001) 'Besoins et Préoccupations des Femmes sur l'Accès à la Terre et à la Propriété Foncière', unpublished report, Kigali: Ministère des Terres, de la Réinstallation et de la Protection de l'Environnement.

Ministère du Plan (1996) 'Notes sur le Problème du Logement dans le Cadre de la Réintégration Sociale des Populations Rapatriées', unpublished document, Kigali: Ministère du Plan.

Ministry of Finance and Economic Planning (2001) *The Government of Rwanda Poverty Reduction Strategy Paper*, National Poverty Reduction Programme, Kigali: Ministry of Finance and Economic Planning.

Ministry of Finance and Economic Planning (2002) *A Profile of Poverty in Rwanda: An Analysis Based on the Results of the Household Living Condition Survey 1999–2001*, Kigali: Ministry of Finance and Economic Planning.

Ministry of Gender and Women in Development (2000) 'The National Gender Action Plan 2000–2005', unpublished document, Kigali: Ministry of Gender and Women in Development.

Muganza, Angeline (2002) 'A Government Acts Against Gender Violence', declaration of the Minister of Gender and Women in Development, Kigali, 6 June.

Ndahimana, Isaïe, Célestin Niseyimana, and Landrada Musabeyezu (2001) 'Données Socio-économiques de Base dans la Zone d'Intervention du Projet SNC', unpublished report, Kigali.

Turshen, Meredeth and Clotilde Twagiramariya (eds.) (1998) *What Women Do in Wartime: Gender and Conflict in Africa*, London: Zed Books.

UNDP (2002) *Human Development Report 2002*, New York: Oxford University Press.

Zucherman, Elaine (2002) *Evaluation of Gender Mainstreaming in Advocacy Work on Poverty Reduction Strategy Papers (PRSPs)*, Washington DC: Gender Action.

Mission impossible: gender, conflict, and Oxfam GB

Suzanne Williams

Introduction

It is now widely recognised among international non-government organisations (INGOs) that working in the context of conflict and turbulence presents them with specific challenges in relation to delivering gender equity in both their humanitarian and development aid programmes. INGOs in general accept the need for gender-disaggregated data, the fact that women and men have different needs and interests, and that conflict and upheaval present women with opportunities as well as threats, and also the chance to renegotiate gender roles following their *de facto* assumption of male responsibilities in the absence of men. However, the analysis is rarely taken further, or deepened. Gender is not identified by INGOs as a key defining factor of identity in relation to how war begins, what it is about, how groups are mobilised to fight, how ceasefires and peace agreements are reached, and what kind of peace can be said to have been achieved. For women, the end of war rarely brings peace, and can in fact bring new levels of violence into their lives.

The power relations which define gender identity, the allegiances, beliefs, and behaviours which are gender-based, are seldom regarded as important for (and even more rarely built into) most INGOs' analysis of war and non-international conflict, or the planning of interventions to address its consequences. The failure to do this can sometimes be attributed to lack of expertise or experience in gender analysis, and sometimes to a profound, often unformulated, resistance to incorporating it into the analytical framework, for a number of reasons that will be examined later in this paper. To address gender relations in the context of conflict entails entering highly contested terrain, not only

First published in Cynthia Cockburn and Dubravka Zarkov (eds.) (2002)
The Postwar Moment: Militaries, Masculinities and International Peacekeeping

within the war-torn society, but also within all the institutions intervening in the situation, including the INGOs.

In this paper I will explore the mission of a large UK-based INGO, Oxfam GB (OGB), and some of its experience in addressing gender inequalities in the institutional structures and policies which govern its activities in situations of conflict and its aftermath.[1] I present some of the contradictions within OGB's organisational culture which have held this work back and continue to provide obstacles to it, in spite of substantial work on the issues within the agency over the years. I also examine some of the recent developments within OGB which are beginning to seek new solutions to the problem of gender-blindness in its interventions, and look at some positive examples of gender-sensitive practice.

My perspective is that of a policy adviser in what is now OGB's Campaigns and Policy Division, with a brief to work on gender, human rights, and conflict. My principal role is to offer advice and support to OGB's programmes at regional or country level, and to contribute to the development of OGB's global programme policy on conflict, gender, and human rights, within which violence against women is a key priority. While this paper represents my own views and not those of OGB as a whole, I draw upon the experiences and concerns of many staff within the organisation – indeed, all of us who believe in and work for the consistent delivery of gender equity in every intervention OGB makes. The next few years will reveal whether this is indeed, or not, a 'mission impossible'.

Having looked at some of OGB's 'institutional imperatives' – in other words its goals and aims, its mandates, policies, and guidelines – which govern its work during conflict and its aftermath, I will discuss some of the problems inherent in several conceptual and programmatic divides which make programme implementation in this area complicated and difficult. These divides, which overlap each other, are the same divides which separate relief and development responses, and technical and social approaches. Interwoven with them are different perceptions within OGB of the division between the public and private domains, and indeed different perceptions of these among those with whom OGB works in the North and the South. The critical feminist insight that the private/public divide has to be broken down, and the personal made political, in order to end discrimination against women and build gender equality is taking a long time to percolate through OGB; and there still remain both perceptual and actual obstacles to making the connections between gender relations in the private and public spheres. However, there is a growing area of work on violence against women in war and in 'peacetime', which has the potential to encourage new ways of thinking beyond these divides, and I look at some of the implications of this work at the end of the paper.

The body of the paper presents examples selected from OGB's programme in Kosovo, Central America, South Africa, and Cambodia, where I look at some of the agency's experience in relation to integrating gender equity into its programme goals for work in the aftermath of war. Both direct operational interventions, especially in Kosovo, and work with counterpart organisations, are considered. While OGB's work is increasingly concerned with campaigning and advocacy, these areas are beyond the scope of this paper. Nonetheless it is true that the many of the contradictions that make it so difficult for gender equity to be at the heart of OGB's direct interventions are equally problematic in its campaigning and advocacy initiatives.

Oxfam GB's institutional imperatives

Founded in 1942, Oxfam GB is based in Oxford in the UK, with a decentralised structure of nine regional offices around the world. Its mandate is to relieve poverty, distress, and suffering, and to educate the public about the nature, causes, and effects of these. It describes itself as a 'development, relief, and campaigning organisation dedicated to finding lasting solutions to poverty and suffering around the world'. OGB works principally with partner or counterpart organisations – international, national, and community-based – supporting them to achieve goals common to both. In the fields of emergency response and campaigning, OGB is also operational, employing its own staff to deliver relief programmes in the field, or to lobby and campaign for changes in policy and public awareness, and working in conjunction with other INGOs and international agencies.

In recent years, OGB has defined its purpose in terms of helping people to achieve their basic rights, loosely in line with articles related principally to social and economic rights within the Universal Declaration of Human Rights, and the two International Covenants. Thus OGB aligns its programmes according to a range of basic rights, including health, education, freedom from violence, and a sustainable livelihood. Additionally, political and civil rights are phrased by OGB as the 'right to be heard', related to governance and democratic representation, while the 'right to an identity' refers to gender equity and discrimination.

OGB has had a corporate gender policy since 1993, but the implementation of this policy throughout the organisation has been patchy, dependent upon the efforts of committed individuals, and limited to its international programme. This has meant that the profound transformations envisaged by the gender policy in human-resources policy and the structure and culture of OGB as a whole have not taken place. Progress in implementing the gender policy within the international programme was mapped in 1997, and pointed to several important lessons. These included that in the absence of clear criteria for measuring progress in implementing gender policies and practices, managers used very different standards, and there was no overall consistency in the integration of gender equity throughout OGB. Strengths revealed by the study were that OGB could demonstrate considerable success in working at grassroots level with women's organisations and in OGB's own gender publishing programme. There has been less success in relation to mainstreaming gender in large-scale emergency or development programmes, and little to point to in relation to gender-sensitive advocacy and campaigning work (Oxfam GB 1998). The mainstreaming of gender throughout OGB and its programme thus remains a challenge, but it is a challenge that the organisation has prioritised, and is beginning to take up in a systematic way through its new framework of objectives, and accountability, related to basic rights and gender equity.

OGB now has a number of sets of guidelines and standards relating to gender for its emergency programming, and these have been implemented successfully in some instances, but are not routinely applied. OGB was a key collaborator in an inter-agency project known as the Sphere Project, which aims to 'improve the quality of assistance provided to people affected by disasters, and to enhance accountability of humanitarian system in disaster response' (Sphere Project 2000). The Project's field handbook lays out a Humanitarian Charter, and a set of minimum standards for the various technical sectors in disaster response – water and sanitation, nutrition, food aid, shelter and site planning, and health services. The 1998 trial edition was gender-blind; a gender review was called for, and OGB, among other agencies, submitted a detailed revision of the handbook from a gender perspective. The published edition (Sphere Project 2000) has incorporated some of these revisions. The Charter itself, however, makes no specific reference to gender or to any specific commitment to gender equity in the delivery of emergency relief, and there is still room for improvement in the guidelines themselves.

OGB is currently developing the concept of 'net impact' or 'net benefit' in relation to humanitarian relief. This has arisen as a result of the work – and the challenge – of Mary B. Anderson's 'Building Local Capacities for Peace' project. The question addressed by Anderson's work is:

> *How can international and local aid agencies provide assistance to people in areas of violent conflict in ways that help those people disengage from the conflict and develop alternative systems for overcoming the problems they face? How can aid agencies and aid workers encourage local capacities for peace?*

(Anderson 1996)

OGB, along with other international humanitarian agencies, has to ask difficult questions: When does our presence do more harm than good, by exacerbating the conflict through diversion of aid, or inadvertent support to perpetrators of human-rights violations in conflict, or perpetuation of the war through provision of humanitarian relief, thus enabling national resources to be allocated to arms and the war itself? What are the alternatives to providing immediate help to victims of violent conflict? How do we balance high-profile advocacy with the security of staff and counterparts? How do we continue to provide humanitarian aid within all these constraints and difficulties?

David Bryer, former Director of OGB, writes:

> *The future of humanitarian aid is now perhaps more in question than at any time since 1945. The providers question whether the abuse of their aid outweighs its benefits; while the donors, at least the official ones, reduce their funding. Yet the need for aid continues; the number of people who suffer needlessly for lack of it rises. Here, we consider some of the practical difficulties and ethical choices involved in judging the 'net impact' of aid that is provided in armed conflicts, where its abuse has become a certainty.*

(Bryer and Cairns 1997:363)

This same question could well be applied to gender equity and the impact of external agencies on women and on gender relations. When do our interventions bring more harm than good to women? Are we exacerbating inequitable gender relations by intervening in ways that do not positively address gender inequality, and tackle male dominance? Are we inadvertently exacerbating male violence against women by acting without a clear analysis of gender power relations? Are we making it easier for male oppression to continue by focusing on women's projects that do not disturb the status quo? Are there times when we should be making a judgement and deciding to pull out of a direct intervention, and focus instead on high-profile lobbying and campaigning for women's rights? In the context of conflict, and in highly militarised societies, both of which can have extreme consequences for women, these dilemmas are particularly acute.

OGB had to address these issues in Afghanistan, when the Taliban took control of Kabul in 1998, and OGB's local female staff were prevented from coming to work. OGB had to scale down its operation, and find a way to balance its presence in the country with a principled stance on the abuse of the rights of women under the Taliban regime. There was considerable debate between those who thought OGB should take a very public position on what was happening to women, rather than implicitly supporting an unjust system by working with 'approved' women, and those who thought OGB should try to find ways of working with women wherever possible, within the constraints. A 1999 internal OGB report states that gender remains a vital concern in the programme, but in the absence of being able to address women's rights directly, health and education remain the most appropriate entry points to work with women. The report points to the dangers of adopting an approach which would aim for quick results, and advocates building on the positive aspects in the situation of women in Afghanistan – for example, that women's voices in local communities are stronger than normally perceived, and that intra-household distribution is more equitable than in many parts of the world. In the end, it was judged that the net benefit to women of OGB staying and working with the opportunities which could be found were greater than radically changing its programme approach, and abandoning direct interventions. (See Clifton and Gell 2001:12–13 for further discussion of these issues.)

This judgement – are we doing more harm than good? – is not, however, routinely applied in OGB's work in conflicts, emergency, or any other situations, and the tools to help staff make such an assessment are not yet developed. But the issue is regularly brought up in debate. A workshop to take forward its work on gender equity took place in Oxford in September 2000 and was attended by staff from all over OGB. Participants emphasised the critical importance of applying much tighter standards, and developing much clearer systems, for assessing OGB's impact on women and gender equity in the areas where it works – and for withdrawing support where it was either of no use to women, or damaging to them. Much research and NGO experience over the last decades has shown how gender-insensitive development and relief interventions damage women and exacerbate their disadvantaged position. The concept of 'net impact' or 'net benefit' in relation to women's basic rights is an important overall guiding principle for OGB in all aspects of its work. Current work on impact reporting is beginning to formalise systematic procedures for asking questions related to the impact on gender equity of every project OGB supports. How this is to be measured, and appropriately recorded, is still work in progress.

Programming in conflict-prone areas: the hard and the soft

'The thing about this programme,' one of the water engineers said to me in Kosovo when I visited in 1999, 'is that it's the soft side of the programme that is the hardest to do'.

The categories of the 'hard' and the 'soft' run through the ways in which different forms of action taken in response to conflict and poverty are seen and thought about. Actions and interventions that are bound by the urgent, which show fast, quantifiable results, and which are predominantly technical in nature, are 'hard'. The inputs are 'hardware'. Those that are associated with more subtle and cautious forms of intervention, whose results are more difficult to measure and take longer to manifest, and which are predominantly social and cultural in nature, are 'soft'. The inputs are 'software'. This dichotomy is closely associated with stereotypical categories of the masculine and the feminine, and runs through not only the ways actions and achievements are perceived in OGB – and indeed, in most institutions – but also how they are valued and rewarded. The 'hard', masculinised, interventions, whether in policy and advocacy work, or humanitarian relief, are generally more visible. The supply lines of the 'hardware', and the context of much policy work, are male-dominated and masculinised. Visible results and high-profile actions carry a premium in NGOs which are struggling in the marketplace for funds and which are under pressure to show concrete and quantifiable results to their donors – many of whom, in their institutional structures and cultures, are subject to the same kinds of masculinised and feminised dichotomies in values. The less visible, 'soft', feminised interventions do not thus attract the same attention or the same amounts of money, and are not valued as highly, either inside or outside the organisation.

This of course becomes a self-perpetuating cycle of highly gendered systems of value and reward, which affects not only the nature of interventions, but also the staff responsible for them.

Gender-equity programming in conflict-prone areas is thus itself prone to conflict in quite complex ways – linked to the opposing categories of the 'hard' and the 'soft'. Other divides intersect or run parallel with this broad dichotomy, as outlined in the introduction. For although organisations like OGB have theorised about the end of the 'development-relief' divide, the division still persists institutionally, and in field policy and practice.[2] The technical ('hard') and social ('soft') approaches to programme planning and implementation are also strongly associated with short-term relief and longer-term developmental approaches within the humanitarian intervention. Threading in and out of these issues, as was mentioned above, is the divide between the public and the private, and the implications for perceptions of violence against women in war, and in 'peace'. Rape as a war crime is perceived as 'hard', a public crime, associated with military strategy; rape as a domestic crime is 'soft', a private crime, associated with social issues and intimate relationships.

The impact of the dichotomies

The short-term versus long-term divide is gradually narrowing but its persistence in both policy and practice means that the implications of the nature of emergency-relief response for the rehabilitation and longer-term recovery and reconstruction work are not always appreciated. Or, to put it another way, the nature of the relief effort is often only peripherally influenced by the longer-term social and economic prospects for the victims of the conflict. The focus is on saving lives, which in OGB's case is principally through the provision of clean water, sanitation, and hygiene promotion. The importance of this aim, and its achievements, cannot be underestimated or undervalued. However, longer-term goals of addressing issues linked to gendered inequalities that sought, for example, to improve women's prospects through education, empowerment, or training, or strategies to prevent further conflict, are secondary to the provision of immediate relief.

Often the aims of relief and recovery themselves thus seem to be in conflict – particularly if resources are limited. Achieving one set of aims may be seen to be at the expense of the other. Moral claims for one or the other raise the temperature. Staff focused on, and responsible for, delivering a quick, large-scale response accuse those emphasising the social complexities of the emergency of fiddling while Rome burns. While the technical staff are saving lives, the social staff are seen to work on non-life-threatening issues, complicating questions, and holding things up, or achieving nothing significant or measurable – or worse still, exacerbating social and political tensions they do not fully understand. Social-development staff, on the other hand, accuse the technical staff of rushing in blindly, treating people like numbers and objects, potentially doing more harm than good by ignoring social and gender differences in the population, creating dependencies, and paying little attention to the long-term consequences of the relief aid itself.

Add gender equity to the mix and the environment may become explosive. It is common to find strong resistance to building in gender-equity goals to emergency response on the grounds that (a) lives have to be saved quickly, information is not available, and there is no time for social surveys; (b) there is immense pressure from donors and the media to show that measures are in place rapidly and having an immediate impact, while the gender dynamics in the society are of less concern, and certainly less visible; (c) while we know distribution is more effective through women, there is often not time to organise it that way, or there is local resistance to it which OGB should not challenge; (d) an emergency is not the right time to challenge gender power relations; and (e) why should special attention be paid to women when everyone is suffering?

I have heard all these arguments in the field. They are arguments that frustrate practitioners on both sides of the debate, all of whom are trying to get the job done as best they can. These are complex issues which are not easily resolved in the clash between speed of response and the social, cultural, and political composition of groups which will determine the quality of that response.

OGB's response to the Kosovo crisis brought these issues out quite clearly, and programme managers made real efforts to work across the relief-development and technical-social divides, and integrate the 'hard' and 'soft' elements into a single programme. The process was fraught with difficulties. And yet, it seemed to have had a good start.

The example of Kosovo

OGB had been in Kosovo since 1995, working closely with women's groups and associations in several regions in the country.

OGB-Priština had strong relationships with local counterparts, and a strong local team. The focus was on long-term development initiatives aimed at the social and political empowerment of women, through capacity building of women activists. With the intensification of the conflict in 1998, OGB's work shifted focus to respond to the needs of displaced women and children. Women's Centres were funded in Viti, Priština, Obiliq, and Gjilan as relief distribution points as well as meeting places for psychosocial support. The programme also included substantial work on water and sanitation and public health.

In March 1999 with the onset of the NATO campaign, OGB evacuated with other INGOs, setting up an office in Skopje with several of its staff from Priština. The existing Albania programme was rapidly expanded to take on the provision of humanitarian relief for the refugees flooding into the country. During the period of exile and displacement, OGB continued to work in Macedonia with its highly committed ex-Priština staff, and some of its Kosovar counterparts, principally in the refugee camps. With the continuity provided by the ex-Priština staff, and programme experience from several years in Kosovo, the chances of a well-integrated programme building the relief response within longer-term strategies for recovery and return, with gender-equity goals at its core, seemed to be high, if not optimal.

However, this integration did not happen, for a number of reasons. A large-scale humanitarian relief programme was mounted, with an enormous budget raised by emergency appeals in the UK, and in the limelight of the high media interest in the crisis. The pressure was on OGB to spend the money, and spend it fast. A large number of expatriate staff, mostly water technicians and engineers, flew into Macedonia to set up OGB's water programme in the camps. Money flowed freely for the emergency response. But the dynamic between the social and technical responses, when I arrived to look at gender, human rights, and protection issues in April 1999, was difficult and competitive. Kosovar staff members, refugees themselves, were dealing with their own personal and family trauma, and with loss and uncertainty, as a result of the war. The problem was heightened by the fact that the new arrivals who arrived en masse to run the emergency-relief response were all expatriates, some with no previous experience of the region. The ex-Priština Kosovar staff felt overrun by the new technical 'expats', misunderstood, and alienated from a programme which had been theirs, and had now inflated beyond recognition.

Kosovar refugees – mostly educated young men and women – were taken on by the technical and social programmes to carry out the work in the camps. There was a heated debate about payment of the young workforce. In the old Priština-based programme, much of the work was based on voluntarism. But in the refugee situation, many of the other international agencies were paying their local recruits. Initially, the debate was played out in gendered terms – the young men working with the water engineers were paid, and the young women were not. This was subsequently adjusted.

The technical staff, running the water programme (the 'hard' side of the programme), were almost exclusively male, and were perceived by the almost exclusively female staff working on gender, disability, social development, and hygiene promotion (the 'soft' side of the programme) to have privileged access to the emergency resources. The technical aspects were thus perceived by those working on the other parts of the programme to be valued more highly than the social aspects. In fact, as in any emergency, all staff were clamouring for more resources, whether logisticians, engineers, managers, or social-development staff. Where all eyes are on the crisis, and the pressure is there externally as well as from the desperate plight of the refugee population, competition over resources is inevitable and where other divisions exist, very difficult to manage.

As is often the case, strong feelings focused on access to vehicles, as key and desirable programme resources. I travelled with staff from all three parts of the programme, and observed that indeed the water-programme staff in each camp had access to their own, new four-wheel drive vehicles, while the hygiene-promotion, disability, and social-development staff had to share older vehicles, one of which was quite unsafe, with a cracked windscreen and a field radio which did not work. I vividly recall sitting on the dusty roadside at the exit from one of the Stankovic camps for some time trying to hitch a lift back to Skopje because the social-development programme did not have its own vehicle. This put extra pressure on the 'soft' teams, and made it harder for them to accomplish all they had to do in the dispersed camps where they worked. There were other specific and more general problems regarding access to programme resources that were not adequately resolved, and this exacerbated the divisions between teams responsible for different components of the programme. This in turn militated against the integration of the social and technical aspects of the programme.

I reported at the time that OGB's programme was a three-pronged effort, comprising community development, with special emphasis on women and disabled people; hygiene and public-health promotion; and the provision of clean water. The programme has many strengths – namely OGB's long and established reputation in the fields of emergency relief and development, and skilled and experienced staff to implement it. The report recommendations included:

> For further development of Oxfam's response, its three elements need to be built into a single integrated programme, with the three aspects based on a clear analysis of the needs and rights of women, men and children. Data collection and appraisal methods sensitive to gender and age are needed to provide the information Oxfam needs for planning of all parts of the programme. Oxfam will then be well-placed to make a significant contribution not only to the current crisis but to the future in Kosovo.
>
> (Williams 1999)

Nonetheless, and in spite of not managing to achieve the desired programme integration, OGB's programme in Macedonia was respected for both its technical and social achievements, and some of the key issues were addressed. Specific needs related to gender and disability were taken into account by the technical team in, for example, the design of washing facilities in the camps. The work of the Social Development and Gender team in providing separate tents for social spaces for women and men set the context for beginning to address the gender-related violence experienced by women and girls, and OGB lobbied UNHCR to fulfil its protection mandate and implement its own guidelines by providing better protection measures for women and girls in the camps.

One of the real difficulties, common to all humanitarian response, was the tension between the pace and style of work of quick-impact emergency relief, and longer-term social processes, and the substantial differences in scale and funding levels of these programmes. Staffing patterns in humanitarian relief are based on rapid scaling-up of numbers, high turnover, and short-term contracts. Induction processes for these staff members are usually sketchy, and the culture of 'hitting the ground running' is not favourable to training in social and gender awareness in the field. In the Kosovo crisis the result was the running of parallel programmes in Macedonia, which was carried forward into the post-conflict work of reconstruction and recovery after the refugees returned. The integration of gender equity into the programme as a whole remains a challenge, although the social-development programme works with previous and new counterparts with the overall aim of the empowerment of women for gender equity in a future Kosovo.

The nature of the funding environment during a crisis and in its aftermath has implications for longer-term work. 'Red' money is tied to specific donor-defined goals; 'green' money is OGB money for programming, and thus offers more flexibility. The 'red' appeal money that sustained the Kosovo humanitarian programme ran out in due course, and the OGB programme had to fund its development and gender work under the Kosovo Women's Initiative (KWI), managed by UNHCR, but which came from an emergency budget-line in the US State Department. Although the KWI project set long-term empowerment goals, the spending for this fund, totalling US$10m, was short-term. This created considerable pressure on Kosovar NGOs as well as on the INGOs, such as OGB, acting as brokers or 'umbrellas' for this fund, to get new projects up and running and spending money, often beyond the organisational capacity of the partner groups. Some women's groups set up in order to create activities the KWI could fund. The KWI was in itself an example of the tension between short-term emergency funding demanding quick and visible returns, and developmental goals whose benefits are only measurable in the longer term. When the emergency money moves on to the next crisis, the gap left can be devastating to organisations which were mobilised, or created, in the plentiful funding climate, and which subsequently find themselves without support, and often collapse, amidst their dashed expectations.

The importance of programme integration was underlined again in OGB's September 2000 workshop on gender equity, referred to above. Joint planning between technical and social intervention teams was identified at the workshop as essential to programming, and it was established that *all* staff operating in emergency relief need to understand the social and gender dimensions of their work, and have clear guidelines to help them. The integration of gender equity would help the planning and design of emergency-relief measures to take into account the longer-term recovery and future development of the population involved, and foster consistency with programme goals designed for the long haul.

Gender assessments were carried out during the Kosovo crisis in both Macedonia and Albania. The Consolidated Recommendations drawn up by gender advisers for the response in both countries hold for OGB programming in general. These included:

- Gender and social development issues need to be fully integrated in the emergency response and future programme development, with every aspect based on a clear analysis of the needs and rights of women, men, and children, and disabled people.

- The social and technical aspects of the programme should inform each other effectively for maximum impact. Social and community services must run hand-in-hand with distribution of non-food items, and water, sanitation, and health/hygiene planning from the start, must be as well resourced and should operate concurrently in Kosovo as soon as OGB has access to the designated sector.

- Unified programme aims and objectives for social and technical interventions need to be set for the region, within the framework of OGB's strategic change objectives, to which gender equity is central, and gender-sensitive indicators for success should be set.

- Setting up a new programme in Kosovo presents an excellent opportunity for OGB to implement best practice in a gender-sensitive programme response in view of the above recommendations. Baseline data and indicators for gender equity should be set at the earliest stage in programme planning for effective monitoring and impact assessment (Clifton and Williams 1999).

Working with counterparts in conflict

OGB's success in integrating gender equity into programming in conflict and its aftermath depends critically not only upon how OGB's institutional dichotomies are resolved (or not), as we have seen above in the case of Kosovo, but also on the relationships with partner organisations and local and national NGOs, and their analysis of the situation. This section looks at some of OGB's experience in Latin America, where its programmes have been notable for the quality of long-standing relationships with local counterpart organisations. Here I focus on the work with counterparts in the immediate aftermath of conflict, where OGB did not have the same level of operationality in its response, and thus the 'technical/social' dichotomy is less evident. The 'hard' and 'soft' elements of the situation, and the programme response through counterpart organisations, however, still had a key influence on the way gender equity was addressed.

From the 1960s and 1970s the country programmes were characterised by intense counterpart relationships, many of which were built around a strong sense of solidarity with the political struggles against brutal military dictatorships and the social injustice and poverty brought about by these regimes. The emphasis was on the long-term transformation of society, by armed or peaceful means, by the real agents of change – the poor and oppressed people of the region. Because of the nature of the regimes, much of the work supported by OGB was initiated by the Catholic church and took place under its umbrella. But the analysis of social injustice did not include an analysis of women's oppression by men.

In El Salvador, OGB's programme focused before and during the war on the strengthening of popular organisations allied to the church and progressive Salvadoran NGOs. In common with many of the liberation struggles of the 1980s, however, gender equity was not seen as part of the liberation goal, and the analysis of gender oppression was often regarded as a 'special interest' issue and potentially divisive to the aims of the movement. The liberation struggle was 'hard', armed, macho, political. Women's specific issues were 'soft', secondary, personal, and for women and men alike, diluted the toughness and authenticity of the armed struggle, whose goal was social justice for all. Moreover, despite the long history of popular feminism and women's struggles in Latin America, both counterparts and some of the OGB staff saw the analysis of gender inequity as having been imported from the developed countries, as yet another example of cultural imperialism, particularly from the USA. Martha Thompson, Deputy Regional Representative for Central America at the time, writes: 'Most counterparts saw the inequalities based on gender relations as a Northern concern, and not one of their priorities' (Thompson 1999:48).

While OGB began to include elements of gender analysis into the El Salvador programme in the 1980s, the extent to which it pushed its gender work was greatly influenced by the position of OGB's counterpart organisations. By 1995, however, OGB's Gender Policy began to require field programmes to show evidence of pursuing gender equity in their work. Thompson (1999:50–3) outlines four basic mistakes made by OGB in trying to incorporate gender analysis into the programme.

- Money was thrown at the issue. Counterparts could access funding if they attached 'gender' to a project. Without a gender analysis, counterparts included projects with women, such as training or micro-enterprises – some of which were effective, some of which were not. Funding agencies went along with this to gain the approval of head office.

- Rather than fully explore the tension between a class and a gender analysis, an uneasy compromise was reached, whereby OGB and counterpart agencies basically continued working as before, but with the addition of specific projects with women, and support to some women's organisations in the popular movement. A broad discussion with counterparts and local women's organisations on gender should have taken place, and would have avoided OGB contributing to the distortion of the concept of gender equity.

- Agencies did not recognise the gains that women had made during the war, gaining visibility in acts of courage, as combatants or resisting the fighting. Nor did agencies understand how transformation of gender roles could be integrated into social transformation. In the refugee camps, and later in the repopulated conflict zones, women began to take on leadership roles, addressing gender relations. But at the end of the war, women were supposed to relinquish their positions, and strategies were not in place to deal with this.

- OGB was unwilling to risk prejudicing its relationship with counterparts by raising gender power differences because of its perceived potential to cause divisions.

In El Salvador, the popular movement was dominated by men; during the war, women became stronger and were able to challenge their position after the fighting had ceased. A narrow political analysis, which did not take gender oppression and the value of internal democracy into account, held women back during the political struggle. Martha Thompson reflects:

> I am struck by a dichotomy: when the popular movement in El Salvador was strong, the development of gender work in member organisations was very weak; it became much stronger in the post-war period, when the popular movement was weaker.

(Thompson 1999:57)

The experience of Salvadoran women in the post-conflict arena is reflected in countries such as Nicaragua, Mozambique, Zimbabwe, or South Africa. Once the war is over, women are sent back to be 'barefoot, pregnant, and in the kitchen', while men make the political decisions about peace and reconstruction, and fill the political positions in the new government order. Women are less likely to accept their subordination once they have experienced relative autonomy and respect during the war, but the obstacles to their advancement are exacerbated by militaristic constructions of masculinity and femininity. The overall message to them is clear: both the war and peace will be dominated by men and masculinist priorities and interests; and this will be maintained as long as women do not have a formal role in peace making and reconstruction. The message to INGOs is that they need to bring their global experience to bear on local and national politics and social relations, and to seek and strengthen counterparts locally, particularly among women's organisations and organisations working for gender equality.

In Central America, OGB supported Guatemalan women's organisations in exile in Mexico, planning the return of the refugee populations to Guatemala. The support included training and organisational strengthening, and women participated in some of the delegations identifying land for resettlement. However, according to Beate Thoresen, then OGB's Programme Co-ordinator in Guatemala,

> *After the return to Guatemala there was a significant decline in the level of organisation of women. This has to do with the dedication to immediate survival in the resettlement process as well as the need to reorganise as the return communities were dispersed and the groups that had lived together in Mexico returned to different places. It could also be observed that there was a change in the attitude of men, saying that things should get back to 'normal' as they were now back in Guatemala. In some cases the leadership in the communities (men) resisted organisation of women after the return.*

(Personal communication)

A central element in this resistance is connected to access to resources, such as land. As women often only have land-use rights through men, widows and single women are dispossessed during and after war. In Guatemala, land is allocated collectively, or in the majority of cases, as individual plots by family. The first post-war land allocations showed that women were not taken into account. Women are demanding joint property rights with men, and their right to become members of co-operatives to acquire land. In response to men's allegation that women have not contributed money or community work to the co-operatives, women are claiming that their domestic work should be accepted as their contribution to the community. On the southern coast of Guatemala, Madre Tierra is an OGB-supported returnee women's organisation that developed in response to women's specific livelihood needs, such as for cooking stoves, and animals for generating income and providing food and milk. Tensions arose with men in the community over the success of the women's projects, but women opted to keep control of them, outside the community co-operatives, which do not represent women's interests. Madre Tierra now employs men to carry out some of the labour for the project.

While many in Guatemala assert that gender relations have not improved, there are considerable differences between one community and another, and women have gained skills and confidence in organisation building and awareness. Thoresen reports help given by an OGB-supported returnee women's organisation, which assisted a neighbouring women's group in preparing a project proposal that included gender training. When asked why they wanted training on gender awareness, 'they said they wanted a better future for their children and they had observed that the returnee women could dance with other men than their husbands at community celebrations!'

The heart of the matter: gender violence and post-war peace

In Africa there is not a universal definition of peace. It is not the clichéd definition of not being at war. In South Africa today there is increasing domestic violence, an increase in child abuse. So we cannot say South Africa is at peace.
(Thandi Modise, ANC Women's League)[3]

Peace does not come with the cessation of armed hostilities and the signing of peace agreements. High levels of social and gender violence are a feature of post-war societies. South Africa has experienced spiralling levels of interpersonal violence, with shocking statistics of sexual abuse of women and children. Violence, like war, is gendered. Its expression is inseparable from female and male gender identities, and the relations between women and men. Gender identities constructed, promoted, and sustained by armed conflict and the impact of militarisation powerfully influence women's and men's attitudes and behaviours in the post-conflict environment.

This section looks at the significance of gender violence and the meaning of peace in the light of the contradictions described in this paper. To address gender violence means overcoming the private/public divide, and bringing together issues commonly categorised as 'hard' – those linked with war, arms, and high-profile, militarised peacekeeping – and 'soft' – those linked to the personal experiences of violence of women, girls, and boys during and after war. It means making the connections between the violence perpetrated in war, within the ambit of relief interventions, and the violence perpetrated outside war, addressed by development programmes. Policies for the construction of post-war peace must also embrace and ensure peace between women and men. In this sense, programming on gender violence goes right to the heart of the matter, bringing the issues described in this paper into stark relief.

The wars in Rwanda and Bosnia brought rape and sexual violence in wartime to the public gaze through intense media coverage. These crimes were in the public domain, and thus became a legitimate focus for the attention of human-rights organisations, and for the interventions of development agencies – although in fact research in Bosnia showed that the majority of rapes and sexual crimes against women were committed by men known to them. The crimes of domestic violence and sexual abuse in societies not at war, or recovering from it, do not attract the same attention, and international organisations show greater ambivalence in addressing issues still widely perceived as too difficult, too complicated, and too private.

Nonetheless, OGB has supported work on violence against women for many years, and in line with the new programme objectives outlined earlier in this paper, a global programme on violence against women was being developed at the time of writing. The programme seeks to overcome the analytic division between the public and the private, and to address violence within a framework of understanding gender relations and the construction of masculine and feminine identities in any sphere, in war and in peace. OGB's experience from all over the world – South Africa, Central and South America, the Great Lakes, Eastern Europe, Cambodia, Viet Nam, South Asia – show that gender violence carries on decades after a war is officially over; peace means different things for women and for men. A closer analysis of gender violence is beginning to inform OGB's work in post-conflict reconstruction and recovery, but gender violence has yet to be tackled strategically, and in an integrated way, as a central element of emergency response.

OGB has supported work by local and national NGOs which tackles violence against women in the aftermath of conflict, or where conflict is endemic, in many parts of the world – notably in South Africa, Rwanda, Bosnia, Indonesia, Cambodia, Guatemala, and Colombia.

In Cambodia, for example, the Alliance for Conflict Transformation, comprised of 19 NGO and government workers, conducts training on conflict resolution for officials from the municipality of Phnom Penh, to be applied to disputes ranging from land issues to domestic violence. Domestic violence is widespread in Cambodia, the legacy of 30 years of war and brutalised relationships. The Project Against Domestic Violence in Cambodia (PADV) has been instrumental in raising awareness of violence against women through education and public campaigning, with government support. A national survey of the incidence of violence against women in 2400 households gained national and international media attention. These organisations make the link clearly between the violence of war and continuing violence against women after the war is over. A victim of violence is quoted in PADV's survey of domestic violence in Cambodia:

> After 1979 men changed. Nine out of ten men are broken, nasty
> ('Khoch'). During the Khmer Rouge period they had no happiness at all.
> So now that they are free, men do whatever they want.
>
> (Quoted in Zimmerman 1994)

There are many examples of the brutalisation of men by extreme nationalism and the experience of military action, and this has been well documented by women's NGOs and international organisations in Bosnia, Uganda, Sierra Leone, and other parts of the world. A chilling case is reported from South Africa, in which a township gang was formed to rape women as a way of bolstering or recovering male identity and status, while at the same time getting back at political leaders by whom gang members felt betrayed. These ex-combatants replicate militaristic patterns of discipline and punishment, and assert their dominance through acts of gendered violence – the sexual abuse and rape of women. The leader of the organisation stated in a television interview:

> I was a comrade before I joined this organisation. I joined it because we
> were no longer given political tasks. Most of the tasks were given to senior
> people. Myself and six other guys decided to form our own organisation
> that will keep these senior comrades busy all the time. That is why we
> formed the South African Rapist Association (SARA). We rape women
> who need to be disciplined (those women who behave like snobs), they just
> do not want to talk to most people ...
>
> (Vetten 1998)

Addressing masculinities and the forces which lead to, promote, and maintain male violence towards women as a defining feature of gender power relations will be part of OGB's mission to have a significant impact on gender equity through all aspects of its programmes. To do this effectively, OGB – as any INGO or international agency – will have to examine closely its own gendered structures and cultures. This paper has identified some of the key areas of difficulty in relation to delivering on gender equity in the context of conflict and post-war programming. The tensions show up at all levels in the institution. The core argument of this paper is that the ways that OGB's organisational imperatives are both conceptualised and implemented are themselves gendered. The 'hard' and the 'soft' run through OGB's structure and culture as metaphors for the masculine and the feminine, and can bump up against each other in the heat of the moment, in the highly charged context of emergencies and post-conflict interventions, and generate tensions over priorities and resources, value, and reward. It is only a thorough and profound commitment to gender equity in all aspects of its structure, culture, and programming that OGB – or any other organisation – can begin to overcome these tensions and avoid the weakening of its effectiveness in fulfilling its mission to relieve human suffering and address its root causes.

Acknowledgement

This article is based on a paper delivered to an Expert Seminar at the Humanist University in Utrecht in October 2000 on gender relations in the aftermath of war, convened by Cynthia Cockburn and Dubravka Zarkov. It subsequently appeared under the title 'Conflicts of interest: gender in Oxfam's emergency response' in their edited volume *The Postwar Moment: Militaries, Masculinities and International Peacekeeping*, published by Lawrence and Wishart (London, 2002).

Notes

1   In this paper, Oxfam GB or Oxfam refer only to Oxfam Great Britain, and not to the wider family of organisations known as Oxfam International.

2   Many writers have emphasised this. Anne Mackintosh, Oxfam GB's Regional Representative for the Great Lakes region from 1991–4, writes: 'even agencies who recognise the inappropriateness of regarding "relief" and "development" as separate phenomena perpetuate this false dichotomy, through resourcing long-term and emergency programmes in different ways and having them managed by different departments and staff. This often leads to unhelpful tensions and rivalry' (Mackintosh 1997).

3   Cited in 'Women and the Aftermath', AGENDA No. 43 2000, Durban, South Africa, a report on a July 1999 conference held in Johannesburg, The Aftermath: Women in Post-conflict Reconstruction.

References

Anderson, Mary B. (1996) *Do No Harm: Supporting Local Capacities for Peace Through Aid,* Cambridge, MA: LCCP.

Bryer, David and Edmund Cairns (1997) 'For better? For worse? Humanitarian aid in conflict', *Development in Practice* 7(4): 363–74.

Clifton, Deborah and Fiona Gell (2001) 'Saving and protecting lives by empowering women', *Gender and Development* 9(3): 8–18.

Clifton, Deborah and Suzanne Williams (1999) 'Gender Assessment of Oxfam's Emergency Response to the Kosovo Refugee Crisis in Albania and Macedonia', unpublished paper, Oxford: Oxfam GB.

Committee on Women's Rights and Equal Opportunities (2000) 'European Parliament: Draft Report on Women's Involvement in Peaceful Conflict Resolution', Brussels: European Parliament.

Mackintosh, Anne (1997) 'Rwanda: beyond "ethnic conflict"', *Development in Practice* 7(4): 464–74.

Oxfam GB (1998) 'The Links: Lessons from the Gender Mapping Project', unpublished report, Oxford: Oxfam GB.

Sorensen, Birgitte (1998) *Women and Post Conflict Reconstruction: Issues and Sources,* War-torn Societies Project Occasional Paper No. 3, Geneva: UNRISD.

Sphere Project (2000) *Humanitarian Charter and Minimum Standards in Disaster Response,* Geneva: The Sphere Project (distributed by Oxfam GB).

Thompson, Martha (1999) 'Gender in times of war (El Salvador)', in Fenella Porter, Ines Smyth, and Caroline Sweetman (eds.) *Gender Works: Oxfam Experience in Policy and Practice,* Oxford: Oxfam GB.

Vetten, L. (1998) 'War and the making of men and women', *Sunday Independent,* South Africa, 16 August.

Williams, Suzanne (1999) 'Gender and Human Rights in the Macedonian Refugee Camps', unpublished report, Oxford: Oxfam GB.

Zimmerman, Cathy (1994) 'Plates in a Basket Will Rattle', Phnom Penh: PADV.

Resources

Serious social upheaval – from political violence to full-scale war – obviously affects all members of society in some measure, whether directly or indirectly. Women are, therefore, inextricably involved. They may be victims of human-rights abuses, or caught in the crossfire, or forced to leave their homes. They may also be fighters, politically or otherwise implicated with one side or another, or stand either to benefit or to lose out from the victory or defeat of one of the warring parties. In this sense, all publications and policies relating to such issues are relevant to women. Yet, as contributors to this volume show, women are often not only invisible in the 'war and peace' literature but absent from detailed consideration in aid programmes or post-war reconstruction processes. The following resources have therefore been selected on the basis of the contribution they make to putting women, and issues affecting them, on the agenda. In particular, we have highlighted works that are written from a feminist perspective. The listing was compiled and annotated by Deborah Eade and Alina Rocha Menocal, Editor and Deputy Editor respectively of Development in Practice.

Leading experts in the field

Cynthia Cockburn

A feminist researcher and visiting professor in the Sociology Department at the City University, London, Cockburn's work focuses on armed conflict and processes of alliance and peace building. Recent publications include *The Space Between Us: Negotiating Gender and National Identities in Conflict* (London: Zed Books, 1998) and *The Postwar Moment: Militaries, Masculinities and International Peacekeeping* (edited with Dubravka Zarkov, London: Lawrence & Wishart, 2002).

Miriam Cooke

Professor of Modern Arabic Literature and Culture at Duke University, Cooke's work focuses on war, gender, and Islam in the post-colonial Arab world. Recent publications include *Gendering War Talk* (edited with Angela Woollacott, Princeton, NJ: Princeton University Press, 1993), *War's Other Voices: Women Writers on the Lebanese Civil War* (Syracuse, NY: Syracuse University Press, 1996), and *Women and the War Story* (Berkeley, CA: University of California Press, 1997). Her work *Hayati, My Life. A Novel* (Syracuse, NY: Syracuse University Press, 2000) is a fictional narrative about three generations of Palestinian women whose lives are torn apart by war, rape, dispossession, and poverty.

Cynthia Enloe

Professor Emeritus in the Government Department at Clark University, Enloe's work has focused on the ways in which militarising processes (local and international) serve to privilege men and certain forms of masculinity, and continue to do so even in 'post conflict' situations. Her research also traces the thinking and strategies of women activists working to create cultures and policies that challenge ongoing militarisation. Relevant publications include *Does Khaki Become You?* (London: Pandora Press, 1988), *Bananas, Beaches and Bases: Making Feminist Sense of International Politics* (Berkeley, CA: University of California Press, 1990), *The Morning After: Sexual Politics at the End of the Cold War* (Berkeley, CA: University of California Press, 1993), and *Manoeuvers: The International Politics of Militarizing Women's Lives* (Berkeley, CA: University of California Press, 2000).

Books

Abdo, Nahla and Ronit Lentin (eds.): *Women and the Politics of Military Confrontation: Palestinian and Israeli Gendered Narratives of Dislocation*, New York, NY: Berghahn Books, 2002, ISBN: 1 57181 459 0, 336 pp.

Based on the (auto)biographical narratives of Jewish and Palestinian women, this collection seeks to provide more nuanced understandings of the Middle East conflict. Each of the essays captures the sense of social, cultural, national, and gender dislocation that characterise this conflict.

Addis, Elizabetta, Valeria E. Russo, and Lorenza Sebesta (eds.): *Women Soldiers: Images and Realities*, New York, NY: St. Martin's Press, 1994, ISBN: 0 31212 704 5, 190 pp.

In this interdisciplinary study of female military service, based on case studies from Libya, Italy, and the first Gulf War, contributors look at how women fare in masculine, authoritarian armed forces; how their presence affects the military; and at the economic consequences of excluding women from military institutions. The book calls for an active policy of integrating women into a military that is willing to accommodate their needs and values.

Anderlini, Sanam Naraghi: *Women at the Peace Table: Making a Difference*, New York, NY: UNIFEM, 2000, ISBN: 0 96795 020 1, 71 pp.

This document argues for the full inclusion of women in peace processes, asserting that their absence from negotiations is likely to undermine democracy and the development of society at large. Drawing on interviews with a range of women peace leaders, the author highlights strategies women have employed to make a positive contribution to peace-building efforts.

Bayard de Volo, Lorraine: *Mothers of Heroes and Martyrs: Gender Identity Politics in Nicaragua, 1979–1999*, Baltimore, MD: The Johns Hopkins University Press, 2001, ISBN: 0 80186 764 9, 304 pp.

Through her analysis of a women's group formed to support the Sandinista revolution in Nicaragua – the Mothers of Heroes and Martyrs of Matagalpa – Bayard de Volo explores 'the dominant but rarely examined maternal identity politics of revolution, war, and democratization'. The author shows how both sides of the civil conflict mobilised mothers and images of motherhood in an effort to win over ordinary Nicaraguans to their cause. While the mobilisation of such identities propelled women into unprecedented levels of collective action, it also channelled them away from feminist priorities.

Bennett, Olivia, Jo Bexley, and Kitty Warnock (eds.): *Arms to Fight, Arms to Protect: Women Speak Out About Conflict,* London: Panos Institute, 1995, ISBN: 1 87067 036 1, 282 pp.

This collection of testimonies concerning the psychological and physical damage of war, and the battle for economic survival, illustrates that women's experiences are not uniform: they can be fighters, participants, refugees, victims caught between warring factions, and peace builders, as well as relatives of the dead and disappeared. The book also explores women's efforts to rebuild their lives and communities once conflict has subsided.

Breines, Ingebord, Dorota Gierycz, and Betty Reardon (eds.): *Towards a Women's Agenda for a Culture of Peace*, Paris: UNESCO, 1999, ISBN: 9 23103 559 2, 265 pp.

Part I of this edited volume explores the problems associated with the role(s) of women in war, peace, and security. Part II provides gendered critiques of peace and security policies and practices, while the chapters in Part III highlight the roles that women have played in different aspects of peace building.

BRIDGE: development – gender: *Cutting Edge Pack on Gender & Armed Conflict*, Brighton: BRIDGE/Institute of Development Studies, 2003.

This pack explores the links between armed conflict and gender inequality and discusses strategies to address these inequalities in working for long-term peace. It includes an overview report highlighting key issues; a supporting-resources collection with summaries of resources, case studies, tools, training materials, websites, and networking details; and relevant articles featured in BRIDGE's bulletin *In Brief*. The pack is available free of charge at: **www.ids.ac.uk/bridge**. Other relevant publications include *Gender, Conflict and Development: Volume I - Overview*, BRIDGE Report 34 (Bridget Byrne, 1995) and *Gender, Conflict and Development: Volume II. Case Studies: Cambodia, Rwanda, Kosova, Somalia, Algeria, Guatemala and Eritrea*, BRIDGE Report 35 (Bridget Byrne *et al.*, 1996).

Corrin, Chris (ed.): *Women in a Violent World: Feminist Analyses and Resistance Across Europe*, Edinburgh: Edinburgh University Press, 1996, ISBN: 0 74860 804 4, 256 pp.

This book offers a feminist analysis of the ways in which women experience male violence in various situations across Europe, including displacement, conflict, and war, and makes connections between violence at the local or 'domestic' level and violence in national and international contexts. Contributors call for public resources to be provided for women who survive violent situations, for protective legislation, and for educational programmes and public awareness campaigns.

Date-Bah, Eugenia, **Martha Walsh** *et al.: Gender and Armed Conflicts: Challenges for Decent Work, Gender Equity, and Peace Building Agendas,* InFocus Programme Crisis Response and Reconstruction Working Paper 2, Geneva: ILO, 2001, ISBN: 92211 246 X, 80 pp.

This document synthesises research and insights based on several country studies undertaken by the ILO between 1996 and 2000. It is intended to guide policy making and effective gender-sensitive programming, as well as to further debate on women and gender issues in the wake of armed conflict. It is available free of charge at: www.ilo.org/public/english/employment/recon/crisis/download/criswp2.pdf

El-Bushra, Judy, **Asha El-Karib, and Angela Hadjipateras:** 'Gender-sensitive Programme Design and Planning in Conflict-affected Situations', London: Acord, 2002, ISBN: N/A, 9 pp.

This research report outlines the findings of an Acord project carried out in Angola, Eritrea, Mali, Rwanda, Somalia, Sudan, Somalia, and Uganda in 2000–1 to enhance gender awareness in the design and management of development programmes in conflict-torn areas. The report, as well as all annexes on case studies and methodology, are available free of charge at:
www.acord.org.uk/Publications/G&CResearch/

Farhat-Naser, Sumaya (translated from German by Hilary Kilpatrick): *Daughter of the Olive Trees: A Palestinian Woman's Struggle for Peace,* Basel: Lenos Verlag, 2003, ISBN: N/A, 220 pp.

Writing in a context of escalating violence with little prospect of sustainable peace, Farhat-Naser provides insights into Palestinian society, its political and social structures, and the problems of its leadership. The author gives an insider's account of the everyday efforts undertaken by Palestinian and Israeli women to achieve peace and justice, and documents ambitious dialogues and conflictual discussions.

Fitzsimmons, Tracy: *Beyond the Barricades: Women, Civil Society, and Participation After Democratization in Latin America,* Hamden, CT: Garland Science, 2000, ISBN: 0 81533 736 1, 205 pp.

This book explores the role of civil society in bringing an end to authoritarian rule in Latin America by tracing the levels and arenas of organised participation among women both before and after 'democratisation'. The author maintains that women have been surprised to discover that democracies do not necessarily yield greater gender equality or more opportunities for participation than did the dictatorships they replaced.

Giles, Wenona and Jennifer Hyndman: *Sites of Violence: Gender and Conflict Zones*, Berkeley, CA: University of California Press, forthcoming 2004, ISBN: 0 52023 791 9, 370 pp.

The rules of war in contemporary conflicts have broken down distinctions between battlefield and home, and between soldier and civilian. In this book, international feminist scholars examine the gendered and racialised dimensions of these changes, and what happens when the body, household, nation, state, and economy become sites of violence, particularly against women. Case studies include the gendered politics of ethno-nationalism in Israel and Palestine, Sri Lanka, and the post-Yugoslav states; 'honour killings' in Iraqi Kurdistan; armed conflict in Sudan; and geographies of violence in Ghana.

Goldstein, Joshua S.: *War and Gender: How Gender Shapes the War System and Vice Versa*, Cambridge: Cambridge University Press, 2001, ISBN: 0 52180 716 6, 540 pp.

This amply illustrated book explores the dynamic relationship between gender and war. The author analyses possible explanations for the near-total absence of women from combat forces over time and across cultures, and explores the history of women fighters, the complex role of testosterone in men's social behaviours, and the construction of masculinity and femininity in the shadow of war.

Guzman Bouvard, Marguerite: *Revolutionizing Motherhood: The Mothers of the Plaza De Mayo*, Wilmington, DE: Scholarly Resources, 2002, ISBN: 0 84202 487 5, 278 pp.

Agentina's 'Dirty War' in the 1970s was prosecuted through the abduction, torture, and disappearance of tens of thousands of civilians. Braving a similar fate, women calling themselves Mothers of the Plaza de Mayo organised to demand information about their children's whereabouts and to spotlight the flagrant violations of human rights. This book traces the Mothers' history and examines how they transformed maternity from a passive, domestic role to one of public strength. See also the 'Asociación Madres de Plaza de Mayo' entry in the **Organisations, Networks, and Websites** section.

Harvey, Neil: 'The Zapatistas, radical democratic citizenship, and women's struggles', *Social Politics* 5(2) (Summer 1998), pp. 158–87.

This article uses social-movement theory and discourse analysis to discuss the Zapatista rebellion in Chiapas. Paying particular attention to the gender-based claims of indigenous women within the movement, Harvey argues that the Chiapas uprising has challenged conventional theories of democracy and citizenship.

Jacobs, Susie, Ruth Jacobson, and Jennifer Marchbank (eds.): *States of Conflict: Gender, Violence and Resistance*, London: Zed Books, 2000, ISBN: 1 85649 656 2, 43 pp.

This book explores gendered violence across layers of social and political organisation, from the military to the sexual, and makes connections between global processes, conflict at the state and community levels, and domestic violence. The contributions look at women as fighters and peace builders, and explore the nature of the public/private divide in the realm of gendered violence.

Kampwirth, Karen: *Women and Guerrilla Movements: Nicaragua, El Salvador, Chiapas, Cuba*, University Park, PA: Penn State University Press, 2002, ISBN: 0 27102 185 3, 194 pp.

Based on extensive interviews, this book focuses on the women who participated in the revolutionary movements in El Salvador and Nicaragua, and the Zapatista insurrection in the Mexican state of Chiapas. The author examines the factors that allowed these women to escape the constraints of their traditional roles to become guerrilla fighters. The final chapter contrasts these experiences with what happened in the Cuban revolution, in which relatively few women participated. Kampwirth is also editor, with Victoria González, of *Radical Women in Latin America – Left and Right* (University Park, PA: Penn State University Press, 2001).

Kasic, Bilijana (ed.): *Women and the Politics of Peace: Contributions to a Culture of Women's Resistance*, Zagreb: Center for Women's Studies, 1997, ISBN: 9 53974 140 8, 155 pp.

Drawing on case studies from Central and Eastern Europe, contributors represent diverse voices and perspectives on women and peace, pacifism, violence, and international security in a context of war.

Kumar, Krishna (ed.): *Women and Civil War: Impact, Organizations, and Action*, Boulder, CO: Lynne Rienner Publishers, 2001, ISBN: 1 58826 046 1, 253 pp.

This book analyses the impact of civil wars on women and gender relations and the different ways in which women have responded. Contributors explore how such wars have affected women's economic, social, and political roles; what types of women's organisations have emerged to promote reconstruction and protect women's rights; and the kind of assistance provided by donor agencies to support women's organising.

Lentin, Ronit (ed.): *Gender and Catastrophe*, London: Zed Books, 1997, ISBN: 1 85649 446 5, 282 pp.

With contributions from feminist scholars and activists, this anthology explores the many ways in which violence has been directed at women. Looking at how women are targeted as ethnic subjects in extreme situations such as war, genocide, mass rape, and 'ethnic cleansing', the book suggests alternative frameworks to analyse events that range from the 1994 Rwandan massacre to reproductive-health policies in Tibet.

Luciak, Ilja: *After the Revolution: Gender and Democracy in El Salvador, Nicaragua, and Guatemala*, Bethesda, MD: The Johns Hopkins University Press, 2001, ISBN: 0 0186 780 0, 336 pp.

This book traces the transformation of women guerrilla fighters in El Salvador, Guatemala, and Nicaragua into mainstream political players in the democratisation process. While women in each country contributed greatly to the revolutionary struggle, their political effectiveness varied significantly once hostilities ended. Luciak considers that women in Guatemala were the least successful in incorporating women's rights into the national agenda for change under the new regime, while women in El Salvador were the most effective.

Manchanda, Rita (ed.): *Women, War and Peace in South Asia: Beyond Victimhood to Agency*, Delhi: Sage, 2001, ISBN: 8 17829 018 9, 304 pp.

This book develops a gender analysis of conflict in South Asia, emphasising women's varied roles in war and their capacity to become agents of social transformation. At one end of the spectrum is the 'woman of violence', symbolised by the 'armed virgin' of the Liberation Tigers of Tamil Ealam (the Tamil Tigers); at the other, the 'woman of peace', embedded in the Naga Mothers' Association struggle for the independence of Nagaland. A recurrent theme is that of 'loss and gain': while protracted conflict opens up new spaces for women, nationalistic projects circumscribe their autonomy by casting them in their traditional role of community guardians.

Matthews, Jenny: *Women and War*, London: Pluto Press in association with ActionAid, 2003, ISBN: 0 74532 073 2, 192 pp.

This photographic tribute to women in times of war is organised by themes including women's relationship to war as mothers; exile; and the opportunities afforded to women in times of war. The images capture the many roles women play, be it watching, avoiding, coping, confronting, or participating. Each photograph carries an accompanying diary entry that tells the story behind it.

Meintjes, Sheila, Anu Pillay, and Meredeth Turshen (eds.): *The Aftermath in Post-conflict Transformation*, London: Zed Books, 2002, ISBN: 1 84277 066 7, 224 pp.

The contributors to this volume argue that the end of conflict does not mean an end to violence against women. The struggle to transform patriarchal gender relations cannot be postponed until the post-war period but must be undertaken during the conflict itself. The book explores how transitions from war to peace and from authoritarian to democratic politics can be used as opportunities for social transformation.

Mertus, Julie A.: *War's Offensive on Women: The Humanitarian Challenge in Bosnia, Kosovo, and Afghanistan*, Bloomsfield, CT: Kumarian Press, 2000, ISBN: 1 56549 117 3, 176 pp.

Drawing on case studies from Afghanistan, Bosnia, and Kosovo, Mertus argues that humanitarian efforts to assist women will be successful only if they incorporate those very women in every aspect of their work. The author also explores how international human-rights law has begun to address gender-based violence, and how agencies can make use of these developments to better protect women.

Moghadam, Valentine M. (ed.): *Gender and National Identity: Women and Politics in Muslim Societies,* London: Zed Books, 1994, ISBN: 1 85649 246 X, 180 pp.

This collection explores gender and national identity within political movements in the Middle East, the Maghreb, and South Asia and argues that, since nationalism, revolution, and Islamisation are gendered processes, women are central to efforts to construct a national identity in periods of political change. The case studies include Algerian women's experience in the national liberation movement; events leading to revolution and Islamisation in Iran; revolution and civil war in Afghanistan; and the Palestinian *intifada.*

Moser, Caroline O.N. and Fiona Clark (eds.): *Victims, Perpetrators or Actors? Gender, Armed Conflict and Political Violence,* London: Zed Books, 2001, ISBN: 1 85649 898 0, 208 pp.

This book analyses the gendered nature of armed conflict and political violence, seeking to deepen understanding of the changing roles and power relations between women and men during such circumstances. Through wide-ranging case studies, contributors address issues such as the complex and interrelated stages of conflict and peace; gendered expressions of violence and of conflict and peace; and the role of women's organisations in conflict resolution and peace building.

Nikolic-Ristanovic, Vesna (ed.): *Women, Violence and War: Wartime Victimization of Refugees in the Balkans,* Budapest: Central European University Press, 2000, ISBN: 9 63911 660 2, 300 pp.

Based on interviews with female refugees from the former Yugoslavia, this book portrays the experiences these women endured, including sexual, physical, and psychological violence, as well as problems of confinement, upheaval, and family separation. Contributors emphasise that violence against women in war is not independent of peacetime abuse and the imbalance of power between the sexes.

Randall, Margaret: *Sandino's Daughters: Testimonies of Nicaraguan Women in Struggle*, Piscataway, NJ: Rutgers University Press, 1995, ISBN: 0 81352 214 5, 252 pp.

Believing that their own liberation was inextricably linked to that of the Nicaraguan nation, many of the women who became involved in the Sandinista revolutionary movement, some of whose stories are recounted in this book, came to experience the personal becoming the political in their struggle against the Somoza dictatorship. Randall is also author of *When I Look into the Mirror and See You: Women, Terror, and Resistance* (Piscataway, NJ: Rutgers University Press, 2002), which chronicles the experiences of two Central American women who survived their abduction by Honduran security forces in the 1980s.

Reed, Betsy (ed.): *Nothing Sacred: Women Respond to Religious Fundamentalism and Terror*, New York, NY: Nation Books, 2002, ISBN: 1 56025 450 5, 433 pp.

Feminist authors and activists examine the ways in which fundamentalism is linked to discrimination and violence against women in countries including Algeria, India, Iran, Israel, and the USA. In particular, they ask whether there is a 'clash of civilisations' between Islam and the West, or rather clashes within civilisations, such as the longstanding struggle between feminists and Christian fundamentalists in the USA.

Rehn, Elisabeth and Ellen Johnson Sirleaf: *Women, War, and Peace: The Independent Experts' Assessment of the Impact of Armed Conflict on Women and Women's Role in Peace-building*, Progress of the World's Women 2002, Volume One, New York, NY: UNIFEM, 155 pp.

Based on extensive interviews with people in conflict areas, this report analyses the impact of war on women and women's contributions to reconciliation. Issues covered include the gender dimensions of violence and displacement, and the need to encourage women's participation in peace building. The report concludes with recommendations on how to better protect and empower women. It is available free of charge at: www.unifem.undp.org/resources/assessment/

Rojas, Rosa (ed.): *Chiapas, ¿Y las Mujeres Qué?*, Mexico City: Ediciones del Taller Editorial La Correa Feminista, 1995, 287 pp.

Contributors to this volume argue that the marginalisation of women in the Mexican state of Chiapas is closely linked to the unjust conditions that led to the Zapatista uprising, but that women remain invisible within the Zapatista cause. Adding 'gender' demands to a list of grievances, as they believe the EZLN has done, amounts only to 'a partial declaration of good intentions' unless women's issues are given due priority. It is available in English free of charge at: www.eco.utexas.edu/Homepages/Faculty/Cleaver/begin.html

Russell, Diana E.H.: *Lives of Courage: Women for a New South Africa*, New York, NY: Basic Books, 1989, ISBN: 0 46504 139 6, 384 pp.

Based on interviews with 24 women activists in South Africa, this book provides a first-hand account of the role that women played in the struggle against apartheid. Across divides of skin colour or age, the women speak of the price they and their families had to pay for their activism, of the difficulties they encountered as women in a racist and sexist society, of the terrors they had to endure, and of their dreams for a new South Africa.

Sajor, Indai Lourdes (ed.): *Common Grounds: Violence Against Women in War and Armed Conflict Situations*, Quezon City: Asian Center for Women's Human Rights, 1998.

Contributors to this volume identify the different types of violence directed at women in times of war; provide a statistical analysis of the violations against women; assess the capacity of women groups to protect women's rights during conflict; and explore legal strategies to defend women in both national and international courts.

Sharratt, Sara and Ellyn Kaschak (eds.): *Assault on the Soul: Women in the Former Yugoslavia*, Binghamton, NY: Haworth Press, 1999, ISBN: 0 78900 771 1.

This collection of contributions by lawyers, activists, and health professionals examines the psychological and legal aspects of women in armed conflict. Recording the experiences of ordinary women and children in such situations, it highlights the significance of women's achievement in getting gender-based abuse recognised as a war crime.

Smith-Ayala, Emilie: *The Granddaughters of Ixmuncané: Guatemalan Women Speak*, Toronto: Women's Press, 1991, ISBN: 0 88961 169 6, 255 pp.

Guatemala's 37-year war was characterised by extreme brutality, particularly against the Mayan population. This book is based on interviews with over 30 women activists, indigenous and *ladina*, describing their experiences of war and their vision for the future: chapters cover rural women and subsistence farmers; Christian nuns and lay-workers; women in human-rights groups; women trade unionists; feminists and members of women's organisations; and women guerrilla fighters. A reflection by Nobel Peace laureate Rigoberta Menchú concludes the volume.

Sorensen, Birgitte: *Women and Post-conflict Reconstruction: Issues and Sources*, War-torn Societies Project Occasional Paper No. 3, Geneva: UNRISD, 1998, ISBN: N/A, 88 pp.

A critical review of the early literature concerning the issues that frequently afflict women in situations of armed conflict and its aftermath, this paper is organised around four topics: political reconstruction, economic reconstruction, social reconstruction, and a consideration of conceptual and analytical frameworks. It is available free of charge at: www.unrisd.org

Stiglmayer, Alexandra (ed.): *Mass Rape: The War Against Women in Bosnia-Herzegovina*, Lincoln, NB: University of Nebraska Press, 1994, ISBN: 0 8032 9229 5, 232 pp.

Originally published in Germany in 1993, this book includes one of the first formal accounts of the magnitude of the atrocities being committed in the former Yugoslavia. Written before disclosures of systematic rapes in the Balkan wars had become public knowledge, the book contains interviews both with rape survivors and with some of the rapists, and offers a legal, psychological, and historical framework for preventing any recurrence of such outrages and ensuring timely intervention and vigorous prosecution of the perpetrators.

Sweetman, Caroline (ed.): *Gender, Development, and Humanitarian Work*, Focus on Gender series, Oxford: Oxfam GB, 2001, ISBN: 0 85598 457 0, 98 pp.

Based on an issue of the journal *Gender and Development*, this collection focuses on the different ways in which armed conflict affects women and men, and on women's involvement in peace building, with brief case studies on the Balkans, Kyrgyzstan, and Nicaragua. Other books in the series include *Violence Against Women* (ed. Caroline Sweetman, 1998), *Women and Emergencies* (ed. Bridget Walker, 1994), and *Women and Conflict* (ed. Helen O'Connell, 1993).

Tadesse, Z.: *African Women's Report 1998. Post-conflict Reconstruction in Africa: Gender Perspective*, Addis Ababa: United Nations Economic Commission for Africa (ECA), 1999, 76 pp.

This report presents a historically grounded analysis of the root causes of conflicts in Africa, examines the changing nature of gender roles in political, economic, and social reconstruction after conflicts have subsided, and identifies gender-balanced strategies that can be replicated as 'innovative experiences'.

Turpin, Jennifer and Lois Ann Lorentzen (eds.): *The Women and War Reader*, New York, NY: NYU Press, 1998, ISBN: 0 81475 145 8, 415 pp.

Challenging essentialist, class-based, and ethnocentric analyses of war and conflict, this volume addresses questions of ethnicity, citizenship, women's agency, policy making, women and the war complex, peace making, and aspects of motherhood. It includes case studies from Afghanistan, India, Israel and the Palestinian territories, Iran, Mexico, Nicaragua, Northern Ireland, South Africa, South Korea, Sri Lanka, and the former Yugoslavia. See also, by the same editors, *The Gendered New World: Militarism, Development, and the Environment* (London: Routledge, 1996), which looks at the connections between militarisation, environmental degradation, and women's rights.

Turshen, Meredeth and Clotilde Twagiramariya (eds.): *What Women Do in Wartime: Gender and Conflict in Africa*, London: Zed Books, 1998, ISBN: 1 85649 538 8, 180 pp.

In a mixture of reportage, testimony, and scholarship, this book analyses the experiences of women in civil wars in Africa, as combatants as well as victims, and describes the groups they have organised in the aftermath. Contributors include women from Chad, Liberia, Mozambique, Namibia, Rwanda, South Africa, and Sudan.

UNDP: *Gender Approaches in Conflict and Post-conflict Situations*, New York, NY: UNDP, 2002, 32 pp.

Charting the shift from aid programmes in which women are treated as an afterthought towards more gender-aware approaches, this manual is designed to support and strengthen the capacity of practitioners working in conflict and post-conflict situations to mainstream gender into intervention strategies. It also provides tools for gender mainstreaming, practical advice on how to conduct gender analysis, and includes a CD-ROM detailing various legal and policy instruments. It is available free of charge at:
www.undp.org/gender/docs/gendermanualfinalBCPR.pdf

UNESCO: *Women Say No to War*, Paris: UNESCO, 1999, ISBN: 9 23003 510 6, 82 pp.

This collection of photographs was inspired by the slogan of the NGO Forum at the 1995 World Conference on Women in Beijing to 'See the world through women's eyes'. The images are accompanied by comments by leading representatives of the peace movement, and portray the impact of war on women, women's resistance, and their efforts to build peace.

Waller, **Marguerite and Jennifer Rycenga** (eds.): *Frontline Feminisms: Women, War, and Resistance*, London: Routledge, 2000, ISBN: 0 81533 442 7, 472 pp.

This edited volume explores women's politics and resistance to war and militarism in an international context. Contributors look at the experiences of local women's groups that have emerged against war, militarisation, and political domination in places as varied as Iran, Israel, Kosovo, the Palestinian territories, and Sudan. Some contributions are memoirs, while others are historical accounts or critical essays.

Zimbabwe Women Writers (ed.): *Women of Resilience: The Voices of Women Ex-combatants*, Oxford: African Books Collective, 2000, ISBN: 0 79742 002 9, 193 pp.

While the role of men in Zimbabwe's liberation struggle has been well documented, women's contributions have been largely ignored. Here, nine women ex-combatants relate their experiences, testifying to the vital importance of women fighters in this war.

Zur, Judith N.: *Violent Memories: Mayan War Widows in Guatemala*, Boulder, CO: Westview Press, 2000, ISBN: 0 81332 799 7, 288 pp.

Based on her 1988–90 fieldwork, Zur examines the impact of political violence on one indigenous Mayan village, focusing in particular on the processes of fragmentation and realignment in a community undergoing rapid and violent change. The author relates these local, social, cultural, and psychological phenomena to the impact of the war on the lives of war widows, for whom 'remembering' is not simply the recollection of the past, but a process allowing them to discover new possibilities for action and for reshaping their own positions in society.

Journals

Accord: An International Review of Peace Initiatives, published twice yearly by Conciliation Resources. Editor: Andy Carl, ISSN: 1365 0742

This journal analyses peace-building processes in conflict areas with each issue focusing on a specific country or process and usually including articles exploring the topic from a gender perspective. Recent relevant articles include Lorraine Garasu (2002) 'The role of women in promoting peace and reconciliation', and Jusu-Sheriff (2000) 'Sierra Leonian women and the peace process'. It is available online free of charge; paid print subscriptions are also available. www.c-r.org/accord/index.shtml

Canadian Woman Studies/les cahiers de la femme, published quarterly by Inanna Publications and Education Inc. Editor-in-Chief: Luciana Ricciutelli, ISSN: 0713 3235

The Winter 2000 issue (Volume 19, Number 4) of this journal on current feminist research and writing is on Women in Conflict Zones and includes articles on women's organisations mobilising for peace, state-sanctioned violence against women, and attempts at political reconciliation in many different settings. In addition to book reviews,

there is also a section on poetry.
www.yorku.ca/cwscf/issues/conflict.html

Development, published quarterly by Sage on behalf of the Society for International Development. Editor: Wendy Harcourt, ISSN: 1011 6370

A thematic journal with a strong feminist focus, which aims to be a point of reference for the dialogue between activists and intellectuals committed to working for a sustainable and just world. Relevant issues include: People's Peace Movements (Volume 43, Number 3, September 2000), and Violence Against Women and the Culture of Masculinity (Volume 44, Number 3, September 2001).
www.sidint.org/journal/

Hypatia: A Journal of Feminist Philosophy, published quarterly by Indiana University Press. Editor: Hilde Lindemann Nelson, ISSN: 0887 5367

A journal of scholarly research at the intersection of philosophy and women's studies, *Hypatia* regularly runs themed issues, which are also available separately. Of particular relevance is Feminism and Peace (Volume 9, Number 2, Spring 1994), which includes essays on feminism and the just war theory, national identity, and collective responsibility for rape.
www.iupjournals.org

International Feminist Journal of Politics, published three times a year by Routledge, Taylor & Francis Group. Editors: Jan Jindy Pettman, Kathleen B. Jones, Gillian Youngs, and Rehka Pande, ISSN: 1461 6742

An interdisciplinary journal of scholarly research at the intersection of politics, international relations, and women's studies which seeks to initiate inquiry and promote debate. The themed issue Gender in Conflict and Post-conflict Societies (Volume 3, Number 1, 2001) contains papers by leading feminists including Chris Corrin, Lene Hansen, Ruth Jacobson, Azza Karam, Julie Mertus, and Marguerite Waller.
www.tandf.co.uk/journals

Organisations, networks, and websites

ABANTU for Development, 1 Winchester House, 11 Cranmer Road, London SW9 6EJ, UK

ABANTU's work focuses on training and resource mobilisation to promote sustainable development in Africa and its programme on Gender and Conflict aims to reduce the consequences of conflict for women by contributing to gender-sensitive peacekeeping and peace-building efforts. Relevant publications include *The Gender Implications of Peacekeeping and Reconstruction in Africa* (2000), and *The International Dimension of Peace Building and Conflict Prevention, Resolution and Management in Africa* (2000).
www.abantu.org

Asociación Madres de Plaza de Mayo (Association of the Mothers of the Plaza de Mayo), Hipólito Yrigoyen 1584 (1089), Buenos Aires, Argentina

During Argentina's so-called 'Dirty War' in the 1970s, a group of women began demonstrating every week in the Plaza de Mayo in Buenos Aires demanding the right to know the fates of their loved ones – a practice that the Madres continue to this day. Several of the Madres, including their founder, were themselves 'disappeared' because of their activism. The organisation's website carries information about its activities and publications, and details on courses and workshops at the Mothers of the Plaza de Mayo Popular University, described by the Madres as a university 'of struggle and resistance'.
www.madres.org/

Black Sash

Formed in 1955, Black Sash began as a women's anti-apartheid movement. Described as 'the conscience of white South Africa' by Nelson Mandela, the organisation fought apartheid through protest vigils, marches, and advice for those deprived of their basic human rights. With special emphasis on the needs of women, Black Sash continues to work for the protection of human rights in South Africa through non-violent individual and collective action.
www.blacksash.org.za/

The Bridge: Jewish and Arab Women for Peace in the Middle East, 57 Horev Street, Haifa, Israel 34343

Founded in 1975, The Bridge was the first association of its kind bringing together Jewish and Arab women to promote women's rights and peace in the Middle East. Through meetings, exchange visits, radio and television programmes, conferences, and other activities, the organisation works to build bridges of culture and understanding among women of different ethnic and religious backgrounds. Its founder, Ada Aharoni, also runs the International Forum for the Literature and Culture of Peace (IFLAC) to promote peace in the Middle East 'with the help of the written word, culture, literature, social activity, and dialogue'.
http://listserv.ac.il/~ada/the-bridge.html
http://listserv.ac.il/~ada/home.html

DAW: United Nations Division for the Advancement of Women, 2 United Nations Plaza, DC2, 12th Floor, New York, NY 10017, USA

Aiming to ensure the participation of women as equal partners with men in all aspects of human endeavour, DAW promotes women as equal participants and beneficiaries of sustainable development, peace and security, governance, and human rights. Relevant publications include *Women, Peace and Security: Study Submitted by the Secretary-General Pursuant to Security Council Resolution 1325* (2002); *Women 2000 – Sexual Violence and Armed Conflict: United Nations Response* (1998); and *Women 2000 – The Role of Women in UN Peace-keeping* (1995).
www.un.org/womenwatch/daw

Human Rights Watch (HRW), Women's Rights Division, 350 Fifth Avenue, 34th Floor, New York, NY 10118-3299, USA

The Women's Rights Division of HRW focuses on documenting and promoting international justice for women who are victims of sexual and other kinds of physical violence and curtailments of basic freedoms, both during armed conflicts and in the post-war and reconstruction phases. The Division has published several reports on the situation of women in Afghanistan, Bosnia-Herzegovina, Iraq, Kosovo, Sierra Leone, and other conflict-affected areas.
www.hrw.org/women/conflict.html

International Alert, Gender and Peacebuilding Programme, 1 Glyn Street, London SE11 5HT, UK

This programme focuses on how international and national commitments to women, peace, and security can be implemented, and how women can further contribute to peace processes. The programme includes the Women Building Peace Campaign, which calls for the protection of women and their full incorporation in all aspects of decision making in peace-building efforts, as well as Gender Peace Audits aimed at improving monitoring and accountability, documenting women's peace building know-how, and developing a toolkit on women, peace, and security.

www.international-alert.org/women/

International Committee of the Red Cross (ICRC), Women and War Project, 19 Avenue de la Paix, 1202 Geneva, Switzerland

The ICRC's Women and War Project, begun in 1998, addresses issues affecting women in war zones and other conflict areas. Reports published as part of this initiative include *Women Facing War: The Impact of Armed Conflict on Women* (2001) and *Women and War: Special Report* (2003), both of which analyse the needs of women in war, the protection afforded by international humanitarian law, and ICRC's activities on behalf of women. The ICRC also keeps a well-maintained webpage on issues related to women and war.

www.icrc.org/eng/women

The International Fellowship of Reconciliation (IFOR), Women Peacemakers Program (WPP), Spoorstraat 38, 1815 BK Alkmaar, The Netherlands

Founded in 1919, IFOR is committed to active non-violence both as a way of life and as a means of social transformation, believing that development and peace are unattainable without the full participation of women. The WPP has supported women's peace-making initiatives in countries such as Armenia, Cambodia, Kenya, and Zimbabwe offering training for grassroots women's groups; regional consultations for women from different sides of armed conflicts; and exchange programmes for women in peace organisations. Its newsletter, *Cross the Lines*, documents women's peace-building activities worldwide and promotes networking among women peace makers.

www.ifor.org

Jerusalem Link

Established in 1994, Jerusalem Link is a partnership between Bat Shalom, Israel's national women's peace organisation, and the Jerusalem Center for Women, a Palestinian women's organisation. While each is autonomous, the two organisations seek to 'promote a joint vision of a just peace, democracy, human rights, and women's leadership'. Their members work to facilitate cross-community dialogue, develop programmes for women from both communities, and pressure policy makers and opinion formers to commit to a just and lasting peace.

www.batshalom.org/

www.j-c-w.org/

Kvinna till Kvinna Foundation, Kristinebergs Slottsväg 8, S-112 52 Stockholm, Sweden

The Foundation supports women in regions affected by war and armed conflict, as well as in building peace. It is active in the Balkans, the Middle East, and the Caucasus, with a main focus on women's health issues and capacity building. Relevant publications include *Engendering the Peace Process: A Gender Approach to Dayton – and Beyond* (ed. Anna Lithander, 2000); *War Is Not Over with the Last Bullet: Overcoming Obstacles in the Healing Process for Women in Bosnia-Herzegovina* (Marta Cullberg Weston, 2002); and *Getting it Right? A Gendered Approach to UNMIK Administration in Kosovo* (ed. Annette Lyth, 2001).

www.iktk.se/english/

LAS DIGNAS: Asociación de Mujeres por la Dignidad y la Vida

A Salvadoran NGO working with women ex-combatants to rebuild women's lives in post-conflict El Salvador. Relevant publications include *Mujeres Montaña: Vivencias de Guerrilleras y Colaboradoras del FMLN* (Cristina Ibañez, 1997).

www.lasdignas.org.sv/

Life & Peace Institute (LPI), PO Box 1520, SE-751 45 Uppsala, Sweden

LPI is an international and ecumenical centre for peace research and action with an extensive publishing division. Titles in its Women and Nonviolence series include: *Linking Arms: Women and War in Post-Yugoslav States* (Maja Korac, 1998), *Mothers, Widows and Guerrilleras:*

Anonymous Conversations with Survivors of State Terror (Victoria Sanford, 1998), *Girls and Warzones: Troubling Questions* (Carolyn Nordstrom, 1997), and *Women, Violence and Nonviolent Change* (eds. A. Gnanadason, M. Kanyoro, and L.A. McSpadden, 1996). LPI's journal *New Routes: A Journal of Peace Research and Action* includes a special issue on Targeting Women – Gender Perspectives in Conflicts and Peace Building (Volume 6, Number 3).
www.life-peace.org

MADRE, 121 West 27th Street, Room 301, New York, NY 10001, USA

MADRE is an international women's human rights organisation that works with women's community-based groups in conflict areas in Latin America, the Caribbean, the Middle East, Africa, the Balkans, and the USA. Its programmes address issues of sustainable development; community improvement and women's health; violence and war; discrimination and racism; self-determination and collective rights; women's leadership development; and human-rights education. Relevant publications include *Indigenous Women and Bush's War on Terror* (2003), *Demanding Justice: Rape and Reconciliation in Rwanda* (Yifat Susskind, 2000), and *Stop the Bombing, Stop the Ethnic Cleansing: A MADRE Guide to the Yugoslav Crisis* (1999).
http://madre.org

Movimiento por la Paz, el Desarme y la Libertad (MPDL), Calle San Agustín, 3 - 3ffl, 28014 Madrid, Spain

The MPDL is an organisation dedicated to pacifism, disarmament, the defence of human rights, and humanitarian assistance, with operations mostly in the Balkans, Central and South America, the Near East, and Northern Africa. Through its Gender and Equity programme, the MPDL strives to incorporate a gender perspective to all aspects of its work, both within the organisation and beyond.
www.mpdl.org

International Peace Research Institute (PRIO), Fuglehauggata 11, NO-0260, Oslo, Norway

PRIO is an independent research body that publishes on a range of peace-related issues, with a particular focus on civil war, small arms, and mine-affected communities. Relevant publications include *Gender, Peace and Conflict* (eds. Inger Skjelsbæk and Dan Smith, London: Sage, 2001) and *Gendered Battlefields: A Gender Analysis of*

Peace and Conflict, PRIO Report 6 (1997). PRIO also sponsors a project on Conflict Studies from a Gender Perspective, as well as two journals, both published by Sage: *Journal of Peace Research* and *Security Dialogue*. www.prio.no

UNIFEM, Women, Peace and Security programme 304 East 45th Street, 15th Floor, New York, NY 10017, USA

UNIFEM established its Women, Peace and Security programme in the early 1990s to assist women in conflict situations and support their participation in peace processes. In particular, the programme has sought to provide strategic and catalytic support to mainstream gender and to strengthen the gender focus in electoral, constitutional, judicial, and policy reform. Relevant publications include Anderlini (2000) and Rehn and Sirleaf (2002), both included in the **Books** section. www.unifem.org

Women and the EZLN

This website provides articles and other useful documents on the role of women in the rebellion in Chiapas and on their ongoing liberation struggle.
http://flag.blackened.net/revolt/mexico/womindx.html

Women in Black, B Corbbelplein 4, 3012 Wilsele, The Netherlands

Women in Black is an international peace network that grew out of silent vigils started in Israel in 1988 by women protesting the occupation of the West Bank and Gaza. The movement was inspired by earlier 'women wearing black' like Black Sash in South Africa and the Madres de Plaza de Mayo in Argentina, and by women refusing violence, militarism, and war, such as the Women's International League for Peace and Freedom (WILPF), formed in 1915. www.womeninblack.net

Women Waging Peace, 625 Mount Auburn Street, Cambridge, MA 02138, USA

Women Waging Peace works to promote the full inclusion of women in peace processes, both through participation in a global network of women peace builders and through the publication of case studies to serve as a basis for policy advocacy.
www.womenwagingpeace.net

Women's Commission for Refugee Women and Children, 122 East 42nd Street, 12th Floor, New York, NY 10168-1289, USA

This Commission is an independent affiliate of the International Rescue Committee set up to defend the rights of refugee women, children, and adolescents, and to advocate for their active inclusion in humanitarian-assistance programmes and policies. To this end, it undertakes fact-finding missions and evaluations of relief and reconstruction programmes.

www.womenscommission.org

Women's Human Rights Network (WHRnet)

A project of the Association for Women's Rights in Development (AWID), WHRnet aims to provide reliable, comprehensive, and timely information and analysis on women's human-rights issues in English, French, and Spanish. The website offers an introduction to women's human-rights issues; an overview of United Nations/Regional Human Rights Systems; a research gateway to relevant online resources; and a full set of related links. A free bulletin service is also available.

www.whrnet.org

Women's International League for Peace and Freedom (WILPF), PeaceWomen

Through its comprehensive web portal, WILPF's PeaceWomen project aims to enhance the visibility of women's peace-building efforts within the United Nations system and the international community more generally, provide a central repository of accurate and timely information on the impact of armed conflict on women, and facilitate communication among women peace activists.

www.peacewomen.org

Women's Learning Partnership for Rights, Development, and Peace (WLP), Culture of Peace Project, 4343 Montgomery Avenue, Suite 201, Bethesda, MD 20814, USA

Through conferences, publications, and other awareness-raising activities, WLP's Culture of Peace Project encourages the cultivation of values, attitudes, and ways of life that promote co-operation and tolerance. Its interdisciplinary anthology, *Toward a Compassionate Society* (ed. Mahnaz Afkhami, 2002) focuses on women's involvement in conflict resolution, peace building, and democracy, and addresses

the importance of cultural pluralism and the role of women in promoting peace in a globalising world. It is available free of charge at: www.cultureofpeace.net/
www.learningpartnership.org/projects/peaceprog.phtml

Women's Peacepower Foundation, Inc., PO Box 1618, Zephyrhills, FL 33539, USA

A foundation offering awards to women and girls who are involved in grassroots projects to bring peace to (or end violence in) the everyday lives of women and their families.
www.womenspeacepower.org

Addresses of publishers

Acord
Dean Bradley House,
52 Horseferry Road, London
SW1 2AF, UK.
www.acord.org.uk

African Books Collective
The Jam Factory,
27 Park End Street,
Oxford OX1 1HU, UK.
www.africanbookscollective.com

Asian Center for Women's Human Rights
Suite 306, MJB Building,
220 Tomas Morato,
Quezon City, Philippines.

Basic Books
10 East 53rd Street,
New York, NY 10022-5299,
USA.
www.basicbooks.com

Berghahn Books
604 West 115th Street,
New York, NY 10025, USA.
www.berghahnbooks.com

BRIDGE
Institute of Development Studies,
University of Sussex,
Brighton BN1 9RE, UK.
www.ids.ac.uk/bridge

Cambridge University Press
The Edinburgh Building,
Shaftesbury Road,
Cambridge CB2 2RU, UK.
http://uk.cambridge.org

Center for Global Peace
American University School of
International Service,
4400 Massachusetts Ave,
NW, Washington, DC
20016-8123, USA.
www.american.edu/academic.
depts/acainst/cgp/

Center for Women Studies –
Zagreb
Berilaviceva 12, 10 000
Zagreb, Croatia.
www.zenstud.hr

Central European University
Press
1397 Budapest,
PO Box 519/2, Hungary.
www.ceupress.com

Conciliation Resources
173 Upper Street,
London N1 1RG, UK.
www.c-r.org

Ediciones del Taller Editorial
La Correa Feminista
Centro de Investigación y
Capacitación de la Mujer A.C.,
Apartado Postal 4-053,
Mexico DF 06400, Mexico.

Edinburgh University Press
22 George Square,
Edinburgh EH8 9LF, UK.
www.eup.ed.ac.uk

Garland Science
4133 Whitney Avenue,
Hamden, CT 06518-1432, USA.
www.garlandscience.com

Haworth Press
10 Alice Street,
Binghamton, NY 13904, USA.
www.haworthpressinc.com

ILO Publications
4 route des Morillons,
CH-1211 Geneva 22,
Switzerland.
www.ilo.org

Inanna Publications and
Education Inc.
York University,
4700 Keele Street, North York,
Ontario, M3J 1P3, Canada.
www.yorku.ca/cwscf/inanna.html

Indiana University Press
601 N Morton Street,
Bloomington, IN 47404, USA.
http://iupjournals.org/

The Johns Hopkins University
Press
2715 North Charles Street,
Baltimore, MD 21218-4363,
USA.
www.press.jhu.edu

Kumarian Press, Inc.
1294 Blue Hills Avenue,
Bloomfield, CT 06002, USA.
www.kpbooks.com

Lenos Verlag
Splalentorweg 12,
CH-4051 Basel, Switzerland.
www.lenos.ch

Lynne Rienner Publishers
1800 30th Street, Boulder,
CO 80301, USA.
www.rienner.com

Nation Books
33 Irving Place,
8th Floor, New York,
NY 10003, USA.
www.nationbooks.com

NYU Press
838 Broadway,
3rd Floor, New York,
NY 10003, USA.
www.nyupress.org

Oxfam GB
274 Banbury Road,
Oxford OX2 7DZ, UK.
www.oxfam.org.uk/publications

Panos Institute
9 White Lion Street,
London N1 9PD, UK.
www.panosinst.org

Penn State University Press
University Park,
PA 16802-1003, USA.
www.psupress.org

Pluto Press
345 Archway Road,
London N6 5AA, UK.
www.plutobks.com

Routledge, Taylor & Francis Group
11 New Fetter Lane,
London EC4P 4EE, UK.
www.routledge.com

Rutgers University Press
100 Joyce Kilmer Avenue,
Piscataway, NJ 08854, USA.
http://rutgerspress.rutgers.edu/

Sage Publications
M-32 Market,
Greater Kailash-I,
New Delhi 110 048, India.
www.sagepublications.com

Scholarly Resources
104 Greenhill Avenue,
Wilmington,
DE 19805, USA.
www.scholarly.com

South-North Centre for Peacebuilding and Development
PO Box HG358, Highlands,
Harare, Zimbabwe.

St. Martin's Press
175 Fifth Avenue,
New York, NY 10010, USA.
www.stmartins.com

UNDP
1 United Nations Plaza,
New York, NY 10017, USA.
www.undp.org

UNESCO
7 Place de Fontenoy,
75372 Paris 07 SP, France.
www.unesco.org

UNIFEM
304 East 45th Street, 15th Floor,
New York, NY 10017, USA.
www.unifem.org

**United Nations Economic
Commission for Africa**
PO Box 3001,
Addis Ababa, Ethiopia.
www.uneca.org

University of California Press
2120 Berkeley Way,
Berkeley, CA 94720, USA.
www.ucpress.edu

University of Nebraska Press
233 North 8th Street,
Lincoln, NE 68588-0255, USA.
http://unp.unl.edu/

UNRISD
Palais des Nations,
CH-1211 Geneva 10,
Switzerland.
www.unrisd.org

Westview Press
5500 Central Avenue,
Boulder, CO 80301-2877, USA.
www.westviewpress.com

Women's Press
c/o Garamond Press,
63 Mahogany Court, Aurora,
Ontario L4G 6M8, Canada.
www.garamond.ca

Zed Books
7 Cynthia Street, London
N1 9JF, UK.
www.zedbooks.demon.co.uk

Index

and the *intifada* 122
Iran, and martyrs 52–3
and war 50–1
Mothers for Peace 135,144,147
Motrat Qiriazi
  education for girls and women
    65,75–6
  and KWN 65
multi-track diplomacy, a systems
  approach to peace building 141

nation, feminist definition differs
  from male 56–7
national identity, of all Palestinian
  women 275
nationalism
  emphasises aspects of masculinity
    31
  Palestinian 110
negative peace 11,252
neutrality 199
  humanitarian 196,203
  key to neutral position (Plattner)
    203
  Red Cross and Red Crescent
    definition 203
  rigorously upheld by UNICEF
    204,205
  temptation to abandon 202–5
NGOs
  accountability 189
  attraction of visible results and
    high-profile actions 239,321–2
  compatibility of humanitarian and
    human-rights positions 200–1
  interventions in Rwanda 303
  Kosovan 96,97
  neutrality abandoned, impartiality
    embraced 204,205
  new codes 198–9
  proliferation of 198
  seen as preferable service-
    providers 262
  women-run more successful 97
Nicaragua 244–5,247–8,259,261–2
  identity mobilisation 261
  impact of conflict 250–1

marriage of women fighters 49
realistic peace-building 257–8
  women's organisations 257
Nolan, Albert, on solidarity 207
non-violence, UK-based training team
  134,137

OGB *see* Oxfam GB
oral testimony (OT), ACORD research
  project 153–5,159,160,169–70
Organisation for Security and
  Co-operation in Europe (OSCE)
  67,68,80
  Gender-awareness lacking in senior
    postings 90
  male ignorance of educated
    Kosovan women 91–2
  Vienna conference on gender
    (1999) 89–90
Oslo Accords (1993) 124,287
Oslo Declaration of Principles 277
Oxfam GB 316–21,318
  2000 gender equity workshop
    320–1,327
  and basic rights 317
  future of humanitarian aid 319
  gender assessments, Macedonia
    and Albania 327–8
  gendered structures and cultures 335
  gender in emergency programming
    318
  global programme on violence 333
  institutional imperatives, gendered
    335
  integrating gender equity in
    post-war work 317
  and Kosovo crisis 324
  net impact or net benefit 319,321
  programming and conflict-prone
    areas 321–32,335
  red money and green money 327
  supports work tackling violence
    against women 333–4
  working with counterparts in
    conflict 328–32
  see also Albania; Macedonia
    refugee camps

positive peace 11–12,29,191,252–3
post-conflict societies, promoting
    human security in 301
post-war reconstruction 54–5
    Rwanda 301–14
poverty
    in Afghanistan 179
    rape and access to property 33
pregnancy from war rape, in Muslim
    societies 112
project effectiveness, evaluation of 145
protection strategies, developed by
    El Salvadorian refugees 225–33

race and cultural issues 145–6
race and gender, intersection between
    147
rape 16,17–18
    as an instrument of war 63,236,304
    as a domestic crime 322
    male rape 32
    recognised as a crime of gender 236
    redefined as a war crime 32,112
    retraining of police officers to deal
        with 29
    of virgin girls by Iranian prison
        warders 49
    as a war crime 322
    see also war rape
refugee camps, new roles for women 116
relief agencies/organisations 198–9
    and the humanitarian imperative
        201
    identity and position in today's
        wars 197
    issue of positioning 196
    and neutrality 203,205
    preserving legitimacy and
        effectiveness in war 210
    selective about humanitarian
        'imperatives' 202
    third-party involvement in wartime:
        moral implications 196–7
relief and recovery 322–3
relief workers/peacekeepers 208–9
    perception of the neutral position
        203–4

repopulation, El Salvador 223–4,229–30
Rwanda 18,333
    changes in marriage practices 162
    CIDA-funded projects 302–3
    common-law marriages 309–10
    homelessness 307–8
    impact of conflict on role
        distinctions 160
    equal access to resources, formal
        recognition of 309
    inheritance problems for young
        females 306,307
    patriarchal society 304
    post-genocide situation 303–4,311–12
    surviving population, majority
        female 20
    violence against women 304
    widowed heads of households 307
    women involved in genocide 164
    young adults as heads of house-
        holds 306
Rwanda, women in
    economic security 307–9
    impact of initiatives 311–12
    initiatives for during reconstruction
        304–5
    personal security of 305–7,311–12
    socio-political security 309–11

security institutions 29
self-determination, right to 297B
sex trafficking, Kosovo 95
sexual violence 111,112,333
    in Rwanda 304,305,311
    see also rape
sexuality, economic strategy or means
    of securing protection 162–3
Sierra Leone, 'warboys' 31
social change, Central America and
    Peru 252
social crisis 15
social disruption, new opportunities
    for women xi,222
social marginalisation and exclusion
    248–9
social responsibilities, shifted to
    women during war 15

Key Titles from Oxfam Publishing

Ending Violence Against Women
A Challenge for Development and Humanitarian Work
Francine Pickup, with Suzanne Williams and Caroline Sweetman

This book makes a sustained case for violence against women to be taken seriously by development organisations as an abuse of human rights and a barrier to development. It offers:

- **various definitions of violence against women, and theories to explain why it happens**
- **an accessible analysis of legal and rights-based approaches to ending violence**
- **case studies from times of war and peace, focusing on strategies to counter violence against women and support the survivors**

2001 • 0 85598 438 4 • paperback 386pp • £12.50 • $19.95

Gender, Development, and Humanitarian Work
edited by Caroline Sweetman

This collection of articles explores the ways in which emergencies affect men and women differently, considering:

- **the particular risks and vulnerabilities they face during disasters**
- **changing roles, relationships, responsibilities, and resources in preparing for and coping with extreme situations**
- **the influence of humanitarian response on gender relations within disaster-affected communities**

While acknowledging the difficulties of integrating gender-equity goals into humanitarian intervention, the authors argue that gender-blind responses can further endanger the survival of women and their families, weaken their long-term position in society, and also deny them the opportunity of exercising their potential as peace-builders.

Focus on Gender series
2001 • 0 85598 457 0 • paperback 98pp • £9.95 • $16.50

Focus on Gender series
Series editor: Caroline Sweetman

The *Focus on Gender* series presents, in book form, each thematic issue of Oxfam's *Gender and Development* journal. This international journal aims to debate best practice and new ideas, in order to inform gender and development research, policy, and practice. Each book features a comprehensive resources section.

For more information on the journal, please visit **www.oxfam.org.uk/go/gad**

TO ORDER

contact **publish@oxfam.org.uk**
or visit our online bookstore at **www.oxfam.org.uk/publications**

Oxfam

Development in Practice Readers

Development in Practice Readers draw on the contents of the acclaimed international journal *Development in Practice*.

> 'The great strength of the Development in Practice Readers *is their concentrated focus. For the reader interested in a specific topic ... each title provides a systematic collation of a range of the most interesting things practitioners have had to say on that topic. It ... lets busy readers get on with their lives, better informed and better able to deal with relevant tasks.'*

(Paddy Reilly, Director, Development Studies Centre, Dublin)

The series presents cutting-edge contributions from practitioners, policy makers, scholars, and activists on important topics in development. Recent titles have covered themes as diverse as advocacy, NGOs and civil society, management, cities, gender, and armed conflict.

There are two types of book in the series: thematic collections of papers from past issues of the journal on a topic of current interest, and reprints of single issues of the journal, guest-edited by specialists in their field, on a chosen theme or topic.

Each book is introduced by an overview of the subject, written by an internationally recognised practitioner, researcher, or thinker, and each contains a specially commissioned annotated list of current and classic books and journals, plus information about organisations, websites, and other electronic information sources – in all, an essential reading list on the chosen topic. New titles also contain a detailed index. *Development in Practice Readers* are ideal as introductions to current thinking on key topics in development for students, researchers, and practitioners.

For an up-to-date list of titles available in the series, contact any of the following:

- the Oxfam Publishing website at www.oxfam.org.uk/publications
- the *Development in Practice* website at www.developmentinpractice.org
- Oxfam Publishing by email at publish@oxfam.org.uk
- Oxfam Publishing at 274 Banbury Road, Oxford OX2 7DZ, UK.

> 'This book [Development, NGOs, and Civil Society] *will be useful for practitioners seeking to make sense of a complex subject, as well as for teachers and students looking for a good, topical introduction to the subject. There is a comprehensive annotated bibliography included for further exploration of many of the issues.'*

(David Lewis, Centre for Civil Society at The London School of Economics, writing in *Community Development Journal* 36/2)

Development in Practice

'A wonderful journal – a real "one stop must-read" on social development issues.'

(Patrick Mulvany, Intermediate Technology Development Group, UK)

Development in Practice is an international peer-reviewed journal. It offers practice-based analysis and research on the social dimensions of development and humanitarianism, and provides a forum for debate and the exchange of ideas among practitioners, policy makers, academics, and activists worldwide.

Development in Practice challenges current assumptions, stimulates new thinking, and seeks to shape future ways of working.

It offers a wide range of content: full-length and short articles, practical notes, conference reports, a round-up of current research, and an extensive reviews section.

Development in Practice publishes a minimum of five issues in each annual volume: at least one of the issues is a 'double', focused on a key topic and guest-edited by an acknowledged expert in the field. There is a special reduced subscription for readers in middle- and low-income countries, and all subscriptions include on-line access.

For more information, to request a free sample copy, or to subscribe, write to Oxfam Publishing, 274 Banbury Road, Oxford OX2 7DZ, UK, or visit: www.developmentinpractice.org, where you will find abstracts (written in English, French, Portuguese, and Spanish) of everything published in the journal, and selected materials from recent issues.

Development in Practice is published for Oxfam GB by Carfax, Taylor and Francis.

'Development in Practice is the premier journal for practitioners and scholars in the humanitarian field who are interested in both practical insights and academic rigour.'

(Joseph G Block, American Refugee Committee, USA)